THE
UNRESOLVED
NATIONAL
QUESTION

THE
UNRESOLVED
NATIONAL
QUESTION

LEFT THOUGHT UNDER APARTHEID

Edited by Edward Webster and Karin Pampallis

WITS UNIVERSITY PRESS

Wits University Press
1 Jan Smuts Avenue
Johannesburg
South Africa

www.witspress.co.za

Published edition © Wits University Press 2017
Compilation © Edition editors 2017
Chapter © Individual contributors 2017
First published 2017

ISBN 978-1-77614-022-0 (print)
ISBN 978-1-77614-023-7 (pdf)
ISBN 978-1-77614-024-4 (EPub: North America, South America, China)
ISBN 978-1-77614-025-1 (EPub: Rest of the world)

Edited by: Monica Seeber
Proofread by: Mirié van Rooyen
Indexed by: Karin Pampallis
Cover designed by: Hothouse South Africa
Book design and layout by: Newgen Knowledge Works (Pvt) Ltd
Printed and bound by: Creda South Africa

NATIONAL INSTITUTE
FOR THE HUMANITIES
AND SOCIAL SCIENCES

The financial assistance of the National Institute of Humanities and Social Sciences (NIHSS) towards this
research is hereby acknowledged. Opinions expressed and conclusions arrived at are those of the authors
and editors and are not necessarily to be attributed to the NIHSS.

CONTENTS

ACRONYMS AND ABBREVIATIONS

AAC	All-African Convention
AB	Afrikaner Broederbond
AMCU	Association of Mineworkers and Construction Union
ANC	African National Congress
Anti-CAD	Anti-Coloured Affairs Department Movement
APO	African People's Organisation
AZAPO	Azanian People's Organisation
ANCYL	ANC Youth League
BAWU	Black and Allied Workers' Union
BC	Black consciousness
BCM	Black Consciousness Movement
BEE	Black economic empowerment
CAD	Coloured Affairs Department
CI	Communist International
CNETU	Council of Non-European Trade Unions
COD	Congress of Democrats
CODESRIA	Council for the Development of Social Science Research in Africa
Comintern	Communist International
COSATU	Congress of South African Trade Unions
CPC	Coloured People's Congress
CPSA	Communist Party of South Africa
CST	Colonialism of a special type
DA	Democratic Alliance
EFF	Economic Freedom Fighters
FCWU	Food and Canning Workers' Union
FDI	Foreign direct investment
FEDSAW	Federation of South African Women
FOSATU	Federation of South African Trade Unions
GEAR	Growth, Employment and Redistribution strategy
GWU	General Workers Union
ICU	Industrial and Commercial Workers Union
IFP	Inkatha Freedom Party
IIE	Institute for Industrial Education
IWW	Industrial Workers of the World
KLA	KwaZulu Legislative Assembly

KZN	KwaZulu-Natal
LGBTQIA	Lesbian, gay, bisexual, transgender, queer, intersex and asexual [community]
MAWU	Metal and Allied Workers' Union
MK	Umkhonto we Sizwe [Spear of the Nation]
MP	Member of Parliament
MWT	Marxist Workers' Tendency
NCW	National Coalition of Women
NDR	National Democratic Revolution
NEC	National Executive Committee
NEDLAC	National Economic Development and Labour Council
NEF	New Era Fellowship
NEUM	Non-European Unity Movement
NGO	Non-governmental organisation
NHI	National Health Insurance
NLL	National Liberation League
NHS	National Health Service
NIC	Natal Indian Congress
NP	National Party
NPC	National Planning Commission
NUM	National Union of Mineworkers
NUMARWOSA	National Union of Motor Assembly and Rubber Workers of South Africa
NUMSA	National Union of Metalworkers of South Africa
NUSAS	National Union of South African Students
NUTW	National Union of Textile Workers
PAC	Pan Africanist Congress
PFP	Progressive Federal Party
RC	Revolutionary Council
RDP	Reconstruction and Development Programme
SAAWU	South African Allied Workers' Union
SABRA	South African Bureau of Racial Affairs
SACC	South African Council of Churches
SACLA	South African Confederation of Labour
SACP	South African Communist Party
SACTU	South African Congress of Trade Unions
SADET	South African Democracy Education Trust
SADF	South African Defence Force
SAIC	South African Indian Congress
SAIRR	South African Institute of Race Relations
SANC	South African Native Congress
SANNC	South African Native National Congress

SARCHI	South African Research Chairs Initiative
SASO	South African Students' Organisation
Spro-Cas	Study Project on Christianity in Apartheid Society
SWANU	South West Africa National Union
SWAPO	South West Africa People's Organisation
TAC	Treatment Action Campaign
TLGFA	Traditional Leadership and Governance Framework Act
TUACC	Trade Union Advisory Coordinating Council
TUCSA	Trade Union Congress of South Africa
UAAWU	United Automobile and Allied Workers Union
UCT	University of Cape Town
UDF	United Democratic Front
UDW	University of Durban-Westville
UF	United Front
UFH	University of Fort Hare
Unisa	University of South Africa
UWC	University of the Western Cape
UKZN	University of KwaZulu-Natal
UN	United Nations
US(A)	United States (of America)
UWUSA	United Workers Union of South Africa
WASP	Workers and Socialist Party
WC	Working Committee [of the ANC]
WNC	Women's National Coalition
WPMAWU	Western Province Motor Assembly Workers Union
WPSA	Workers Party of South Africa

PREFACE

This volume grew out of an initiative of the National Institute for the Humanities and Social Sciences (NIHSS). The NIHSS was established by the minister of higher education and training to re-invigorate the humanities and social sciences in South Africa. Launched in 2014, it has two goals. The first is to promote postgraduate studies and to contribute to the development of a new generation of academics. The second is to reinvigorate the humanities and social sciences through a series of catalytic research projects which aim to open up new avenues for scholarship and to assist in and promote the development of relevant research.

This edited volume, *The Unresolved National Question: Left Thought Under Apartheid*, is part of a broader catalytic project – Hidden Voices: Left Thought under Apartheid. That project's overall aim is to recover some of the lineages of knowledge production from 1950 to 1990. The project emerged out of an interest in left intellectual contributions towards discussions on race, class, ethnicity and nationalism in South Africa. Specifically, the idea is to look at Hidden Voices – academic voices suppressed by apartheid pressures, and organic intellectual voices outside of the university system, similarly silenced by apartheid.

A number of excellent publications have made available documents from the liberation struggle. In the early 1960s, for example, Gwendolen Carter, Gail Gerhardt and Thomas Karis started collecting documents to begin what is now a seven-volume series – *From Protest to Challenge*. The Democracy Education Trust has published its six-volume *Road to Democracy in South Africa*. Allison Drew has edited two volumes of *South Africa's Radical Tradition: A Documentary History*. Unisa Press has its Hidden History Series, Jacana Media has its Pocket Biographies, and HSRC Press has its Voices of Liberation Series.

None of these, however, is devoted specifically to publishing left thought under apartheid. The first phase of the Hidden Voices project examines the way in which various strands of left thought have addressed the National Question, especially during the apartheid years. We wanted to ensure that the volume represented the broadest possible range of left South African thought since 1950, so instead of imposing a particular understanding of the National Question we identified and selected a number of political traditions, and allowed the authors the freedom to define the question as they believe appropriate – in other words, to explain what *they* thought was the Unresolved National Question.

We had two successful workshops in Johannesburg – in June 2014 and May 2015 – to discuss the content of papers. Discussions were lively at both workshops – a foretaste, we hope, of the interest and debate that the *Unresolved National Question* will catalyse.

The volume is structured in two parts. The first section examines four foundational traditions – Marxism-Leninism (as typified in the Colonialism of a Special Type thesis), the Congress tradition, the Trotskyist tradition and Africanism. The second part of the volume explores the various shifts in this debate from the 1960s onwards, and includes chapters on Afrikaner nationalism, ethnic issues, black consciousness, feminism, workerism and constitutionalism.

We struggled to decide what contributions to include in this collection. After all, the boundaries of the nations of Africa are an artificial construct of nineteenth-century colonialism. This broader vision is reflected in the powerful Pan Africanist tradition in South Africa and the presence of South African exile communities throughout Africa during the apartheid period. In the end, however, we decided to limit contributions to South Africa.

We argue in this volume that the questions raised by the National Question debate over a century ago remain unresolved. The goal of one united nation living prosperously under a constitutional democracy remains elusive. We hope that by revisiting the debates hidden from the scholarly mainstream this volume will become a catalyst for an enriched debate on our identity and our future.

We would like to thank our funders, the National Institute for the Humanities and Social Sciences, for making this publication (and the entire project) possible. We also thank the Chris Hani Institute, and Anthea Metcalfe and Priscilla Magau in particular, for their support during the first phase of this project. The second phase of the Hidden Voices project envisages the publication (and in some cases re-publication) of other Hidden Voices – key texts and original sources that were never published under apartheid, or seminal books that have gone out of print. This phase of the project will be located in the Society, Work and Development Institute (SWOP) at the University of the Witwatersrand.

We hope that this publication will make a valuable contribution to the decolonisation of knowledge production in South Africa.

Edward Webster and Karin Pampallis

Johannesburg, September 2016

REVISITING THE NATIONAL QUESTION

Edward Webster and John Mawbey[1]

The 2015 academic year seemed to begin on a familiar note as students struggled to find sought-after places at South Africa's top universities. Then a protest broke out in February at the University of Cape Town (UCT). The target was the prominent statue of Cecil John Rhodes (the arch-imperialist of the British Empire) which had occupied a central position in the university for nearly a century. The trigger for the protest was the deep sense of injustice felt by black students by this 'celebration' of the symbol of colonial conquest, exploitation and land dispossession. The demand, named 'Rhodes Must Fall', rapidly spread across South African universities, culminating in the dramatic removal of the statue. In October a demand for no university fee increases – 'Fees Must Fall' – took centre stage. By the end of the year the protest had developed into a broader call for the decolonisation of universities, with the issue of race at the centre of nationwide campus protests (Habib, 2015).

Seized with the challenge of the present, the architects of this new movement, not surprisingly, seemed impatient with the narratives of the past. But we have to grasp 'the present as history' (a phrase drawn from *The Eye of the Needle* by political philosopher and anti-apartheid activist Richard Turner, initially published in 1972).[2] The National Question – the drive to build one united, democratic nation – is a 'century-long discourse on South Africa's nationhood' (Mistra, 2014: 49) framed by a number of popular narratives or stories:

- Colonialism of a Special Type (CST) – the notion that South Africa consists of two nations, the colonising and the colonised, in the same territory;

- the approach that recognises the numerical superiority of indigenous Africans as the most oppressed and exploited members of society, and places special emphasis on African leadership, as well as prioritising the conditions of African people;
- the 'rainbow nation' approach, which emphasises the multiple identities that constitute South Africa's diverse population (Mistra, 2014: 49–50).[3]

Studies of nationalism, race and ethnicity, and their relationship to class, lie deep in the intellectual history of South Africa (Marks and Trapido, 1987). What is striking, however, is the limited academic study of the intellectual history of the National Question.[4] To some in South Africa there never was a National Question (or, if there was one, it has long since been resolved), insisting that South Africa has become a fully independent sovereign nation exercising the right to determine its own future (if not in 1910, then at least by 1934).[5] The issues at stake were about internal democracy and economic power.

Why, twenty-three years into our democracy, should we revisit the history of this debate? The rationale for this volume is that the central challenge of forging a united, democratic nation remains unresolved. We boldly declare in the Constitution that 'South Africa belongs to all who live in it, both black and white, united in our diversity'. In 2012 the National Social Cohesion and Nation Building Summit confidently declared, 'South Africa is a unitary and sovereign state based on democracy, the rule of law, pursuit of equal human rights, non-racialism, non-sexism, and the equality of all persons' (cited in Mistra, 2014: 80) However, the declaration went on to identify the many obstacles to uniting South Africans. The contribution of this collection of essays is to show how the foundational traditions of the past continue into the present, and how new approaches to the National Question have emerged.

In order to capture the dynamic nature of this debate around the National Question we first (in this Introduction) trace its origins to nineteenth-century Europe's attempt to grapple with the colonial nature of South African society. The rest of the volume is divided into two parts. In Part One we identify four foundational traditions that emerged from a broadly left position to address the National Question in South Africa–Marxism-Leninism, the Congress tradition, Trotskyism and Africanism.[6] Part Two examines the debate from the mid-1960s to the present. Although there are continuities between the two periods, there are also distinctive challenges arising from Afrikaner nationalism's implementation of the bantustan policy as well as the rise of Inkatha and Zulu-ness, the New Left, black consciousness, feminism and liberal constitutionalism. At the centre of these challenges is a complex process of continuity and rupture with the National Democratic Revolution (NDR) narrative of class struggle and national struggle. We turn now to a brief history of the debate on the National Question.

THE PRESENT AS HISTORY

Most of the major debates within the Tripartite Alliance and the trade union movement continue to be framed in terms of the National Democratic Revolution[7] and its unfulfilled second, socialist stage. South Africa remains riven by debates which foreground 'race' or hint at 'ethnic' cleavages, and there are repeated outbreaks of xenophobia against 'other Africans' or immigrants from East Asia.

Twenty-three years beyond the demise of formal apartheid, we still continue to use four racially defined categories as central descriptors in our statistics, and seek to deal with issues of redress using these statistics as a proxy for 'advantaged' and 'disadvantaged' because of a lack of alternative socio-economic indicators. The distribution of wealth is unequal nationally and within classes, but remains colour-coded. Capital remains predominantly white, though this is changing; the working class is still predominantly black, but this is also changing as a growing number of whites experience downward mobility. The economic entrenchment of inequality is clearly something built up since the earliest days of colonialism and it cannot be reduced to the legacy of apartheid – on the contrary, multinational control of the economy has, if anything, been reinforced with the relocation of most of our 'indigenous' major corporations to listings on global stock exchanges.

There are many who now feel that the African National Congress (ANC), a liberation movement that, at the height of the struggle against apartheid, represented a 'radical vision of non-racialism, social liberation and equality', has betrayed that vision (Lissoni et al., 2012). Mazibuko Jara, a key figure in the United Front, an initiative to link unions to the community, argues that:

> ...the ANC's NDR theory is an exhausted Marxism that is denuded of both its radical impulses and emancipatory logics, particularly when it comes to resolving the national question. The ANC's nation building project, whether in its 'rainbow nation' or 'home for all' or 'liberation of Africans in particular' versions, has not been based on a conscious political strategy which understands and addresses the structural socio-economic base of national oppression. Where critical structural interventions could have been made, we saw equivocation and even a retreat to racialised strategies (Jara, 2013: 568).

As the Declaration of the 11th National Congress of the Congress of South African Trade Unions (COSATU) in 2012 put it:

> Workers are demanding that the People Shall Share in the Country's Wealth (as promised by our Freedom Charter). Our members are speaking through our

structures, demonstrating their lack of patience through wildcat strikes and service delivery protests (Craven, 2014: n.p.).

Academics are beginning to debate again the significance of the National Question. In a fascinating use of Fanon's concept of the 'colonial unconscious', Peter Hudson uses it to understand the resistance of whites to the NDR in post-apartheid South Africa. He analyses Brett Murray's controversial painting of President Zuma, *The Spear*, to illustrate the return of the 'colonial repressed' through the colonial symbolic – as Fanon puts it, 'the black man is penis' (Hudson, 2013: 271). Gill Hart more recently wrote:

> I was inattentive to the National Question – a profoundly evocative term that for many South Africans conjures up struggles against colonialism and imperialism, the indignities and violence of racial injustice and dispossession, the sacrifices and suffering embodied in movements for national liberation, and the visions of social and economic justice for which many fought and died. I also failed to take seriously a key phrase of the ANC alliance – the NDR – the meanings and ownership of which have become an increasingly contentious site of struggle within the ANC alliance over the decade of the 2000s (Hart, 2013: 157).[8]

The origins of the National Question go back to the struggles for national liberation and the formation of nations which dominated Europe in the late nineteenth and early twentieth centuries (Mawbey, 2014). The treaties signed in the aftermath of the First World War saw the breakup of three predominantly feudal empires – the Austro-Hungarian Hapsburgs, the Russian Tsars and the Turkish Ottomans. In their place a number of ethnic-linguistic national states were created, according to the then prevalent belief in the right of nations to self- determination (Hobsbawm, 1995: 31). The Bolsheviks, in the course of the Russian Revolution, also supported the recognition of ethnic-linguistic nations as put forward by Stalin, but ended up with a multicultural Union of Soviet Socialist Republics (USSR) (Stalin, 1913; Hobsbawm, 1995).

In South Africa, the National Question was first articulated in meetings of political organisations, movements and trade unions, or in what were called social debating clubs and other informal sites, rather than in the context of formal knowledge production within the academy. Early debates on the South African National Question were led by the Communist Party of South Africa (CPSA), their theory having been shaped from the 1920s by the Marxist-Leninist debates taking place within the Communist International (Comintern). In 1920, Lenin had argued that anti-colonial national independence movements were objectively allies of the global socialist struggle, even if led by the bourgeoisie and based on underdeveloped peasant societies. There were 'oppressing' and 'oppressed' nations, and therefore a potential existed for national revolutionary struggles to undermine capitalist imperialism. He also held that it was possible for such nations, on gaining independence, to skip the capitalist stage of development and move directly towards implementing socialism. This debate took place in the context of India, with the Indian communist Roy opposing it on the basis that indigenous capital was already too strong and would dominate the national independence struggle (Carr, 1974: 629, 675). Lenin's position was adopted. The debate resulted, in 1929, in South African communists taking up the slogan of an independent native South African Republic, which was envisaged as eventually leading to a non-racial workers' and peasants' republic (Filatova, 2012). In essence, this was the first expression of a two-stage national democratic revolution – the first stage bringing universal democracy, the second giving rise to the advance to power of workers and peasants.

KEY FOUNDATIONAL TRADITIONS

As we indicated earlier, the first part of the volume deals with four foundational traditions.[9] We begin with the Marxist-Leninist tradition developed by the CPSA in the twenties. 'The distinguishing feature of South Africa', the CPSA reported in January 1950, 'is that it combines the characteristics of both the imperialist state and the colony within a single indivisible, geographical, political and economic entity' (quoted in Filatova, 2012: 526). Michael Harmel (1953) expanded on this position in a 1953 paper titled 'Observations on Certain Aspects of Imperialism in South Africa'. He identified whites as having settled in South Africa, contrasting this with India where the colonialists went out to make a quick profit and then returned home. The result, he claimed, was that white South Africa had an imperialistic relation with black South Africa, which was its colony. He pointed to the system's rapacious demand for cheap labour and then argued that the system was increasingly being challenged by the growth of 'a non-white national liberation movement'. He saw this as the 'advanced progressive anti-imperialist force in our country', arguing that it was a movement of workers and peasants, professionals, middle and commercial classes with no developed large bourgeoisie (Harmel, 1953: 10; Mawbey, 2014). By the time the South African Communist Party (SACP), the successor to the CPSA, issued its programme, 'The Road to South African Freedom', in 1962, much had changed. Repression had intensified, and an armed struggle had begun, directed mainly at infrastructural sabotage. For the first time, the SACP's programme mentioned the theory of 'Colonialism of a Special Type' (CST) and linked it to the 'national democratic revolution'.

In the first chapter of this volume, Jeremy Cronin and Alex Mashilo revisit the National Question through a critical engagement with the concept of CST. The roots of this concept are located in a 1928 resolution of the Communist International on 'The South

African Question' characterising South Africa as a 'British dominion of the colonial type'. They argue that while it is no longer relevant to characterise South Africa as CST, the concept is useful in considering the programmatic tasks required to resolve the National Question. Certainly, as part of the answer to the National Question, it is crucial to resolve the questions of 'race', 'nationality', 'ethnicity' and 'identity'. However, they also argue that South Africa's political economy was cast in a colonial mould and inserted within the global circuit of capitalist accumulation and reproduction, and that this has shaped the National Question.

The second tradition we identify is the Congress tradition. Robert van Niekerk examines the National Question from the perspective of the ANC's social policies. Through an examination of key foundational policy documents such as the African Claims (1943, in Karis and Carter, 1973: 209–211) and the Freedom Charter (1955, in Karis and Carter, 1977: 205–208), as well as the writings of presidents-general A.B. Xuma and Albert Luthuli in the same period, he argues that the ANC had a clearly articulated social democratic agenda for the post-apartheid good society, as a basis for the resolution of the National Question.

Luli Callinicos continues this focus on the Congress tradition through an examination of Oliver Tambo's concept of the South African nation. She explores challenges posed by race and ethnicity from the time that Tambo helped to found the ANC Youth League in 1943 through to the organisation's unbanning in 1990, and argues that scholars have neglected the influence of indigenous culture on Tambo's commitment to collective decision-making and style of political relations.

Shortly after the Comintern-induced approach to the National Question was adopted by the CPSA, an alternative left project developed, mainly in the west and east of the Cape Province. It came to be known as the Unity Movement, discussed in this volume by Basil Brown and his colleagues. It brought together a number of left groupings, in particular the All-African Convention (AAC) and Anti-CAD[10] movement, to form the Non-European Unity Movement (NEUM). Bill Nasson (1990: 194) characterises the umbrella organisation, the NUEM, as consisting of a 'coloured intelligentsia' and 'tough-minded amateur scholars' operating outside of white academia, many of them teachers.[11] Some members of the network were influenced by Trotskyism. Trotsky posited that, based on the theory of 'permanent revolution', all social struggles were 'interconnected due to their common reproduction in the capitalist system, so the resolution of one struggle shaped the outcome of others. Social change developed continuously and unevenly, rather than proceeding through discrete stages, enabling a proletarian revolution to occur in a relatively undeveloped country like Russia before it took place in more advanced capitalist countries ... Contradictions ... could only be resolved ... through world revolution' (Drew, 2000: 137).

The NEUM adopted a very different approach to the National Question from that of the CPSA and the African and Indian Congresses. Where the Congress movement believed that it was necessary to organise four national groups – black, coloured, Indian, white – separately for tactical reasons, the NEUM advocated a non-racial approach, but organised on the basis of three ethnic-based pillars, Africans, coloured and Indian, hoping over time to build broader unity around their ten-point programme.[12] It promoted boycotting any forms of separate representation or organisation. It was a seedbed of discussion and reading groups, and a variety of small-circulation polemics such as the *Discussion,* the *Torch* and the *Education Journal.*

Siphamandla Zondi's chapter explores Africanist discourses on the National Question in twentieth and twenty-first century South Africa. He argues that Africanists regard the National Question as an artefact of a global problem – the problem of the colour line as W.E.B. Du Bois announced in the early twentieth century. The nation state and national territories are all, Zondi suggests, the product of Western modernity as it enveloped the world through imperialism and colonialism. Drawing on Frantz Fanon, Africanists stress the limits of the African bourgeoisie and its tendency to mimic and emulate its Western counterpart. Africanism can be found in various political platforms, from the African National Congress to the Pan Africanist Congress (PAC). Africanists emphasise the solidarity of Africans and other subaltern peoples as an important solution to the national problems generated by a global problem: global colonialism, global racism, global capitalism, global cultural imperialism, global epistemic imperialism, global ecological imperialism, and so forth.

The crushing of the movements of national liberation inside South Africa in the early 1960s was to change the context within which the National Question was pursued profoundly. Forced underground and into exile, these movements no longer had a public presence in South Africa, and made way for a number of new responses.

CONTINUITY AND RUPTURE

This volume examines, in Part Two, how these foundational traditions both endured and changed. The first direct challenge to the National Question emerged with the implementation of the apartheid government's bantustan policy, specifically the establishment of the Transkei as a self-governing territory in 1963 and later, in 1976, as an 'independent' state. Dunbar Moodie's chapter in this volume examines how there was, within Afrikaner nationalism, an abiding contradiction between the moral and spiritual affirmation around which they built their own nation and their inability to apply the same values to other 'nations'. In response to decolonisation in the 1940s and 1950s, Afrikaner nationalists developed the apartheid project of promoting ethnic identities and asserting a 'right' to independent nationhood in the form of bantustans. Moodie sets out the 'liberal nationalist' views that underlay the cultural basis of Afrikaner approaches to the National Question. Afrikaner arguments about culture, however, were always at odds with the white racism that emerged starkly from debates within Afrikaner circles about whether to admit Afrikaans-speaking coloured people into the Afrikaner fold. In 1960, Hendrik Verwoerd used political power to settle this debate along racial lines. However, after the National Party and the Afrikaner Broederbond split irrevocably in the early 1980s, progressive Broederbond intellectuals engaged in an intense debate about whether Afrikaner cultural survival required Afrikaner domination of the state. The final constitutional settlement decided this matter by abandoning ethnic notions of 'group rights' in the new South Africa.[13]

Neville Alexander wrote *One Azania One Nation* (1979) in response to the many discussions on the National Question in which he participated while a prisoner on Robben Island. He sought to understand and refute the theory of nationality that informed the National Party's attempt to implement the bantustan policy. He criticised those who discounted the notion of 'the nation' – perhaps, Enver Motala and Salim Vally suggest in this volume, *the* seminal contribution to this question.

The chapter by Martin Legassick takes Alexander's critique a step further by applying to South Africa Trotsky's theory of permanent revolution. The chapter focuses on the origins of the Marxist Workers Tendency (MWT) of the ANC and the expulsion from the ANC of four of its members. The MWT maintained that the methods and ideology of nationalism could not end national oppression, and that to undertake the abolition of apartheid and capitalism the working class would need to build and transform the ANC on a socialist programme. Such a programme, they argued, should not be based purely on class but should also include national liberation and other 'democratic' tasks. Legassick concluded[14] by pointing out that the National Question has not been resolved in South Africa to this day. Just as national oppression is rooted in capitalist exploitation, he argued, so national liberation is rooted in class struggle.

Gerhard Maré explores the tension between ethnicity and nation through the challenge of the Inkatha movement in KwaZulu-Natal. One way of resolving this tension is to argue that, as Samora Machel once put it, 'For the nation to thrive the tribe must die' (cited in Mangcu, this volume). Maré, drawing on the SACP activist intellectual Mzala, captures a more nuanced view when he writes:

> ... denunciation of tribalism and ethnic exclusiveness is not denunciation of the ethnic communities themselves. People's democracy does not mean that all cultural and traditional distinctions between the various groups must disappear ... what is not needed are bantustans to preserve their cultural heritage (Mzala, cited in Maré, this volume).

Similarly, Ari Sitas, in a wide-ranging historical account of Zulu-ness, persuasively argues for the need 'to stop thinking that a national consciousness is a deficit, some "misrecognition" of interest, or a distorted ideology'. Drawing on the concepts of parallelism, inflection and rupture, he shows how pliant the symbolic landscape of nationalism and ethnicity has been in KwaZulu-Natal and he suggests that the 1970s and 1980s created ruptures which have been re-absorbed by the ANC leadership in its drive to establish its hegemony in competition with Inkatha.

Xolela Mangcu's chapter provides a critique of the National Question from a black consciousness perspective. He argues that both liberal and Marxist dismissals of culture as merely an expression of primordial identities and false consciousness have deprived South Africa of the proto-nationalist values that have been the foundation of nation building in other countries. The dominant economistic conception of the nation has left us with a procedural, constitutional democracy and a public philosophy of economic growth and service delivery that pays little or no attention to human solidarity as a public value. Mangcu argues that we must seek inspiration in the cultural values of human solidarity that provided the spirit of survival and informed black struggles against colonial and apartheid oppression. He suggests that we find a revitalised conception of the nation in Steve Biko's idea of a 'joint culture' among blacks and whites.

A central unresolved issue within the National Question is the role of women. Within the liberation movement, the priority was seen as the anti-apartheid struggle, which was rooted in a two-stage theory of social change – and this meant postponing the issue of gender equality. In other words, the specific problems facing women were seen as secondary to and contingent upon national liberation, as Shireen Hassim argues in her contribution to this volume. However, within the national liberation movement in exile, there were challenges to the argument that the Women Question should be postponed. Tessa Marcus (1988: 102), for example, argued that 'women are oppressed as women' and that 'women's oppression, as a question of social justice, has to be overcome'. This meant that women had to organise as women and that 'the women's struggle is an integral part of, and not in contradiction with, the national liberation struggle' (Marcus, 1988: 102). This is what Shireen Hassim describes in this volume as the socialist-feminist position. It had become increasingly common among activists inside the country by the end of the 1980s, especially in the trade union movement, where it was 'argued that women's organisations need to be influenced by feminism but should be cognisant of class and race differences that produce different interests amongst women' (Hassim, 2014: 34).

Hassim explores this uneasy relationship between feminism and nationalism through an analysis of the Federation of South African Women (FEDSAW) and the National Coalition of Women (NCW). The aim of FEDSAW, she argues, was primarily to harness the energies of the resurgent women's organisation to the nationalist cause, whereas the NCW embraced a more diverse set of organisations in elaborating new forms of citizenship. Hassim concludes that it is wrong to present feminism and nationalism as two separate processes. Rather than polarise a rights-based approach to feminist theorising (the dominant approach in the First World) with a needs-based approach (the dominant approach in the Third World), she shows how 'gender politics in South Africa suggests ways in which rights-based activities can facilitate and enhance struggles to meet needs' (Hassim, 2014: 45).

Alec Erwin, a key architect of the largest of the post-1973 trade union groupings, the Federation of South African Trade Unions (FOSATU) and later COSATU, explores how the exigencies of the time shaped an organisational practice and political approach that focused on building strong unions based on the shop floor. While a superficial analysis might have viewed this emphasis on workers' control and industrial unionism as a form of syndicalism, Erwin argues that it conceived of itself as a distinct form of working-class organisation as was spelled out in a 1982 speech by Joe Foster. Tensions with the liberation movement emerged, encapsulated by the 'workerist vs populist' debates of the 1980s. Erwin argues, however, that COSATU was able to unify unions across widely different political views and objective conditions and, as such, was an exercise in nation building and, therefore, relevant to the National Question.

In their chapter, Sian Byrne, Nicole Ulrich and Lucien van der Walt argue that although FOSATU's 'workerist' approach has been caricatured, it was a cohesive, class-based, left-wing current. It challenged apartheid, racial inequality, capitalism and nationalism, promoted bottom-up industrial unions as the basis of a larger working-class movement and identity, and played a central role in fighting *both* class exploitation and national oppression. In the new South Africa, the working-class movement was to create, from below, a new, working-class nation. Workerism was, they argue, not economistic, as sometimes claimed. Its eclecticism contributed to workerism's internal tensions, exacerbated by the lack of an adequate medium- and long-term strategy; both weaknesses led to its eventual eclipse by African nationalism and Marxism-Leninism.

Daryl Glaser concludes the volume with a chapter on the challenge of liberal constitutionalism. He explores the relationship between the theory of the National Democratic Revolution and South Africa's post-1994 constitutional democracy. There are clearly a range of tensions between these two fields of discourse and practice, which arise from differing accounts of institutional form, of procedures and rights, of power, and of the nation and people whose liberation is sought. An analysis of the sources and character of these tensions helps to clarify whether the two fields are inherently adversarial in a way that must result in one superseding the other, or whether terms can be found for their coexistence. The chapter argues for the latter point of view, but only if the NDR is construed in a particular way. Glaser also argues that terms of coexistence *ought* to be found, given the historical failure of Marxist-Leninist governments that were rationalised by versions of NDR theory which treated democratic constitutionalism in a hostile or instrumental way. The attractiveness of coexistence is boosted by evidence that social justice gains can be made on a constitutional-democratic terrain.

THE UNRESOLVED NATIONAL QUESTION: CATALYSING
A NEW RESEARCH AGENDA

In this volume we have identified a variety of intellectual traditions that address the questions of nationalism, race and ethnicity during the apartheid period. We have also identified a range of challenges that emerged in the 1970s and 1980s to the four foundational traditions that have addressed the National Question in South Africa. These challenges are re-emerging and key figures of the left such as Frantz Fanon and Steve Biko are being re-discovered and re-interpreted in the context of the renewed drive to decolonise knowledge production.

In a recent intervention on the National Question, Gill Hart reflects on the constraints that what she calls 'denationalisation' imposes on South Africa's ability to deal with its socio-economic challenges. Denationalisation, she argues, encompasses 'the terms on which heavily concentrated corporate capital re-engaged with the increasingly financialised global economy starting in the early 1990s, and the ways in which these forces are driving increasing inequality and the generation of surplus populations' (Hart, 2013: 156). This includes massive capital flight, permission for powerful conglomerates to disinvest from the economy and move their primary listings to London, and the formation of a small but powerful black capitalist class allied with white corporate capital.

But the 'unresolved National Question' goes beyond the constraints imposed by the neoliberal global economy. Today we have to ask why, given the chiefs' complicity with the apartheid administration, did the ANC endorse these traditional bantustan rulers post 1994? The chiefs and tribal authorities that were created were authoritarian, deeply undemocratic and often corrupt, and yet they have survived into the post-apartheid era. Ntsebeza's (2005) answer is that it has been politically expedient for the ANC to strengthen traditional authorities. Indeed, as Gibbs (2014: 53) suggests, '[t]oday, these densely populated rural areas have become a dominant part of party caucuses'.

And then there is the question of race. Historically, the Unity Movement was the most assertive in its rejection of the notion of race. There was only one race, they argued – the human race (Kies, 1953). Xolela Mangcu, in his chapter on the black consciousness approach, rejects as 'irrational' the Unity Movement's 'denial of the ontological reality of people's self-understanding'. The existence of physical differences between races is not a myth, Mangcu observes; the myth is the notion that there are pure races. In their day-to-day interaction, activists and analysts recognise the reality of race. Mazibuko Jara reinforces this argument when he writes:

> In my analysis the CST thesis did not sufficiently explain the development of, nor develop strategies to address, racial identities in colonial and apartheid South Africa, together with the concomitant fears and perceptions of working-class

coloured people about the reduction of their privileges due to deracialisation (Jara, 2013: 267).

Shireen Hassim suggests that women's organisations have made major attempts to ensure that gender inequalities are understood and addressed as part of the struggle for a free South Africa. However, much of the scholarship of political movements and ideas on the left has tended to treat gender as subordinate to race or class or sometimes both, rather than as a constitutive element of both race and class. The result has been consequential for how politics is conceived as well as for how a non-oppressive society is imagined. She argues for the gendered nature of the economy to be addressed, and for attention to be paid to sexualities as variables that structure political and social subjectivities and political practice itself.

The role of trade unions in the national democratic revolution remains contested, as the current divisions in COSATU attest. The issues raised earlier on the idea of a working-class politics re-emerged in December 2013 when the National Union of Metalworkers of South Africa (NUMSA) decided not to give logistical support to the ANC in the 2014 elections. Following independence, trade unions in postcolonial Africa have tended to submit to the ruling party that drove the liberation struggle. However, growing marginalisation led unions in countries such as Zambia and Zimbabwe into opposition and the formation of separate political parties. In the case of Zambia's Movement for Multiparty Democracy, it won state power in elections. However, there has generally been a low level of political tolerance for political opposition in postcolonial Africa. Unlike established democracies, these new governments are engaged in the complex task of nation building. The result is a culture of 'us' versus 'them', and union-backed oppositional parties have often been labelled 'counter-revolutionary' and 'imperialist'. The union-backed Movement for Democratic Change, for example, soon became the focus of organised violence inflicted by the Zimbabwean state.

Could South Africa be a special case in postcolonial Africa? The existence of a relatively large industrial working class, strong civil society organisations and an independent trade union movement with a political culture of shop-floor democracy makes the survival of a workers' party more likely.

In this volume we have suggested that a range of theoretical approaches developed during the anti-apartheid struggle. These approaches still inform current debates within the ruling Alliance, but is there not a need to go beyond them? Many unresolved questions arise when one revisits the National Question. How can the national space of South Africa be transformed in a globalised world of transnational capitalism? Is building a nation not inimical to a pan-African project and an invitation to xenophobia? Does the resolution of the National Question mean the replacement of capitalism? Where in discussions about the National Question are the conceptions of gender and the gendered nature of poverty? How can we find answers to these questions while still measuring development in terms of gross domestic product and, in all probability, still seeing socialism as a matter requiring the same type of linear industrial or post-industrial economic growth (Cock, 2007)? Can the call by Callinicos, Sitas, Mangcu and Zondi for an emphasis on cultural values and indigenous knowledge take us beyond the National Question into current debates around decolonisation?

Does the Marxist tradition provide the tools for answering these questions? The conventional view is that nationalism represents Marx's greatest failure (Nairn, 1975; Laclau, 1991). In a recent article, Mike Davis (2015: 51) recovers what he sees as a theory of nationalism in the writing on the concrete strategies that Marx and Engels 'recommended in specific political contexts'. But class, Davis argues, remained the unit of analysis which Marx and Engels used to look at nationalism. With few exceptions – such as Martin Legassick's (2007) magisterial manuscript on socialist democracy, the project on class in Soweto (Alexander et al., 2013) and the work of Jeremy Seekings and Nicoli Nattrass (2006) – there has been little academic attempt in post-apartheid South Africa to engage in class analysis, and less on the intersection between race, class, gender and nationalism. Above all, there is the unresolved issue of how to develop the 'forces of production' in economically underdeveloped societies, an issue that lay at the core of Lenin's initial formation of the National Question (Nzimande, 2015).

In spite of the bad press received by liberalism in the liberation movement,[15] it has done surprisingly well in the new South Africa. Indeed, it could be argued that 'the first stage' of the NDR has been substantially achieved with the adoption of a liberal democratic constitution based on checks and balances of power between different parts of government, the judiciary and oversight bodies.

Daryl Glaser asks in this volume whether the ANC's goal of socio-economic transformation can be pursued on the terrain of the democratic constitution or whether it is just an instrument that was useful in the first stage of the NDR, one to be pushed aside if it hinders a state-led implementation of developmental goals. He emphasises the social rights contained in the Constitution, and argues for seeing constitutional democracy as permanent, a path which makes it possible to achieve a socially egalitarian democratic outcome. An example is the property clause in the Bill of Rights which recognises the right to expropriate both for a 'public purpose' (such as building a dam) and for what it calls 'public interest' (which it defines as including 'the nation's commitment to land reform').[16]

Towards the end of his life, Frederick Van Zyl Slabbert, a leading liberal thinker, wrote of the tensions between pursuing a market economy and the NDR. He concluded optimistically: 'Out of the current confusion, something extraordinarily creative may yet emerge' (Slabbert, 2006: 12). We would argue that 'something creative' has already occurred with the expanded social rights of the Constitution. Indeed, to call our Constitution liberal is to miss the point that it contains the potential for a far more radical transformative project than traditional liberalism. As Glaser suggests in this volume, our failure to reach these social goals has 'less to do with the Constitution than with political will and structural constraints'.

But what is the ultimate goal of the national democratic revolution? The Communist Party formulation in the 1950s and 1960s was of a two-stage revolution. The first stage was the achievement of constitutional democracy based on essentially liberal precepts, placing the working class in a position to advance, in the second stage, to the achievement of socialism and, eventually, communism. Were the two stages to occur separately and chronologically, or could they occur simultaneously? With the adoption of the NDR by the ANC, the emphasis came to be placed on the fact that it was not a programme for socialism. For Albert Luthuli, the goal of the NDR was to build a 'democratic welfare state' (Van Niekerk, this volume). For Oliver Tambo, it was to build a democratic, non-racial nation (Callinicos, this volume). Not surprisingly, the ultimate goal of the NDR ended up being a hotly debated issue in the 1980s, both in exile and in South Africa (Hudson, 1986; Slovo, 1988; Wolpe, 1988). Recently, ANC intellectuals have focused on debates on social cohesion, emphasising the creation of a South African nation with a multiplicity of identities (Mistra, 2014: 49–82).

For Cronin and Mashilo (this volume), '[t]he neoliberal agenda of the Mbeki-ites consisted in reducing the core task of the National Question to the modernising and de-racialisation of monopoly capital in South Africa – the former by opening up to global markets, and the latter by promoting a black bourgeoisie'. The national democratic revolution was portrayed, they argue, as a stage that required the 'completion' and consolidation of a 'capitalist democracy' in South Africa. They reject the 'explicit two-stage-ism' of the CPSA conference of 1929 and emphasise instead the two interrelated processes of combined and uneven development of South Africa as a semi-peripheral country within the imperialist system, with an 'internal articulation reproducing a racialised cheap labour system'.

In 1993, the SACP adopted the slogan 'Socialism is the future: Build it now'. It was, Cronin and Mashilo suggest, a shift away from stage-ism to a socialist struggle seen as being fought in and through a Gramscian-type national democratic 'war of position' across all key sectors of power. This, they assert, must also involve a struggle for national sovereignty through a 'relative delinking' from the global order and democratic popular sovereignty over the capitalist market through 'progressive de-commodification', including the 'solidarity economy'.

We hope that by approaching this debate through the 'hidden voices' of the past this volume will act as a catalyst in developing a new research agenda and political project that takes the debate forward in the context of a democratic state in the twenty-first century. Such a project, we argue, should begin by revisiting the National Question.

NOTES

1 We would like to thank John Pampallis and Allison Drew for their useful comments on earlier drafts of this Introduction.

2 Tony Morphet, in his Afterword to the recently re-published edition, interprets Turner's phrase 'the present as history' as placing 'all aspects of the present social life as provisional and already in movement in the processes of change' (Morphet, 2015: 242).

3 We do not see non-racialism as a distinct political project. Instead, it underpins to a greater or lesser extent virtually all of the political discourse. As Soske argues in his comprehensive analysis of the ambiguous and contested nature of the term non-racialism, it is not possible to 'reduce non-racialism to a single, definite idea (as)... there are Marxist, liberal, and African nationalist versions of (non-racialism)' (2015: 3).

4 There are four notable exceptions: Neville Alexander (1979), Andrew Nash (1999, 2014), Peter Hudson (2009, 2013, 2014, 2015) and Peter Vale, Lawrence Hamilton and Estelle Prinsloo (2014).

5 In 1934 the Dominion colonies were given full independence and legislative powers equal to Britain.

6 During the workshops leading up to this manuscript, we included discussions (led by Chris Saunders) of the democratic liberal tradition. However, we eventually decided not to include that strand in this volume, interesting as it is, since South African liberals never directly addressed the National Question.

7 Jeremy Cronin and Alex Mashilo argue for a socialist struggle fought in and through a Gramscian-type national democratic 'war of position' across all key sectors of power; see Chapter One in this volume.

8 There has also been a revival of interest in Marxism (Burawoy and Von Holdt, 2012; Williams and Satgar, 2013; Friedman, 2015). The establishment of the Mzala Nxumalo Centre for the Study of South African Society in Pietermaritzburg in 2015 is another example of scholarly interest in the National Question and Marxism.

9 Traditions, as distinct from narratives or stories, are handed down from generation to generation and have deep symbolic significance. We do not see non-racialism as a distinct tradition; it underpins much of the contemporary political discourse.

10 The CAD was the Coloured Affairs Department established by the government; it was seen as a segregationist institution. The Anti-CAD movement was begun in February 1943 at a conference in Cape Town called by the Teachers League of South Africa.

11 Bill Nasson's depiction of the NUEM as a 'coloured intelligentsia' is a stereotype. Their best-known leader was I.B. Tabata, who was not 'coloured', nor were Livingstone Mqotsi, Andrew Lukele, etc. I would like to thank Allison Drew for pointing this out.

12 We would like to thank Allison Drew for helping us formulate a more nuanced view of the Unity movement.

13 See Dan O'Meara (1983) for a different interpretation that focuses on how Afrikaner nationalism laid the foundations for the rise of an Afrikaner bourgeoisie.

14 Martin Legassick died while this volume was being edited.

15 'Liberalism', Maloka (2014: 273) argues, 'is not a product of the anti-colonial struggle, but an anti-thesis to the latter. In its various manifestations, its ambition was to capture black nationalism, subvert it, and dilute it of its radical content. It wanted to subordinate the anti-colonial struggle to its leadership. Thanks to its political choices and strategy, it distanced itself from the liberation movement, opting instead for participation in the white-only parliament'.

16 A robust debate took place in the letters columns of the *Business Day* newspaper on the land question. Jeremy Cronin, deputy general secretary of the SACP, cited the property clause as evidence of the 'eminently progressive Constitution, which acknowledges that the majority of

South Africans continue to suffer from a colonial history of prolonged and systematic expropriation' (Cronin, 2015: 10). John Kane-Berman (2015: 11), a traditional liberal, vehemently disagreed, arguing that the recently proposed Expropriation Bill 'seeks to prevent the courts from pronouncing on this very issue. The victim of an expropriation is thus empowered to go to court only to contest the amount of compensation offered, not to question the validity of the expropriation itself or even whether it is constitutionally compliant'.

REFERENCES

Alexander, Neville (writing as No Sizwe) (1979) *One Azania, One Nation.* London: Zed.

Alexander, Peter, Claire Ceruti, Keke Motseke, Mosa Phadi and Kim Wale (2013) *Class in Soweto.* Pietermaritzburg: UKZN Press.

Burawoy, Michael and Karl von Holdt (2012) *Conversations with Bourdieu: The Johannesburg Moment.* Johannesburg: Wits University Press.

Carr, E.H. (1974) *Socialism in One Country 1924 to 1926,* Second edition. Harmondsworth: Pelican.

Cock, Jacklyn (2007) *The War against Ourselves: Justice, Nature and Power.* Johannesburg: Wits University Press.

Craven, Patrick (2014) Speaker's Notes for COSATU Spokesperson, Mayday 2014. Unpublished document.

Cronin, Jeremy (2015) Constitutional Gripe (Letter). *Business Day,* 20 May 2015, page 10.

Davis, Mike (2015) Marx's Lost Theory: The Politics of Nationalism in 1848. *New Left Review,* 93 (May/June): 45–66.

Drew, Allison (2000) *Discordant Comrades: Identities and Loyalties on the South African Left.* Pretoria: Unisa Press.

Filatova, Irina (2012) The Lasting Legacy: The Soviet Theory of the National Democratic Revolution and South Africa. *South African Historical Journal,* 64(3): 507–37.

Friedman, Steven (2015) *Race, Class and Power: Harold Wolpe and the Radical Critique of Apartheid.* Pietermaritzburg: UKZN Press.

Gibbs, Timothy (2014) *Mandela's Kinsmen: Nationalist Elites and Apartheid's First Bantustan.* Martlesham: James Currey.

Habib, Adam (2015) Habib's Eight Key Strategies to Fix Wits. Getting Ahead, *Mail & Guardian,* June 12 to 18.

Harmel, Michael (1953) Observations on Certain Aspects of Imperialism in South Africa. *Viewpoints and Perspectives,*1(3): 27–38. Part of the Johannesburg Discussion Club papers, held in the African Studies collection, Jagger Library, University of Cape Town.

Hart, Gillian (2013) *Rethinking the South African Crisis: Nationalism, Populism and Hegemony.* Pietermaritzburg: UKZN Press.

Hassim, Shireen (2014) *The ANC Women's League: Sex, Politics and Gender.* Johannesburg: Jacana.

Hobsbawm, Eric (1995) *Age of Extremes.* London: Abacus.

Hudson, Peter (1986) The Freedom Charter and the Theory of National Democratic Revolution. *Transformation,* 1: 6–38.

Hudson, Peter (2009) Taking the Democratic Subject Seriously. *Social Dynamics,* 35(2): 394–410.

Hudson, Peter (2013) The State and the Colonial Unconscious. *Social Dynamics,* 39(2): 263–77.

Hudson, Peter (2014) Liberalism, Colonialism and National Democracy. *Theoria,* 61(3): 89–101.

Hudson, Peter (2015) Colonialism and Capitalism in South Africa Today. Unpublished paper, Department of Political Studies, University of the Witwatersrand.

Jara, Mazibuko K. (2013) Critical Reflections on the Crisis and Limits of ANC 'Marxism'. In *Marxisms in the 21st Century: Crisis, Critique & Struggle,* edited by Michelle Williams and Vishwas Satgar. Johannesburg: Wits University Press.

Kane-Berman, John (2015) Cronin's Red Herrings (Letter). *Business Day,* 21 May 2015, page 11.

Karis, T. and Carter, G.M. (eds) (1973) *From Protest to Challenge: A Documentary History of African Politics in South Africa 1882–1964. Volume 2: Hope and Challenge 1935–1952.* Standard University: Hoover Institution Press.

Karis, T. and Carter, G.M. (eds) (1977) *From Protest to Challenge: A Documentary History of African Politics in South Africa 1882–1964. Volume 3: Challenge and Violence 1953–1964.* Standard University: Hoover Institution Press.

Kies, B.M. (1953) The Contribution of the Non-European Peoples to the World Civilisation. A.J. Abrahamse Memorial Lecture held under the Auspices of the Teachers League of South Africa, Cape Town, November 1953.

Laclau, Ernesto (1991) Introduction. In *Marxism and Nationalism: Theoretical Origins of a Political Crisis,* by Ephraim Nimmi. London: Pluto.

Legassick, Martin (2007) *Towards Socialist Democracy.* Pietermaritzburg: UKZN Press.

Lissoni, Arianna, Jon Soske, Natasha Erlank, Noor Nieftagodien and Omar Badsha (2012) *One Hundred Years of the ANC: Debating Liberation Histories Today.* Johannesburg: Wits University Press.

Maloka, Eddie (2014) *Friends of the Natives: The Inconvenient Past of South African Liberalism.* Durban: Third Millennium.

Mapungubwe Institute of Strategic Reflection (Mistra) (2014) *Nation Formation and Social Cohesion: An Enquiry into the Hopes and Aspirations of South Africans.* Johannesburg: Mistra.

Marcus, Tessa (1988) The Women's Question and National Liberation in South Africa. In *The National Question in South Africa,* edited by Maria van Diepen. London: Zed.

Marks, Shula and Stanley Trapido (1987) *The Politics of Race, Class and Nationalism in Twentieth Century South Africa.* London and New York: Longman.

Mawbey, John (2014) The Unresolved National Question in Left Thinking: Seeking Lineages and Hidden Voices. Concept paper commissioned by the Chris Hani Institute for the First Workshop on 'The National Question under Apartheid, Hidden Voices: Unpublished Works 1950s to 1990', Johannesburg, June 2014.

Morphet, Tony (2015) The Intellectual Reach of The Eye of the Needle. In *The Eye of the Needle: Towards Participatory Democracy in South Africa.* Calcutta: Seagull.

Nairn, Tom (1975) The Modern Janus. *New Left Review,* 94 (November/December).

Nash, Andrew (1999) The Moment of Western Marxism in South Africa. *Comparative Studies of South Asia, Africa and the Middle East,* X1X (1): 66–82.

Nash, Andrew (2014) The Double Lives of South African Marxism. In *Intellectual Traditions in South Africa: Ideas, Individuals and Institutions,* edited by Peter Vale, Lawrence Hamilton and Estelle Prinsloo. Pietermaritzburg: UKZN Press.

Nasson, Bill (1990) The Unity Movement: Its Legacy in Historical Consciousness. *Radical History Review,* 46(7): 189–211.

Ntsebeza, L. (2005) *Democracy Compromised: Chiefs and the Politics of Land in South Africa.* Cape Town: HSRC Press.

Nzimande, Bonginkosi E. (2015) The People's Republic of China: An Opportunity for Delinking from Imperialism? Reflections from Beijing. *Umsebenzi Online,* 11(25), July 23.

O'Meara, Dan (1983) *Volkskapitalisme – Class, Capital and Ideology in the Development of Afrikaner Nationalism 1934–1948.* Johannesburg: Ravan.

Seekings, Jeremy and Nicoli Nattrass (2006) *Class, Race and Inequality in South Africa.* Pietermaritzburg: UKZN Press.

Slabbert, Frederick Van Zyl (2006) *The Other Side of History.* Johannesburg: Jonathan Ball.

Slovo, Joe (1988) The South African Working Class and the National Democratic Revolution. *Umsebenzi,* Discussion document published by the South African Communist Party.

Soske, J (2015) The Impossible concept: Settler Liberalism, Pan-Africanism, and the Language of non-racialism, *African Historical Review* Volume 47, Number 2, pp. 1–36.

Stalin, Josef (1913) Marxism and the National and Colonial Question. In *Stalin as Revolutionary, 1879–1929. A Study in History and Personality,* edited by Robert Tucker, 1973. New York: W.W. Norton.

Vale, Peter, Lawrence Hamilton and Estelle Prinsloo (editors) (2014) *Intellectual Traditions in South Africa: Ideas, Individuals and Institutions.* Pietermaritzburg: UKZN Press.

Williams, Michelle and Vishwas Satgar (2013) *Marxisms in the 21st Century: Crisis, Critique and Struggle.* Johannesburg: Wits University Press.

Wolpe, Harold (1988) *Race, Class and the Apartheid State.* Paris: Unesco.

PART ONE

KEY FOUNDATIONAL TRADITIONS

DECENTRING THE QUESTION OF RACE: CRITICAL REFLECTIONS ON COLONIALISM OF A SPECIAL TYPE

Jeremy Cronin and Alex Mohubetswane Mashilo

In much activist and academic discussion, the National Question tends to be dominated by matters of race, nationality, ethnicity and identity – not least in South Africa, and for obvious reasons. These emphases are not misplaced. 'Race' and especially racism, along with related issues like ethnic rivalries and xenophobia, continue to be burning concerns in contemporary South Africa. However, an overemphasis on race (that is, on one or another form of identity politics) coupled with the second word in the term 'National Question' might further suggest that essentially we are dealing here with a puzzle, the persistence perhaps of backward prejudices, resurgent and problematic ethnic identities, or 'race relations' that require delicate management. Several recent African National Congress (ANC) Strategy and Tactics documents travel in this direction.

All this might then encourage us to conceptualise the National Question as a matter of 'false consciousness' as is the case with a colour-blind, liberal humanism which states that 'there is no such thing as race' – which in bio-genetic terms is of course true. This in turn grounds other contemporary arguments about 'irrational' voter behaviour based on 'identity'. The association of the National Question with false consciousness also occurs in various more left-leaning perspectives, one of which could be summarised thus: 'Nationalism is inherently and ultimately a bourgeois trick to obscure class exploitation'. Or, as Benedict Anderson (1991) asserts, nations are 'imagined communities'.

We do not intend to engage directly and in detail with the substantial South African and international literature that has dealt with these important issues of race, ethnicity, nationality, the concept of the nation, and the like.[1] Rather, we hope to shift somewhat the central focus of the discussion on the National Question. In doing this we are not entering into an old South African debate that surfaced in activist circles in the 1980s: 'class versus race'. On the contrary, we are seeking to illustrate how the configuration of both class realities and racial/national identities have been shaped by the manner in which the capitalist political economy of South Africa has been (and remains) inserted within the global circuit of capitalist accumulation and reproduction. Although it is no longer relevant to describe the South African reality as 'colonialism of a special type' (CST), we will argue that critically re-examining the contested idea of CST can contribute to a better appreciation of the National Question. In shifting focus in this manner, we seek to illustrate that understanding the pre-1994 South African capitalist political economy as grounded in colonial-type articulations helps to clarify South Africa's concrete specificity within a general world capitalist system. This, in turn, should contribute to a better understanding of the possibilities and challenges of advancing democratic, working-class and popular struggles.

A central thesis of this chapter is that CST and the political economy of South Africa are best understood as the interrelationship between two colonial-type core/periphery relations. The first is an *external* colonial relationship determining the semi-peripheral positioning of South Africa's emergent monopoly capital sector. It involves South Africa's incorporation into and subordination within the global imperialist accumulation chain, essentially as an exporter of primary commodities produced on the basis of super-exploited (cheap) labour. The second is an *internal*, racialised articulation between what was formerly an oppressed black majority and a white minority. This internal articulation was grounded through the first half of the twentieth century in what Harold Wolpe (1972) insightfully analysed as a core/periphery relation between two distinct modes of production.

These systemic features of South Africa's political economy are the consequence of a complex history of domination and resistance in the wider context of the global expansion of capitalism. They include the relatively effective and prolonged resistance of pre-colonial African societies to colonial settlement. Despite the genocidal intent of much of the colonisation process, by the beginning of the twentieth century, the overwhelming majority of those living in South Africa were of indigenous African descent. (This is clearly an important specificity when compared to other areas of extensive European settlement in temperate zones of the New World.) Other early specificities of the South African reality were the Anglo-Boer War and the particular challenges of industrial mining requiring high levels of capital investment and significant quantities of low-paid manual labour. The 'special' in Colonialism of a Special Type should refer not so much to the mistaken notion of South Africa's exceptionalism but, rather, to the specific features of its political economy within a general context.

COLONIALISM AND ITS VARIANTS

Colonialism in the capitalist epoch was first implanted into what later became South Africa in the mercantilist phase of expanding capitalism, with European settlement at the Cape under the aegis of the Dutch East India Company. A second, relatively distinct dimension of colonial settlement was the direct result of the advancing development of a new phase of capitalism – industrial capitalism, with its early epicentre in Britain. The great flows of European migration to the New World in the nineteenth and twentieth centuries were part of the solution to the dramatic expansion of a European relative surplus-population.[2] Much of this migration went to North America, Australasia and the temperate zones of Latin America. But some of it came to South Africa, with the 1820 British settlers an important early wave in this process.

These earlier colonial realities have affected modern South Africa in many profound ways. However, it was in a third phase of the global expansion of capitalism – its imperialist phase, dominated by monopoly finance capital – that the core systemic features of our contemporary political economy were laid down.

From a Marxist perspective, colonialism (in its imperialist stage) and its variants – semi-colonialism,[3] settler colonialism, internal colonialism, colonialism of a special type and neocolonialism – all refer essentially to articulations of dominance/ domination. This relational structure also has a spatial dimension (core/periphery) which is underpinned by a political economy involving the extraction of surplus (colonial or imperialist rent) by the core from the periphery. The latter may or may not be developed or partially modernised in this process of domination, but it is a skewed and essentially blocked development – that is, underdevelopment rather than simply no development.

In the capitalist era, these colonial-type relations are embedded in the nature of capitalist expansion and accumulation that invariably involves development and underdevelopment, or combined and uneven development. It is important to note that combined and uneven development is a generalised feature of capitalism, and does not apply only to those core/periphery relations that might be more usefully described as variants of colonialism.

There is no Chinese Wall between colonial and non-colonial instances of combined and uneven development. Colonial variants, we suggest, are characterised in the politico-ideological domain by two factors. First is the evocation of national/racial/ethnic identity and difference – although often in quite different ways – by both the hegemonic power bloc and the oppressed. The former may, for instance, invoke racial superiority, or manifest destiny, or a civilising mission; the latter may, as in South Africa, seek to overcome narrow ethnic identities with mobilisation and a discourse of a common African – or black – national identity. These identities are not pre-determined, nor are they stable. They draw upon a range of pre-existing realities (language, culture, geography, real or attributed human physical features, historical narratives and, above all, traditions of struggle) and articulate these into colonially oppressive identities (ethnic divide-and-rule strategies, for instance) and/or a national emancipatory discourse. How these identities consolidate is contested and is ultimately the product of struggle, including struggle within and between classes.

The second and more important politico-ideological factor which characterises colonial-type formations is the presence of colonial administrative apparatuses distinct from but articulated with the metropole state – the Raj in India or, in South Africa, separate Native (later Bantu) Affairs administrations plus – here comes the double articulation on which we will elaborate later – tribal authorities, bantustan administrations and a range of racially separate municipal black local authorities. In the case of so-called semi-colonialism (as in China), the distinct administrative apparatus may be centred on foreign concessions at strategic ports, bestowing on the foreign powers a choke-hold over the political economy of the interior. In the case of neocolonialism (post-independence Latin America is the classical case), the subordinate administrative apparatus might be a nominally independent national state characterised by deeply compradorist features, making it little more than a client state. The common factor in all of these cases is the existence of at least two distinct (and nationally/ethnically shaded) administrative apparatuses that reinforce the pattern of combined and uneven development.

Incidentally, the constitutional disappearance of racially distinct state apparatuses in post-1994 South Africa is one reason why we argue that the attribution of colonialism, or CST, or even neocolonialism to the current South African reality would be inaccurate. This is not to deny the existence of serious compradorist tendencies and dangers within the state and among the new political elite, but the post-1994 democratic state has a relative measure of autonomous capacity partly linked to the significant democratic majority that the ruling party still enjoys. It cannot simply be dismissed as a client state. However, this measure of sovereign capacity certainly needs to be used with a greater degree of strategic coherence and determination (and, indeed, patriotism) if the dangers of full-scale neocolonisation are to be avoided.

To anticipate the central theme of this chapter, we are trying to ground the argument that overcoming an apartheid legacy is not the unique challenge of the National Question in the present. At the heart of addressing our contemporary National Question is the struggle against a persisting and specific pattern of combined and uneven development that precedes apartheid, that was reproduced in new variations during apartheid, and which is being continuously and actively reproduced, and in some respects aggravated, in the present.

THE CPSA AND THE COLONIAL QUESTION

The National Question was first incorporated into the programmatic perspectives of the Communist Party of South Africa (CPSA) in 1929 with the adoption of the so-called Native Republic thesis (later often referred to as the Black Republic thesis). This was an endorsement of the line developed at the 6th Congress of the Communist International (CI, or Comintern) meeting in August and September 1928. More specifically, it meant acceptance of the resolution on 'The South African Question' emanating from the CI's Executive Committee after the plenary congress. The resolution argued that the role of communists in South Africa was to work with the nascent national movements (the ANC was specifically mentioned). It called on the CPSA to adopt the 'correct slogan ... for an independent native South African republic as a stage towards a workers' and peasants' republic with full, equal rights for all races' (SACP, 1981: 94).

The CI resolution was hotly debated, and accepted with varying degrees of enthusiasm or resignation by the CPSA national conference in 1929.[4] In recent decades, the Black Republic thesis, the commitment to working with national liberation organisations, and the explicit two-stage-ism of the CI resolution have been the subject of considerable debate. Many commentators regard the Black Republic thesis as the original (Stalinist) sin of the Communist Party in South Africa, one which has marked and compromised its politics ever since (Bond, 2007; Harvey, 2014).

Although we certainly concur with the criticism of the rather mechanical stage-ism of the CI resolution, we believe that it contains seminal insights, and these require de-linking from any notion of stage-ism.

The opening paragraph of the CI's Executive Committee resolution reads:

> South Africa is a British Dominion of the colonial type. The development of relations of capitalist production has led to British imperialism carrying out the economic exploitation of the country with the participation of the white bourgeoisie of South Africa (British and Boer). Of course, this does not alter the general colonial character of the economy of South Africa, since British capital continues to occupy the principal economic positions in the country (banks, mining and industry), and since the South African bourgeoisie is equally interested in the merciless exploitation of the negro population (quoted in SACP, 1981: 91).

This is the passage that seeks to ground the new strategic line. Central to the argument that will be advanced here is the insistence by the Communist International on the *colonial* character of South Africa, notwithstanding the 1910 Union settlement, and notwithstanding the emergence of a 'white bourgeoisie'. This formulation begins to lay the basis for understanding South Africa's colonial character as resting on two interrelated processes of combined and uneven development – although this is not developed in the 1928 resolution. The important consequences of this double ('external' and 'internal') colonial-type articulation implicit in the Comintern resolution were obscured partly because of the controversy that the resolution triggered both within the CPSA at the time and continuously in broader debate ever since.

For a variety of reasons – notably, debilitating factionalism within the CPSA in the first half of the 1930s, and a major shift in the CI line to an anti-fascist popular front strategy in 1935 – the 'colonial' characterisation and the imperative of a national democratic struggle failed to receive any substantive theoretical development in the Communist Party's programmatic perspectives for some decades.

THE SACP'S 1962 PROGRAMME AND THE CONCEPT OF CST

The next time in which colonialism and the National Question receive significant programmatic treatment in the Communist Party is with its 1962 programme, *The Road to South African Freedom*. It is in this programme that the concept of 'colonialism of a special type' is introduced in an extended section in the *South African Communists Speak* collection. South Africa, the 1962 programme asserts:

> ... is not a colony but an independent state. Yet masses of our people enjoy neither independence nor freedom. The conceding of independence to South Africa by Britain, in 1910, was not a victory over the forces of colonialism and imperialism. It was designed in the interests of imperialism. Power was transferred not into the hands of the masses of people of South Africa, but into the hands of the White minority alone. The evils of colonialism, insofar as the non-White majority was concerned, were perpetuated and reinforced. A new type of colonialism was developed, in which the oppressing White nation occupied the same territory as the oppressed people themselves and lived side by side with them (SACP, 1981: 299).

This return to a colonial-type analysis of the South African reality marked a recalibration of the Party's strategic posture. It laid the basis for a more explicit foregrounding of a national liberation struggle. From the mid-1930s the Communist Party had embraced in its domestic strategy and tactics the Comintern's 1935 strategic shift to popular fronts against fascism. The CPSA in the 1940s and the underground South African Communist Party (SACP) in the 1950s tended to analyse the emergence of the National Party (NP) and its apartheid policies less in terms of the modernisation of a colonial-type system and more as the emergence of a racist fascist regime (Bunting, 1964). Undoubtedly, there was a strong fascist lineage within the apartheid regime, and there were abundant influences of German Nazism (dating back to the 1930s) on leading figures within the National Party. However, an over-emphasis on the fascism of the apartheid regime opened the way to two potential errors. In the first place, characterising it in this way tended to treat it as a post-1945 global anomaly rather than a regime that reproduced the semi-peripheral character of South Africa's political economy within a general imperialist system. Secondly, the fascist characterisation tended to deflect attention from the proactive and not just repressive measures that the apartheid regime introduced in order actively to reproduce a racialised (internal-colonial) cheap labour system.

HAROLD WOLPE'S 1975 INTERVENTION

While the conceptual shift of 1962 (in many respects a return to the strategic perspective of the late 1920s) was an important advance for the SACP, the CST concept itself, as Harold Wolpe was to argue in 1975, tended to remain largely descriptive. In particular, Wolpe noted the disjuncture between passages like the following that asserted: 'Power was transferred [in 1910] not into the hands of the masses of the people of South Africa, but into the hands of the White minority alone' (SACP, 1981: 299) and other passages that said something rather different:

> All Whites enjoy privileges in South Africa... This gives the impression that the ruling class is composed of the entire White population. In fact, however, *real power* is in the hands of the monopolists who own and control the mines, the banks and finance houses, and most of the farms and major industries (SACP, 1981: 300; our emphasis).

Wolpe was correct to understand conceptual wobbles like this as a symptom of an insufficiently grounded analysis of South Africa's political economy in which 'race' and 'class' categories awkwardly substitute for each other. But in our view, Wolpe did not go far enough in his critique. There is, for instance, another wobble in the 1962 programme that Wolpe does not highlight:

> ... in mining, industry, commerce and farming, monopolists dominate the country's economy. They are also closely linked with *state monopoly capital* ventures, such as Iscor (Iron and Steel), Escom (Electricity) and Sasol (Petrol)... These monopolists are *the real power* in South Africa (SACP, 1981: 301; our emphasis).

But then the programme continues:

> The South African monopolists act as *allies and agents of foreign imperialist interests* (SACP, 1981: 301; our emphasis).

This suggests that 'real power' ultimately rests with foreign imperialist interests, who nonetheless 'find common ground' with their local agents 'in the perpetuation of the colonial-type subjugation of the non-White population' (SACP, 1981: 301).

In his 1975 intervention, Wolpe sought to give greater theoretical rigour to what he rightly regarded as the still largely descriptive evocation of CST in the SACP's 1962 programme:

> While the internal colonial thesis purports to rest on class relations of capitalist exploitation, in fact it treats such relations as residual. That is to say, the conceptualisation of class relations, which is present in the theory, is accorded little or no role in the analysis of relations of domination and exploitation which are, instead, conceived of as occurring between 'racial', 'ethnic', and 'national' categories ... In so far as the theory of internal colonialism does accord relevance to relations of capitalist exploitation it does so in a manner which denudes the analysis of all historical specificity and thereby deprives the concept of analytical utility (Wolpe, 1975: n.p.)

In his 1975 essay, Wolpe endeavours to ground the concept more effectively by applying the analysis in his earlier seminal contribution (Wolpe, 1972; Legassick and Wolpe, 1977).

CST (or 'internal colonialism') was, in Wolpe's argument, historically based in the 'articulation between two modes of production' upon which South Africa's mineral-based industrial revolution was grounded. This was an 'internal', 'racialised' articulation between an oppressed black majority and a white minority. It was based through the first half of the twentieth century in a core/periphery relation between what Wolpe analyses as an articulation between two modes of production – an advanced industrial capitalist mode centred on mining on the one hand, and subsistence farming based in a patriarchal mode in the reserves on the other. At the heart of this articulation was the reproduction of cheap migrant labour.

By the mid-twentieth century the reproductive capacity of the subordinate patriarchal mode in the reserves was in considerable decline as a consequence of overcrowding and land degradation. Its centrality within the reproduction of the dominant capitalist mode of production was also challenged by growing African urbanisation, and the somewhat different labour market reproductive needs of industrial and commercial capital (for semi-skilled workers and urbanised mass consumers). So, was the concept of 'internal colonialism' still valid in the 1960s as the SACP's 1962 programme explicitly argues?

Wolpe's (1975) intervention becomes elusive at this point. 'Apartheid may be seen as the attempt of the capitalist state to maintain the system of cheap migrant-labour ... by means of the erection of a "perfected" and "modernised" apparatus of political domination' (Wolpe, 1975: n.p.). Then, Wolpe writes in a concluding footnote:

> I leave open whether the notion of 'internal colonialism' has any proper application in conditions of racial discrimination where, however, the internal relations within society are overwhelmingly capitalist in nature, that is, where non-capitalist modes of production, if they exist at all, are marginal (Wolpe, 1975: footnote 45).

In his tribute to Wolpe, Dan O'Meara (1997) touches on these concluding passages in Wolpe's intervention, suggesting that they are symptomatic of his impossible endeavour to reconcile a commitment to rigorous Marxist scholarship with his loyalty to the SACP and its programmatic perspectives.

Michael Burawoy attributes to Wolpe a similar inner conflict between the Marxist scholar and the loyal SACP supporter. In dealing with CST, Burawoy writes:

> [Wolpe] did not have the courage of his class convictions ... and could not imagine separating the socialist project from the national bourgeois project. At most, he saw this as a clash of short term and long term interests so that the National Democratic Revolution would be the first stage and the socialist revolution the second revolution. He didn't see what Frantz Fanon saw: two very different, opposed projects that existed side by side, that vied with each other within the decolonisation struggle (Burawoy, 2004: 665).

However, it is Burawoy who is confused here, and his confusion includes a misrepresentation of Frantz Fanon as well.[5] Burawoy is right to assert that two very different class projects are likely to be found within any decolonisation struggle. But, precisely for that reason, it is not pre-ordained that an internally contested national democratic revolution will be captured by a national bourgeois project although it may well become hegemonised by a bourgeois project (a point to which we shall return later).

Wolpe's grounding of the early variant of CST in an articulation between two modes of production certainly represents a major advance in the Marxist analysis of the post-1910 South African capitalist social formation. However, the full potential of this breakthrough, and particularly the possibilities of extending its underlying approach into the apartheid period in order better to analyse both the strategies of apartheid-era monopoly capital and those of the popular resistance, was weakened by several lacunae in Wolpe's 1975 intervention.

First, by treating the 1962 SACP's perspective as based on the struggle against 'internal colonialism' (rather than the actual term used in *Road to South African Freedom* – that is, 'colonialism of a special type'), Wolpe tends to foreclose on the possibility of understanding the interdependence of the twin (internal and external) colonial-type articulations in shaping South Africa's political economy. We have conceded that in both the 1928–1929 characterisation (with its largely external colonial focus) and the 1962 characterisation (with its largely internal colonial focus), this double set of articulations is implicit but remains largely undeveloped. Wolpe narrows the field even further.

A second shortcoming in Wolpe's 1975 paper is the assumption that a colonial (or at least an 'internal colonial') reality could only really be ascribed to a situation in which there was a significant articulation between a dominant capitalist and a dominated non-capitalist mode of production. But are colonial-type relations of dominance/domination necessarily grounded in two different modes of production? The following is the passage in Marx's *Capital* upon which Wolpe relies in order to advance his 'two modes of production' insight into the foundational internal colonial character of South African capitalism:

> Within its process of circulation … the circuit of industrial capital whether as money-capital or as commodity capital crosses the commodity circulation of the most diverse modes of social production, so far as they produce commodities. No matter whether these commodities are the output of production based on slavery, of peasants … of state enterprises … or of half-savage tribes, etc., as commodities and money they come face to face with the money and commodities in which industrial capital presents itself and enter … into its circuit. The character of the process of production from which they originate is immaterial. They function as commodities in the market, and as commodities they enter into the circuit of industrial capital as well as into the circulation of the surplus value incorporated into it … To replace them they must be reproduced and to this extent the capitalist mode of production is conditional on modes of production lying outside of its own stage of development (cited by Wolpe as: Marx, *Capital*, vol. 2, pp. 109–110).

This seminal passage, prefiguring one aspect of what later Marxists would refer to as the law(s) of combined and uneven development within capitalism, is used by Wolpe (we think fruitfully) to advance the related dialectical proposition of a conservation/destruction tendency within capitalist development. Specifically within the South African reality, the expanded reproduction of mining monopoly capitalism was premised on the conservation of a subordinate patriarchal, non-capitalist mode of production in the reserves (and wider southern African hinterland), while the very development of capitalism at the same time tended to erode this subordinate mode.

However, several things need to be noted about this passage. It is not intended to be a characterisation of a colonial-type relationship per se but, rather, a description of how the expanded reproduction of industrial capitalism may involve the entry of commodities emanating from less advanced forms of production into the circuit of capitalist production and reproduction. This may even involve the need, from the perspective of industrial capital, to conserve such less-advanced forms of production within a national or global setting. Secondly, although Marx here uses the term 'modes of production', it is clear that at least some of what he lists under this rubric, notably 'state enterprises', would not now normally be considered a separate mode of production.

More critically, following Luxemburg, Lenin and others, imperialist-era colonial and neocolonial relations are clearly understood to involve, inter alia, the extraction of imperialist rent not just from pre-capitalist formations, but also and increasingly from subordinated capitalist production in the periphery. An obvious contemporary example would be sweatshops in Asia linked into the value chains of major transnational corporations.

Related to the above, Wolpe's conceptualisation of the capitalist mode of production tends to be grounded rather exclusively in Marx's *Capital* Volume 1 which uncovers the 'secret' of capitalist surplus production through a 'willing-seller, willing-buyer', 'freely contracted' appropriation of surplus labour-time from 'free' waged labourers at the point of production. However, as David Harvey (2003: 114) has argued in recent times, Volume 1 of *Capital*, for the purposes of analytic explication, treats the capitalist mode of production abstractly as a closed system, as a 'thing' rather than a process. It is only in the lesser-read Volume 2 that the conditions for the expanded reproduction of capitalism – that is, the challenge of actual surplus, 'realisation' – are considered:

> The disadvantage of these assumptions [in Volume 1] is that they relegate accumulation based upon predation, fraud, and violence to an 'original stage' [of 'primitive accumulation'] that is considered no longer relevant or, as with Luxemburg, as being somehow 'outside' of capitalism as a closed system (D. Harvey, 2003: 144).

Harvey argues that the 'primitive accumulation' – the extraction of surplus associated with, for instance, colonial dispossession – is a continuing (and expanding) feature of contemporary capitalism in a variety of old and new forms of dispossession. These include commodification of land and water resources, debt peonage, structural adjustment and other austerity programmes involving privatisation and the rolling back of welfare gains.

In the South African reality, the tendency to treat the capitalist mode of production largely from the perspective of point-of-production surplus extraction runs the risk of seeing apartheid as 'outside' of a capitalist logic. Of course, we should guard against excessive structuralism but, as we will argue later, the mass education (Bantu Education) and mass township housing initiatives during the apartheid era were not external to the need for the expanded reproduction of capital; rather, they were critical interventions to sustain a racially segmented reproduction of labour for the capitalist South African reality of the 1950s and 1960s.

Furthermore – and this will become more central in our later arguments about the relevance of all of this to the current struggle for socialism in South Africa – there are the important insights into the capitalist reproduction of labour power developed by Marxist feminists. Diane Elson lays the groundwork for such an understanding:

> In a capitalist economy labour power is separated from the means of subsistence, and the process of production and reproduction is a dependent variable, shaped by the accumulation process. The fundamental antagonism between buyer and seller [of labour-power] is that between households as sellers of labour power and enterprises as buyers of labour power (Elson, 1988: 27–8).

Elson's concern here is to develop a socialist agenda. She goes on to argue that this will require an inversion (what we will later refer to as a 'partial de-linking') of the articulation between capitalist enterprise and proletarianised household, in which 'the process of production and reproduction of labour power is the independent variable to which the accumulation process accommodates' (Elson, 1988: 28). Put another way, Elson is arguing that a socialist struggle needs to invert the enterprise-household relationship, prioritising the production of use-values for proletarian households (and, we would add, communities), making this the 'independent variable' to which the capitalist accumulation process is increasingly subordinated. Essentially, this involves the free (or at least de-commodified) social production of a range of basic services to the household/proletarian community (health, education, water, sanitation, a basic minimum money income *and* the socialisation of household and community work).

We will touch on these perspectives in the concluding section of this chapter. For the moment, we are simply arguing that the exploitative reproduction of labour power under capitalism involves a variety of social and economic activities which may, or may not, involve an articulation between two separate modes of production. Although Elson is not dealing with a colonial-type interaction between a household and a capitalist enterprise, where this interaction is over-determined by racial/national features it may also be integral to a colonial-type reality.

In short, in our view Wolpe's hesitation in extending the concept of 'internal colonialism' to the post-1945 reality in South Africa (on the grounds that the reproductive capacity of a separate mode of production in the reserves was considerably diminished) is not well-founded.

APARTHEID'S SOCIAL WAGE AND EXPLOITED LABOUR POWER

Another gap in Wolpe's 1975 intervention is his view that, with the decline of the reproductive capacity of the reserves, the apartheid capitalist system paid scant attention to
other ways of reproducing racialised (black) labour power. Although the regime did seek
to conserve the residual capacity of the reserves, Wolpe writes:

> The diminution of the product from these Reserve economies generates rural
> impoverishment and, also, in the absence of the assumption by the capitalist
> sector of responsibility for indirect wages, extreme urban impoverishment. The
> consequence is increasing African pressure on wages and on rural conditions,
> pressure which becomes elaborated into an assault on the whole political and eco-
> nomic structure in the 1940s and 1950s. Apartheid may be seen as the attempt of
> the capitalist state to maintain the cheap migrant-labour system, in the face of this
> opposition, by means of the erection of a 'perfected' and 'modernised' apparatus
> of political domination (Wolpe, 1975: n.p.).

These perspectives are partially correct. The deepening crisis in South Africa in the articulation between two modes of production became increasingly evident in the 1940s and
1950s. It certainly led to growing popular and working-class mobilisation and struggle in
both rural and urban areas. Similarly, the apartheid phase can be understood as a direct
response to the rising tide of popular and class struggle through the intensification of
racially oppressive domination through state power.

However, this reading of the apartheid phase of white minority rule neglects the not
insignificant (if always racially specific) capitalist state interventions into the reproduction of cheap labour power. Wolpe simply asserts there was an absence of the assumption
by the capitalist sector of responsibility for indirect wages. Although this might have
been largely true of the 1940s and first half of the 1950s, as the apartheid system gathered
momentum increasingly vicious state oppression was complemented by major 'social
wage' or reproductive interventions – particularly with the mass roll-out of education
and the mass construction of (peri)-urban township housing.

The apartheid regime vastly expanded education infrastructure and secondary schooling in these semi-peripheral township locations under the aegis of Bantu
Education. The inferior character of this education system is often and correctly criticised, but the scale of the roll-out is sometimes forgotten. When the National Party
took power in 1948, the average black child spent only four years in school, and only a
quarter of black children of schoolgoing age were enrolled as pupils. Under the Bantu
Education system the number of places for black pupils increased rapidly. But the racial
inequalities in terms of government spending were massive, and with the growing

intake of black pupils the per capita inequality increased. In 1953 government spending per African pupil was 14 per cent of that for each white pupil; by 1968 it had declined to 6 per cent (Giliomee, 2012).

This significant expansion of education for blacks was not, of course, due to any enlightened philanthropy on the part of the apartheid regime. It was a strategic response to the growing demand for more literate, more numerate semi-skilled labour, while professional training and qualifications in the expanding but limited black universities ('bush colleges') was intended to be reserved for staffing 'homeland' administrations in the bantustans. In short, the mass-based education and training dispensation that was rolled out under the apartheid regime was a systematic intervention that formed part of its overall state-led industrial policy and labour market planning. While modernising, it actively conserved the exclusion and simultaneous inferior inclusion of the black majority. The peri-urban township (rather than the reserves) became the main peripheral location for the reproduction of semi-skilled labour. These apartheid capitalist housing and education interventions constituted key elements of the modernising (but not abolition) of an internal colonialism. In many respects, while the articulation between rural reserves and the capitalist core continued, these developments increasingly underpinned the development of a new form of labour migrancy – 'daily migrancy' to evoke Michael Denning's (2010) term – and the expanded reproduction of a cheap reserve army of labour in peri-urban locations.

CST AND INSURRECTION IN THE 1970s AND 1980s

We have already noted that colonialism in its various forms, like the broader category of uneven development, involves a spatial relationship (core/periphery). This is not merely a metaphorical use of a spatial reference. Space was always a feature of earlier forms of racial segregation in South Africa and of apartheid itself. But, perhaps because of this very self-evidence, spatiality has not always been sufficiently theorised, or adequately incorporated into an understanding of the nature of popular political struggle in South Africa.

The 1962 SACP programme characterised CST as 'a new type of colonialism ... in which the oppressing White nation occupied the same territory as the oppressed people themselves and lived side by side with them' (SACP, 1981: 299). This is not entirely accurate, since the nationally oppressed were separated spatially from the white minority but within the borders of the same nation state. Nor is it entirely accurate to say that the oppressor and the oppressed 'lived side by side'. Spatial exclusion of the black majority was always interlinked with various mechanisms of simultaneous inferior inclusion – as wage labourers and retail consumers – within the dominant capitalist system.

This dialectic of racialised exclusion and simultaneous disadvantaged inclusion became absolutely critical for the semi-insurrectionary struggles that unfolded in a series of rolling waves from the mid-1970s through the 1980s and into the negotiations period of the early 1990s. The South African liberation struggle assumed a form that was somewhat different from the classical national liberation struggles of the twentieth century. The latter tended to be based on a rural peasant base in the remote countryside (China, Cuba and Vietnam, for instance). In South Africa from the mid-1970s, however, the epicentres of much popular struggle occurred along the axes of CST's exclusion/inferior-inclusion fault-lines. The proletarian township, the Bantu Education school and the bush college became the loci of popular power and partially liberated zones. The maximum weapon of struggle, even for the active working class which used the work-place as a point of organisation, was the temporary withdrawal of participation in disadvantaged inclusion – the general stay-away, consumer boycotts, bus boycotts, school boycotts, and so on. Because these were essentially centred on proletarianised communities, they could not be sustained indefinitely. Households were dependent on wages and on consumer items. However, localised productive/reproductive social activities (burial societies and other forms of cooperative savings initiatives such as stokvels, subsistence farming, the taxi industry, and a variety of semi-legal and illegal economic activities), and the petty surplus they produced, provided some buffering support to the struggle. Much of this remains under-researched.

We note these points because new questions now arise in the present. Understandably, overcoming the apartheid legacy and addressing the National Question are often conceptualised as a process of integration – integrating our urban spaces to overcome racial divides; integrating the 'informal' economy into the 'formal'; 'banking' the 'unbanked'; and so on. Yet, these initiatives often fail. That is largely because integration is liable to toss marginalised individuals and households into sink-or-swim situations, exposing them to the inequitable power relations that pre-exist within the labour, property, retail, agricultural and financial markets.

This raises a critical strategic and tactical question. How can integration occur on different terms, on the terms of the working class? That is to say, how do we alter the class balance of forces? It means, in part, building working-class and popular power not only through integration into existing capitalist markets, but also through a relative de-linking of proletarian households and communities from absolute dependency for survival on these very markets (Elson, 1988). This includes building sustainable livelihoods and producing community use-values, services and assets through cooperatives, public employment work guarantee schemes and other initiatives. The legacy of an internal CST geography might, in the case of land still under communal land tenure, for instance, assist this partial de-linking from the capitalist markets through the effective use of state power and community mobilisation.

EXTERNAL ARTICULATION? SOUTH AFRICA'S POLITICAL ECONOMY

We believe that this relatively long exploration of the concept of CST can help us better to understand both the challenges and the potential opportunities confronting progressive forces in South Africa. In particular, we believe that a critical re-examination of CST's key features can assist in countering a widespread failure to grasp the dominant strategic agenda of monopoly capital in South Africa in the post-1994 period.

The SACP's 1962 programme stated that, with the 1910 Union settlement, a new form of colonialism had been developed in South Africa with 'power transferred to the hands of the White minority alone'. But who transferred this power, and did they transfer all power? Although the 1962 programme does not ignore the persisting reality of imperialism, it fails to lay the basis for a deeper understanding of the ongoing subordination of South African monopoly capital to the core centres of advanced capitalism.

In ANC Strategy and Tactics documents of the 1990s, the concept 'imperialism' disappeared. The hegemonic reading of post-1994 South Africa is one of a prodigal returning to the bosom of a happy family (Mandela, 1999). It is the same perspective that led then president Thabo Mbeki in 2002 to hail the outcome of a G8 Summit as the 'birth of a more equitable system of international relations' and 'the end of the epoch of colonialism and neo-colonialism' (*Sunday Times*, 30 June 2002). Such statements are symptoms both of the mistaken assumption that the end of the Cold War also marked the end of imperialism, and the related misreading of the global trajectory of capitalism over the past half century. This has led to serious strategic and tactical errors, based on the illusion that post-1994 South Africa is located in the geopolitical West and that we are still living in the 'golden years' of capitalism that followed the Second World War.

The welfare state democracies in the advanced capitalist countries of the North from 1945 to the early 1970s occurred within a specific set of realities including the challenge of an alternative global Soviet bloc, and powerful domestic left and labour formations emerging from the anti-fascist struggles in much of Western Europe. The dominant capitalist power, the United States (US), and the advanced sections of capital had learned the negative lessons of the reparations that had followed the First World War, and were now committed to major investments into war-torn Western Europe and Japan. Marshall Plan aid and domestic Keynesian policies were the order of the day. Explicit or implicit national social pacts prevailed, ensuring productive investment, high tax contributions, commitments to near full employment and extensive social wage measures. However, by the mid-1970s slowing growth and inflation were the early indicators of a deepening systemic crisis. National monopoly capital in Western Europe increasingly led the charge against domestic social compacts – the turn to neo-liberalism, the rolling back of the welfare state and high domestic taxation, the taming of trade unions, the trans-nationalisation of corporate structures, the globalisation of investment in pursuit of low-wage markets, and growing financialisation were all part of this shift.

A subordinate but by no means insignificant South African monopoly capital sector echoed this global trajectory, but with its own specificities. In many respects South Africa's post-Second World War white polity constituted a racialised welfare state, ensuring privileges that helped to secure the relative cross-class coherence of a white power bloc. In the 1970s, apartheid South Africa, like other semi-peripheral economies, was also the beneficiary of globalising foreign direct investment (FDI) into industrial sectors such as auto manufacturing, chemicals and textiles. However, the global capitalist crises, marked among other things by the two oil shocks (1973 and 1979), also made an impact on the profitability of South African monopoly capital. Deepening working-class and popular unrest that coincided with these developments compounded the challenges.

Economic and financial sanctions against apartheid South Africa, and the regime's defensive responses – exchange controls and widening security fiscal requirements – meant that South African monopoly capital found itself locked in and paying taxes at home. This was at a time when other monopoly corporations were globalising, escaping domestic tax obligations and pursuing low-wage market opportunities. These low-wage markets had burgeoned dramatically in the 1980s with China's economic liberalisation and, after 1989, with the dismantling of socialism in Eastern Europe. With significant surplus bottled up within South Africa, local monopoly capital enterprises increasingly conglomerated and diversified, with mining and finance capital expanding into retail, forestry, agro-processing, logistics and property. However, any sustained inward industrial strategy was constrained by the small size (and racialised poverty) of the domestic market, and by the continued destabilisation of the region.

This was the context in which key sectors of South African monopoly capital from the mid-1980s began to explore the possibilities of a negotiated transition to a non-racial 'democracy'. However, their strategic objective was less about democracy and more about escaping the discipline of a national state. Under the aegis of the globally acclaimed Mandela transition, private South African monopoly capital successfully lobbied the new government for major liberalisation, conceding important labour rights on paper while undercutting many of these through retrenchments, labour brokering and casualisation. Most of South Africa's major corporations have rapidly trans-nationalised, and the new democratic state is compelled to engage with them more and more as foreign investors. While the upper managerial echelon of the remaining South African end of these corporations remains overwhelmingly white and male, it is increasingly irrelevant to describe the ownership as 'white'.

Trans-nationalisation through dual listings, mergers and acquisitions, dividend out-flows, transfer pricing, and the use of tax havens has deprived South Africa of major rev-enue sources at the very time that it has huge developmental challenges and a non-racial responsibility to all citizens, including those in townships and rural areas, which played a leading role in the crisis of apartheid. Monopoly capital which, as we have argued (following Wolpe and others), historically absconded from carrying the full cost of the reproduction of labour by dumping a major share of the costs onto labour reserves, has now increasingly dumped the challenge of restive townships onto the new democratic government.

WHAT IS TO BE DONE? THE NATIONAL QUESTION TODAY

The importance of breaking with stage-ism, without abandoning many of the core stra-tegic and tactical features associated with the CST thesis (the centrality of a national democratic revolutionary struggle, in particular), was to come dramatically to the fore in the years immediately following the 1994 democratic breakthrough. From around 1996, a leadership group around then deputy president Thabo Mbeki achieved a contested but undeniable dominance within both the ANC and the state. In opposition to this devel-opment, the SACP and the Congress of South African Trade Unions (COSATU) char-acterised this tendency as 'the 1996 class project', alluding to the announcement in 1996 of government's neoliberal macro-economic package, the Growth, Employment and Redistribution strategy (Gear). For the 1996 class project the National Question was essen-tially conceived of as the task of 'normalising' – which is to say, 'de-racialising' – South Africa's political economy. In particular, this underpinned the energetic promotion of black economic empowerment (BEE), seen largely as the creation of a new black, patri-otic bourgeoisie.

When the neoliberal and BEE interventions failed to address the continued repro-duction of racialised inequality, poverty and unemployment, those associated with the 1996 class project sought to provide an explanatory analysis with the notion of a 'first economy' and a 'second economy'. The first (capitalist) economy was claimed to be func-tioning well, but a supposed second economy needed state-led (or state-facilitated) inter-ventions to 'promote' it into the first economy. A series of one-off interventions were introduced to bring the denizens of the second economy into the formal, capitalist mar-ket. These included taxi recapitalisation, land reform and restitution, short-term public employment work opportunities, and (later) micro-credit. The assumption was that a new minibus, or a parcel of land, or sixty days of work opportunity would somehow promote second economy members into active and successful formal capitalist market activity as workers or entrepreneurs.

It is possible to recognise in this idea of first and second economies the shadow of what we have characterised as the historical internal colonial-type articulation between monopoly capital and the reproduction of a cheap labour regime through the racialised reproduction of a labour army. However, the 1996 class project conceived of this as two separate economies at different stages of development, with the second economy requiring 'developmental state' interventions to allow it to 'catch up'. Missing in this analysis was precisely the understanding of the dialectical process of development and under-development. It is the character of South Africa's monopoly capitalist economy and the double articulation (external and internal) associated with it that actively reproduces a second economy (or, rather, the crises of underdevelopment).

The neoliberal agenda of the Mbeki-ites consisted in reducing the core task of the National Question to the modernising and de-racialisation of monopoly capital in South Africa – the former by opening up to global markets, and the latter by promoting a black bourgeoisie. In short, the national democratic revolution was portrayed as a stage that required the completion and consolidation of capitalist democracy in South Africa.

Faced with this problematic stage-ism, the SACP re-visited its own programmatic understanding of the national democratic revolution. As far back as the early disputes around the Native Republic thesis within the CPSA, there had been voices querying the notion of stages. S.P. Bunting, for instance, in a 1928 letter to Eddie Roux referred to stage-ism as 'verbiage' and stated that 'no black republic in SA could be achieved without overthrowing capitalist rule' (cited in Hirson, 1989). In the 1970s Ruth First (1978: 97), a prominent SACP-aligned theorist, rejected the idea of stages. Joe Slovo stretched the notion of the interrelationship of a national democratic and socialist stage to the extreme, arguing that there was 'no Chinese Wall' between them, without, as Legassick (2007: 182) has correctly noted, ever quite abandoning a residual notion of two stages. In September 1993, addressing the Special Congress of COSATU, then SACP general secretary, Charles Nqakula (1993), advanced the theme 'Socialism is the Future...Build it Now!' Speaking on behalf of the SACP on the eve of the April 1994 elections, Nqakula began to develop the theme of actively building capacity for and momentum towards socialism in the midst of the national democratic revolution. These themes were taken forward programmatically by the SACP's ninth national congress in Soweto in November 1995, signalling a decisive break with two-stage-ism.

In breaking with a mechanical two-stage-ism the SACP was, it might seem, converging with a position long advanced by those associated with the Marxist Workers' Tendency (MWT) who, drawing on a Trotskyist legacy, argued for a national democratic struggle but in the context of a 'permanent revolution'. Here it might be useful to introduce the Gramscian distinction between a 'war of manoeuvre' and a 'war of position' – the former envisaging a rapid, frontal and typically anti-state insurrectionary advance, and the latter striving for systemic and cumulative transformations towards socialism, waged simultaneously across a range of sites of struggle including the state itself (P. Anderson, 1976). It would be wrong to imagine that there is a mechanical and unbridgeable gap between these two postures, but they do helpfully underline different strategic calculations. Since 1994, the SACP has adopted essentially a 'war of position' strategic posture which informs its participation in the state and Parliament as part of the ANC-led Tripartite Alliance. This strategic perspective is not rooted in a two-stage approach to the National Question but, rather, in the strategic calculation that a socialist democracy in South Africa has to be fought for through a national democratic war of position across all key sites of power.

But what exactly are the critical systemic transformations that are decisive for any socialist advance in the South Africa reality? This returns us to the central focus of this chapter. We have argued that South Africa's political economy continues to be dominated by what was formerly a colonial-type double articulation that still reproduces crises of underdevelopment – our inclusion as a semi-peripheral exporter of commodities within the world capitalist system, and the reproduction of a racialised cheap active and reserve army of labour. The former articulation is based on the latter, and vice-versa. Strategically, as the SACP's 2014 document *Going to the Root* argues, any socialist-oriented systemic transformation of this reality must involve a 'relative de-linking'– or, if you like, the progressive disarticulation – of these two axes of underdevelopment. This means a major state-led re-industrialisation of our economy to break out of our continued global semi-peripheralisation on the one hand, and the forging of a 'social' or 'solidarity' economy on the other hand. In the latter, the social production of use-values for the proletarianised majority increasingly trumps the production of commodities (exchange value) for private profit, and socially useful work trumps employment for a boss.

These struggles are essentially about building the capacity for democratic – that is, both popular and national – sovereignty. In the current South African reality, we argue, this goes to the very heart of the National Question.

NOTES

1. For a useful summary of recent debates on these topics, see Mike Davis (2015).
2. See Marx's *Capital* (volume.1, chapters XV ff.) for the classic analysis of these processes and the elaboration of the concept of a 'relative surplus-population'.
3. Imperialist enclave domination of the late-nineteenth and early twentieth centuries in China is often cited as an example of semi-colonialism.
4. There is an extensive literature on the debates within the CI and the CPSA around the 'Native Republic' thesis. Source documents can be found in SACP (1981) and Davidson et al. (2003). For a first-hand account from one CPSA participant, see Roux (1944). A useful historical survey of the debates can be found in Legassick (2007).

5   Fanon did not collapse a national liberation struggle unilaterally into a 'national bourgeois project' as Burawoy does. Fanon understood the importance of a progressive, social, humanist struggle within the national liberation movement: 'If (post-independence) nationalism is not explained, enriched and deepened, if it does not very quickly turn into a social and political consciousness, into humanism, then it leads to a dead end' (Fanon, 1963: 204).

REFERENCES

Anderson, Benedict (1991) *Imagined Communities: Reflections on the Origin and Spread of Nationalism.* London: Verso.

Anderson, Perry (1976) The Antinomies of Antonio Gramsci. *New Left Review,* I/100 (Nov–Dec): 5–78.

Bond, Patrick (2007) Introduction: Two Economies – or One System of Super-exploitation? *Africanus, Journal of Development Studies,* 37(2): 1–2.

Bunting, Brian (1964) *The Rise of South African Reich.* London: Penguin African Library.

Burawoy, Michael (2004) From Liberation to Reconstruction: Theory and Practice in the Life of Harold Wolpe. *Review of African Political Economy,* 31(102): 657–75.

Davidson, Apollon, Irina Filatova, Valentin Gorodnov and Sheridan Johns (eds.) (2003) *South Africa and the Communist International,* vol.1. London and Portland: Frank Cass.

Davis, Mike (2015) Marx's Lost Theory: The Politics of Nationalism in 1848. *New Left Review,* 93 (May–June): 45–66.

Denning, Michael (2010) Wageless Life. *New Left Review,* 66 (Nov–Dec): 76–97.

Elson, Diane (1988) Market Socialism or Socialisation of the Market? *New Left Review,* 172 (November–December): 3–44.

Fanon, Frantz (1963) *The Wretched of the Earth.* New York: Grove Press.

First, Ruth. (1978) After Soweto: A Response. *Review of African Political Economy,* 5(11): 93–100.

Giliomee, Hermann (2012) Bantu Education: Destructive Intervention or Part Reform? *New Contree,* 65: 67–86.

Harvey, David (2003) *The New Imperialism.* Oxford: OUP.

Harvey, Ebrahim (2014) COSATU crisis has its roots in 'colonialism of a special type'. *Business Day,* 24 November 2014.

Hirson, Baruch (1989) Bukharin, Bunting and the Native Republic Slogan. Originally published *Searchlight South Africa,* 1. Available online at https://www.marxists.org/archive/hirson/1989/native-republic.

Legassick, Martin (2007) *Towards Socialist Democracy.* Pietermaritzburg: University of KwaZulu-Natal Press.

Legassick, Martin and Harold Wolpe (1977) The Bantustans and Capital Accumulation in South Africa. *Review of African Political Economy,* 7: 87–107.

Mandela, Nelson (1999) Address by President Nelson Mandela at the Opening of Parliament, Cape Town, 5 February 1999. Available online at www.mandela.gov.za/mandela_speeches (accessed 29 October 2015).

Nqakula, Charles (1993) Socialism is the Future...Build It Now. Address to COSATU Special National Congress. *The African Communist,* 134: 9–14.

O'Meara, Dan (1997) The Engaged Intellectual and the Struggle for a Democratic South Africa – The Life and Work of Harold Wolpe. Address to inaugural conference of the Harold Wolpe Memorial Trust, April 1997. Available online at www.wolpetrust.org.za.

Roux, Edward. (1944) *S.P. Bunting: A Political Biography.* Cape Town: The African Bookman.

South African Communist Party (SACP) (1981) *South African Communists Speak. Documents from the History of the South African Communist Party, 1915–1980.* London: Inkululeko.

South African Communist Party (SACP) (2014) Going to the Root: Towards a Radical Second Phase of the National Democratic Revolution. *The African Communist,* 187 (4th Quarter): 4–40.

Wolpe, Harold (1972) Capitalism and Cheap Labour Power in South Africa: From Segregation to Apartheid. *Economy and Society,* 1(4): 425–56. Available online at www.wolpetrust.org.za.

Wolpe, Harold (1975) The Theory of Internal Colonialism: The South African Case. In *Beyond the Sociology of Development,* edited by Ivar Oxaal, Tony Barnett and Kegan Paul. London: Routledge and Kegan Paul. Available online at www.wolpetrust.org.za.

2

THE AFRICAN NATIONAL CONGRESS: SOCIAL DEMOCRATIC THINKING AND THE GOOD SOCIETY, 1940–1962

Robert van Niekerk

This chapter will build on previous research on the African National Congress (ANC) and the National Question rather than restate it (Suttner and Cronin, 1986; Van Diepen, 1988). It will focus on public goods and the idea of the 'good society' embedded in two foundational policy documents of the ANC: African Claims of 1943 and the Freedom Charter of 1955. It will discuss the thinking that informed these documents in the context of the struggle to overcome the racial and class inequalities of the apartheid era.

I chose this approach because I consider that the framing of the National Question is not reducible only to the struggle to end white domination. It is also about the idea of an alternative 'good society' – that is, a society planned and organised with particular social and economic arrangements to meet the needs of its citizens. The ANC, in the struggle to construct a nation, had defined an understanding of what the 'good society' was; this is reflected most significantly in African Claims and the Freedom Charter. These ANC policy documents are embedded in the idea that the state should actively intervene in the market to secure the social rights of citizenship for all citizens – which included rights to healthcare in the form of a national health service (NHS), the rights to education in the form of a comprehensive system of education, and rights to welfare in the form of a national system of welfare provision. These historical policy statements also directly imply or call for economic arrangements that are consistent with a neo-Keynesian social democratic strategy of economic development, where the state intervenes to secure decent employment for its citizens, including through investment in public goods such as health and education which are universally free at the point of delivery. They articulate a clear 'strategy of equality' for the society which the socialist and historian Richard Tawney described as

> ...the pooling of its surplus resources by means of taxation, and the use of the funds thus obtained to make accessible to all, irrespective of their income, occupation, or social position, the conditions of civilization which, in the absence of such measures, can be enjoyed only by the rich (Tawney, 1952: 130).

These two policy documents spoke to the rights of workers to organise themselves and to be decently housed in a manner concomitant with the prevailing living standards acceptable to the wider society. This 'strategy of equality' has been clearly embedded in the ANC's policy trajectory since at least African Claims in 1943; had it been implemented it would have led to the establishment of a social democratic welfare state. If we are to take these foundational ANC policy documents seriously, the resolution of the 'National Question' is thus the establishment of a constitutional democracy in a non-racial, unitary state based on a universal franchise, where public goods such as health, education and welfare are provided by the state as an entitlement of citizenship (and not dependent on the financial means of the citizen).

The debate on the relationship between the National Question and ideas of postcolonial social policy is one that has received little systematic attention in the scholarly literature on national liberation struggles. It was, however, an issue that was prominent in the thinking of radical intellectuals and scholars in the context of the struggle against Nazism and fascism during the 1940s and discussions on the new world order which was to replace it. For example, as early as 1942 the African-independence political activist George Padmore identified the strategic importance of the call by the anti-fascist Atlantic Charter to make global democratisation and extension of welfare part of the struggle against colonialism (Padmore and Cunard, 1942). The failure to articulate ideas of the good society more fully into the political programmes of anti-colonial and national liberation movements requires further research. In a valuable paper, Thandika Mkandawire (2009) concludes that the struggle for national liberation involved subsuming the social question within the imperatives of the National Question to create a coalition of class and social forces around a nationalist agenda that could overthrow colonial rule. The crisis of the development model in Africa following structural adjustment programmes, growing social differentiation and the rise of ethno-nationalism has led, however, to a new wave of democratisation and the possibility of new coalitions emerging; these could be focused on egalitarian social policy which requires 'decoupling struggles for recognition (Black Empowerment) from struggles for redistribution and equality' (Mkandawire, 2009: 154). The historian Frederick Cooper (1996) also draws attention to the displacement of social questions during struggles for economic rights by workers in the French and British colonies, in favour of a unifying nationalist discourse.

The reason such a social democratic agenda failed to be implemented has been the subject of significant scholarly discussion. The failure has been chiefly located in the post-apartheid government's adoption of a neoliberal policy framework of fiscal conservatism which has privileged market-based economic and social policies (Adelzadeh, 1996; Bond, 1996a, 1996b, 2005; McKinley, 1997; Fine, 2001; Alexander, 2002; Saul, 2005; Marais, 2011).

The attempts by Dr Aaron Motsoaledi, the minister of health, to establish a national health service funded by general taxation (referred to as National Health Insurance or NHI), revisits the social democratic policy trajectory embedded historically in ANC social policy. Based on the objective of achieving free universal healthcare provision for all inhabitants of South Africa at the point of delivery and based explicitly on social democratic principles of equity and social solidarity, the NHI policy proposals have created an opportunity for the ANC potentially to reconnect with its displaced social democratic 'strategy of equality' (Van Niekerk, 2012).

My key argument is thus that the social policy agenda of the ANC in the 1940s established an unmistakably social democratic agenda, rooted in the primacy of universal public goods provided by a unitary state as an entitlement of citizenship – public goods such as a national health service, a comprehensive system of national education, quality state-provided housing, a system of income maintenance for those who are unemployed or who could not work, and state-provided employment. This is the radical implication of African Claims (ANC, 1943), a document prepared under the leadership of perhaps the most significant political strategist of a modernising ANC, Alfred Bitini Xuma, president-general of the ANC between 1940 and 1949.

The substance of Xuma's policy positions on the good society were far more decisively radical than those of the ANC Youth League (ANCYL) – at least the Youth League in its earliest incarnation under Anton Lembede in the late 1940s – and were taken up by Albert Luthuli in the 1950s and expressed in the 1955 Freedom Charter. Both Xuma and Luthuli represent significant 'hidden voices' of social democratic thought in the ANC. An engagement with these ideas may create the possibility of reclaiming the ANC as a movement (and, now, political party) committed to the universal provision of public health, education and welfare to all its citizens, provided by a democratic, constitutional state as an entitlement of social citizenship – with accompanying economic arrangements which are unequivocally redistributive and give effect to the good society. In other words, a social democratic welfare state. Its achievement may also provide a meaningful solution to the still unresolved National Question.

A.B. XUMA AND AFRICAN CLAIMS

Between 1912 and 1952, the ANC attempted to secure citizen entitlements using non-violent strategies. Historically, the dominant concern of the ANC and allied movements was seeking civil and political rights for the African majority. A.B. Xuma, himself a medical doctor, took health and social policies seriously. Xuma's interest in social policies and the 'public good' that met the needs of disenfranchised blacks in segregation-era South Africa was evident in his statement as ANC secretary general in 1941, issued as *The Policy and Platform of the African National Congress – Statement by Dr A.B. Xuma*. Alongside the demand for franchise and representation rights for Africans are the following positions on social policy:

> D. Social Welfare: (1) Eligibility of Africans to enjoy all benefits from Social Welfare Departments of the Union Government on same principles as other sections (2) Pensions for aged and physically disabled Africans (3) Adequate hospital facilities for general and special purposes (4) Full extension of public health and preventative health measures to Africans (Xuma, 1941, in Karis and Carter, 1973: 169).

In 1942 Dr Xuma led an ANC deputation to the then United Party deputy prime minister, Jan Hofmeyr, to petition for full representation in government as well as other claims:

> We pressed, on principle, for the application of full benefits of social legislation to the Africans according to the human needs of the individual and not on a racial or colour basis ... [W]e urged the extension of the benefits of the Children's Act to African children, the application of disablement pensions, Blind pensions and Old age pensions to Africans ... we were told [in response] it was the policy of the Department of Social Welfare not to give the indigent African child more than he would receive on the basis of his father's wages of about three pounds. [B]esides we were told that it was the intention of the department not to take away the urge on the part of the mother to go out to work for her child (in Karis and Carter, 1973: 190–191)

The segregation government's response reminds one of the 'less eligibility' principle of the English Poor Laws of 1834, which ensured that state assistance was kept to a level which would not place the indigent in a better position than they would be in if they had stayed in, or entered into, employment. As T.H. Marshall (1950: 24) argued in his pioneering essay, the Poor Law was a substitute for the claims of the poor as a social right of citizenship: the claims could only be met if the claimants ceased to be citizens. Claimants to the Poor Law social grants were placed in a stigmatised, exclusionary social position by surrendering the civil and social rights they possessed. The application of English Poor Law principles in segregation-era South Africa resulted in the conflation of the poor with blacks (notwithstanding the large portion of the poor white community who lived in poverty in the same period but who were still considered full citizens); thus the poverty of blacks reinforced their citizenship disentitlement. Segregation legislation not only reproduced white economic domination by bifurcating the nation by race and class but also consolidated it through racialised social policies that reinforced unequal citizenship; to acknowledge blacks as full citizens in a single nation would undermine the entire fiscal and political edifice of the system of racialised capitalism during the era of segregation (and, later, apartheid).

Although it was to change in the later war years, the 'claims' to equality employed by the ANC in the early 1940s acknowledged the legal boundaries of the segregation-era state (and, in effect, a racial and class-bifurcated nation). The ANC thus sought access to health, social welfare and education for blacks in the reformist language of 'eligibility', 'adequacy' and 'extension' (Karis and Carter, 1973: 89). This legal strategy of the ANC – claiming equality and thus the social rights predicated on its achievement – proved unachievable, however, in the face of a state committed to maintaining white domination through a strategy of racial paternalism based increasingly on repressive political rule.

Tawney (1964: 103) comments on reliance on legal strategies to achieve equality:

> [I]n reality of course, except in a sense which is purely formal, equality of opportunity is not simply a matter of legal opportunity. Its existence depends, not merely on the absence of disabilities, but on the presence of abilities ... [I]n proportion as the capacities of some are sterilized or stunted by their social environment, while others are favoured or pampered by it, equality of opportunity becomes a graceful, but attenuated figment.

Xuma clearly understood the political significance of the struggle for an inclusive citizenship based on a universal franchise. He was aware that only a mass-based unified movement for national liberation could secure the 'claims' of disenfranchised blacks to universal franchise:

> Without a strong, active, and militant African National Congress, even our parliamentary representative and our members of the Native Representative Council, with their talented membership, can accomplish nothing unless they have the backing of a strong national organization (Xuma, 1942, ABX 421221a).

Within a year, his position was to become more radicalised, as reflected in his presidential address to the ANC's annual conference in 1943. He argued that white 'domination' over blacks was enshrined in the words 'control and segregation' which had brought the 'most oppressive and discriminatory colour and race legislation' and which had been 'responsible for acts that in our minds seem hardly different from those of fascism and Nazism' (Xuma, 1943, 431216a).

In the same address, Xuma discussed black disenfranchisement in the following unequivocal terms:

> In the political sphere, the African has no status. He is a South African national but not a citizen. He is a part of the population but not counted among the people of South Africa. He has no right to vote, no right to represent himself in the councils of the state ... Like a crying child who must be quieted ... he has been given the Native Representative Council – a 'toy parliament' ... it gives but a shadow of political rights and is intended to eliminate forever, if our European rulers can help it, the influence of the Africans over the governing councils of the states [sic] and therefore eliminates him as a factor in using his franchise ... to compel legislators to grant him his citizenship rights and pay heed to his demand [sic] (Xuma, 1943, 431216a).

This position, that social rights of citizenship could only be realised by a full, unqualified franchise was to be reflected in the African Claims policy document. It was based on the extension of the universal franchise as the cornerstone of the post-war, post-segregation good society as reflected in the section on a Bill of Rights. Echoing the American Declaration of Independence, it set out the most direct and unequivocal statement of African expectations for full, unqualified rights to citizenship:

> We, the African people in the Union of South Africa, urgently demand the granting of full citizenship rights such as are enjoyed by all Europeans in South Africa' (African Claims, 1943, quoted in Karis and Carter, 1987: 217).

African Claims and the Freedom Charter were the most significant ANC policy documents before the unbanning of the ANC in 1990. Their formulations reflected a gathering pro-independence nationalism in Africa that was inspired by the war against Nazism and fascism and the call in the 1941 Allied Atlantic Charter for post-war democratisation for societies under Nazi and fascist occupation and the global extension of welfare (Cooper, 2002). The committee which drew up African Claims comprised twenty-eight key intellectuals and political activists from varying ideological positions who were active members of or aligned to the African National Congress. They included James Calata, secretary general of the ANC; Moses Kotane, secretary general of the Communist Party of South Africa (CPSA) and member of the ANC; Z.K. Matthews, executive member of the ANC; Govan Mbeki, trade secretary of the Federation of Organised Bodies in Transkei; Edwin Mofutsanyane, member of the National Executive of the ANC and member of the CPSA; Gana Makabeni, trade unionist and president of the Council of Non-European Trade Unions (CNETU); Pixley ka Isaka Seme, attorney and executive member of the ANC National Executive; R.V. Selope Thema, editor of the *Bantu World*, member of the Native Representative Council and speaker of the ANC; and A.B. Xuma, chairperson of the committee.

The Atlantic Charter was an anti-Nazi document drafted in 1941 which advocated certain political, civil and social rights in relation to countries under Nazi occupation in Europe; it established the ideological foundations for a democratic, post-war settlement. African Claims attempted to explicitly apply the Atlantic Charter to the disenfranchised position of Africans in South Africa:

> We urge that if fascism and fascist tendencies are to be uprooted from the face of the earth, and to open the way for peace, prosperity and racial good-will, the 'Atlantic Charter' must apply to...all the nations of the world and their subject peoples. And we urge that South Africa as a prelude to her participation at the Peace Conference in the final destruction of Nazism and Fascism in Europe, must grant the just claims of her non-European peoples to freedom, democracy and human decency... since charity must begin at home, and if to quote B.B.C Radio news reel: 'We Fight for World Democracy' (African Claims, 1943).

The Atlantic Charter deeply influenced anti-colonial and South African opposition political movements. Its recognition of full citizenship as a *right* was applied, in African Claims, to South Africa. For example, in the Bill of Rights section adequate medical and health services for the entire population is regarded as a *duty of the state*.

African Claims was specifically concerned with the form of post-war South African society and the relationship of the state to citizens mediated through public goods such as health, education and welfare. Implicit in its formulations was the social democratic idea that the postcolonial and post-segregation 'nation' could only be realised through the universal extension and provision of public goods by a democratic state to *all* universally enfranchised citizens regardless of race or class (or gender).

This position, linking universal public goods for all to the idea of an inclusive national liberation struggle is most tellingly reflected in the preface by Xuma:

> On behalf of my Committee and the African National Congress I call upon chiefs, ministers of religion, teachers, professional men, *men and women of all ranks and classes* to organise our people, to close ranks and take their place in this mass liberation movement and struggle, expressed in this Bill of Citizenship Rights *until freedom, right and justice are won for all races and colours* to the honour and glory of the Union of South Africa whose ideals – freedom, democracy,

Christianity [sic] and human decency cannot be attained *until all races in South Africa participate in them* (A.B. Xuma, 1943, quoted in Karis and Carter, 1987: 1, my emphasis).

This inclusive approach to non-racial political collaboration was consistently applied by Xuma during his tenure as ANC president in the 1940s, and further reflected in his initiation of the Joint Declaration of Cooperation or 'Three Doctors' Pact' of 1947. The Pact was a political response to the Asiatic Land Tenure Act of 1946, a particularly repressive law passed by the United Party government which restricted the residency and trading rights of Indians to particular areas in Natal. The Land Tenure Act provoked militant opposition led by the Natal Indian Congress (Karis and Carter, 1987: 114; Davenport, 1991: 328). The Pact took the form of an agreement between Xuma, Monty Naicker and Yusuf Dadoo on the need for political alliance and cooperation between the African National Congress and the Natal Indian Congress in the struggle for a universal franchise, including freedom of movement, the right to recognition of trade unions, removal of land restrictions and the 'provision of adequate housing facilities' and the 'extension of free and compulsory education' (Joint Declaration of Cooperation, in Karis and Carter, Volume 2, 1987: 272) .

What then was the ANC view on public goods in a post-segregation society as reflected in its African Claims policy statement? Alongside an unequivocal demand for full rights to universal civil and political citizenship were the following demands for social rights:

The establishment of *free medical and health services* for all sections of the population.

The *right of every child to free and compulsory education* and of admission to technical schools, universities and other institutions of higher education.

Equality of treatment with any other section of the population in the State social services, and the inclusion on an equal basis with Europeans in any scheme of social security.

The *extension of all industrial welfare legislation* to Africans engaged in Agriculture, Domestic Service and in Public institutions or bodies

(African Claims, 1943, quoted in Karis and Carter, 1987: 217–222, my emphasis).

For the ANC led by Xuma, the limits of liberalisation were reached with the publication of African Claims in 1943. After repeated failed attempts to secure a meeting with Smuts to discuss the implications of the Atlantic Charter, Xuma sent him a copy of African Claims and its Bill of Rights (Gish, 2000: 128). Smuts sent a reply through his private secretary in September 1944 rejecting the application of the Atlantic Charter to South Africa.

Smuts's rejection of an inclusive non-racial welfare state and the drift to more extreme forms of repression in the post-year wars, exemplified in the ruthless repression of the 1946 mineworkers' strike, led to Xuma's inclusive social policy trajectory being subsumed by the political struggle. The ANC leadership were compelled to change their stance of strategic diplomacy as protest actions grew out of the poor living conditions of urban blacks in the mid-1940s. The Alexandra Bus Boycott of 1943, the anti-pass campaign of 1944 and the movement of squatters seeking better housing in 1944 were the most prominent of the protest actions and contributed significantly to the further radicalisation of the ANC.

THE SEARCH FOR AN AFRICANIST SOLUTION TO THE NATIONAL QUESTION

The increased use of repression in response to these forms of mass-based opposition contributed significantly to the dynamics of black resistance to segregation, which developed a more confrontational stance. In the 1950s, constitutional approaches in the form of deputations to the government gradually gave way to civil disobedience campaigns. The shift in the ANC to political mobilisation around a universal franchise as a precondition for establishing the good society was consolidated with the coming to power of the apartheid regime in 1948. Accompanying this was an initial shift to a more exclusionary Africanist and anti-communist discourse under the earliest incarnation of the ANC Youth League under the intellectually brilliant philosopher Anton Lembede and skilful political organiser A.P. Mda, alongside a young Nelson Mandela and Oliver Tambo (Glaser, 2012). A forerunner of the Black Consciousness Movement, the ANC Youth League's 'Programme of Action: Statement of Policy' was adopted at the ANC National Conference of 1949. Its principle objective was 'the right to direct representation' through 'raising national consciousness' and 'to assist, support and reinforce the African National Congress, in its struggle for National Liberation of the African people.' In this programme of action, the precise formulations of African Claims for universally-provided public goods are replaced with somewhat vaguer formulations around, for example, the 'consolidation of the industrial organisation of the workers for the improvement of their standard of living'.

The intransigence of the Smuts government to the demand for a universal franchise shifted the National Question. It moved from the possibility of resolution through an inclusive non-racial agenda to one that focused on Africanist identity politics and the unrealised political interests of young university-educated intellectuals who were increasingly attracted to non-violent resistance and confronting state power.

MASS-BASED POLITICAL MOBILISATION AND THE FREEDOM CHARTER

This exclusionary Africanist position was to change with the 1952 Defiance Campaign against Unjust Laws and the increasing crystallisation of a politics of non-racialism under Oliver Tambo and Nelson Mandela. The return to a non-racial, politically inclusive agenda established in embryonic form by Xuma in the mid-1940s was due in part to lived experience based on political activism. Mandela and Tambo worked closely with communists such as Bram Fischer, Moses Kotane, J.B. Marks, Denis Goldberg, Harold Wolpe, Ismail Meer, Ruth First, Joe Slovo, and Rusty and Hilda Bernstein who demonstrated a political commitment to overthrow apartheid which matched their commitment. In his speech at the Rivonia Trial in 1964, Mandela refers to this as follows:

> ... for many decades communists were the only political group in South Africa who were prepared to treat Africans as human beings and their equals; who were prepared to eat with us; talk with us, live with us, and work with us. They were the only political group which was prepared to work with the Africans for the attainment of political rights and a stake in society. Because of this, there are many Africans who, today, tend to equate freedom with communism (Mandela, 1964: 181).

It was perhaps in the crucible of the mass politics of defiance during the 1950s that the dialectic of race and class became increasingly evident. The struggle to overcome national oppression had to confront the class relationships that reproduced inequality in South African society and was not reducible to a struggle against apartheid racism. By implication it had to confront the nature of the post-apartheid state and the good society offered as an alternative to racial capitalism.

The ANC's campaigning around rights of political citizenship became a primary focus of its political activities in the 1950s, with the specific concerns of social policy gradually subsumed under this political objective. In 1952 Albert Luthuli became the president-general, and he was to lead the ANC until his death in 1967. Luthuli commented in 1952 on the shift to militant opposition to citizenship demands as follows:

> In so far as gaining citizenship rights and opportunities for the unfettered development of the African people, who will deny that thirty years of my life have been spent knocking in vain, patiently, moderately and modestly at a closed and barred door? What have been the fruits of my many years of moderation? Has there been any reciprocal tolerance or moderation from the Government, be it Nationalist or United Party? No! On the contrary, the past thirty years have seen the greatest number of laws restricting our rights and progress until today we have reached a

stage where we have almost no rights at all... It is with this background and with a full sense of responsibility that... I have joined my people in the new spirit that moves them today, the spirit that revolts openly and boldly against injustice and expresses itself in a determined and non-violent manner (Luthuli, 1952, quoted in Karis and Carter, 1987: 487).

This period of militant opposition was met by the introduction of repressive legislation that curbed civil and political rights. These included the Suppression of Communism Act of 1950 mentioned earlier, the Criminal Law Amendment Act of 1953 which was aimed at anyone who protested against the repeal or modification of any law, and the Riotous Assemblies Act of 1956 which prohibited public gatherings in open spaces if they threatened the public peace (SAIRR, 1978: 418, 431).

In this climate of repression, social policy, the public good, was subordinated to the political objective of achieving an unqualified franchise. This was illustrated in the case of education by the presidential address of Nelson Mandela to the Transvaal Congress of the ANC in 1953. Mandela first criticised the objective of the Bantu Education Bill – 'The aim of this law is to teach our children that Africans are inferior to Europeans' – and then proposed undermining the intentions of Bantu Education by replacing it with an alternative system of education under the control of African parents within their communities:

> You must defend the right of African parents to decide the kind of education that shall be given to their children. Teach the children that Africans are not one iota inferior to Europeans. Establish your own community schools where the right kind of education will be given to our children. If it becomes dangerous or impossible to have these alternative schools, then again you must make every home, every shack or rickety structure a centre of learning for our children. Never surrender to the inhuman and barbaric theories of Verwoerd (Mandela, 1953, quoted in Karis et al., 1987: 113).

This approach to social policy located it as a site of contestation with the ruling National Party regime over social rights, and the system of community schooling (implemented unevenly in the East Rand townships and eastern Cape, was outlawed (Lodge, 1983)). However, in the period of mass-based political activism of the 1950s, the ANC was moving towards formalising its position on the place of democracy, social policy and the public good in relation to the state in a post-apartheid nation. The ANC's position took the form of a public Congress of the People in 1955 in Kliptown which the ANC was instrumental in organising and which inaugurated the Freedom Charter.

The Freedom Charter gave expression to the increasingly militant civil disobedience campaigns in favour of civil and political rights. It contained a series of demands framed by the primary citizenship demand that 'the people shall govern'. In addition to civil and political rights, it contained demands for social rights, which were framed as follows:

> The state shall recognise the right and duty of all to work, and to draw full unemployment benefits;
> Men and women of all races shall receive equal pay for equal work;
> There shall be a forty-hour working week, a national minimum wage, paid annual leave, and sick leave for all workers, and maternity leave on full pay for all working mothers;
> Education shall be free, compulsory, universal and equal for all children;
> Higher education and technical training shall be opened to all by means of state allowances and scholarships awarded on the basis of merit;
> All people shall have the right to live where they choose, be decently housed, and to bring up their families in comfort and security;
> Unused housing space to be made available to the people;
> Rent and prices shall be lowered, food plentiful and no-one shall go hungry; A preventive health scheme shall be run by the state;
> Free medical care and hospitalisation shall be provided for all, with special care for mothers and young children.
> (Congress of the People, 1955, in Karis and Carter, 1987: 205–208)

The Freedom Charter also contained demands about the control of wealth, which was predicated on public ownership and presupposed nationalisation as the mechanism to achieve it.

Gavin Williams (1988: 81) argues that there are important continuities between the Freedom Charter and previous ANC statements such as the Bill of Rights of African Claims in that they both represented the interests of working people who were 'unified by the structures of racial discrimination and oppression'. Williams makes the point that the Freedom Charter was distinctive in

> ... explicitly claiming South Africa for all its people, in its concern for the rights of all 'nationalities' among the people and in taking up demands of women ... and it puts forward in a cogent series of declarations which resonate with a wide range of people's experiences and aspirations in a way that no previous documents ever did (Williams, 1988: 80).

The Freedom Charter represented a programme for a future post-apartheid society, but did not specify how this was to be achieved. Its declamatory tone suggested that it would involve a protracted political struggle, and its ideals would not be the subject of negotiation. Substantively, the goals of the Freedom Charter could not be achieved without a redistribution of wealth and resources. This does not imply that the major beneficiaries would necessarily be the working class and the poor, as the Freedom Charter was not a class-based, socialist programme. It incorporated demands on individual rights to land and property that were compatible with a liberal democracy; at the same time, its demands were nationalist but also compatible with a social democratic approach. These demands included the nationalisation of mineral wealth, banks and monopoly industry which, at a minimum, implied an interventionist state. It would be in the emphasis placed on the implementation of economic and social policies that the limits of the Freedom Charter's objectives would be revealed. Albert Luthuli's comments to the 44th Annual Meeting of the ANC in December 1955 are instructive as to the interpretation of the Freedom Charter within the leadership of the ANC. Arguing that the Freedom Charter should be ratified by the ANC Annual Meeting, Luthuli asked:

> What is the implication of the charter? The charter definitely and unequivocally visualises the establishment of a socialistic state. It therefore brings up sharply the ideological question of the kind of state the African National Congress would like to see established in the Union of South Africa ... My own personal leanings are towards the modified socialistic state, patterned on the present-day Great Britain, a middle-of-the-road state between the extreme ultra-capitalistic state as we see it in the United States, and the ultra-socialistic state as we see it in Communist Russia ... My advice to the conference would be to accept the charter with the qualification that it does not commit itself at present until further discussion on the principle of nationalisation, of means of production, as visualised in Section 3 of the charter (Luthuli, 1955, in Pillay, 1993: 84–85).

Although Luthuli's comments suggest there was contestation within the ANC over the redistributive emphasis of the Charter, the document was ratified at the Annual Conference. Its strong advocacy of social rights and state intervention in securing such rights made it compatible with the development of a Keynesian, social democratic welfare state based on the social rights of citizenship. This represented an unequivocal continuity with the social democratic agenda established in the 1940s by the ANC. Far from being a 'minimal programme', the Freedom Charter suggested such a far-reaching transformation of South Africa that it would take a social revolution to achieve the goals of the good society it implied.

Unsurprisingly, the Charter was met with a hostile response from the ruling National Party under Verwoerd, which viewed it as a direct challenge to state authority and arrested the leadership of all the major constituent political groups which had been involved in the Freedom Charter campaign, foremost of which was the ANC. Over a period of four years it attempted to prove that the demands of the Freedom Charter could be achieved only by violent overthrow of the ruling government, but failed to prove this and released the leadership in 1960. The ANC was committed to civil disobedience campaigning which it hoped would lead the ruling party to agree to a National Convention which would allow for meaningful negotiations with the National Party on a future constitutional order based on the universal extension of the franchise.

The National Party regime, having substantially increased its parliamentary majority among the white electorate in the 1958 elections, rejected the proposal for a National Convention and resorted to increased violent repression of political protest, culminating in the indiscriminate shooting of unarmed anti-pass-law protesters in Sharpeville on 21 March 1960. Nine days later, the government declared a State of Emergency, effectively outlawing all opposition political activity, and introduced the Unlawful Organisations Act No. 34 of 1960 which outlawed the ANC and the PAC.

The ANC's response to the banning was contained in a statement by an Emergency Committee of the ANC released on 1 April 1960. Recording that the ANC had historically attempted a non-violent, peaceful solution to resolving South Africa's political problems, it indicated that such a solution was not possible under the current government:

> The first essential towards resolving the crisis is that the Verwoerd administration must make way for one less completely unacceptable to the people, of all races, for a Government which sets out to take the path, rejected by Verwoerd, of conciliation, concessions and negotiation (ANC, 1960, in Karis and Carter, 1987: 573).

The statement reiterated political citizenship as its primary demand, and listed a set of proposals calling for the end of the State of Emergency, the system of pass laws, and laws curbing civil and political rights, as well as the release of political prisoners. The statement concluded with the demand for a new national convention

> ... representing all people on a fully democratic basis, [which] must be called to lay the foundations of a new union, a non-racial democracy, belonging to all South Africans, and in line with the United Nations Charter and the views of all enlightened people everywhere in the world (ANC, 1960, in Karis and Carter, 1987: 573).

The banning of the ANC in 1961 ended all chances for dialogue between the opposition movement and the government on a new democratic constitutional order based on a universal franchise. The banned ANC was left with no alternative but to rely on mass mobilisation and underground forms of struggle as a means of overthrowing the apartheid regime, including the use of armed struggle.

By 1962 Luthuli was more categorical about the form of interventions that the state should support to realise the post-apartheid good society.

> The solution to the South African problem will call for radical reforms, some of them of a really revolutionary nature. The basic reform will be in the form of the government. At present, there is a government by whites only. This should be replaced by a government which is truly a government of all the people, for the people, and by the people. This can only be so in a state where all adults – regardless of race, colour or belief – are voters. Nothing but such a democratic form of government, based on the parliamentary system, will satisfy (Luthuli, 1962).

Luthuli then expressed the belief that nationalisation was necessary to achieve the social policy goals of free education, affordable municipal housing, state-provided employment for 'the bulk of people' who would also enjoy unqualified rights to unionisation. In a free South Africa:

> State control will be extended to cover the nationalization of some sectors of what at present is private enterprise. It will embrace specifically monopoly industries, the mines and banks, but excluding such institutions as building societies (Luthuli, 1962).

Luthuli then advocated that the new government should have as its objective the creation of a *'democratic social welfare state'* (my emphasis). He stated, 'It will be the paramount task of the government to bring it about and advance it without crippling industry, commerce, farming and education' (Luthuli, 1962).

In short, the discourse within the ANC between 1940 and 1962 regarding how to overcome the legacies of segregation and apartheid was premised on a state that was democratic and would intervene in the economy to secure redistributive social policies in health, education and welfare. The substantive form of such a state was a social democratic welfare state. This is reflected in the policy formulations of the 1955 Freedom Charter, which demonstrated a reconnection with the inclusive discourse of the 1943 African Claims and unequivocally in social policy with a social democratic vision of the post-apartheid good society.

CONCLUSION

The economic and political demands of the war against fascism in the early 1940s and the democratic alternative to fascism represented by the Atlantic Charter of 1941 acted as a decisive catalyst for developing a post-war vision of global democracy and social secu-rity. The ANC under A.B. Xuma interpreted the global extension of political and social rights in the anti-Nazi Atlantic Charter as applying to disenfranchised blacks in South Africa, and it was on this basis that the ANC participated in the war against Nazism and fascism, based on the policy document African Claims.

The response of Xuma and the ANC to the political possibilities presented by the Atlantic Charter was to extend the call for social rights to a fundamental demand for civil and political rights for blacks. In this regard, the most significant statement on social citizenship to emerge in the war years was the African Claims document, which called for the comprehensive extension of political, civil and social rights – including health, welfare and education – to all citizens regardless of race, class or gender by a democratic state as an entitlement of citizenship. The ANC, swelled by the urban dwellers whose housing, social welfare and health needs remained unmet, increas-ingly turned to direct action to secure the political rights demanded in African Claims. The increasing use of repression by the Smuts administration in the late 1940s to quell these demands alienated blacks and led to the rise of an uncompro-mising, militant, Africanist opposition to white minority rule and the displacement of the nascent non-racial, social democratic politics supported by the ANC under A.B. Xuma in the 1940s. The intensification of repression in the late 1940s revealed that the promise of inclusive social policies in the early war years consolidated in African Claims, and predicated on the extension of social rights to Africans, could not be realised in the absence of their political rights. This conclusion was reinforced when the National Party came to power in 1948 and removed the limited civil, polit-ical and social rights previously enjoyed by blacks. The political practices of alliance politics across political organisations and the mass struggles of the 1950s, such as the Defiance Campaign against Unjust Laws, led to a rejuvenation of a non-racial politi-cal tradition in the ANC.

The Freedom Charter, unveiled in 1955 by the anti-apartheid opposition as the pro-gramme for an alternative society to apartheid, contained demands for social rights to universal healthcare, education and welfare that were compatible with the establishment of a de-racialised social democratic welfare state in South Africa, but these demands for social rights were now predicated on the prior establishment of democratic rule. Albert Luthuli specifically argued for a democratic social welfare state, alongside state interven-tion in the economy to secure employment for the majority of citizens and to establish comprehensive health, education and welfare services. By the time of its banning in 1962, the ANC had a firmly-established policy framework on the universalisation of public goods which would be provided as an entitlement of social citizenship by a democratic, constitutional state – a framework that if implemented would have established a social democratic welfare state.

REFERENCES

Adelzadeh, A. (1996) From the RDP to GEAR: The Gradual Embracing of Neo-liberalism in Economic and Social Policy. *Transformation*, 31: 66–95.

African National Congress (ANC) (1943) African Claims in South Africa, including the 'Atlantic Charter from the Standpoint of Africans within the Union of South Africa' and 'Bill of Rights'. Adopted by ANC Annual Conference. Document 29b. In T. Karis et al. (1987) *From Protest to Challenge: A Documentary History of African Politics in South Africa 1882–1964: Volume 2: Hope and Challenge 1935–1952*. Stanford University: Hoover Institution Press.

African National Congress (ANC) (1960) Statement by the Emergency Committee of the African National Congress. In T. Karis et al. (1987) *From Protest to Challenge: A Documentary History of African Politics in South Africa 1882–1964: Volume 2: Hope and Challenge 1935–1952*. Stanford University: Hoover Institution Press.

Alexander, N. (2002) *An Ordinary Country*, Pietermaritzburg: University of KwaZulu-Natal Press.

Bond, P. (2005) *Elite Transition. From Apartheid to Neoliberalism in South Africa*. Durban: University of KwaZulu-Natal Press.

Bond, P. et al. (1996a) The State of Neo-liberalism in South Africa: Economic, Social and Health Transformation in Question. *International Journal of Health Services*, 26(4).

Bond, P. (1996b) The Making of South Africa's Macro-economic Compromise. In *Development Strategies in Southern Africa*, edited by E. Maganya. Johannesburg: IFAA.

Congress of the People (1960) 'Freedom Charter'. In T. Karis et al. (1987) *From Protest to Challenge: A Documentary History of African Politics in South Africa 1882–1964: Volume 2: Hope and Challenge 1935–1952*. Stanford University: Hoover Institution Press.

Cooper, F. (1996) *Decolonization and African Society: The Labour Question in French and British Africa*. Cambridge: Cambridge University Press.

Cooper, F. (2002) *Africa Since 1940: Past and Present*. Cambridge: Cambridge University Press.

Davenport, R. (1991) *South Africa: A Modern History*, 4th edn, Basingstoke: Macmillan Press.

Fine, B. (with Padayachee, V.) (2001) A Sustainable Macroeconomic Growth Path for South Africa? In *Development: Theory, Policy and Practice*, edited by J. Coetzee et al. Oxford: Oxford University Press.

Gish, S. (2000) *Alfred B. Xuma: African, American, South African*. New York: New York University Press.

Glaser, C. (2012) *The ANC Youth League*. Jacana Pocket History. Johannesburg: Jacana.

Karis, T. and Carter, G.W. (eds) (1973) *From Protest to Challenge: A Documentary History of African Politics in South Africa 1882–1964, Volume 2: Hope and Challenge 1935–1952*. Stanford, CA: Hoover Institution Press.

Karis, T. and Carter, G.M. (eds) (1987) *From Protest to Challenge: A Documentary History of African Politics in South Africa 1882–1964. Volume 2: Hope and Challenge 1935–1952*, Stanford University: Hoover Institution Press.

Lodge, T. (1983) *Black Politics in South Africa since 1945*. London and New York: Longman.

Luthuli, A. (1952) The Road to Freedom is via the Cross: Statement issued by Chief A.J. Luthuli, issued after the announcement on November 12, 1952 of his dismissal as chief [n.d.]. In *From Protest to Challenge: A Documentary History of African Politics in South Africa 1882–1964: Volume 2: Hope and Challenge 1935–1952*, edited by T. Karis and G.W Carter (1987). Stanford University: Hoover Institution Press.

Luthuli, A. (1955) The Implications of the Freedom Charter. In Voices of Liberation, Volume One, Albert Luthuli, edited by G.L. Pillay (1993). Pretoria: Human Sciences Research Council Press.

Luthuli, A. (1962) What I Would Do If I Were Prime Minister. *Ebony*, February.

Mandela, N. (1964) *No Easy Walk to Freedom*. London: Heinemann.

Marais, H. (2011) *South Africa Pushed to the Limit: The Political Economy of Change.* Cape Town: UCT Press.

Marshall, T.H. (1950 [1992]) *Citizenship and Social Class.* London: Pluto.

McKinley, D. (1997) *The ANC and the Liberation Struggle.* London: Pluto.

Mkandawire, T. (2009) From the National Question to the Social Question. *Transformation,* (69).

Padmore, G. and N. Cunard (1942) *The White Man's Duty: An Analysis of the Colonial Question in the Light of the Atlantic Charter.* London: W.H. Allen.

Saul, J.S. (2005) *The Next Liberation Struggle: Capitalism, Socialism, and Democracy in Southern Africa.* New York: Monthly Review Press.

SAIRR: SAIRR (South African Institute of Race Relations) (1978) Laws Affecting Race Relations in South Africa (to the end of 1976), Johannesburg: SAIRR.

Suttner, R. and J. Cronin (1986) *30 Years of the Freedom Charter.* Johannesburg: Ravan Press.

Tawney, R.H. (1952) *Equality.* London: George Allen and Unwin.

Tawney, R.H. (1964) *Equality.* London: George Allen and Unwin.

Van Diepen, M. (1988) *The National Question in South Africa.* London: Zed.

Van Niekerk, R.D. (2012) The Historical Roots of a National Health System in South Africa. In *Universal Health Care in Southern Africa: Policy Contestation in Health System Reform in South Africa and Zimbabwe,* edited by G.D. Ruiters and R. van Niekerk. Durban: UKZN Press.

Williams, G. (1988) Celebrating the Freedom Charter. *Transformation,* 6: 73–86.

Xuma, A.B. (1941) The Policy and Platform of the African National Congress – Statement by Dr A.B. Xuma in Inkululeko (Freedom), August 1941. In *From Protest to Challenge: A Documentary History of African Politics in South Africa 1882–1964: Volume 2: Hope and Challenge 1935–1952,* edited by T. Karis and G.W. Carter (1987). Stanford, CA: Hoover Institution Press.

Xuma, A.B. (1942) Report of a Deputation from the ANC to the Deputy Prime Minister and others on March 4, 1942 by Dr A.B. Xuma. In *From Protest to Challenge: A Documentary History of African Politics in South Africa 1882–1964: Volume 2: Hope and Challenge 1935–1952,* edited by T. Karis and G.W. Carter (1987). Stanford, CA: Hoover Institution Press.

Xuma, A.B. (1943) Presidential Address Delivered by Dr A.B. Xuma, President-General African National Congress on December 15, 1943. ABX 431215a, A.B. Xuma Papers, William Cullen Library, University of the Witwatersrand.

OLIVER TAMBO AND THE NATIONAL QUESTION

Luli Callinicos

Oliver Tambo's steadily widening and inclusive concept of the nation in the history of the African National Congress (ANC) is a familiar narrative. Pixley ka Isaka Seme's rallying cry in 1911 – 'We are one people. These divisions, these jealousies are the cause of all our troubles and of all our ignorance today' – attracted traditional leaders as well as educated liberals and nationalists. It inspired the many generations that followed the launch of the South African Native National Congress in 1912 (renamed the African National Congress in 1924).

Despite its uneven and slow progress against racial hostility and segregation in the years that followed, the ANC was the organisation that young Africanists joined some thirty years after its inception. By the 1940s, however, the voice of the ANC had become muted, confined to eloquent 'cap-in-hand' petitions. That approach had failed to counter increasing legislative aggression against blacks, and Africans in particular. The 1936 Natives' Representations Act had removed the direct vote from the few black men who (in the Cape Province only) were still entitled to a qualified franchise, whereas all white adults, women and men, had access to the vote.

In 1949, the year after the apartheid government was voted into power by a white electorate, the ANC Youth League issued its programme of action. Founded by Walter Sisulu, Oliver Tambo and Nelson Mandela, the ANCYL was first led by the passionately articulate political philosopher and law clerk, Anton Lembede. The young, predominantly male, African-elite initiators of the Youth League concluded that the answer lay in mass action.

Above all, they were unapologetically Africanist. 'The problems of African churches, trade unions, teachers, traders, industrialists, farmers and peasants represent merely certain aspects of our colonial national struggle which is one, single and indivisible,' asserted Lembede (1944) in sketching out the task of uniting a nation.

The formation of the ANC Youth League was strongly informed by a rejection of the paternalism of missionaries and liberals, who assumed that Africans had a primitive, simple culture riddled by superstition and unbridled self-indulgence and were unable to discern the civilising influence of the values of indigenous humanism, and the sophistication of oral skills in the transmission of knowledge. In the eyes of Europeans influenced by centuries of slavery, non-Europeans were inferior to the Europeans who had developed the technology of trade and weapons as a means of domination. Like most of the Youth League founders, Oliver Tambo had attended missionary schools and stridently exposed these colonial prejudices. Lembede emphasised that the Youth League would insist on Africans 'going it alone' (Edgar and Msumza, 1996).

For Oliver Tambo's part, the need to defend humanism, dignity and self-esteem, and to empower the most oppressed and exploited, Africans, was self-evident. He was particularly interested in indigenous knowledge, and consistently used cultural African experiences to illustrate concepts and strategies. Earlier, he had wanted to study medicine in order to enrich it with the holistic and alternative healing of indigenous knowledge, but had been prevented by the University of the Witwatersrand (Wits) medical school's racial exclusion during the 1930s. The ANC Youth League identified indigenous values that were under threat. It firmly rejected attempts by both Ruth First (Communist Party) and Isaac Tabata (Unity Movement) to recruit them into their respective Marxist organisations. The Youth League firmly rejected 'foreign' ideologies as well as a divisive class analysis. Strategically, however, they audaciously borrowed tactics and campaign programmes from their rivals.

The war years brought unprecedented urbanisation of Africans, resulting in dire housing shortages and imaginative forms of resistance. James Mpanza led the Sofasonke movement in 1944 in land invasions adjoining Orlando to set up the first major 'informal' yet firmly controlled settlement. The Youth League also supported the 1946 African miners' strike. They drew upon boycott, non-cooperation, strike and 'stay-away' tactics from the Non-European Unity Movement and the Communist Party, and civil disobedience – satyagraha or passive resistance – from the South African Indian Congress to formulate their programme of action. Lembede was articulate in reinventing African traditions and consummately tailoring them to the challenge of modern urban life in a hostile system of racial oppression. During the high noon of apartheid, the Youth League's documents became the inspiration of the Pan Africanist Congress (PAC) and the Black Consciousness Movement (BCM). In 1947 Lembede died suddenly, and his leadership was taken over by the committed Africanist A.P. Mda.

Years later, Tambo revealed in an interview that Mandela (and by implication himself) 'was not at one with Lembede on those portions which could be described as ultra-nationalistic'.[1] In practice, Mandela and Tambo embraced Western skills that could be marshalled strategically in the defence (literally) of their people when in 1952 they joined forces to set up their law firm, Mandela and Tambo, Attorneys at Law. Together, they reconnoitred, like their peers, an amalgam of indigenous and Western culture, while keeping their gaze firmly focused on the advancement of African nationalism.

This greater sense of nuance and syncretism began to express itself incrementally. The signing of the Doctors' Pact in 1947 between A.B. Xuma (ANC), Monty Naicker (Natal Indian Congress) and Yusuf Dadoo (Transvaal Indian Congress) was accepted with some reluctance by the Youth League, which continued to be suspicious of domination by any 'non-African' organisations. And when Sisulu began talking to black communists in 1948, both Tambo and Mandela were indignant that Sisulu had agreed to meet with them again without first consulting the Youth League's committee. They were also angry with Ismael Meer, an articulate member of the Indian Congress and a communist to boot, whom they accused of 'flattering' Sisulu.

Reminiscing about that period, Sisulu explained that he eventually succeeded in persuading Mandela and Tambo that 'African nationalism need not be contradicted by communism. Moses Kotane was a convincing example' (interview with the author, 27 June 1990). In 1929, the Communist Party of South Africa (CPSA) had decided to promote an 'independent Native republic as a step towards a workers' and peasants' government'.[2] Kotane wanted to turn this into reality, beginning with the need for the Communist Party to Africanise its Marxism. In pursuit of that objective, Kotane and J.B. Marks, another leading African CPSA member, became active members of the ANC. Kotane's strategic example, and his commitment and integrity, were persuasive. In 1949, the anti-Indian riots in Durban took many Indian as well as African lives. The scale of popular rage and violence shocked the ANC leadership. They appointed Tambo – calm, professional, an intelligent listener and scrupulously fair – as a member of the ANC Working Committee formed to ascertain the causes of the riot; also on the committee were Albert Luthuli, George Champion, Kotane, Gana Makabeni and others (*The Leader,* 13 February 1949). It was in Durban that Tambo first met Chief Luthuli, a church minister in Groutville where he lived. Observing his responses to the social conditions and distress on both sides of the conflict, Tambo was struck by Luthuli's humanity and his intellect.[3] Tambo, I.C. Meer, Luthuli and Champion toured the riot area in an open van. On a loudhailer, they called on the communities for peace and dialogue. The resulting statement issued by the Working Committee concluded:

> ...the Union [of South Africa] policy of differential and discriminatory treatment of various racial groups is the fundamental contributing cause of racial

antagonisms ... The WC is of the opinion that the situation demands a round-table conference of African and Indian leaders including the representatives of Indian commercial groups (Desai and Vahed, 2010: 236).

The dramatic event proved to be historic on several levels. The trauma that the Working Committee had encountered sensitised the ANC leadership to the need to look more holistically at damage inflicted by the authorities. This was clear evidence that, even on a local level, municipal authorities were systematically imposing apartheid, and fine tuning segregation among the black communities themselves. Ismael Meer commented:

> This is the first time that O.T. acts on a national terrain and not only in the Transvaal. So he comes to Durban in the midst of the riots and we stand together, addressing the people in my van. What has been opposed by the ANCYL, to work together with the Indian Community, here were the riots which caused them to change their minds (interview with the author, 2000).

It was also the start of the ANC's identification of Tambo as the movement's lifelong chief problem solver.

The Youth League's programme of action, spelling out a systematic plan of organised, collective and direct action, was adopted by the ANC at its December Congress in 1949 after intensive lobbying and support from an unexpected source. Phyllis Ntantala remembers:

> Xuma got up and he said, 'Well, we don't want this thing in Congress ... We want a dignified organisation.' The kids [the Youth League] fought every inch of the way to put their programme through ... The CP members who had dual membership – CP and Congress – were laid back throughout that whole day. It was only after dinner that they came back and threw in their lot behind the Youth League – fellows like Kotane, J.B. Marks threw in their lot; Mofutsanyane, Lucas Phillips who came from Cape Town; and it was because of *their* support that the Programme of Action was accepted by Congress (interview with the author, 6 December 1993).

These Communist Party members, concluded Ntantala, knew that the Party was about to be banned, and they wanted to work with and influence the militant Youth League in the future.[4] The programme of action proved to be brilliantly timed. The National Party had come into power in May 1948, and had already begun systematising apartheid through its brutal tightening of segregation laws while rapidly expanding well-paid job opportunities for Afrikaners in the police force and the growing government bureaucracy.

Walter Sisulu was now secretary general of the ANC's National Executive Committee (NEC), and Oliver Tambo was a respected member. Borrowing from the effective Passive Resistance Campaign, they recast their first initiative – the Defiance Campaign – to emphasise active rather than passive protest (interview with the author, 1993). Although the ANC worked with the Indian Congress, which had pioneered the method of passive resistance under Gandhi and others such as Thambi Naidoo, they made it their own campaign by virtue of rallying many thousands of African volunteers. In June 1951 the ANC achieved a breakthrough by inviting other 'National Organisations of Non-European Peoples' to take part (Desai and Vahed, 2010: 213). This initiative was strongly influenced by the experience in Durban of the ANC's Working Committee, which had alerted them to the racial divide and rule policies of the colonial and apartheid governments. The ANC's new office bearers now found themselves working with communists. This experience was to pave the way for a pragmatic alliance with communists within the ANC and in related organisations of non-Africans.

The 1952 Defiance Campaign proved to be extremely popular. It was presented as an inspiring opportunity for the oppressed to gain power by demonstrating their collective agency through disobeying Six Unjust Laws symbolically selected to introduce a culture of pride and self-respect for being jailed in the cause of freedom. Mandela was volunteer in chief. Tambo, who also had to keep the law practice functioning, was among the leading mobilisers, conceptualising the strategy of creating a united resistance through common and collective action. He was a good negotiator, and skilfully maintained coherence in the ANC during the 1950s.

An additional development during the Defiance Campaign was the noticeable contingent of non-Africans who participated. Members of the newly formed South African Indian Congress (SAIC) responded with particular enthusiasm. The 1946 Passive Resistance Campaign was still vivid in their memories; men and women were eager to relive it and to demonstrate to a much bigger populace the power of disciplined collective action. In late 1952, dozens of whites – including members of the Liberal Party and former members of the CPSA (by this time banned) who were clamouring to participate – were also given the go-ahead. Nearly 9 000 defiers (including a good few hundred Indians and coloured workers and several dozen whites) were sentenced to prison. Their defiance was to enter black 'locations' or segregated public buildings without permission.

For many of the founders of the Youth League, participation in the campaign proved to be a turning point in their attitude towards white 'comrades' and defused their suspicion of communists. During the following year, with Chief Luthuli now the newly elected president, the ANC began to formalise the groups who had demonstrated their commitment in opposing apartheid. The thinking was to draw in unaffiliated whites tactically in order to strengthen focused action. However, as Sisulu had emphasised earlier, the ANC should lead, as the representative of the African people.

The ANC had invited all white 'democrats' interested in influencing other whites to join them in actively challenging apartheid. During the Defiance Campaign, a number of whites (including Ronald Segal, editor of *Africa South*, lawyer Albie Sachs and Patrick Duncan, the Second World War veteran and son of South Africa's first governor general) had tried to join the ANC directly. President Luthuli had turned them down. 'Being a national movement, we really couldn't deal with individuals,' explained Luthuli as a witness in the Treason Trial five years later. Some Africanist members had also criticised the high-profile exposure of non-Africans in the press. It seemed to confirm the suspicion that whites, in particular, consciously or otherwise, wanted to dominate Africans – revealing their intrinsic assumption of white supremacy. The increasing number of those anti-white and even anti-Indian voices worried the leadership. Lucas Phillips, chairperson of the Western Cape ANC, supported the inclusion of white members, commenting that it was necessary to 'dispel the idea among Africans that all whites are oppressors' (Everatt, 2010: 102).

In November 1953 the Johannesburg Congress of Democrats (COD) was formed on the initiative of the ANC. Bram Fischer, highly respected Queen's Counsel and former Transvaal chairperson of the now-banned CPSA, was elected to chair the new national body. In October 1953, Oliver Tambo chaired a meeting for whites held in Darragh Hall adjoining St Mary's Church in Johannesburg. This was 'the first white meeting to be addressed by Congress leaders' (Everatt, 2010: 102). The meeting attracted white liberals, but they were wary of the number of well-known communists attending. In that year, a Liberal Party had been formed, as well as the Torch Commando; the latter consisted of militant former Second World War soldiers and the more left-wing ex-combatants of the Springbok Legion. Unknown to most of the audience and speakers, an underground South African Communist Party (SACP) had also been formed in that year, but this was not revealed – even to former communists who had not joined the revived party.

Speakers at Darragh Hall included Yusuf Cachalia representing the SAIC, the ANC secretary general, Walter Sisulu, and Tambo himself. Rusty Bernstein recalled Tambo's impact:

> Tambo's address was delivered with great eloquence and charm... The Congress opposed all racism, including black racism against whites. But they could not fight it alone. The time had come for those who sincerely shared the Congress aim of ending apartheid to take up their share of the burden (Bernstein, 1999: 137).

Tambo dealt deftly with difficult questions raised from the floor. Trade unionist Dan Tloome recalled the occasion clearly:

> Congress... called upon [Europeans] to form an organisation which would work for Congress principles for freedom and equality among their own people. One

section present at the meeting asked whether Congress insisted on a policy of full equality or whether it would be satisfied with, for example, a qualified franchise. They were told by Mr Tambo on behalf of the ANC, that nothing less than full equality would be acceptable, and thereafter they went their own way (Everatt, 2010: 103).

This was neither the first nor the last time that the diplomatic Tambo displayed an unanticipated hard-hitting coup de grace that decisively silenced opponents.

But it was not only the cautious liberals who were dismayed. The ANC was steadily widening its concept of the nation and the invitation to whites was a significant step in the process. In the meantime, there were bitter campaigns against further onslaught by the apartheid regime. There were passionate protests against the removal of the black community from Johannesburg's Sophiatown and its destruction, and brave resistance to what Tambo described as the most devastating of the apartheid laws, the Bantu Education Act, as well as the start of the Women's Federation campaign against the introduction of passes for women. Multiracial support and even international exposure was given in all of these campaigns.

On 26 June 1955, the Congress Alliance was launched at the Congress of the People at Kliptown, the day that the Freedom Charter was presented to the people who had participated in its formulation. The Charter was regarded by many as a generous, inclusive national embrace in the face of a barbaric, inhuman regime, and they were moved by its lofty message of *Ubuntu*.[5] Certainly, Tambo, Mandela and Sisulu, who served on the Working Committee of the Congress of the People, sanctioned the multiracial (rather than non-racial) structure of the Congress Alliance as agreed by the NEC. Four of the affiliates of the Congress Alliance were racially defined – the African National Congress, the South African Indian Congress, the Coloured People's Congress (CPC) and the tiny white Congress of Democrats. (The fifth affiliate was defined by class: the non-racial South African Congress of Trade Unions, SACTU.) It was a sharp, historic move away from the Africanism of the early years of the Youth League, but a trajectory that can be steadily traced in the thinking of Sisulu, Mandela and Tambo.

The Africanist tendency within the ANC was outraged by the provocative introduction to the Freedom Charter: 'South Africa belongs to all who live in it, black and white.' The colonisers had seized the land by conquest and theft and violently continued to exploit and oppress the indigenous people, they argued. Indeed, the difference raised the fundamental 'National Question'. Whereas the ANC prided itself on the 'broad humanism' of the Freedom Charter, to the ordinary African in the street, this was 'a mere abstraction', argued P.H. Molotsi in *The Africanist* (cited in Gerhart, 1979: 162). The Africanists insisted that the absurd opening statement of the Freedom Charter could only have come about with the influence of non-Africans participating in its composition. Gerhart summed up *The Africanist's* critique of the Freedom Charter's essential error:

> The correct nationalist definition of the South African struggle [w]as one of 'the dispossessed versus the dispossessors'; whereas the Freedom Charter 'defined the conflict as one of "the people" against "a system"' (Gerhart, 1979: 158).

The Freedom Charter's abstract concept, no doubt influenced by the Marxist theory of class, obfuscated 'the truth', which was simply that 'the African people have been robbed by the European people' (Raboroko and Mothopeng, cited in Gerhart, 1979: 158).

The Africanists were also developing Lembede's theory of pre-colonial indigenous culture and values. One of its proponents, Victor Sifora, a close school-friend of Tambo's, had joined the breakaway Pan Africanist Congress. Though committed to the Anglican Church since his school days, Sifora simultaneously traced African identity back to a time when people enjoyed confidence and self-reliance. As Lembede had advocated:

> For us, the slogan for African Nationalism was not, as it is not, a formula of hate, but rather a formula of reconstruction; the reconstruction for the soul of the African without which all battles, moral, economic and political, must be lost ... [We] ourselves, for ourselves and by ourselves, hold the key to our salvation to our progress and glory, whether the white man, his law, his government, his church are with us or not (Sifora, 1956, in Gerhart, 1979: 162).

Later, however, when the PAC was formed in 1958, the 'white man' was to be firmly excluded until Africans had achieved liberation on their own terms, without compromise. 'After it is all over, we will grant those who accept African hegemony their full rights as private citizens of an African State' (*Contact*, 8 March 1958, in Gerhart, 1979: 162).

The Congress Alliance was simply reproducing the structures of apartheid through its 'four nations' structure, argued its critics, particularly the Unity Movement, bitter foes of the CPSA. The ANC responded by arguing that under apartheid's draconian segregation laws, it was impossible not to employ pragmatism in its long-term strategy. Years later, Tambo recalled how he spent an entire night of debate and discussion yet was unable to persuade his fellow youth leaguer, Robert Sobukwe, of the necessity of inclusiveness, which would strengthen power and influence for the heavy task that lay ahead (verbal communication to the author, February 1993). The increasingly strident criticisms by Africanists eventually led to the breakaway movement, the Pan Africanist Congress. Tambo's astute chairing of rowdy meetings might well have saved greater haemorrhage of membership and discouraged the Africanists from their attempts to seize control of the ANC (Callinicos, 2004: 237–49). Instead, they broke away to form their own organisation.

A direct outcome of the Freedom Charter was the Treason Trial. The arrest of 156 men and women across the racial spectrum in December 1956 gave the stamp of popular legitimacy to the accused. During the long and tedious court case in the following four years, a lasting bond was formed among them. In the end, all were acquitted.

The December 1959 congress of the ANC proved to be an historic event: it was to be the last legal national gathering of the elected leadership in South Africa for more than three decades. In that year, with an ailing Chief Luthuli living under constant banning orders and a sense that the regime was ready to do its worst, the congress elected Oliver Tambo as deputy president to assist Luthuli in his duties. Assessing recent developments, the congress also considered opening up membership to all races. Most welcomed the idea in theory; they agreed that such a move would not only accord with the Freedom Charter but would also solve the problem of the 'multiracial' critique. However, the PAC breakaway was a clear warning that a significant portion of their members would not countenance such a step. In short, the ANC leadership dared not depart from its traditional collective decision-making or rush ahead of its constituency.

Once again, with a knotty problem, consensus prevailed; it meant carefully listening to grass-roots members, reassuring them that their opinions carried weight. Consensus accompanied tactical compromise, patience and strategic pragmatism.

Within three months, the massacre of Sharpeville changed the political landscape for South Africa and the liberation movements. The latter were immediately banned, and the leadership went underground or into exile. The narrative is well known. While Mandela led the underground movement, Oliver Tambo was chosen as diplomatic head of the ANC's External Mission to alert the world to the evil of apartheid and to mobilise against it. In his first visit to the newly independent state of Ghana, Tambo met the president and visionary Africanist, Kwame Nkrumah. Tambo agreed that under the circumstances – the banning of the liberation movements, and with leading figures of the PAC already having introduced themselves to independent African countries – it was imperative to work together against the apartheid regime.

This was the first of many examples where, with most of the leadership underground or in jail, Tambo would need to make a principled decision for which he had not been given a specific mandate. The two organisations in exile formed a United Front (UF) together with the South West Africa National Union (SWANU) (the Namibian forerunner of the South West Africa People's Organisation (SWAPO)) and the SAIC, ironically a non-African organisation whose president, Yusuf Dadoo, was also a member of the underground SACP.

By all accounts, Tambo's sensitive handling of the way forward encouraged constructive cooperation.[6] With no official leader, the United Front made a good start: a high-profile protest campaign allied to the UK's Labour Party was successful in attracting attention. Its legitimacy as a new, united opposition to the South African regime made possible dramatic appeals to the United Nations (UN) in New York; the United Front argued successfully for the exclusion of apartheid South Africa from the UN and the Commonwealth (Callinicos, 2004: Chapters 8–12).

But in Africa differences were manifested. Although the ANC had the advantage of a proven historical record of struggle, in the dawn of independent Africa the PAC tended to be regarded as the movement of the future. The ANC's multiracialism and the compromising opening statement of the Freedom Charter were seen as pandering to oppressors. Tambo was scrupulously respectful of the PAC's identity. However, when Mandela arrived in 1962 to pursue the new ANC policy of armed struggle, he brought a message from the internal leadership: the United Front must be abandoned. The formation of Umkhonto we Sizwe (MK) demanded new imperatives and one of its first conditions was its non-racial composition. Tambo relocated to Tanzania and set about securing material and moral support for MK.

The National Question was to be a perennial issue for the ANC on the African continent for the following three decades (Callinicos, 2004: Chapter 13).[7] Tambo had to exercise patient diplomacy with the ANC's multiple audiences. 'People must understand you have to be many things to many people,' he once told Tami Mhlambiso, the ANC representative in New York. Having to manage international relations, the army and the underground, as well as keeping in touch with the leaders in prison and underground back home, called for holistic thinking.

Tambo's strategic approach was to use an indigenous metaphor to take small, incremental steps, ensuring on the way that he had everyone's support. This was cited by several of his comrades and was to become legendary. Wilton Mkwayi very clearly recalled its genesis:

> It was during the stay-at-home of 1958. The late [Stephen] Segale from Sophiatown was saying, 'We must stay away forever until we are free.' So O.R. says, 'You know, you come from Rustenburg; you have a piece of land there. When you are ploughing it, you always take one acre at a time. You plough it. You take another acre. That is *sekindima* – one by one. You can't say this strike must go forever until we are free. What are we going to eat?' (interview with the author, 2000).

The first fifteen years moved very slowly. Indeed, it seems in hindsight that Tambo was operating cautiously from a position of weakness, particularly as the death of Chief Luthuli elevated him without formal approval from home and from Robben Island, where most of the elected ANC leadership was incarcerated for life. Tambo, meticulous lawyer and agent of correct democratic procedure, had to feel his way forward. That he had to be pragmatic was a lesson he had learned during the contestations over the National Question following the gradual acceptance of the communists, the various non-Africans and the adoption of the Freedom Charter.

During the years which followed, ethnicity was emerging as a divisive issue, fuelled by the Hani Memorandum, written collectively following the first engagement in combat at Wankie in Southern Rhodesia (now Zimbabwe). It condemned both the MK and the ANC leadership and complained about preferential treatment along ethnic lines. Tambo's response (without his being able to consult with the leadership underground on Robben Island) was to arrange a consultative conference of all the ANC branches in exile. This took place in Morogoro, Tanzania, in 1969 and included the venerated ANC leaders J.B. Marks and Moses Kotane. Tambo stepped down, but was re-elected and confirmed as the acting president of the ANC.

It was then that non-Africans (Joe Slovo and Reg September) were elected onto a new structure, the Revolutionary Council (RC), with considerable powers to fulfil an important new resolution – that the political imperative should take precedence over the military. The other symbolically significant resolution prioritised the working class as the motive force, and formally acknowledged the Revolutionary Council as the structure that would drive change inside South Africa. The non-African members of this sub-committee were also members of the SACP, as indeed were the African members, Joe Matthews and Duma Nokwe.

Tambo explained how the opening of membership came about in an exile setting, where official apartheid constraints did not apply:

> We were taking the decision outside; we thought the time had come ... The formula that was adopted was this: all patriots who support the Freedom Charter and the policy of our movement could become members of the External Mission. [S]o therefore, non-Africans can perform any duties and fill any positions – except on the National Executive Committee, because their membership of the NEC would need consultation with the leadership at home and, in general, our people. That is how the thing stands (interview with Howard Barrell, 1985).

The Morogoro conference seemed to resolve some of the issues raised by the Hani Memorandum. However, another group emerged to express their dissatisfaction that the exile movement had unconstitutionally changed its foundational definition of 'African' in the ANC. A group of eight disgruntled senior members met with Tambo, who appeared to be sympathetic to their concerns. He had of course been through this process ten years earlier while still at home, and was anxious to listen carefully to their grievances and forestall another breakaway. For him, more than ever in exile, the liberation movement had to strive to remain united against the real enemy.

Almost all of the 'Gang of Eight' (as they were then labelled) had been members of the SACP, but had been castigated or sidelined in the party for 'corrupt behaviour'. Party members claimed that denunciation of non-Africans by the Eight was a smokescreen for power struggles over leadership. The outcome, distressing for Tambo but vigorously pursued by Duma Nokwe and agreed to by the majority in the NEC, was expulsion. The 'Gang of Eight' were bitter that Tambo had not supported them. They sent a message to the leadership incarcerated on Robben Island that Tambo had 'betrayed the revolution'. The reply eventually came, a message from Mandela. It confirmed support for the ANC in Lusaka, 'whose leader is O.T.' (interview with Mac Maharaj, 1 August 1995, cited in Callinicos, 2004: Chapter 12).

However, the tensions exemplified by the Eight did not disappear with their expulsion. Ideological struggles related to the 'unresolved National Question', for 'the soul of the ANC' were to continue in a more muted form. The National Question had another, deeply embedded stream of ethnicity and kinship, with a disconcerting habit of surfacing in surprising ways – perhaps because imposed exile heightened the longing for one's familial roots. These aspects of ethnicity were to be a complex challenge for those who had a broader vision of the South African nation. In the ANC, as well as in debates on Robben Island, ethnicity was linked to the issue of bantustans – was it acceptable to engage with them? Certainly, both in strategy and in practice, the ANC and MK were already engaging with the bantustans. The plan was to enter South Africa through the bantustans to conduct guerrilla warfare (Gibbs, 2014: 6). Tambo did not hesitate to seize any opportunity to talk discreetly to heads of bantustan states. He explained his thinking about bantustan chiefs and township initiatives to call for 'independence' to the Revolutionary Council:

> To castigate them because they are not measuring up to revolutionary standards would be wrong. They are people of some influence ... We must not turn them into enemies. If they are enemies, we can surely neutralise them – they and the ANC have plenty in common (Callinicos, 2004: 388).

He was, of course, referring to the National Question of their common African identity and history, accentuated more than ever under apartheid.

Bantustans remained a tricky question. However, following a visit by an ANC delegation to Vietnam in 1978, Tambo was encouraged by the accomplishment of the National United Front in that country. Against great odds, it had managed to build up an impressive mass resistance movement. Tambo was also heartened by the example set by Thembuland's King Sabata Dalindyebo, who opposed independence for the Transkei homeland. Tambo praised him for effectively '[holding] high the banner of genuine national liberation in one of the bantustans, an outstanding leader of our people' (Callinicos, 2004: 394). As tensions escalated at home, Tambo consistently urged people to 'define who is the enemy, who the ally – actual and potential. This policy should be enunciated on every possible occasion' (Callinicos, 2004: 394).

Ethnic consciousness was not only evident in the camps, where a majority of cadres had been recruited regionally in rural areas, but also among more urbane ANC members. To many in the ANC, including non-Zulu-speakers, Chief Buthelezi had brilliantly demonstrated his skill in ambiguity. He was able to outsmart the apartheid system by refusing to allow Zululand to become a formal 'independent homeland', and had succeeded in obliging the South African government to revise its legislation. In 1972, KwaZulu was designated a 'territorial authority', with Buthelezi as its chief minister. Tambo's discreet meetings with Buthelezi on rare occasions in the preceding years seemed to confirm for the ANC leadership that Buthelezi, former member of the Youth League and an admirer of Chief Luthuli, was 'their man' in Zululand.

In that same year, Buthelezi was granted a passport and duly arrived in London. The tricky issue of the Zulu bantustan 'of a special type' was tested in 1979 between two masters of strategy, Buthelezi and Tambo, in their secret meeting in London. This complex attempt at rapprochement came to naught, and indeed was to trigger hostilities that were later to bring South Africa to the brink of civil war (Callinicos, 2004: 390–401). A decade later, open warfare broke out between urban and migrant workers in townships and hostels, and spilled over into political rivalry between Buthelezi's Inkatha, black consciousness activists and the ANC underground.

In the meantime, the explosive events initiated by school students in Soweto in 1976 resounded throughout the world and had a dramatic impact on the ANC in exile. Within months, events began to escalate. Thousands of fleeing students arrived at the offices of the PAC, MK and the ANC, clamouring to take up arms against the apartheid regime, or to call for liberated education. At home, Umkhonto we Sizwe had developed a reputation based on the narratives of prisoners from Robben Island. As prisoners were beginning to be released after long sentences, organised support for the struggle was growing in the face of structural contradictions in the system. The apartheid regime responded with a mixture of reform and repression. Every frontline state was bombed or invaded by the South African Defence Force (SADF), suffering civilian loss as well as ANC and PAC casualties. Dozens of cadres were assassinated. MK camps were also directly attacked, and a conviction grew that heavy infiltration had occurred. Extreme anxiety gripped the intelligence unit and a clamour was raised, sometimes violently, by cadres demanding to return home to fight for freedom. A detention camp was set up, where severe torture took place to extract confessions (Callinicos, 2012). When he began to apprehend the gravity of the problem, Tambo took careful steps in order not to split the movement asunder. He put into place the protection of human rights. First, while directing the Stuart Commission to report on the dissatisfaction of cadres in the camps, he also ensured in 1982 that the ANC signed the Geneva Convention. The move served to protect captured MK cadres as well as suspected informers apprehended in the MK camps and in ANC structures. This was followed by Tambo's initiation of an ANC Bill of Rights. Concerned by emerging evidence of continuing abuses of dissidents in the MK detention camps, Tambo guided the ANC's legal experts to provide protection for individuals and minorities. This, commented the veteran Albie Sachs, legitimised human rights as an instrument that would protect everyone and would protect South Africans in future from abuse (Callinicos, 2004: 578).

To ensure the ANC's ownership of its commitment to human rights, Tambo initiated a long overdue consultative conference in Kabwe, finally held on 16 June 1985. There, the National Question was again foregrounded in all its dimensions of race, ethnicity and class. The turn to armed struggle had demanded a systematic reinvention of the public image of the movement, which had been incorporated into its MK structures. However, as we have seen, the ANC was not able to extend membership fully at the consultative conference in 1969. The issue was resurrected formally in 1985 with the third full consultative ANC conference to take place in exile – the largest, most diverse and most representative of the exile movement. A number of difficult and pressing issues were on the agenda, with prepared responses from branches around the world, one of which was the outstanding issue of a racially open membership. Surprisingly, opposition to the motion came from seasoned members of the SACP, based on the sense that not everyone was ready to entertain such a move (Brian and Sonia Bunting, interview with the author, 2000). In the end, the conference opened all membership, regardless of 'race' and at every level of the organisation. The ANC was now formally a non-racial organisation, twenty-five years after the leadership first raised the possibility. Tambo had never lost sight of an inclusive ANC whose members participated in defining its identity:

> This is the wisdom that came from the National Executive committee in 1959: that we have to have regard for whether the masses of the people also understand correctly the need to go along with you. That is the only reason why the matter is coming up. We want to test opinion. In practice, the ANC has moved forward; it has not marked time (interview with the author, 1985).

The elephant in the room within the movement, though, was an issue that engaged many ANC supporters around the world. How much influence did the SACP wield over the national organisation? This question was put to Tambo by the Friedrich Ebert Stiftung, the social democrat institution of West Germany. They had avoided supporting the ANC over that very question until, in 1986, the funding organisation invited Tambo to visit Bonn. 'The ANC is not the Communist Party,' Tambo pointed out first of all. The SACP had its own position and the ANC its own identity, he explained, the latter guided by the Freedom Charter, which, he observed, was closer to a social democrat view of society and economy (Callinicos, 2004: 514). This was an argument he had made two decades earlier to the Scandinavians, who had wholeheartedly put their trust in the ANC leadership. The debate, therefore, was an old one. As the cold war in Africa intensified, however, emerging African states were fought over by Western capitalism and Soviet and Chinese communism. The situation required immense skill and leadership from the ANC, whose armed struggle and equipment were funded by the Eastern bloc.

Tambo's steadfast emphasis on a united liberation movement was also demonstrated by his willingness to explore the tenets of the Marxist Workers' Tendency (MWT), a small group of ANC members, left-wing interpreters of black consciousness and critics of the Soviet Union and the SACP. In 1973, the scholar Martin Legassick accompanied Tambo and Mazisi Kunene on a fundraising trip to Scandinavia. During this period Tambo read Legassick's paper, in which he argued that '[a] fusion of cultural, political and economic nationalism into a revolutionary program is still *the* revolutionary form, for South Africa's form of capitalism based on racism', a wrong 'conflation', Legassick observed later, 'of national and class struggle into revolutionary nationalism'. Tambo was fascinated, and wrote to Legassick asking for more of his work. 'As it happens the matter of "race" and "class" in South Africa is very much with us at the moment' (Legassick, 2007: 12–13).[8]

A decade later, the MWT's provocative approach angered the NEC.[9] Tambo opposed their expulsion, which nevertheless occurred in 1985 (conversation with Norman Levy, 14 March 2015). On principle, he was anxious to avoid a second damaging split in the ANC, although the MWT was less influential than the 'Gang of Eight' had been in 1975. Tambo was outvoted on this issue.

Tambo's invitation to the South African business community shortly after the Kabwe conference is another indication of his inclusive approach. To left-wing critics, dialogue with big business was going too far. He replied that they were South Africans, too, and that it was pointless talking only to the converted. One of the representatives of that group was the tycoon Tony Bloom, who was deeply impressed by Tambo's response to his somewhat anxious query on whether the ANC would nationalise businesses. 'Oh, that depends', responded Tambo, 'on what the people decide during elections.'[10]

Ellis's portrayal of Tambo as 'weak' and Breytenbach's labelling him as a 'useful idiot' for the communists (interview with the author, 1993) betray a rudimentary lack of understanding of the collective nature of the ANC – in a different way from the collectivism of the less flexible Comintern – and the more profoundly interactive, ongoing nature of consensus decision-making. Like Luthuli, Tambo's sophisticated and subtle process of drawing in diverse opponents who shared the common objective of defeating apartheid was more nuanced, strategic and process-driven by humanism rather than by dogma.

Tambo's steadily widening concept of the nation reveals how, in the process, his pragmatism and nuanced style of consensus decision-making, even in the face of the SACP's powerful democratic centralism, prepared the way. Tambo's use of indigenous skills in the pursuit of an all-embracing democracy has not been sufficiently acknowledged by historians, and in contemporary South African politics, where rural tradition still sits uneasily side by side with other forms of decision-making and modern democracy. The tensions that underlay Tambo's commitment to an holistic and inclusive nationalism remained, and were to re-emerge from time to time in post-apartheid South Africa. But the legacy of Oliver Tambo continues to be evoked; by drawing on the skills of his homestead culture, tried and tested over the centuries, he demonstrated that a cooperative, inclusive culture resulted in strengthening the social relations of the community and, by sharing resources, keeping it together. Tambo is widely credited with the remarkable and perhaps unique feat among exiled liberation movements, of holding the ANC together during its thirty years in exile. He can be best understood when one takes into account that unity was his bottom line, an essential component in the push for liberation.

Tambo used the inherited social skills of careful listening, which reinforced collective consciousness through inclusiveness and consensus decision-making. By embedding indigeneity – a neglected and under-explored aspect of the National Question – into his syncretic style, Tambo was able, subtly and incrementally, to expand his notion of the nation and to prepare a post-apartheid South Africa for the task of inclusive nation building for democracy.

NOTES

1   Unpublished notes to Gail Gerhart and Tom Karis on manuscript for brief biography of N.R. Mandela, Wits Historical Papers.
2   According to Jack and Ray Simons, in *Class & Colour 1850–1950* (IDAF} 1983: 352.
3   Author's conversation with O.R. Tambo, 9 February 1993.
4   In the following fifty-five years, scholars, observers and members of the movement had much to say about the influence of the communists on the strategy and tactics of the ANC. The topic continues to be relevant to the 'unresolved national question'. This brief chapter, however, cannot do justice to the issues involved and therefore confines itself to a more limited focus on race and nationalism.
5   Roughly translated as 'humanity', demonstrating respect and empathy for all human beings.
6   Interviews by the author with Peter Molotsi, Victor Sifora and Joe Matthews.
7   See also www.sahistory.org.za/topic/umkhonto-wesizwe-mk.
8   The issue was shortly to develop into a gripping debate for ANC members with the resurgence of the democratic labour movement inside South Africa when a series of black workers' strikes exploded in the factories of Natal in early 1973.
9   I have in my possession a copy of a note on an otherwise unmarked, undated sheet of paper in Tambo's writing. It is inscribed. 'Leave Martin alone!' See also Martin Legassick's chapter in this volume.
10 Tony Bloom, 'Notes of Meeting at Mufuwe Game Lodge', 13 September 1985, courtesy late Gavin Relly.

REFERENCES

Bernstein, Rusty (1999) *Memory Against Forgetting: Memoirs from a Life in South African Politics, 1938–1964.* New York: Viking.

Callinicos, Luli (2004) *Oliver Tambo: Beyond the Engeli Mountains.* Cape Town: David Philip.

Callinicos, Luli (2012) Oliver Tambo and the Dilemma of the Camp Mutinies in Angola in the Eighties. *Historical Journal, Special Issue: The ANC at 100* (3), September 2012.

Desai, Ashwin and Goolam Vahed. (2010) *Monty Naicker: Between Reason and Treason.* Mkondeni, KZN: Shuter.

Edgar, Robert and Luyandaka Msumza (eds.) (1996) *Freedom in our Lifetime: The Collected Writings of Anton Muziwakhe Lembede.* Athens, OH and Johannesburg: Ohio University Press and Mayibuye Books.

Everatt, David (2010) *The Origins of Non-racialism: White Opposition to Apartheid in the 1950s.* Johannesburg: Wits University Press.

Gerhart, Gail M. (1979) *Black Power in South Africa.* Berkeley, CA: University of California Press.

Gibbs, Timothy (2014) *Mandela's Kinsmen: Nationalist Elites and Apartheid's First Bantustan.* Johannesburg: Jacana.

Legassick, Martin (2007) *Towards Socialist Democracy.* Pietermaritzburg: UKZN Press.

Lembede, Anton (1944) Congress on the March. *Bantu World,* March 1944. Cited in *Freedom in our Lifetime: The Collected Writings of Anton Muziwakhe Lembede,* edited by Robert R. Edgar and Luyandaka Msumza (1996). Athens, OH, and Johannesburg: Ohio University Press and Mayibuye Books.

Sifora, Victor (1956) I Will Arise... *The Africanist,* December 1956. Cited in Gail Garhart (1979) *Black Power in South Africa.* Berkeley, CA: University of California Press.

INTERVIEWS

Breyten Breytenbach, telephonic interview with the author, 4 August 1993

Brian and Sonia Bunting, interview with the author, Cape Town, 3 July 2000

Norman Levy, conversation with the author, 14 March 2015

Joe Matthews, interview with the author, Pretoria, 31 August 1994

Ismael Meer, interview with the author, Durban, 20 January 2000

Wilton Mkwayi, interview with the author, King Williams Town, 20 June 2000

Peter Molotsi, interview with the author, Johannesburg, 1 August 1995

Phyllis Ntantala, interview with the author, Sandown, 6 December 1992

Walter Sisulu, interview with the author, 27 June 1990

Walter Sisulu, interview with the author, Shell House, Johannesburg, 8 February 1993

Oliver R. Tambo, interview with Howard Barrell and Jenny Cargill, Salisbury (Harare), 10 August 1981

Oliver R. Tambo, interview with Howard Barrell, Lusaka, 12 January 1985

Oliver R. Tambo, conversation with the author, February 1993

Victor Sifora, interview with the author, Rustenburg, 4 October 1994

ARCHIVAL MATERIAL

Taped memoir, cassette 1, UFH Archives.

Unpublished notes to Gail Gerhart and Tom Karis on manuscript for brief biography of NR Mandela, Wits Historical Papers.

THE UNITY MOVEMENT AND THE NATIONAL QUESTION

Basil Brown, Mallet Pumelele Giyose, Hamilton Petersen, Charles Thomas and Allan Zinn

INTRODUCTION

Capital accumulation in South Africa started off as a process of 'accumulation by dispossession' (Harvey, 2010: 48–49). War, violence, predation, thievery, criminality, fraud...these were the means by which the indigenous people were dispossessed of their communal lands, and by which the basis to wealth in this country passed into the hands of the capitalists.

South Africa was incorporated into the world economy as an *enclave* – as a colonial economy established by imperialist class interests primarily for the exploitation of its raw material resources (Mhone, 2001). Our economy was typically characterised by a capital-intensive sector co-existing with a capital-starved traditional economy. Although often described as 'dual', they are by no means 'separate'. The capitalist sector, particularly the gold mining industry, was critically dependent on the traditional economy for the ongoing supply of 'ultra-cheap, ultra-exploitable' supplies of labour (Johnstone, 1976). By providing a subsistence base, the traditional economy in effect lowered the minimal acceptable wage threshold of labour (Wallerstein, 2003), thereby ensuring the very existence and sustainability of the capitalist system in this country.

Herein lies the root of our so-called National Question for, historically, class rule in South Africa has been about institutionalising 'systems of duality' in our society in order to extend and maintain the conditions of exploitation. It is against this background that *divide and rule* as a fundamental mechanism of class rule needs to be understood.

Capitalism's interests were served by dividing the nation, by perpetuating a core-periphery duality in society and the economy.

Historically, this has created the conditions of struggle in South Africa. It explains why opposition that was predicated on the principle of 'one single South African nation' has had revolutionary implications – why a call for a non-racial democracy was a fundamental threat to the very basis of capital accumulation.

THE NEUM AND THE NATIONAL QUESTION

The Non-European Unity Movement (NEUM) had a clear-cut position on what constituted the Nation. In a 1951 'Declaration to the People of South Africa' the following was stated:

> Who constitutes the South African nation? The answer to this question is as simple as it would be in any other country. The nation consists of the people who were born in South Africa and who have no other country but South Africa as their mother-land. They may have been born with a black skin or with a brown one, a yellow one or a white one. They may be long-headed or round-headed; straight-haired or curly-haired; they may have long noses or broad noses; they may speak Xhosa, Zulu, Sotho, English or Afrikaans, Hindi, Urdu or Swahili, Arabic or Jewish; they may be Christians, Mohammedans, Buddhists, or of any other faith. So long as they are born of a mother and belong to the human species, so long as they are not lunatics or incurable criminals, they all have an equal title to be citizens of South Africa, members of the nation, with the same rights, privileges and duties. In a nation it is not necessary that the people forming it should have a common language or a common culture, common customs and traditions. There are many nations where the people speak different languages, consist of different nationalities with different cultures. All that is required for a people to be a nation is a community of interests, love of their country, and pride in being citizens of their country (quoted in Wessels, 1991a: 68).

From the outset, the Movement was uncompromising in its demand for the full franchise as 'the most important right of all and, indeed, [as] *the* fundamental right' of all in an undivided South Africa (Wessels, 1991a: 4). Moreover, it was noted:

> In Africa and in Asia 'independence' conferred by the former colonial power, accompanied as it has been by the granting of the full franchise, has not meant national liberation for the populations of these countries. They have remained in

economic bondage to their former masters and this has meant, necessarily, the continued wretched poverty and exploitation of the peasants and workers of these countries ... if national liberation is to be obtained then there has to be the establishment of an equal citizenship by abolishing the old colonial land system, the old unequal legal system, the old exploitative system of taxation, indeed every form of inequality – educational, social and economic. A change that is concerned only with the political, that is, only with the franchise, far from abolishing the yoke of oppression and exploitation results in a double harness. The burden of carrying the independence elite is added to the old heavy load of exploitation by the Colonial masters (Wessels, 1991a: 4–5).

Thus, for the NEUM, the National Question has always meant nothing less than the establishment of equal citizenship for the entire population *as well as* the abolition of 'rightlessness, poverty and inequality of the nationally oppressed and economically exploited mass' (Wessels, 1991a: 22).

PRECURSORS TO THE NEUM

In the inter-war years, two major developments occurred which were to have a profound effect on the ideas of the Unity Movement, especially with regard to the National Question. The first was the spread of the ideas of Mahatma Gandhi. Gandhism became an ideological tendency which would have far-reaching effects on the fledgling national movement in South Africa. The second was the impact of the Bolshevik revolution on the question of imperialism. The nascent movement in South Africa was forced to deal with this issue. As it is today, the hour in the early 1930s was ripe for one direction or another. In his seminal study of the All-African Convention, *The Awakening of a People*, I.B. Tabata (1950) noted that this period saw the sprouting of a range of political organisations among the oppressed. There was already a body known as the National Liberation Front, soon to be followed by the Non-European United Front. To the left of these were smaller intellectual groupings (clearly inspired by the revolution in the USSR) such as the Lenin Club and the Spartacist Group. It was these bodies, principally formed by immigrants from Eastern Europe, which resulted directly in the formation of the Workers Party of South Africa and of the Fourth International Organisation of South Africa. In the middle of that political maelstrom, there arrived in December 1935 the All-African Convention (AAC).

Propelled by the three Hertzog Bills enacted late in 1935, the AAC was a spontaneous response to legislation which, according to its authors, would 'solve the native question once and for all'. In the eyes of the South African ruling class, no problem was more

critical than that of land, labour and the banishment of liberty. Their response was evoc-
ative of the final solution offered by Hitler to the Jewish question. The three Hertzog Bills
were the Native Representation Bill, the Native Trust and Land Bill, and the Urban Areas
Amendment Bill. The first banished the political rights of the oppressed masses, and
circumscribed them in a dummy electoral vote and a dead advisory council. The second
took away their rights to land, pretending that a trust fund would improve on the provisions of the 1913 Land Act – soon demonstrated to be a forlorn hope. The third aimed
at regimenting the labour of the African masses, driving it to those areas (the mines
and the farms) where it was needed most. The intellectual clubs such as the Lenin Club,
already in full bloom, now had an opportunity to mingle with the dynamics of a real and
spontaneous mass movement.

In the 1930s the industrial working class had not yet been created in the political
economy. To be sure, this was the creation of the secondary industries which came
into being only after the Second World War, thanks to the newly discovered drive for
import substitution. So far, the 'working class' was but a nascent concept actualised
only by mine labour and labour in the communications sector. The masses of the
people, more than four-fifths of the population, remained rural, living on residual
land pockets in the native reserves (later, bantustans). The small organisations which
had come to life in the 1930s now suddenly became important as the social leaven
that would convert the AAC into a politically conscious mass movement. In an essay
written in 1941, entitled *Five Years of the All-African Convention,* Tabata drew these
lessons very clearly so that all could realise the dynamics of the new situation. It was
within this milieu that a new cadre of politicos arose. Goolam Gool was shaped by the
immigrant movement that came from India. A doctor, he learned much from the revolutionary working-class movement in Europe, where he had studied. He became the
pre-eminent 'man of ideas' who provided a direction to the new forces. Tabata himself
was a young student from the Eastern Cape who had come to Cape Town in search
of employment, and soon became enmeshed in the intellectual ferment as a trade
unionist. Ben Kies, a younger man sprung from the traditional teacher association of
the time, became one of the 'Young Turks' who would transform the Teachers' League
of South Africa (TLSA) into an organ of liberation. S.A. Jayiya, also an ex-student
from the Eastern Cape, was the typical young man come to Cape Town in search of
employment. This is the group of young revolutionaries who were joined by Dorah
Taylor, A.C. Jordan, Allie Fataar and Hosea Jaffe. Later still, in the early 1940s, others
came in from Natal, the Witwatersrand and the hinterland of the Eastern Cape. The
broader dynamic was that smaller intellectual clubs in the Western Cape were multi-
plying in depth and in numbers through the arrival of the National Liberation Front,
the Non-European United Front and the All-African Convention. A mass movement
was in the offing.

THE ROOTS OF THE NATIONAL QUESTION

In 1937 a significant event occurred. The intellectual circles of the Western Cape formed an organisation known as the New Era Fellowship (NEF). It was at NEF gatherings that the problems of theory and strategy for the immense political tasks at hand were subjected to the most scrupulous examination and debate. The same applied to the even more gnawing problems of programme development. At that time there were four aspects of the National Question. First was the question of racialism. How could the new nation be constituted when clearly its constituency, the people, saw themselves as distinctly divided and disparate groups? In particular, the oppressed saw themselves as Indians, coloureds and Africans, quite apart from the whites. How could anybody build a nation out of such mutually exclusive splinters? Above all, how could the oppressed be united for the purpose of overcoming their separation, building a united consciousness and overcoming their backwardness? It was clear that the central problem lay at the door of the racial idea, and concerted efforts were made to examine the problem of race with the immediate aim of unifying the oppressed as the first block in the building of one human entity, one human race. When the NEUM was formed in the early 1940s, studies on this question were pursued further.

The second element of the National Question which came up for examination in the NEF was that of tribalism. The tribal question was associated with the residual powers and authority of tribal chiefs. In the course of the resistance to conquest, both chief and tribe had been central points of focus around which ruling-class military strategy had been orchestrated. The idea of tribe was sometimes associated with that of nationality, and both had been principal focuses of social cohesion. For the imperial conquerors, it was critical to destroy the power of the chief and, with it, that of the tribe. In order to conserve the solidarity of the imperial taxpayer, however, colonial administrators soon devised the stratagem of indirect rule. This meant a plan to co-opt the chiefs and convert them into 'allies' (actually, tools) of the conqueror. Sometimes the artifice included the conversion of the tribes of such chiefs into 'friendly buffers' to the colony in the manner of the divide-and-rule tactics so ably developed by Julius Caesar in Gaul. The point of the matter, however, was that the surviving tribe was a fiction, important only in so far as it gave its members a false consciousness about the real social essence of tribal identity in a society now controlled by a single capitalist economy – indeed, in the Cape Colony such deception was successfully employed by the conquerors against the Mfengu refugee tribal entities. It was important, therefore, that the AAC should be employed politically to destroy such myths among the 'African' people. In the modern struggle against the capitalist, fictitious tribal divisions had to be overcome so that the 'African' people should unite into one coherent social whole. A united African people were but a step towards the building of a united non-European people. (The term 'non-European' did not signify a social conglomerate of 'races' – it was a descriptive term segregating all people, whether black or white in complexion, who lived outside the continent of Europe. At its core, the term was an attack on *Herrenvolk* racialism propagated by imperialism. Over time, and in the cut-and-thrust of political struggle these demographic studies were as much a conscious effort to undermine the human divisions brought by the colonial system as they were a political weapon designed to cement a new humanism. Emancipating the mind of the oppressed was part of the liberation of the mind of the nation.)

The third element of the National Question rested on the land question. Historically the land in South Africa had been occupied by and belonged to African societies, tribally organised and governed by chiefs. In the 1930s, the struggles over the land question were still fresh in the minds of the oppressed. The violence of conquest was only twenty years old. The 1913 Land Act, with its painful social dislocations, together with the fraud of the Native Trust and Land Bill, were a current reality. The resolution of the land question would therefore be a basic component of resolving tribal bickering over 'the land of our ancestors'. All these cries were fast disappearing and becoming irrelevant in a land stock which was rapidly being gobbled up by capitalist farmers, big corporations and new non-colonial immigrant populations. The new division of the land currently being applied by the ruling class was as grossly wicked and cruel as it was unjust to the majority of the citizens who desired to live by the land. The problem of land was thus an urgent matter of social reconstitution in the nation. Social criticism on this score was urgent and inescapable.

The fourth element was the stark one of imperialism. How would the new nation be built in a world in which every aspect of life was controlled by the British imperial system? The issue was not irrelevant; the current conflict at that time was between British imperialism and an Afrikaner population that was demanding in manifold ways to become the junior partner of imperialism. The competing policy controversies between segregation and apartheid were part of the capitalist problematic that constituted the nature of imperialism in South Africa.

In the resolution of all these issues the debate between Gandhism and Marxism took centre stage. For Gandhism, the strategy of satyagraha was only a component of a long-term policy leading to peaceful negotiations with colonialism and a rearrangement of economic activities between British companies and their colonial counterparts in which the capitalist system would be preserved under new management. For instance, in India where Gandhist principles had had an opportunity to have a 'trial run', by 1948 the country's national bourgeoisie had already concluded company-to-company business arrangements with British firms, in advance of the political negotiations. The Indian leadership itself was clearly a servant of its own national bourgeoisie and the granting of independence became a political formality in which the masses of the Indian working class and peasantry (the very strike force of the Gandhist movement) were completely betrayed. The Indian example was taken by Britain as the blueprint for the settlement of the colonial question throughout its empire. In South Africa, where Gandhi had a committed following among the Natal merchant class, these ideas found easy access to the leadership of the ANC.

In contrast, the Marxist critique implied a revolutionary overturn of the entire system of capitalism. The analysis in the NEF, following closely on the experience of the Bolshevik Revolution, understood the imperialist reality in South Africa to be an example of the expansionist tendency of capital at its highest stage of development. Control of the South African economy by British capital and large Western capitalist companies meant a denial of national economic rights to the mass of South Africans.

The fledgling national movement in South Africa would have to proceed along one axis or another, between the Gandhist and Marxist approaches. It would be on those terms that the National Question would be resolved. Indeed, the hour could no longer be postponed. A clarion call would have to be sounded, calling the nation to arms.

FORMATION OF THE NEUM

As a united front with the AAC and Anti-CAD[1] as its principal constituents, the NEUM's emergence in 1943 was a seminal development in the history of struggle in South Africa. It was accompanied by a set of clearly-formulated principles and demands which were encapsulated in the NEUM's Charter of Liberty – its ten-point programme of non-negotiable minimum demands.

The emergence of the NEUM signalled a break with the politics of reform and collaboration that had hitherto dominated the approach of the leadership of the oppressed. The NEUM was uncompromising in its commitment to a non-racial, democratic society, and sought to unite the organisations of the oppressed on this platform.

The demand was for a full franchise rather than a qualified franchise, which was considered 'no franchise at all' (Wessels, 1991a: 3). Moreover:

> The purpose of granting dummy representation was ... more than that of masking the absence of rights; it was more than the old slave-holders' injunction of 'giving the slave a bone to suck lest he, in his hunger, should demand meat'. It had two further purposes. It has always been a means of fostering division between various groups of the oppressed and so preventing and hampering the growth of the unity of the oppressed people which is indispensable for any struggle against oppression and exploitation. Dummy representation has thus always meant separate representation and accepting dummy representation has meant accepting segregation not only between the citizens and non-citizens but also between the various sectors of the oppressed people. It has always been part of the strategy of 'divide-and-rule' (Wessels, 1991a: 81).

And:

> ... The third, and perhaps most fundamental, aim of the system of dummy representation is to secure an acceptance in practice of the inferior status of the non-citizens by getting the non-citizens themselves to work the system of dummy representation. While they accepted inferiority by accepting dummy representation they were naturally unable to struggle for equality for, clearly, no struggle for equality is possible while inequality is being accepted. You cannot simultaneously accept and reject inferiority. No people working the instruments of their own oppression can wage a struggle against that oppression (Wessels, 1991a: 81).

These were the cornerstones on which the NEUM attempted to unite the leadership of the organisations of the oppressed. It meant that organisations then participating in the dummy representational structures would have to forswear such participation.

The ANC was neither willing to terminate its participation in the Native Representative Council or to elevate the unity of the oppressed as a whole above the unity of the African people. In the words of R.V. Selope Thema (himself a member of the Native Representative Council), speaking for the ANC at a meeting with an AAC delegation:

> ... the unity of the African people [is] of primary importance. Charity began at home. They, the Africans, wanted to unite in their economic and social life, and therefore they had to unite as a race. We had a purpose to fulfil as a united African race. Our aims might be opposed to those of other people, it did not matter. We should follow the law of self-preservation. We should love each other first before we loved other people (ANC and AAC, 1949: 40).

The South African Indian Congress had no appetite for principled unity or the demands of the ten-point programme. Speaking on their behalf at the Second Unity Conference in 1943, Mr A.I. Kajee, dealing with the question of the franchise as contained in Point 1 of the ten-point programme, stated:

> ... that as the Indian Congress stands by the policy of compromise, they could not commit themselves on this point. He stated that in their negotiations with the Judicial Commission now sitting in Natal, they had accepted the principle of a 'Communal' vote based on educational and property qualifications ... [he] made it clear that the Merchant class leadership had no interest in building a movement for liberation from economic exploitation and political domination. They wanted a loose 'unity' that could be manipulated to improve their bargaining position in various negotiations with the ruling class. What mattered to them were their

trading rights and they would make any compromise (read sell-out) to secure these. Thus they were quite prepared to sell out the franchise rights of all the oppressed, including the vast majority of the Indian people, in order to secure the trading rights of the few merchants (Wessels, 1991b: 42).

The rest, as they say, is history.

THE (RE)EMERGENCE OF THE UNITY MOVEMENT

Following two decades of repression by the apartheid government – with cadres banned, banished, detained and imprisoned – the Unity Movement re-emerged as an active organisation at the beginning of the 1980s, in a decade that witnessed a massive turna-round in the dynamics of struggle.

At this stage, a key strategic objective of the liberation movement was to counter the National Party (NP) government's balkanisation policy of separate nation states, or ban-tustans. The Unity Movement noted that both the 'national unity of the oppressed' and the 'dismantling of the homelands' – i.e. the reunification of South Africa – are problems central to the national question' (Dudley, 1983: 23).

This was the era of 'grand apartheid', when ruling-class ideology and policy were char-acterised by the oppression and exploitation of the working class along racially defined lines, and when divide and rule was taken to its ultimate conclusion – the separation of the 'races' in strictly demarcated homelands and urban ghettos. The vision of the ruling class for South Africa was, as Neville Alexander (1979: 12) put it, 'the bogus claims of the National Party's theory and practice ... which postulates the existence in South Africa of eight (sometimes nine) "bantu nations", one "white nation", one "Indian" and one "coloured nation-to-be"'.

In 1984, a new Constitution came into force in South Africa. The single House of Parliament was replaced by three constituent bodies: a 178-member (all-white) House of Assembly, an 85-member (coloured) House of Representatives, and a 45-member (Indian) House of Delegates.

As already mentioned, a cornerstone of Unity Movement politics was the positing of one South African nation, with 'full democratic rights for all, regardless of colour, 'race' or sex' (NUM, 1985: 1). The New Unity Movement's *Declaration* went on to say:

We strive for the dismantling of apartheid in all walks of life; for the dismantling of the location and homelands system and for the re-unification of South Africa. Equally importantly we strive to put an end to the oppression and exploitation by local and foreign interests, of the mass of rural poor who bear the brunt of the evil system that dominates South Africa at present. We strive for principled unity and a programmatic struggle to liberate the oppressed from the yoke of servitude and the daily insults of colour and 'race' discrimination. The rulers have intensified their divide-and-rule policies ... Under the pretence of 'power sharing' and the fraud of 'independent national states' (homelands) the rulers have set up more elaborate machinery both to divide the oppressed and to harness gutless collaborators to work that machinery (New Unity Movement, 1985: 1–2).

In line with Ellen Meiksins Wood's observations, the national democratic revolution was the form that the class struggle took in this period:

> ... modern revolutions have tended to take place where capitalism was less, rather than more, developed. Where, for example, the state itself is a primary exploiter where, say, the state exploits peasants by means of taxation ... economic and political struggles are hard to separate, and in cases like that, the state can readily become a focus of mass struggles. It is, after all, a much more visible and centralized class enemy than capital by itself could ever be ... the state's growing complicity in capital's anti-social purposes might mean that the state would increasingly become a prime target of resistance in advanced capitalist countries ... (Wood, 1997: n.p.).

And, according to Neville Alexander,

> National liberation came more and more to be presented in terms of a national democratic movement, i.e. the nation was conceived as being oppressed or stultified by the bourgeois rulers of the country. Liberation of the nation meant consistent and total democratization of the society, a task which the bourgeoisie, 'white' or 'black', was incapable of performing. Consequently, it was the task of the workers to bring about this historic transformation (Alexander, 1979: 185).

CONJUNCTURES IN THE 1980s

By the beginning of the 1980s, capitalism in the metropolitan countries of North America and Western Europe had succeeded in reining in their high inflation of the 1970s. This caused:

> ... unemployment to jump to levels not seen since the Great Depression ... in spite of high unemployment and rapid de-industrialization caused, among other things, by a restrictive monetary policy. In both the US and the UK, disinflation

was accompanied by determined attacks on trade unions by governments and employers, epitomized by Reagan's victory over the Air Traffic Controllers and Thatcher's breaking of the National Union of Mineworkers. In subsequent years, inflation rates throughout the capitalist world remained continuously low, while unemployment went more or less steadily up... In parallel, unionization declined almost everywhere, and strikes became so infrequent that some countries ceased to keep strike statistics (Streeck, 2011: 12–13).

In South Africa, the mass of unfranchised citizenry was not falling for the ruling-class fraud of 'separate nations', and was boycotting the dummy representative bodies (management committees, urban councils, the Tricameral Parliament), effectively rendering them unworkable. For example, in elections in 1984 for the House of Representatives and the House of Delegates, only 30 per cent of registered coloured voters and only 20 per cent of registered Indian voters cast ballots (US Federal Research Division, 1979: n.p.).

Reduced economic activity in the metropolitan countries (South Africa's chief markets for mineral exports) meant reduced economic activity in South Africa. As a result, the South African currency lost value, the gold price dropped, and unemployment and inflation rates rose (SAHO, 2011).

> ...the resistance movement gain(ed) momentum. The economic crisis, which ordinary people felt in the rising cost of living, gave momentum to the resistance movement for political change which grew dramatically. Trade union strikes, stayaways, boycotts, factory occupations, and other forms of protest spread throughout the country (SAHO, 2011).

Simultaneously, forces in the global political economy that were to have a determining effect on capital accumulation in the 1990s were taking shape. Apart from the demise of the USSR, there was the so-called 'Third World debt crisis' and, perhaps more importantly, the ruling-class response to it. This is nicely encapsulated by David Graeber:

> ...during the '70s oil crisis, OPEC countries ended up pouring so much of their newfound riches into Western banks that the banks couldn't figure out where to invest the money... Citibank and Chase therefore began sending agents around the world trying to convince Third World dictators and politicians to take out loans (at the time, this was called 'go-go banking')... they started out at extremely low rates of interest that almost immediately skyrocketed to 20 percent or so due to tight U.S. money policies in the early '80s... during the '80s and '90s, this led to the Third World debt crisis... the IMF then stepped in to insist that, in order to obtain re-financing, poor countries would be obliged to abandon price supports

on basic foodstuffs, or even policies of keeping strategic food reserves, and abandon free health care and free education ... all of this had led to the collapse of all
the most basic supports for some of the poorest and most vulnerable people on
earth ... thirty years of money flowing from the poorest countries to the richest was
quite enough ... these loans had originally been taken out by unelected dictators
who placed most of it directly in their Swiss bank accounts ... the justice of insisting that the lenders be repaid, not by the dictator, or even by his cronies, but by
literally taking food from the mouths of hungry children ... Or to think about how
many of these poor countries had actually already paid back what they'd borrowed
three or four times now, but that through the miracle of compound interest, it still
hadn't made a significant dent in the principal (Graeber, 2011: 7–8).

For South Africa, the stage was set for a neoliberal coup. On the one hand, the ruling
class's 'separate nations' divide and rule strategy was completely and utterly rejected by
the working-class masses. At the same time, international capital needed to secure a solution that would safeguard its interests in the country, in terms of which:

- There would be a political settlement between the classes, such that the aspirations of all would be accommodated in a single parliament, yet without altering
  the economic interest of the ruling class.
- South Africa would commit to the emerging regime of 'liberal markets', in effect
  reducing any obstacles to free investment by foreign corporations (including privatisation of state assets).
- Most importantly, there would be total commitment to honouring the foreign debt.

What the rulers needed was a partner to assist them in selling the hoax of 'one South
African nation' (but whose wealth-generating machine would remain firmly in the hands
of the capitalists). Enter the ANC.

In a hard-hitting article in 2003, Phyllis Ntantala (wife of the late A.C. Jordan and
mother of ANC stalwart, Pallo Jordan) had the following to say of the negotiated
settlement:

> The Agreement cobbled by the South African regime and the ANC at Kempton
> Park is one of the biggest Frauds that was ever sold to a people ... It was agreed to
> give the reins of power to the ANC on condition that (1) The Economic Structure
> was left intact. This meant that besides the conglomerates that own the wealth of
> South Africa, the 11% of South Africans would still control 80% of the economy.
> This 11% is all WHITE. (2) That the Land Act of 1913 would not be touched;

only the land affected under the Group Areas Act of 1950 would be negotiable. This meant that the 87% of African land, stolen by Whites would still be in their hands and the African population, the majority would still be confined in the 13% of the land. The Mandela Constitution further entrenches the rights of Whites in the 87% of the land, in that under the Constitution, Rights to Private Property are Entrenched ... (Ntantala, 2003: n.p.).

Writing on this fraud, Albie Sachs, an acute and honest ANC leader, says:

We have achieved a great victory. We have accomplished what the Apartheid regime never did. We have deracialised Oppression and legalized Inequality.
The Agreement was the 'Changing of the Guard' – white faces replaced by black faces – all Gate-keepers at the Treasure Trove, South Africa, whose wealth still belongs to the Global Conglomerates with a sprinkling of Whites in South Africa and now, a few black Elites (quoted in Ntantala, 2003: n.p.; emphasis in the original).

In a review of Hein Marais' (2011) *South Africa Pushed to the Limit: The Political Economy of Change*, Helena Sheehan says of South Africa under ANC rule:

There has been privatization of public property, regressive taxation, and facilitation of capital flight. This expatriated capital represents wealth amassed from South African labor and from resources extracted from South African soil. Redistribution has been conflated with black economic empowerment, which has brought the enrichment of a layer of black 'tenderpreneurs,' who provide black cover for white capital and engage in conspicuous consumption, simultaneously representing collusion in the impoverishment of the masses and embodying the secret aspirations of many of them (Sheehan, 2011: n.p).

THE NATIONAL QUESTION AFTER 1994

The 1996 Constitution of the new 'united and democratic' South Africa goes a long way in reversing the discriminatory provisions of the previous regime. On the face of it, the National Question would seem to be resolved in provisions such as '... South Africa belongs to all who live in it, united in ... diversity', from the Preamble, and the citizenship clause which refers to '... a common South African citizenship'. The Bill of Rights 'affirms the democratic values of human dignity, equality and freedom' and tasks the state with protecting them.

However, there are several 'buts'. In the first place, apart from various affirmative-action-type reforms, the prevailing property relations were left intact (and were, in fact, protected by the Bill of Rights). Thus, the basis for the ongoing (and intensified) exploitation of South Africa's working class was laid, and today the devastating effects of this can be seen in numerous indicators, such as the following (Klein, 2007: 215):

- Since 1994, the year the ANC took power, to 2006, the number of people living on less than $1 a day has doubled, from 2 million to 4 million.
- Between 1991 and 2002, the unemployment rate for black South Africans more than doubled, from 23 per cent to 48 per cent.
- Of South Africa's 35 million black citizens, only 5 000 earn more than $60 000 a year. The number of whites in that income bracket is twenty times higher, and many earn far more than that amount.
- The ANC government has built 1.6 million homes, but in the meantime 2 million people have lost their homes.
- Close to 1 million people have been evicted from farms in the first decade of democracy. Such evictions have meant that the number of shack dwellers has grown by 50 per cent (and the number of shanty towns to more than 2 600). In 2006, more than one in four South Africans lived in shacks located in informal shanty towns, many without running water or electricity.

It was as if the Constitution had issued a new licence to foreign and local capitalists to pick up where their predecessors had left off. Thus, it would be true to say that the Constitution does not prevent this attack on the living standards of the mass of the working class people – it *facilitates* it.

The second 'but' addresses the role of the so-called democratic provisions of the Constitution. An article in *The Bulletin* has the following comment about democracy South Africa-style:

What we have today – parliamentary democracy – should be called parliamentary demockery, because that is what it is, a mockery of democracy. Through voting, all we end up doing is legitimising the rule of an elite who have anything but our interests in mind and who will continue to exploit our hopes for as long as we let them. Surely not another twenty years?

The system that we have in this country comes packaged as part of a liberal agenda that offers personal and social freedoms with one hand (e.g., freedom of speech) and economic exploitation with the other (i.e. capitalism, private property, free trade, free circulation of capital, freedom of investment, etc.). The reason that voting changes nothing can be ascribed to three major reasons

Firstly, the system decrees that we the people will do nothing but cast our ballots – that is the extent of our participation under the system. Secondly, the system provides for a parliament which is little more than a talk-shop whose main role is to ensure a climate conducive to capitalist profit-making. Thirdly, management of the economy remains in private hands, unhindered by parliament and the voting public. For the capitalists – local and foreign – it's business as usual.

By granting the nation liberal freedoms, the constitution has achieved two major benefits for capitalism: It has forestalled socialist revolution by providing parliamentary or bourgeois democracy in its place, and it has legitimised private property and capitalist profit-making. So, we have freedom of speech, freedom of organizing, and freedom of exploitation (New Unity Movement, 2014: 25–26).

A third concern with the Constitution is that it provides for the institution of traditional leadership and customary law. This flies directly in the face of liberal democratic principles. It is the back door by means of which the ANC's historical ambivalence on the question of 'race' or 'nationalities' asserts itself. As stated by Unity Movement stalwart, M.P. Giyose:

> The collaborationist politics of the ANC towards the Chiefs was part of its general ambivalence on the matter of traditionalism and traditional customs. This was the root of its nationalist outlook. It is a position which derived directly from the ANC theses of four nations inside the structure of South African society, namely 'Africans', 'Coloureds', 'Indians' and 'Whites'. This was a multi-racial nation in which the four 'races' or national groups had long and old cultural origins. The need of the moment was to make a rational unification of these strands, articulated as they were like Archbishop Tutu's rainbow colours. In reality, these were the views upheld by unredeemed tribalists and racists who wanted to create rational order out of a divergent human past. They offered intractable resistance to the Unity Movement position of one human race and one Nation. Even such eminent leaders of the ANC Youth League as Anton Lembede and A.P. Mda denounced the Unity Movement insistence in 1948 on non-European Unity as a 'fantastic notion.' It was only the abrasive condemnation of racialism and the governance of the chiefs by Steve Biko and a hegemonic Black Consciousness movement in the 1970s that forced the ANC into temporary retreat on this issue. However, once in power after 1994, the ANC went back to its traditional position on African Chiefs. It is no accident that today on its 100th anniversary, it is resuscitating the ghost of the 1951 Bantu Authorities Act in the form of a Traditional Leadership and Governance Framework Act where the Chiefs will enjoy even more powers than they did in the Bantustan regimes of the Nationalist Party. In a sovereign Republic,

resting on a non-racial Constitution, this position amounts to a 'contradictory republican monarchy' (Giyose, 2012: n.p.).

This dramatically ramps up the potential for xenophobia in South African society. Previously, the 'multiple nations' theories of the apartheid rulers created an ever-present competition for (scarce) jobs that could degenerate into 'race'-based conflict among the surplus unemployed. In the modern context, this is more likely to occur at the level of South Africans versus foreigners – meaning unemployed workers of Zimbabwean or Somalian or Mozambican descent – for scarce jobs. In other words, the policy of divide and rule is alive and well.

THE WAY FORWARD

The current reality suggests that the National Question will not be resolved as long as capitalist relations of production are dominant (Alexander, 1979: 13). In other words, the National Question amounts to far more than the constitutional acceptance of a single South African nation (a necessary but not sufficient condition). As long as the ruling capitalist order persists, not only will historical imbalances in the distribution of wealth continue, but future imbalances are guaranteed to persist and, most likely, deepen. The answer, then, is unequivocal: transition to a socialist order.

In this regard, the Unity Movement has responded strategically in two key ways. First, it revised its ten-point programme from a set of minimum demands to a transitional programme (New Unity Movement, 2012). Second, it adopted an action programme underpinned by the slogan 'Towards a People's Democracy'.

In the preamble to the revised ten-point programme, the following statement positions the Movement for its intended direction:

The Nature of Our Struggle
In the era of capitalist parliamentary democracy following the abrogation of apartheid legislation in South Africa, our struggle continues to be both the national and class struggle of a people dominated by imperialism. It is a struggle by the entire working class of this country for nothing less than total emancipation – emancipation from all forms of deprivation and discrimination, from all forms of enslavement and victimization. It is an anti-capitalist and anti-imperialist struggle; it is a struggle for the socialist transformation of society. Our struggle is based on a transitional programme, one that raises demands for the immediate transformation of society such that the disabilities of the working class are immediately addressed, as well as one that raises demands that will

lead to the democratic transition of society to a post-capitalist order (New Unity Movement, 2012: 68).

The slogan 'Towards a People's Democracy' is designed to guide political action in local communities across the length and breadth of the country as they build united, democratic 'people's structures' with the view to self-empowerment. It is critical that such people's structures be independent and not susceptible to co-optation by reactionary forces. Such democratic structures would then form the vehicles through which the working people would pursue not only their demands for immediate redress of their capitalist-induced disabilities, but also their transitional demands for the new socialist society.

Critically, 'Towards a People's Democracy' is posited as an *alternative* to bourgeois democracy and the current parliamentary system in South Africa. In a nutshell, the Unity Movement is saying that building a movement for direct democracy at grass-roots level is a vital precursor to the working class entering Parliament, where the purpose will be not to participate in it but to destroy it, and to replace it with a genuine socialist democracy.

At the time of writing, dynamics within the organised working-class movement (following the massacre of mineworkers at Marikana in 2012) are centred on the emergence of the Workers and Socialist Party (WASP) and United Front being built by the National Union of Metalworkers of South Africa (NUMSA). While it is far too early to predict which way events will shift, it is not unlikely that forces in favour of worker participation in the bourgeois Parliament will surface under both the WASP and NUMSA banners. Given its commitment to building the people's power base *outside* of Parliament, this is something that the Unity Movement will definitely seek to contest via democratic processes within the working-class movement.

In addition, it is not unlikely that the Freedom Charter will be put forward as a programmatic option for the United Front. This, too, will have to be contested, as the Freedom Charter is not a working-class programme, and cannot therefore be used as a signpost to socialism.

CONCLUSION

The Unity Movement's trajectory of struggle will see it on the path sketched out by the Communist Manifesto. Capitalist globalisation has ensured the primacy of class over nation. Thus, in the words of the Manifesto, 'the working men have no country'. Capitalism needs to be conquered country by country – 'the proletariat must first of all acquire political supremacy, must rise to the leading class of the nation, and must constitute itself the nation ... though not in the bourgeois sense of the word' (Tucker, 1978: 488).

NOTE

1   The Anti-Coloured Affairs Department (Anti-CAD) was a people's movement formed to oppose the intensification of the government's segregation strategy when, in the late 1930s, the latter established the Coloured Advisory Council.

REFERENCES

African National Congress (ANC) and All-African Convention (AAC) (1949) Minutes of the Joint Meeting of the National Executive Committees of the ANC and the ACC, 17–18 April 1949. In *Majority Rule: Some Notes (XIII): The Enemies of Principled Unity: The ANC and SAIC.*

Alexander, Neville (writing as No Sizwe) (1979) *One Azania, One Nation: The National Question in South Africa.* London: Zed.

Dudley, R.O. (1983) The Nature of South African Society and the Nature of our Struggle. Keynote Address delivered at the Preliminary Conference of the New Unity Movement, Pietermaritzburg, December 1983.

Giyose, M.P. (2012) *The Antinomies of National Liberation Movement Theory and Practice*: The African National Congress, 1910–1960. Unpublished article.

Graeber, David (2011) *Debt: The First 5000 Years.* New York: Melville House.

Harvey, David. (2010). Enigma of Capital and the Crises of Capital. London: Profile Books.

Johnstone, F.A. (1976) *Race, Class and Gold.* London: Routledge and Keegan Paul.

Klein, Naomi (2007) *The Shock Doctrine: The Rise of Disaster Capitalism.* London: Penguin.

Marais, Hein (2011) *South Africa Pushed to the Limit: The Political Economy of Change.* London: Zed.

Mhone, G.C. (2001) Enclavity and Constrained Labour Absorptive Capacity in Southern African Economies. Draft paper prepared for the discussion at the United Nations Research Institute for Social Development (UNRISD) meeting on 'The Need to Rethink Development Economics', 7–8 September 2001, Cape Town, South Africa. Available online at http://www.unrisd.org.

New Unity Movement (1985) *A Declaration to the People of South Africa.* Durban: African Peoples Democratic Union of Southern Africa (APDUSA).

New Unity Movement (2012) *Ten Point Programme.* Published in Cape Town in December 2013 by the New Unity Movement in its Anniversary Bulletin: '1943–2013, Unity Movement: 70 Years of Struggle'.

New Unity Movement (2014) Our Democracy in South Africa should be called a Demockery. *The Bulletin,* 21(1).

Ntantala, Phyllis (2003) Mistakes and Miscalculations: The Agreement. Unpublished article.

Sheehan, Helena (2011) *The Left Must Launch a Counteroffensive. Monthly Review,* 63(6). Available online at http://monthlyreview.org/2011/11/01/south-africa-the-left-must-launch-a-counteroffensive/ (accessed 28 February 2015).

South African History Online (SAHO) (2011) *How South Africa Emerged as a Democracy from the Crises of the 1990s.* Updated 10 March 2015. Available online at http://www.sahistory.org.za/grade-12/how-sa-emerged-democracy-crises-1990s (accessed 1 April 2015).

Streeck, Wolfgang (2011) The Crises of Democratic Capitalism. *New Left Review,* 71 (Sep-Oct).

Tabata, I.B. (1941) Five Years of the All-African Convention.

Tabata, I.B. (1950) *The Awakening of a People.* All-African Convention. (Republished in 1974 by the Bertrand Russell Peace Foundation for Spokesman Books, Nottingham, UK.)

Tucker, Robert C (ed) (1978) *The Marx-Engels Reader,* Second edition. New York: WW Norton & Co.

United States Federal Research Division (1979) *History of South Africa: Government in Crisis1978–79. Area Handbook of the US Library of Congress.* Available online at http://lcweb2. loc.gov/frd/cs/cshome.html (accessed 28 February 2015).

Wallerstein, Immanuel (2003) *Historical Capitalism,* Eleventh edition. London: Verso.

Wessels, Victor (writing as Sarah Mokone) (1991a) Majority Rule: Some Notes. In *The Educational Journal,* Volume I, edited by H.N. Kies.

Wessels, Victor (writing as Sarah Mokone) (1991b) *Majority Rule: Some Notes.* Second edition. Cape Town: TLSA. (This is a collection of articles originally published in various volumes of *The Educational Journal,* and now collected in a single booklet.)

Wood, Ellen Meiksins (1997) *Labor, the State, and Class Struggle. Monthly Review,* 49(3). Available online at http://monthlyreview.org/1997/07/01/labor-the-state-and-class-struggle/.

5

THE AFRICANIST TURN IN SOUTH AFRICAN
NATIONAL QUESTION DISCOURSES

Siphamandla Zondi

The basic factor which assures their [Africans'] regeneration resides in the awakened race-consciousness. This gives them a clear perception of their elemental
needs and of their undeveloped potential. It therefore must lead them to the
attainment of that higher and advanced standard of life (Pixley ka Isaka Seme,
1906: n.p.).

We, however, move from the deeply held conviction that the people of Africa
share a common destiny and must therefore, at all times, seek to address their
challenges in a concerted manner, as a united force (Thabo Mbeki, 1998:
198–9).

Our contention is that South Africa is an integral part of the indivisible whole that
is Afrika. She cannot solve her problem in isolation from and with utter disregard
of the rest of the continent (Robert Sobukwe, 1959a: n.p.).

INTRODUCTION

In his address to the inaugural meeting of the Pan Africanist Congress in 1959, founding president Robert Mangaliso Sobukwe posed what would be central questions for

Africanists in South Africa, questions that link them to Africanists throughout the continent and beyond. He asked:

> In the course of the past two years we have seen man breaking asunder, with dramatic suddenness, the chains that have bound his mind, solving problems which for ages have been regarded as sacrilege even to attempt to solve... The question then arises, where does Africa fit into this picture and where, particularly, do we African nationalists, we Africanists in South Africa, fit in? (Sobukwe, 1959a).

Sobukwe was observing changes taking place in the world in the middle of the twentieth century, following two terrible wars that had devastated physical infrastructure, human lives and the dream of a better world. He observed the massive changes taking place then as pregnant with many possibilities for Africa's dream of a new world, a world for all. Pixley ka Isaka Seme's 1906 essay also speaks of hope for the birth of a new civilisation, one that would have Africa at the centre. Thabo Mbeki writes in 1998, at the dawn of a new millennium, another time of great changes in the world, a period in which it seemed timely to pose the question whether the twenty-first century would indeed be an African century. There are many Africanist voices in-between and after the three that I highlight in this chapter. The point here is to illustrate three themes. The first is how global changes in the past century (or more) have inspired a rekindling of the African dream for a new world with Africa at the centre. The second is that the Africanist turn in the discourses on the National Question was remarkable for its longevity, the consistency of its central message and the simplicity of its agenda. The third theme is that this Africanist turn included voices in both the African National Congress (ANC) and the Pan Africanist Congress (PAC) precisely because, as Issa Shivji (2003) has convincingly argued, the African nationalism with which the ANC is associated is in fact pan-Africanist and anti-imperialist in orientation. The questions that Sobukwe posed at the moment of change – What is Africa to do to respond to the challenges and opportunities globally? How does it solve national problems in a united and pan-African way? – drew ANC and PAC Africanists closer than they often realised.

In this sense, I want to argue here that for Africanists in general the National Question is in essence also supranational and global. It is tied to the dual history of how Africa was brought against its will into the periphery of the modern (Western) world. First was the tragedy of the trans-Atlantic slave trade, when Africa lost millions of its people for the service of Western centres of the world. Second was 'the curse of Berlin' (Adekeye, 2010), when it was cut into largely unviable nation states for the service of the globalised Western economy. Hence, the 'national' as it relates to the idea of nation state is tied to the very invention of the nation state in the form of colonies in service of global imperialism and colonialism. The notion of the national as a geopolitical imaginary around which power is organised today has its genesis in the very belly of modernity for which the colonisation of time and space was crucial. The national, in the modern sense, therefore, first appears outside Europe as colonies were invented to service European imperial interests, and this logic does not automatically fall away at independence.

Independence amounted to handing over the colonial modern nation state to African political formations or leadership structures without the transformation of their underlying logic and purpose. This chapter posits that it is difficult to see this point on the basis of discourses and analytical tools within the various pockets of modernity as a narrative, left or right wing. This is because both the left and right wings of Western discourses take the nation state and the national economies for granted, and thus become largely ahistorical in their interpretation of the National Question as it presents itself in Africa (Headley, 2008). Such discourses fall into the old trick of modernity, which is to present itself in the language of progress and civilisation when it fact it hides its darker underside, coloniality (Mignolo, 1995). (Anibal Quijano (2000) has shown how, below the veneer of modernity, there emerged a new model of power that naturalised racist, capitalist, patriarchal, Eurocentric, Christian-centric, heterosexual and sexist hierarchies, a model of power he calls coloniality.) In turn, this model of power resurrected ideas about the constitution of power in terms of the logic of dominance, from Plato's idea of philosopher-king through Machiavelli's prince to Friedrich Nietzsche's 'will to power' that naturalise inequality (Golomb, 2002). It was encounters with this hidden side of modernity that created conditions for resistance, African nationalism and pan-Africanism as combative ideologies, paradigms, instruments of counter-power and liberatory thought and action. Therefore, the National Question resides in Africanist paradigms about the very constitution of the problem that spread throughout the world, and not merely its manifestation in national territories. If imperialism takes the form of a colossal octopus with multiple tentacles in various parts of the world, simultaneously effecting its interests everywhere its tentacles can reach, then no manifestation of the problem at national level can be understood outside global designs of coloniality.

Broadly, the Africanist narrative is one that is sceptical of the very idea of the National Question being bounded by national borders but, instead, sees it as global because it emanates from the global designs that have produced the malaise witnessed at continental and national levels. It is a problem of a colonial global humanity that Western Europe's modernity takes credit for constructing, in the name of 'progress'. The haunting question relates to the persistence of coloniality and its manifestation as imperialism well beyond the end of colonial rule, giving rise to the idea of the total liberation of Africa and its nations through self-discovery, combative consciousness, psychic emancipation, epistemic disobedience and pan-African unity and solidarity. 'Total liberation' suggests that where Africa is freed from one of the many hands of the global colonial octopus the liberation is inadequate. Total liberation goes beyond the emancipation of the dominated: from the visible and physical strictures of coloniality to liberation of the mind, the soul, the spirit and culture – and therefore it is not synonymous with political independence. It implies the remaking of the whole of common humanity rather than the insertion of Africans into the zone of Western human beings. This chapter, therefore, argues that the discourses about National Questions in Africa cannot be understood outside discussions about the decolonisation of the world as a whole, the de-imperialisation of the world system.

CONTEXT, CONCEPTS AND CONTOURS

In the African context, the mainstream National Question discourse is a conversation that is taking place among Africans and others, but largely within the confines of modernity because it is a concern about what to do with the national territory, economy and society produced by modernity and including its dark underbelly, coloniality. It is a discourse that is imposed on countries coming out of colonial rule by the historically determined condition of the nation state and the national society. It is associated with discussions that took place in what Issa Shivji (2003) calls territorial nationalisms, especially in the period after independence.

Pan-Africanism has always been a grand narrative of liberation from global imperial designs in their different forms, from capitalist domination to Eurocentric negations in the knowledge environment, and from colonial political domination to coloniality of being and identity; from neocolonial manipulations of the post-independence period to globalisation. Inspired by humanist ideals of liberty, justice and emancipation, pan-Africanism had its roots in resistance to the very arrival of coloniality, although it was articulated as a philosophy, theory and ideology at the dawn of the twentieth century. Pan-Africanism emerges as a global movement for the transformation of the world the West made for its own glory into a world for all, through the efforts of Africans in the western hemispheric Diaspora, especially in the Caribbean and the southern United States. The partition of Africa by Europeans at the Berlin Conference of 1884 sparked denunciation by African Diaspora activists. This evolved into a movement to express solidarity with mother Africa that produced the African Association, formed in 1897 by a group of activists led by the Trinidadian lawyer, Henry Sylvester Williams who, three years later, would serve as the convenor of the Pan-African Congress in London. Between 1900 and the 1930s this involved mainly Africans in the Diaspora, although its influence is evident in the pan-Africanist ideas of early activists, including in Seme's 1906 essay. Only in the 1940s did this movement see prominent participation by continental Africans, but contact between some from the continent and Africans in the Diaspora involved in the pan-African movement (or generally in resistance to anti-black racism) helped to give expression to pan-Africanism as a philosophy of liberation (Walters, 1997).

Coloniality has produced this phenomenon of the African Diaspora, a people forcibly removed from their land, separated from their kin and divorced from their cultures. It was a Diaspora haunted by the pain of separation, in contrast to the Diaspora of Europeans who had expanded by choice in search of opportunities for their own development. This worldwide model of power had introduced a deeply racist conception of humanity by codifying differences between the conquered and the conqueror, so that categories of inferior and superior were naturalised on the basis of phenotypic traits, making inequality, subordination and exploitation permanent. The invention of racially based inferior-superior categories would also find meaning in the new form of control over labour and resources – the enslavement of Africans in support of the colonial economic enterprise that the Americas came to represent was thus crucial for global coloniality. It is because this happened under the veneer of modernity as a narrative of rights, progress and salvation that Seme posed the question: 'Whither is fled the visionary gleam ... where is it now, the glory and the dream?' (Seme, 1906). Modernity promised progress but produced regress; it promised the salvation of souls but delivered the enslavement of bodies and souls; it promised civilisation but delivered barbarism. Encounter with what Walter Mignolo (2007) calls coloniality as the darker side of modernity dashes the dream of freedom and a better life. Modernity produced conquered people of double souls – at once inspired by the narrative of progress and dismayed by the reality of unfreedom. The African encounter with this deeply racist modernity and coloniality led W.E.B. du Bois (1903) to declare that the problem of the twentieth century was the problem of the colour line. Skin colour had been used as a line of distinction between civilised and uncivilised, inferior and superior, Christian and heathen, human and sub-human. While modernity constructed many lines, the most fundamental of these was the colour line. Seme's (1906: n.p.) insistence at the beginning of his essay that 'I am an African, and I set my pride in my race over against a hostile public opinion' underlines that the colour line had been used to disparage the black in order to exalt the white, to affirm whiteness by demeaning blackness. As Carter G. Woodson (2012: 2–7) points out in *The Mis-education of the Negro*, this racist project produced a negro in a troubled seat, one educated by a system that dismisses him as nonentity, a people that W.E.B. du Bois (1903: 9) says carry the burden of 'accumulated sloth and shirking and awkwardness', a people who are a problem in the modern world. The barbarism of anti-black racism produced self-disparagement, self-hate, low self-esteem and even melancholy among oppressed blacks, while it generated racist confidence, self-love and pride among whites. This later point about benefits of whiteness in a racist colonial setting applies (albeit to different degrees) to both those who actively embraced the colonial project and those who rejected it, according to Albert Memmi (2013).

The construction of coloniality as modern model of power precedes physical colonial conquest and tends to outlast the duration of colonial administration. Coloniality existed more than two centuries before Jan van Riebeeck landed on the Cape coast in 1652. The presence of European explorers and traders is thought to have contributed to the convolutions that took place in coastal areas in the eastern interior that are sometimes called the *mfecane* and *difaqane*, the consolidation of nationalities. Indeed, the conquest required mutually reinforcing actions by the colonial administrator, the imperial army, groups of missionaries and colonial business enterprises. The colonial administration, the mine, the plantation, the church and the school were among the most powerful mechanisms used to subdue Africans intellectually, psychologically, culturally, spiritually and physically. This complicated nature of coloniality imposed upon liberation struggles the need to look beyond the mere achievement of national independence, for this did not entail the attainment of freedom. Independence in this sense simply makes coloniality invisible rather than non-existent. As Ramon Grosfoguel (2009: 21) puts it: 'The old national liberation and socialist strategies of taking power at the level of a nation state are insufficient to the task because global coloniality is not reducible to the presence or absence of a colonial administration.' Archie Mafeje (2002) speaks of an umbilical cord between the independent states and former colonial empires that did not break on the occasion of independence; blaming it for the failure to generate alternatives in the organisation of political power, economy, education, knowledge and so forth. For Nzongola-Ntalanja (1987), it was a continuity that produced national liberation without social liberation because the goal of ending foreign direct rule came to supersede that of fundamentally transforming the state, economy and society in order to deliver on the right of the people to a better life. Issay Shivji (2000) suggests that this led to liberal democracy instead of social democracy.

Coloniality is the continuum connecting different orders of the modern world system that produces clashes between hope and despair, aspiration and exasperation, independence and freedom, dream and illusions. As Ndlovu-Gatsheni (2013: 12) has shown, in a neocolonised world, decolonisation and independence present 'illusions of freedom and a terrain of unfinished nation-building, fragmented identities and failing economic development'. What he calls the 'postcolonial neocolonised world' is 'an arena of frustrated dreams and shattered visions'. It is in this context that the Africanist turn is at once a message of hope and a narrative of frustration. It celebrates the glory of independence and decries neocolonialism. It praises as heroes of liberation those who conspire with the global bourgeoisie in the deferment of the African dream.

No wonder African nationalism, as a response to imperial reason, showed two broad ambitions in the 1960s. One was to reverse the imperial order that has governed the world on the basis of hierarchies of race, gender, class, culture and power in order to bring about a free, equal, just and fair world order. This was because it was thought that, as

Amilcar Cabral, the leader of the Guinea-Bissau liberation movement, said: '... so long as imperialism is in existence, an independent African state must be a liberation movement in power, or it will not be independent' (quoted in Shivji, 2003: 3). The second ambition was a desire to speedily achieve continental unity in the form of a supranational state sometimes called the Union Government or the United States of Africa, as proposed by Ghana's Kwame Nkrumah. It was sceptical of territorial nationalism because it invested in making inherited nation states work in an international environment where global imperial forces were powerful enough to subvert them. Nkrumah feared that if African nationalists focused wholly on newly independent states they would be vulnerable to neocolonial manipulations. Even though Tanzania's Julius Nyerere preferred a gradual process of continental unity by first building regional federations of states, he too was worried that if African countries delayed the process of building unity, sovereignty, the flag and the anthem would become difficult to jettison when the time came for regional and continental unity (Shivji, 2003: 7).

Africanists in various political formations in South Africa identified with this, pushing for the struggle against global imperialism and for pan-African unity. In his crucial speech inaugurating the Pan Africanist Congress, Robert Sobukwe (1959a: n.p.) made the point that the dispute between the West and East in the Cold War masked and abetted the bigger demon of imperialism through their 'terrible competition, use of tough language and tactics ... brinkmanship stunts which have the whole world heading for a nervous breakdown'. He echoed calls for 'positive neutrality' by refusing to 'change one master (Western imperialism) for another (Soviet hegemony).' He also underlined the fact that what united Africanists in South Africa, in Africa as a whole and in the Diaspora was the unity of Africa placing its destiny firmly in the hands of Africans themselves. On this basis, the underlying imperative of the South African liberation struggle was that South Africa could not solve its National Question in isolation from the rest of Africa.

The pan-Africanist dream was frustrated as independence saw the rise of military governments and dictatorships that would haunt Africa until the 1980s. This decimated the capacity of the states to respond to social crises, further weakened as they were by neocolonial and imperial manipulations of domestic policies through loan agreements and structural adjustment programmes that helped discredit independent African states in the eyes of ordinary people. As donors saturated the policy space, African states lost their self-determination in making critical policy decisions about the pertinent challenges of their time.

African nationalism with a pan-Africanist slant became an ideological home for all kinds of resistance against imperial and neocolonial designs in independent states, as well as in colonies like South Africa. Linkages with Third-World nationalism provided useful energy to the African efforts (as the Cuban involvement in Angola shows) but it was weakened by the onslaught of the neoliberal agenda under the guise of globalisation that emerged in the late 1980s. The policy prescriptions through aid conditionality, corporate penetration of the African state and cultural imperialism helped weaken the agency of African nationalism. In some cases, Shivji (2003) argues, African nationalism was forced to retreat and become entangled in territorial nationalism that had a weak understanding of global designs. It was a form of nationalism that would nurture and promote tribalist and ethnic tendencies, and parochial responses to the demand for continental unity.

Because coloniality, both in the form of colonial rule and in post-independence neocolonialism, entailed a comprehensive project of domination, the national liberation agenda had to become a humanist endeavour, seeking to undo the very basis on which colonial and neocolonial distortions are built. It had to be a rejection of the idea of humanity bifurcated into beings and non-beings. It had to reject racism and other Eurocentric myths, while insisting on the ontological density of blacks merely because it had been denied. This was not always what African nationalist and pan-Africanist struggles entailed in practice, of course, for many reasons. The task of this chapter is to outline the Africanist turn in the National Question discourses rather than to reflect extensively on its impact in the practical pursuit of liberation.

The key contribution of Africanist discourses on the National Question is to disabuse the concept of territorial limitations by arguing that it is, in essence, a global question, a question about the deconstruction of the model of global power as described above. It also poses questions relating to African being and governance outlined below.

A PERENNIAL QUESTION: WHO IS AN AFRICAN?

The Africanist discourses fundamentally hope for true and full decolonisation, true liberation. Without the birth of a new world humanity and philosophy of humanism, colonialism evolves into new forms, including neocolonialism. Therefore, central to Africanist interjections in the discourses on the National Question is the need to rethink matters of ontology in order to free the concepts of blackness and whiteness, Africanity and *Ubuntu* from racist distortions. In this thinking, Seme (1906: n.p.) said, 'Each race is self.' This is why the idea of human brotherhood as the basis of true human solidarity permeates the works of early thinkers on pan-Africanism (see, for instance, Du Bois, 1903). The question that arises in this regard is how Africanists respond to the perennial question: Who is the African? (The question is posed in the context of the presence in Africa of peoples from Europe, Asia and the Middle East.) Sobukwe explained a broadly shared perspective on Africanness as a human category this way:

> We aim, politically, at government of the Africans by the Africans, for the Africans, *with everybody who owes his only loyalty to Afrika and who is prepared to accept*

the democratic rule of an African majority being regarded as an African (Sobukwe, 1959a: n.p., my emphasis).

Thus, Africanness was not a fixed biological attribute, unattainable for those from elsewhere. This strips the concept of race of the dehumanising features it carries in Westernised modern thought and practice, and Seme (1906: n.p.) could use race in a way that fundamentally challenged this dominant conception when he said, 'I am an African, and I set my pride in my race over against hostile public opinion.' In this sense, race is not a category for exclusion but a term for people who make a certain choice about their identity and stance on humanity. It distinguishes people who decide consciously to go against the hostile colonial public opinion that defined Africanness on the basis of biological features and related it to inferiority. Years later, Thabo Mbeki suggested the basic script for the birth of a new, post-apartheid nation in a speech to Parliament on the occasion of the adoption of the South Africa's democratic Constitution. He characterised the Constitution as a declaration by the new citizens that they were Africans. The African race Mbeki conjured up was one of loyalty rather than biology, of consciousness rather than accident of birth, and of commitment rather than condemnation to fixed human categories.

Closely related to this point of rehumanising the world, is the idea that Africa is actually central to building a new world. Archaeological discoveries showed that Africa was the cradle of humankind; pan-African thought had long reasoned that Africa had given humanity to the world. At the height of apartheid and colonialism, it was thought that because Africans had experienced how a people could be victims of progress they were best suited to thinking about a new humanity, a new human civilisation founded on true dignity, peace, justice, fairness and freedom. As Sobukwe (1978) put it in his speech: 'We breathe, we dream, we live Africa; because of Africa and humanity.' He went on to say, 'On the liberation of the African depends the liberation of the whole world.' He reasoned further, 'The future of the world lies with the oppressed and the Africans are the most oppressed people on earth.'

This is linked to questions of pan-African consciousness and African loyalty. The idea is that the pan-Africanist project cannot survive unless it rejects the imposed consciousness of a people as objects, as inferior, and as a people whose self-perception is organised into tribal illusions. Pride in Africa thus demands appreciation of African history – the history before Eurocentric distortions and negations, the history of a people as agents rather than subjects. This narrative envisages self-discovery and self-writing, enabling Africans to echo Seme's contention that the regeneration of Africans was in essence a march out of the imposed hellish zone of being fashioned by Western civilisation. 'The basic factor which assures their regeneration,' he said in his 1978 speech to university students, 'resides in the awakened consciousness' (Sobukwe, 1978).

It is also central to pan-Africanist orientation on the National Question that the necessary rebirth has a spiritual dimension. This sets the pan-Africanist proposition apart from other related discourses on the National Question because Western modernity presupposes a difference between body and spirit, and therefore between reason and inspiration. Often, the dominant discourses understate the importance of the spiritual dimensions of the decolonisation process, the need for spiritual liberation. Sobukwe (1978) once underlined the duty of the conscious African as being a mission to build a nation, to glorify God and to contribute to the blessing of mankind. It is remarkable to note that those concerned about the rise of Africanist sentiments among the restless and conscientised youth on university campuses – members of the ANC Youth League and Sobukwe when at Fort Hare University College in the 1940s – were already describing this development as a 'naughty spirit of nationalism'. They saw it as more as a spirit than as a philosophy or a mere campaign (Pogrund, 2006: Chapter 1).

Pan-Africanists also underline the importance of the psychic liberation of a people haunted by coloniality in all its forms. Central to the interjections of Africanists to the discourse of liberation is the call that Bob Marley made in song, and which Marcus Garvey repeatedly made in speech: 'Emancipate yourself from mental slavery; None but our self can free our minds' (Marley, 1979). In a wide-ranging speech to the newly-formed Pan Africanist Congress entitled 'The State of the Nation', Sobukwe eloquently placed the question of mental liberation at the centre of the Africanist argument about conditions for liberation. He recognised the coloniality of being by which the colonial system taught Africans that they were inferior, teaching them to accept white superiority. Therefore, he said, it was the very task of Africanists to 'exorcise slave mentality' and impart the spirit of 'self-reliance' that made them choose to starve in freedom rather than have plenty in bondage. He called upon Africans to embrace what Nkrumah called the African personality, and to pursue what Kenneth Kaunda called African humanism. Nkrumah and Kaunda called this a status campaign, and emphasised that there is no national liberation without the liberation of the status of being African.

Failure to de-imperialise common humanity reproduces imperialisms of new kinds. 'The essence of neocolonialism,' wrote Kwame Nkrumah (1965: 1), 'is that the State which is subject to it is, in theory, independent and has all the outward trappings of international sovereignty. In reality, its economic system and thus its political policy are directed from outside.' As Sobukwe would put it in 1959, Africanists had learned that it was not enough to fight colonialism; one also had to fight imperialism because while the former manifested practically at national level, imperialism was the force behind it all over the world (Sobukwe, 1959b). This realisation drew Africanists closer to the critics of narrow national liberation such as Amilcar Cabral and the Argentinian revolutionary Che Guevera. The latter once argued, 'As long as Imperialism exists it will, by definition, exert its domination over other countries. Today that domination is called neocolonialism' (Guevara, 1965: n.p.). As we have shown, at the heart of the connections between the apparent system and its hidden forms was the question of race, in particular the assumed superiority of the white race. Therefore, Africanist discourses link the dethroning of the national colonial situation to the defeat of racist imperialism in the world (Shivji, 2011: n.p.).

Central to the message of Africanists on the National Question is the argument that the question is not national in essence even though it manifested in a nation state that the Euro-centric world system created. Rather, the essence of the question is global. The very idea of nation states and nations as we know them today is an invention of Western modernity following the traumatic experience of Europe through decades of internecine wars which sought to reorganise the existing political space. At the end of the Thirty Years War in 1648, European states gathered in Westphalia to agree the famous Peace of Westphalia where the notion of nation states was born. Narrow versions of nationalism, often inspired by the German and French ideas of a nation state, are misplaced with regard to the colonial question haunting Africa. Problems of poverty, underdevelopment, violence and alienation are produced by imperialism globally, and colonialism or neo-colonialism is only a tool by which it does so at the national level. This is the argument Julius Nyerere (1966) put forward strongly in the late 1960s, but which came up against the trappings of national independence and positions of power that were just too strong for African politicians to resist. Therefore, pan-Africanist struggles must of necessity be international and global at the same time. This militates against understanding the problem facing the South African state today only in terms of manifestations of imperialism; it is essential to understand their totality in terms of global machinations and the responses to them.

In this context, Africanists have argued consistently for economic freedom based on the understanding that imperialism has evolved – from something that used physical force to dispossess and impoverish, to a force that uses subtler means of achieving the same aim – what Paul Nye (1990) terms 'soft power'. Sobukwe described this as evident in development programmes from the centre of imperialism, which used attractive slogans of development for all in order to ensnare Africa in the new global economic agenda (Pogrund, 2006). Imperialism had shifted its tactic from coercion to enticement. It understood the limitation of the African bourgeoisie, which in Fanon's (1961: 105) view, sought to emulate its Western counterpart in taste, thought and conduct. No wonder Africanists emphasised the return of control over the economy, natural resources and the land. At a level of ideology, this was designed to rob imperialism of entry points for subverting the sovereignty of newly independent African states. The idea of pan-African unity is a response to the nagging National Question as manifest in the neocolonial nature of the inherited state and economy, the continued cultural dislocation of the former colonial subjects, the corruption of independence by the African national bourgeoisie, and shattered dreams as the ideal of freedom remained elusive for ordinary Africans.

Nyerere's idea was that African nationalism was anachronistic and unhelpful unless it was at the same time pan-Africanism (Fanon, 1961). He believed that the major stumbling block to concretising African unity was the strength of territorial nationalisms that had led to the willingness of the political class to renege on commitments to African integration in order to preserve their national flags and national anthems. This was a true scandal of independence and a vindication of Nkrumah's discomfort about celebrating national independence when it promised only an illusion of sovereignty. As Ndlovu-Gatsheni (2013: 12) has shown, in a neocolonised world, decolonisation and independence present 'illusions of freedom and a terrain of unfinished nation-building, fragmented identities and failing economic development'. In his view, the 'postcolonial neocolonised world' is 'an arena of frustrated dreams and shattered visions'. It is under these conditions that Africanist discourses on the National Question are taking place, engendering hope for the birth of a new African, a new Africa and a new world.

Africanist perspectives also place on the table the important question of epistemic disobedience. They understand the implications of coloniality for knowledge and its production. As Sobukwe implied, education was used to mis-educate Africans, to turn them into subjects instead of citizens, into objects of someone else's designs rather than active agents capable of fashioning their destiny. Knowledge was important in the spread of coloniality. By homogenising all knowledge into one Eurocentric knowledge, other knowledges were denied and denigrated. To achieve this, imperialism needed to move on the premise that Africans could not think and were therefore not beings with souls. It had to accuse Africa of having no scientific heritage, no body of knowledge and no thinkers, so as to justify importing knowledge. This is what Archie Mafeje (2011) calls Eurocentric negations that legitimised erasure and other forms of epistemic injustices committed against the Other. He said that there would be no need for Africans to claim the renewal of their heritage of knowledge and to insist on Afrocentric epistemologies if these were not denied them by Eurocentric negations. Therefore, the decolonisation of knowledge and its production, which links to the decolonisation of the mind, is seen as an important terrain of disobedience of coloniality, a rebellion against the neocolonised order of things.

WHAT STRUCTURES INCUBATED PAN-AFRICANIST DISCOURSE ON THE NATIONAL QUESTION?

The Africanist or pan-Africanist narrative on the National Question is not a monolithic discourse, but a variety of discourses joined together by what I suggest are running themes. In South Africa, these discourses prevail in platforms associated with African nationalist, African leftist/Marxist spaces and in pan-Africanist/black consciousness terrains.

Although the formation of the Pan Africanist Congress was inspired by almost all of the thematic discussions outlined above – discussions in which its founding president, Robert Sobukwe – played a principal role, it would not be a consistently reliable platform for the flourishing of the idea of pan-Africanism in the sense proposed above. A number of reasons can be proffered for this. One of them is that after Sobukwe there did not emerge a body of thinkers within the PAC to keep the organisation interested in the philosophical and ideological questions that instigated its establishment. In the difficult terrain of exile politics, and haunted by raids conducted by apartheid forces in neighbouring countries such as Botswana, Swaziland and Mozambique, the young PAC found it difficult to settle down sufficiently to nurture this ideological and philosophical response to the National Question. The politics of militarism overshadowed militancy, and dominant leaders did not develop a cadre of thought leaders in the frame of Sobukwe. Factionalism and the turning of the organisation into a mass movement also ate away at the PAC as a platform for input into the national, continental and global discourses on pan-Africanist propositions.

In many ways, the ANC, which survived the exile years much better and with a strong domestic front, provided a home to many of the Africanist ideas. It was in the nature of the ANC to be a 'broad church' and thus provide space for the competition between ideas born within modernity, from liberalism to Marxism, as well as those seeking to transcend it, like black consciousness and Africanism. From Pixley ka Isaka Seme in the early decades of the ANC through the emergence of Africanist voices in the Youth League of the 1940s to the recruitment of black consciousness activists into the ranks of the ANC, especially on Robben Island, the ANC was able to appropriate the ideational space of the PAC. It came as no surprise that the ANC government after 1994 implemented many of the Africanist ideas, principally the projection of a strongly Africanist foreign policy and the rhetoric of radical land reform. Thabo Mbeki joined together Seme and Sobukwe in his political persona, advocating African renaissance and urging South Africa to face up to its African identity and destiny.

The Africanist orientation would also prevail among critical African scholars, from Jordan Ngubane to Herbert Vilakazi and Ben Magubane to Archie Mafeje. This, however, has been the weakest element of the Africanist pursuit because the Eurocentric negations of Africa as an archive of ideas, and Africans as capable of thinking, were perhaps more successful than we often recognise. There is a rebirth taking place, principally through the connection of South African scholarship to the broader continental and Diaspora counterparts through conferences and the Council for the Development of Social Science Research in Africa (CODESRIA). The birth of the Thabo Mbeki Institute for African

Leadership in close proximity to the Institute for African Renaissance Studies and the Archie Mafeje Institute for Social Policy is making the University of South Africa, which has a thriving campus in Ethiopia, a key centre of this African intellectual renaissance. Initiatives like the South African Research Chairs Initiative (SARCHI) Chair on African Diplomacy and Foreign Policy at the University of Johannesburg, which has worked closely with the Concerned Africans Forum to raise issues of the subordination of Africa under global imperial designs masked as humanitarian interventions, have also stimulated interest in Afro-centric thought, Africanity and Africanisms. The Africa Institute of South Africa, which is sadly being closed, has been the most consistent champion of Africanist narratives through its lively dialogue programmes, aggressive publishing of African authors and field research in various parts of Africa.

CONCLUSION

The Africanist orientation of the National Question is to this day underpinned by the ideas of de-imperialisation on a global scale and the demands to understand Africa from its cultural context in order to recognise how it could be an agent of its own transformation. This orientation found an institutional home as a political ideology of the PAC, but had taken root in the ANC much earlier. For this reason, on his release from jail Nelson Mandela proclaimed that Africa was South Africa's destiny, and his successor, Thabo Mbeki, drove a national agenda underlined by the belief that South Africa's problem was Africa's problem, and therefore South Africa needed to place itself at the centre of the African pursuit of solutions. This ideological and theoretical lens on the National Question has survived and expanded, thanks to the fact that it was not monopolised by one political formation, but inspired a cross-section of individuals and institutions.

REFERENCES

Adekeye, Adebajo (2010) *The Curse of Berlin: Africa after the Cold War.* New York: Columbia University Press.
Du Bois, W.E.B. (1903) *The Souls of Black Folks.* New York: Start Publishing.
Fanon, Frantz (1961) *The Wretched of the Earth.* New York: Grove.
Golomb, J. (2002) How to De-Nazify Nietzsche's Philosophical Anthropology. In *Nietzsche, Godfather of Fascism? On the Uses and Abuses of Philosophy*, edited by J. Golomb and R.S. Wistrich. Princeton: Princeton University Press.
Grosfoguel, Ramon (2009) A Decolonial Approach to Political Economy. *Kult, 6 (Special Issue. Epistemologies of Transformation)*: 1–38.
Guevara, Ernesto (1965) Speech delivered at the Second Economic Seminar of Afro-Asian Solidarity. Available at https://www.marxists.org/archive/guevara/1965/02/24.htm (accessed 12 April 2008).

Headley, J.M. (2008) *Europeanisation of the World: On the Origins of Human Rights and Democracy.* Princeton: Princeton University Press.

Mafeje, Archie (2002) Democratic Governance and New Democracy in Africa: Agenda for the Future. Paper presented at the African Forum for Envisioning Africa, Nairobi, 26–29 April 2002.

Mafeje, Archie (2011) Africanity: A Combative Ontology. In *Post-colonial Turn: Imagining Anthropology and Africa*, edited by R. Devisch and F.B. Nyamnjoh. Leiden: Langaa.

Marley, Bob (c.1979) Redemption Song Lyrics. Available at www.lyricsfreak.com.

Mbeki, Thabo (1998) *Africa: Time has Come,* Johannesburg: Tafelberg.

Memmi, Albert (2013) *The Colonizer and the Colonized.* New York: Plunkett Lake Press.

Mignolo, Walter (1995) *The Darker Side of Modernity: Literacy, Territoriality and Colonization.* Ann Arbor: University of Michigan Press.

Mignolo, Walter (2007) Coloniality and Modernity/Rationality. *Cultural Studies,* 21(2–3): 155–67.

Ndlovu-Gatsheni, S. (2013) *Coloniality of Power in Postcolonial Africa: Myths of Decolonisation.* Dakar: CODESRIA.

Nkrumah, Kwame (1965) *Neocolonialism: The Last Stage of Imperialism.* New York: International.

Nye, Paul (1990). *Bound to Lead: The Changing Nature of American Power.* New York: Basic Books.

Nyerere, Julius K. (1966) The Dilemma of the Pan-Africanist. In *Freedom and Socialism*, edited by J.K. Nyerere. Oxford: Oxford University Press.

Nzongola-Ntalanja, G. (1987) *Revolution and Counter-revolution in Africa.* London: Zed.

Pogrund, B. (2006) *Robert Sobukwe: How Can Man Die Better?* Johannesburg: Jonathan Ball.

Quijano, Anibal (2000) Coloniality of Power, Eurocentrism and Latin America. *Neplanta: Views from the South*, 1(3): 533–80.

Seme, Pixley ka Isaka (1906) Regeneration of Africa. Available at www.sahistory.org.za/archive/regeneration-africa-5-april-1906 (accessed on 2 March 2007).

Shivji, Issa (2003) The Rise, Fall and Insurrection of African Nationalism. Keynote Address to the CODESRIA East African Regional Conference, Addis Ababa, Ethiopia, October 29–31. Unpublished.

Shivji, Issa (2011) The Struggle to Convert Nationalism to Pan-Africanism. *Amandla!*, 25 August. Available at www.amandla.org.za (accessed 2 July 2015).

Shivji, Issay G. (2000) Critical Elements of a New Democratic Consensus in Africa. In *Reflections on Leadership in Africa: Forty Years after Independence*, edited by H. Othman, and M. Halfani. Brussels: VYB University Press.

Sobukwe, Robert M. (1959a) Robert Sobukwe Inaugural Speech, April 1959. Available at http://www.sahistory.org.za/archive/robert-sobukwe-inaugural-speech-april-1959 (accessed 12 July 2014).

Sobukwe, Robert M. (1959b) The State of the Nation. Available at www.ilizwe.files.wordpress.com (accessed on 3 October 2014).

Sobukwe, Robert M. (1978) Address on Behalf of the Graduating Class at Fort Hare College Delivered at the Completers Social, 21 October 1949. In *Speeches of Mangaliso Robert Sobukwe*, edited by the Pan Africanist Congress. Maseru: PAC Information Bureau.

Walters, R.W. (1997) *Pan Africanism in the African Diaspora: An Analysis of Modern Afrocentric Political Movements.* Detroit: Wayne State University.

Woodson, Carter G. (2012) *The Mis-Education of the Negro.* New York: Start Publishing.

PART TWO

CONTINUITY AND RUPTURE

VICISSITUDES OF THE NATIONAL QUESTION: AFRIKANER STYLE

T. Dunbar Moodie

In *One Azania, One Nation,* his classic study of the National Question, discussed elsewhere in this volume, Neville Alexander (1979) relies heavily on my early work, *The Rise of Afrikanerdom*, to argue for the impact of Afrikaner nationalist understandings of the world on what he calls the apartheid 'bantustan strategy'. My book posits that for Afrikaner intellectuals separate development theory relied greatly on their experience of their own struggle to free themselves from the demeaning and condescending attitudes of English-speaking white South Africans by asserting their own national identity.

Later, Aletta Norval (1996) also picked up on this, arguing, memorably, that Afrikaner discourse around 'the Afrikaner myth' fed directly into ideas of 'the apartheid imaginary'. Debates among Afrikaners about their own cultural calling, then, provided a model to impose their understanding of 'national identity' on coloureds, Indians and the various African 'cultural entities' – themselves to a large extent creations of colonial imagination about 'tribal identities'.

Thus, despite the misery wrought by the South African state's pursuit of white racial interests, the origins of apartheid ideology in what I called 'the Afrikaner civil religion' meant there were always those who sought to justify apartheid's fundamental precepts in moral terms (Moodie, 1975). However cruel apartheid was in its effects, and however blind its adherents were to the suffering it caused, many Afrikaners (especially Afrikaner intellectuals) saw the policy as tackling a moral dilemma rooted in their own experience of colonial domination. Indeed, some of the very ruthlessness of apartheid's implementation may be attributed to wilful avoidance of the moral predicament it evoked. Much of it, of course, was simply self-interested blindness.

From its inception, the full implications of separate development ideology engendered intense debate among Afrikaner intellectuals. This chapter makes no attempt to argue that debates among Afrikaner intellectuals *caused* the transition of the 1990s (there were many much more concrete causes), but F.W. de Klerk clearly articulated his direction and marshalled his support along the lines of those debates, both for and against separate development.

Moreover, it is striking how *internal* these debates were to a narrow intellectual community of Afrikaans-speaking white South Africans. Moral debates among Afrikaners were referenced in the Afrikaans press and published in widely read collections of essays, but with little or no participation from Afrikaans-speaking coloureds, let alone Africans or English-speaking whites. Such inwardness, compounded by the very effects of apartheid itself, closed off the majority of even morally aware Afrikaners from full comprehension of the suffering their policy had occasioned.

I begin this chapter with a discussion of N.P. van Wyk Louw and his plea for a just nationalism. His writings develop the notion of separate development as the framework through which Afrikaners might find moral justification for apartheid. I go on to discuss tensions between the racist assumptions of apartheid and the cultural nationalist assumptions of separate development, which became explicit in the 1950s during the course of internal conflict among Afrikaners about the 'coloured question'. Eventually, after the Soweto uprising, both the National Party and the Afrikaner Broederbond split over the Tricameral Parliament. A central question became whether Afrikaner cultural independence could survive without control of the national state, which had been a pivotal goal of the Afrikaner struggle since the 1930s. I conclude with an account of intense debates in the 1980s within the Afrikaner Broederbond between those who believed the future of Afrikaners could be retained in a post-apartheid South Africa through constitutional guarantees and those who believed Afrikaners could retain their identity only if they controlled the state.

VAN WYK LOUW

N.P. Van Wyk Louw was an Afrikaans-language poet, playwright and scholar. Among his writings are some of the most striking (and earliest) examples of an Afrikaner intellectual struggling with the moral predicament of Afrikaner nationalism in South Africa.[1]

Van Wyk Louw engaged with the fundamental question of the exact nature of the Afrikaner 'calling'. Afrikaner nationalism, he wrote, 'has found no reasonable answer to the fundamental political question, "What moral right has a small nation (*volk*) to wish to survive *as a nation*?"' (Louw, 1986: 500).[2]

His own answer to this question in *Liberale Nasionalisme* was twofold: national calling demands both that there be cultural values worth defending and that the realisation of that calling should not oppress others. In the first place, Louw pointed to social movement nationalists like Piet Meyer (Moodie, 1975: 164). They were important, he believed, 'active and faithful on the purely political level: good organizers, wide awake, going to meetings, voting when it is necessary to vote ... [nonetheless] defence on this front opens our flanks from other directions' (Louw, 1986: 461). Indeed, if this is all that is done 'then one day we will discover that we no longer wish to defend our city, because there is nothing valuable *within* that we want to keep'. This is why, for Louw, literature and art were so important.

Important as are the artist's language and the history of his or her nation, these are but means for the artist. The end is to convey with integrity, movingly and powerfully, insight into the depths of the human condition in all its grandeur and its pettiness. That is the artist's vocation. It coincides with the calling of his or her nation. It provides the reason for his or her existence. When it is realised (and it seldom is – and never perfectly), then social context, language, ethnic aspirations and realisations are all enhanced. Only through such creative work can a nation claim a right to exist. For Van Wyk Louw, then, it is cultural creativity with its deep insight into the human condition that ensures that a nation has valuable assets worth preserving.

If a majority of Afrikaners considered it no longer worth the trouble to continue to exist as a nation, Louw (1986: 458) added, Afrikaans-speaking 'individuals each will be able to continue – indeed, perhaps survive in prosperity – but they will no longer make up a separate nation'. By 1952, however, Louw was insisting:

> A nation is not *one being*. It has no unity of judgment, no unity of will; it does not make *one* decision. It exists out of countless individuals, and where it thus 'decides' or 'chooses', this is the result of countless judgments and decisions, half judgments and lame decisions (Louw, 1986: 455).

In the second place, Louw (1986: 460) argued, the Afrikaner nation would not survive 'if a large part of the nation are in danger of reckoning that we do not need to live in justice with our fellow nations in South Africa':

> Suppose that a nation has come into the narrows – finding that it must mount a life or death defence; it summons up all material and political powers, guards and marshals its spiritual, technical, intellectual assets, does everything it can to survive ... Then it comes before the last temptation: to believe that bare survival is preferable to *survival in justice* ... This is the lasting temptation awaiting a nation in their desert days – the biggest almost mystical crisis before which a nation can

stand. I believe that in a strange way this is the crisis from which a nation appears, reborn, young, creative. This 'dark night of the soul' in which it says: I would rather perish than survive through injustice (Louw, 1986: 462).

This is a theme Afrikaner intellectuals, especially after 1976, would return to again and again.

At this point in his essay, Van Wyk Louw turns to practice. How is it possible to know and understand such a complex, chaotic, uncontrollable thing as a community, he asks (Louw, 1986: 484). Such complexity had led many to conclude that big decisions should be taken out of the hands of the ignorant masses and assumed by a smaller elite better able to judge what should be done. Although Louw himself had implied the same in some of his earlier writings, now he asserted:

> *No person* and *no group* can truly see through the chaos of a large community and make proper decisions on its behalf; human partiality and murky insight clings to everyone – even the greatest spirits … Precisely because all knowledge and insight is relative and one-sided, the elite must eternally be pulled by the dull demands, the confused but different insights of the masses.

Hence Louw insisted on the importance of democracy, especially of open polemical struggle, public argument, ongoing debate (*oop gesprek*).

He was opposed to simple majority rule, which is itself, he said, a form of dictatorship by the masses. Instead, he advocated majority rule within a framework of checks and balances (*remmende factore*) such as 'a free press; party politics; established rights for subordinate bodies: provinces, municipalities, individual persons: an independent judiciary and relatively entrenched written laws' (Louw, 1986: 488).

Van Wyk Louw was a devoted nationalist. He was deeply committed to an evolving interpretation of Afrikaner sacred history and to creative use of the Afrikaans language – indeed, to the survival of the Afrikaner nation. He made three important points that would be picked up by Afrikaner intellectuals and politicians committed to reinterpretation of the civil religion. First, Afrikaner survival must be earned by inhabiting a local cultural context but transmuting it to create genuinely moving insights into the human condition. Second, ethnic survival without just relations with neighbouring cultures is empty (for him this amounted to a proclamation of the necessity for separate but equal development). And third, both insight and justice are best served by open discussion guaranteed by checks and balances.

These are very general guidelines. They could be, and were, used in very different ways by Afrikaner intellectuals, politicians, and church and cultural leaders. How could one ensure both survival and justice, for instance, and what did 'justice' imply in South

Africa? What does 'cultural survival' mean? What sorts of checks and balances made the best sense in the South African context? What were the implications for others of a single 'cultural' group having captured the state?

THE 'COLOURED QUESTION'

Van Wyk Louw was one of the first Afrikaner intellectuals publically to suggest the notion of 'separate development' as a just policy to accommodate all the nations of South Africa. He had argued in 1946 that liberal demands for individual rights threatened the survival of Afrikaner ethnicity. The only alternative, he wrote, would be 'the separate development of the different groups – with as final goal something other than the current centralized Union'. The ethical impasse between ethnic and individual rights came down 'in practical terms in South Africa to a balance of forces between the numbers of the natives and the cultural, economic and military preponderance of the whites (especially Afrikaners)'. Louw concluded:

> The task of liberal thought in South Africa is to develop a policy for the future that remains true to the great European liberal principles but demands that there be no injustice in our multi-national state; perhaps indeed the construction of a form of state unknown in Europe – if it comes to that, the total transformation of the artificial South African 'Union' (Louw, 1986: 505–6).

This argument, or something very like it, was the logical and moral basis for Hendrik Verwoerd's later argument – perhaps formulated most immediately in response to Harold Macmillan's 'wind of change' speech – that South Africa must move to self-determination for its many African 'nations'. Apartheid was more than a negative system of racial separation, Verwoerd argued. It also contained the seeds of a response to 'the National Question' – ethnic 'independence' for Africans as an extension of the Afrikaner myth.[3]

There was a tension in Verwoerd's thought and practice between racism and cultural pluralism. It was directly from Dutch Reformed Church concerns for cultural and racial separation that the South African Bureau of Racial Affairs (SABRA) was formed by the Afrikaner Broederbond in the late 1940s as a counter to the liberal South African Institute of Race Relations (SAIRR). SABRA's purpose was to investigate the practical possibilities of separate development as an alternative moral ideal.

The Tomlinson Commission was a creature of SABRA's efforts to give practical implementation to separate development. As it turned out, the commission insisted that 'survival with justice' along ethnic lines was going to be a costly affair, if it could be realised at all. As minister of native affairs at the time of the release of the Tomlinson Commission's report, Verwoerd seems to have calculated that it was a price white voters would not be willing to pay – but that did not stop him adopting 'separate development' on an ideological level.

Verwoerd's mind seems to have operated on two levels – a political and pragmatic racial level and a moral and theoretical cultural level (Steyn, 2002: 123). Thus, he oversaw one of the most ambitious township construction projects for Africans in South African history while at the same time convincing himself that African urbanisation could be stopped in its tracks. Immensely intelligent, he comes across as a combination of administrative competence, theoretical rigour and moral self-righteousness based on premises that shifted, apparently seamlessly, from culture to race depending on the context. In theory, for Verwoerd, cultural assumptions were central, but in practice race trumped culture at every turn.

The tension between race and culture in separate development theory and apartheid practice is perhaps most clearly exemplified by the example of the 1960 Afrikaner squabble over coloured policy. Afrikaans-speaking and Dutch Reformed, sharing common everyday cultural practices, 'brown persons' in South Africa were culturally Afrikaner. They even shared many aspects of the Afrikaner sacred history. In the words of D.P. Botha:

> They fought alongside us, as members of the militia, as associates on the borders, as allies against Mzilikazi, as confidants at Blood River. They were fellow creators of our language and fellow educators of our children. They were our play mates in our youth and caregivers in our old age. They suffered together with us ... Their blood flowed for our communal freedom ideal. They were cut down with us ... more than two hundred by the Zulus at Bloukrans; at Hloma Amabutha the bones of thirty of them lie buried in one grave with the bones of Piet Retief and his seventy. When we needed them, they were with us, even to the death (Botha, 1960: xv).

Despite this common history, coloureds were increasingly racially alienated from their white Afrikaner culture-mates.

The Sharpeville massacre in early 1960 and the subsequent march on Parliament in Cape Town elicited great concern in Afrikaner intellectual circles. The fact that coloureds refused to participate in the unrest was noted with approval in Cape Broederbond and Sabra circles. Cape Afrikaner intellectuals embarked on a movement to grant political rights to coloureds – to have 'brown people representing brown people on Parliament' (Steyn, 2002: 143). However, at a Broederbond meeting in Cape Town in April 1960, Verwoerd was distinctly cool to the idea, arguing that there could be no turning back on the path to racial separation.

Writing in his political column, Piet Cillie, editor of *Die Burger*, nonetheless stated that it was his impression 'that the National Party was already more than half-way to supporting the principle [of coloureds in Parliament representing coloureds]. With strong leadership the Party could be completely won over' (Louw, 1965: 182–3). Phil Weber, the managing director of *Die Burger*, wrote to Verwoerd on August 26 to reassure him about the ferment of thought that was happening in the Western Cape – especially in the Broederbond. 'Here and there,' he wrote, 'there is talk of "a genuine movement in Coloured policy" and it is hoped that the country can get away from job reservation, the Immorality Act, apartheid rules in post offices, and so on.'

Verwoerd was alarmed. He had no objection, he replied to Weber, to people sharing ideas in limited circles, but he 'worried that our friends[4] will do our nation's cause harm ... by seeking broader publicity for their ideas too quickly or at the wrong time'. He added that direct representation of 'brown persons' could only cause trouble – concessions would simply lead to more demands. Weber shared Verwoerd's letter at the next Cape Town Broederbond meeting (Steyn, 2002: 145).

In October, D.P. Botha's (1960) book appeared with a Foreword by Van Wyk Louw. Louw had recently returned from the Netherlands to take the chair in Afrikaans/Dutch at the University of the Witwatersrand. He was not in the Cape Broederbond circle, but he shared their most adventurous ideas and argued them passionately in his Transvaal Broederbond circle (which included Piet Meyer). The cultural logic of separate development should not be applied to coloured people, Louw wrote:

> Brown people are our people, they belong with us ... I have a sincere desire – no, a passionate *will* – that my nation, white and brown, and the language we speak, survive in this land ... In a wider context, I am concerned about all who represent *human* values in this country. [One hears committed Afrikaner and South African nationalists spontaneously saying that] we have acted wrongly against the brown people; we have neglected, and indeed repulsed them; we must make right the wrongs that were done ... Our leaders must take care to remain *au fait* with this turn in ethnic feeling; otherwise a wretched estrangement will ensue (Botha, 1960: v–vi).

Verwoerd was livid. Racial apartheid was at stake, he said. Representation of brown people by their own in the white Parliament would ultimately lead to racial integration – indeed, to 'biological assimilation'. The racial foundations of his conception of Afrikanerdom came adamantly to the fore. 'The Government and the leaders must stand like walls of granite. The survival of a nation is at stake,' he declared with implacable insistence (Van Rooyen, 1971: 103).

Cape Afrikaner intellectuals were shocked at the flat bleakness of Verwoerd's announcement. Verwoerd nonetheless elicited unanimous support from the Cabinet, although it went against the grain of some ministers. Letters to the editor of *Die Burger* came in overwhelmingly, and often crudely, in favour of Verwoerd's appeal to racial attitudes.

Cillie was unrepentant. He warned publically against a 'heresy hunt' against Nationalists who had supported the idea of coloured inclusion (Louw, 1965: 199). Besides, he added in an editorial, Verwoerd's position was not official National Party policy. The official party line was simply that coloureds should be represented by whites in Parliament. That could be subject to change or reform in changed circumstances (Steyn, 2002: 153).

Verwoerd could not let this appeal pass. It did not help that the Cottesloe Declaration intervened at this point, insisting on theological grounds that there could be no biblical justification for apartheid (Walshe, 1983). Verwoerd mobilised the full power of Broederbond connections, in the church and in the party. All the provincial Dutch Reformed Church synods firmly rejected the Cottesloe Declaration. On 21 January 1961, the Federal Council of the National Party unanimously and flatly denied as a matter of principle that coloureds could be represented by coloureds in Parliament. However, the moral dilemma remained: since coloureds had no homeland, racial restrictions on them became blatantly repressive (Steyn, 2002: 179).

The question of the *Afrikanerskap* of 'our brown nation' became the logical and ethical Achilles heel of the entire policy of ethnic separate development. There was no way of getting around it if culture were the basis for separate political rights. Perhaps Verwoerd was correct politically in the short term, given the racial attitudes of most of the white population at the time, but he made no effort to educate his white supporters.

Meanwhile, the forced removals, the devastation of District Six, the international embarrassment of charges under the Immorality Act, and the humiliation of coloured cultural, social and political leaders continued unabated. Rights of citizenship rested firmly on racial rather than cultural foundations. Whatever moral claims might be made for separate freedoms, as long as culturally Afrikaner coloured people were excluded from Afrikanerdom, separate development with its cultural claims remained racist apartheid. Black consciousness was indeed a logical response to apartheid racial discrimination.

SOWETO 1976: A FUNDAMENTAL TURNING POINT

Verwoerd had managed to close down debate even within Afrikaner circles. Race trumped culture, and party politics overruled moral dissent in the Broederbond, the Afrikaner churches and Sabra. For a decade and a half, the Broederbond toed the party line and *oop gesprek* among Afrikaners moved out to small circles, such as that around philosophy professor, Johan Degenaar, at Stellenbosch (Moodie, 2009: 200–10).

However, the Soweto uprising in 1976, was to change all that, albeit slowly and with much infighting during the decade before 1985. Gerrit Viljoen, the rector of the Rand Afrikaans University, was chairperson of the Broederbond in 1976. A careful chronological reading of his published speeches suggests a fundamental shift took place in his thinking after July 1976 (Viljoen, 1979). The student revolt, as a sort of protest *oop gesprek*, had revealed to him the bankruptcy of Verwoerd's claim that black urbanisation would be turned around during the 1970s. Blacks were obviously in the South African cities to stay (Smit and Booysen, 1981).

In the course of a 1977 speech given on the Day of the Vow (*Geloftedag*), for instance, Viljoen (1979: 54–5) proclaimed that the actual significance of Blood River lay not in the Voortrekkers' physical survival against Zulu attack but rather in the values and culture they represented. Four sets of values were paramount, he argued: the political values of freedom for all nations; the economic values of the Protestant ethic; a fundamental (Christian-based) humanity in dealings with other nations and persons; and a rich spiritual life of cultural appreciation and open, critical conversation (*loyale verset*). Viljoen admitted this was an idealisation. Basic humanity had been transgressed, he conceded, in job reservation, the application of the Group Areas Act, migrant labour, the quality of life in black townships and the handling of political prisoners, but these issues were being raised and debated. One might well wonder what remains of Afrikaner 'Christian humanity' after this list.

In 1979, Viljoen became administrator of South West Africa and then minister of education in South Africa. He resigned as chairperson of the Broederbond and was eventually succeeded in that position by Carel Boshoff, who argued that South African whites should abandon their dependency on black labour and establish a genuinely white (if not Afrikaner) economy. (Eventually, Boshoff established the exclusively Afrikaner settlement at Orania.)

Political division among Afrikaners in the early 1980s hit the Broederbond as hard as all other Afrikaner institutions. The establishment of the Tricameral Parliament in 1982 was a turning point not only because it precipitated uprisings in the African townships, but also because the establishment of the Conservative Party under Andries Treurnicht irrevocably divided Afrikaners against themselves. Although this split has been read, quite correctly, along class lines, it also reveals the internal debate around the bankruptcy of apartheid along racial and cultural lines. An effort was made through the Tricameral Parliament to grant representation for coloureds and Indians under white control. Chris Heunis and his cohorts began to spin constitutional plans for political representation for urban Africans. Many 'petty apartheid' laws were in fact scrapped. 'Grey areas' emerged in the large cities. The National Party was feeling its way towards accepting South African social reality.

The Broederbond was equally split. Boshoff resigned as chairperson in 1983, followed by the resignation of many conservative members. Pieter de Lange, the newly elected chairperson and rector at the Rand Afrikaans University, returned the organisation to a reformist path that had been pioneered by Gerrit Viljoen. It was not until 1985 that he was able to restore a modicum of order to the organisation and to refocus its deliberations.

BROEDERBOND DEBATES

Since at least the establishment of Verwoerd's republic in 1961, the Broederbond Executive Council had appointed various committees to consider the question of the 'constitutional development of the black man' (*staatkundige ontwikkeling van die swart-man*). In earlier years, such deliberations had dealt with the separate development of black 'homelands', but under De Lange the committee changed its focus toward constitutional reform more generally. Now named the Committee for Constitutional Policy (*staatkundige aangeleenthede*), hereafter Staatkundige Committee, this task force addressed the question of constitutional change for South Africa as a whole. The debates make for fascinating reading.

In June 1986, the Staatkundige Committee circulated to all local branches a document which echoed Van Wyk Louw's famous passage about survival with justice. Entitled *Basiese Staatkundige Voorwaardes vir die Voortbestaan van die Afrikaner* (Basic Political Policy Conditions for the Survival of the Afrikaner), hereafter BSV, the document posited a contemporary version of Van Wyk Louw's argument for just survival (AB, 1986a). Continued Afrikaner domination in South Africa spelled both a political and moral 'dark night of the soul'. Moreover, policies proposed by the Conservative Party under Treurnicht represented 'bare survival ... in their desert days'.

The BSV document was the Broederbond's response to the crisis. Rights claimed by Afrikaners must apply to all other groups and individuals in South African society. No group should dominate any other. Entrenched racial or ethnic rule must be abolished. The state must rule on behalf of all its subjects, regardless of race or ethnicity, favouring none. Indeed, the document added, black participation at every level of the political process was essential for Afrikaner (and white) survival. This meant that the head of state would not necessarily be white, although the power of that office should be limited so as to avoid group domination. Thus, the document added, 'the rights and aspirations of groups must be protected and satisfied'. Eventual constitutional negotiations for a new system should include wide participation from all groups, else their exclusion doomed it to failure. The document added that group boundaries were not absolutely fixed:

> Freedom of association, including the right to associate and the right not to do so, is relevant – this includes thus also recognition of the formation of an open group. Ethnicity is important and also a reality in regard to the identification of minority

groups and communities, but it does not imply the reification [*verabsolutering*] of group rights.

Freedom of association thus also implied a right to voluntary 'open' urban neighbourhoods. While this would not necessarily threaten the survival of the Afrikaner, the document was nonetheless cautious on the matter. 'Separate neighbourhoods are currently desirable', it read, 'from an order point of view', but could not be justified as a matter of principle. The document ended on a dramatic note. 'Humanly speaking, there are no guarantees', it stated:

> We have to think in terms of likelihoods, of reasonable risks. The greatest risk we face today is to take no risks at all. Our will to survive as Afrikaners and our energy and faith is the strongest guarantee. If the Afrikaner is not able through his own creative power to bring negotiated structures into being that are strong and supple enough to accommodate the clashing forces of South African ethnic differences, then it is inevitable that structures will be forced upon him in which he will have no say. That will make self-defence impossible. It is essential that representatives of different power groups participate in the writing of a new constitution ... The acceptance of such a new system for the majority of our fellow-countrymen, and ultimately also for the majority of Afrikaners, is one of the most important conditions for our survival.

The document, which was approved in principle by 96 per cent of the 1012 branches (10 230 members) that responded to a head office survey, became official Broederbond policy (AB, 1986b). Thenceforth BSV, with all its internal contradictions, provided the principles on which the Staatkundige Committee based its intellectual and educational work.

Central contradictions in the BSV centred on how 'groups' should be defined for political purposes if 'race' were not an acceptable category. The document itself used racial categories in referring to Afrikaners as members of the white group. 'Survival' was still understood in racial rather than ethnic or cultural (historical, language, religious) terms. Racial categories were challenged in the document on at least two fronts, however. First, it noted that on grounds of culture and language, many coloured persons are ethnically Afrikaner and, second, accommodation of freedom of association and the notion of 'open' groups surely opened Pandora's box. Suppose all blacks joined together into one open group? Would that not ensure a black majority?

Many Broederbond members submitted written responses to BSV when it was first circulated in 1986 (AB, 1986b). I shall pay close attention to two of them, because contrasting them will provide useful guidelines to at least some of the debates that ensued within the Broederbond during the next three or four years.

Given the abandonment of race as a viable category, the debate turned to the question of group rights, the legal basis for defining 'groups' and, especially, the question of state power. What was really at issue was whether it was possible to retain the *volkstaat* as the culmination of the Afrikaner myth – or at least maintain some legal basis for representation of cultural groups. At what level, then, might Afrikaners retain some hold on state power?

I shall consider at some length the contradictory responses to the BSV of Piet Cillie, by now in retirement in Cape Town, and Danie Strauss, an expert on philosopher and juridical scholar Herman Dooyeweerd and professor at the University of the Orange Free State.[5] Cillie's trenchant comments (reflecting, we are told, the opinions of his Cape Town Broederbond branch) begin with a clear statement of contradictions inherent in the traditional Afrikaner points of view:

> The most basic [traditional] position is that South Africa must belong in the first place to the Afrikaners – or, with less enthusiasm, to the whites – and, if that gets seriously meddled with, everything is over for the Afrikaner nation ... Equally traditional, nevertheless, is more or less sincere lip service to the freedom ideal, in terms of which 'the Afrikaner must grant to other nations or groups in South Africa the same as they demand for themselves' ... Tension between the demands of justice and self-defence has been brought sharply into focus in our time both through the West's world-wide decolonization and the developing thought of the Afrikaner churches and intelligentsia (AB, 1986b).

The outcome of these developments, Cillie argued, is that 'realism compels Afrikaners to try the alternative path of mutual freedoms which they had been taught to reject as suicide'. His Broederbond branch, Cillie said, accepted the broad principles set forth in BSV with little enthusiasm but also with scant opposition:

> We see it as an honest attempt by the best available thinkers to shift Afrikaner institutions from a largely out-of-date policy perspective to an order of freedom, equality and brotherhood and to see whether we can manage it without driving our civilization, including the Afrikaner nation, into the ground. We know that we must try because we have no other choice.

Cillie thus affirmed a version of nationalism in which state and nation are irrevocably intertwined. Hence the reluctance with which Afrikaners of his generation confronted 'power-sharing'. In this regard, Cillie and his colleagues agreed with Treurnicht and the Conservative Party (and with P.W. Botha, for that matter). Power-sharing (*magsverdeling*) between 'nations' in the central state was the core issue. The question was whether Afrikaners as a 'nation' could survive if they did not dominate the central state.

For Danie Strauss this should not have been a problem. While he also agreed in general with the principles of the BSV, he started at a different place: with the conservative reformist politics of Abraham Kuyper[6] as further specified by Herman Dooyeweerd. His cardinal point was that the state as such must be conceptually and practically separated from various spheres of corporate social life (*lewensverbindnesse*) such as cultural communities, families, schools, churches and universities. Afrikaners, for Strauss, ought not to need to control the state in order to survive as a cultural community.

Failure to make a clear distinction between the state (as a set of freedoms[7] and obligations that define citizenship and maintain order) and other social formations (*lewenskringe*) such as cultural communities, churches, educational institutions and welfare organisations, was the primary cause for 'the crisis in which the Afrikaner nation' now found themselves, said Strauss. Afrikaners, Strauss argued, had cherished false expectations (*foutiewe verwagtinge*) of political order in South Africa:

> Before and after 1948, among many Afrikaners, the conviction took hold that Afrikaners owned the state. Membership in the nation [*volkgenootskap*] was the most central bond [*verbintenis*] in human life, so that all other social forms including the state, were embedded in the soil of the Afrikaner nation ... The elaboration of this ethnic ideological line [*volksideologieselyn*] has resulted in our not learning correctly to distinguish between state and nation [*volk*] on the one hand and government and political party on the other (AB, 1986b).

Although he cited various characteristics to describe the uniqueness of a nation – a common history, geographical location, language and/or religion – Strauss insisted that 'the only uniquely differentiating characteristic of ethnicity (*volkwees*) is given in the typical cultural style of a specific nation. While formation of this cultural style 'takes place in inescapable conjunction with other social forms ... the nation must not be lifted up as the fundamental basis of our entire life ... No person's life is inexhaustibly contained within the nation to which he belongs' (AB, 1986b). He or she was necessarily at the same time at least a citizen of a state, a member of a church community, a friend in a circle of friends and part of a family.

Moreover, although it does have a solidarity unity, a nation (as a cultural entity) possesses no permanent structure of authority. The state, however, does have authority in addition to its unity and thus is an obligatory association (*verband*) – as opposed to communities, even if they are real and historically constituted. Thus, in Strauss' terms it is not difficult to conceive of various nations as communities with a particular cultural style, living within the bounds of the authority of a single state. 'The core problem for the future of South African politics', Strauss insisted, 'is how the constitutional interests [*regsbelange*] of, among others, ethnic groups can be meaningfully held together in one public order' (AB, 1986b).

The major differences between Cillie and Strauss were significant and continued to haunt debate in the Staatkundige Committee throughout its life. For Cillie, freedom was both cultural and political, achieved with the establishment of the republic in 1961. Having lived through the long Afrikaner cultural struggle for freedom, he was only too aware of the importance of political power for cultural survival, and was willing to abdicate it only reluctantly – although he was also troubled by the racial exclusions built into the system. Strauss had a very different political philosophy, and domination of the state was irrelevant (if not morally problematic) for the survival of cultural community – as long as the state followed through on its obligation to protect and guarantee communal life. After that, communities (whether cultural, religious, familial or other associational entities) needed to take responsibility for their own flourishing – sovereign in their own spheres.

Although I perhaps state the alternatives too starkly here, in the end it was Strauss's general position that won out in the constitutional negotiations of the early 1990s.[8] Contemporary South Africa is a constitutional state (*regsstaat*) with entrenched protections for individual rights; group rights are a matter for freely associating individuals. The Afrikaner nation–state of Piet Cillie now lies in shreds. The future of Afrikaner ethnic identity remains uncertain, but it cannot now be rescued by political power.

BROEDERBOND PRAXIS

Judging from copies of minutes scattered through the boxes dealing with *staatkundige aangeleenthede* in the Broederbond archives, the five years after the circulation of the BSV document were a period of intense intellectual debate among members of the committee. They produced multiple documents on constitutional policy to be sent to the Executive Council for approval and then circulated to the branches. Not only was the committee struggling to come up with intellectual solutions for constitutional problems, it was also distributing such debates within the organisation so as to educate Broederbond members about difficult political policy issues facing Afrikaners. 'Political literacy' became the watchword. Branches were kept very busy debating the merits of policy drafts about various constitutional models, which deliberately posed questions rather than providing set answers. Ordinary Broederbond members I have met have told me that this was an enormously stimulating process for them. It was also, of course, conscientising them in preparation for constitutional change. 'Friends in responsible positions' – that is, Broederbonders in government positions – were also contacted and drawn into the debate.

VALUES AND NORMS

For this chapter, it is not possible to summarise the many *studiestukke* (position papers) sent out by the Staatkundige Committee over the course of the 'political literacy' programme. It is, however, worth considering a controversy within Broederbond ruling circles occasioned by a paper (*Waardes en Norme van die Afrikanerstaatkunde* – Values and Norms of Afrikaner Constitutional Policy) commissioned as a *studiestuk* from Francois Venter, a constitutional law professor at Potchefstroom University. I do so because revisions of the paper represented what I am calling the Cillie/Strauss divide within the committee, and because Venter was an influential member of Roelf Meyer's team that negotiated the final constitutional settlement. Meyer told me personally that it was a position paper from Venter (along the lines of the original draft of *Waardes en Norme*) that turned the negotiations around at their most difficult point right after the Boipatong killings.[9]

Venter (AB,1992b) argued that the state should be representative of all its citizens (the inhabitants of the country), and that its government should exercise specific functions on behalf of citizens according to the law. The state should not enforce either racial or ethnic divisions. In this regard, he was fully with Danie Strauss in the Dooyeweerd camp. Among whites at the time, of course, there was no ethnic legal bond. Race was the means by which whites were constitutionally classified. Venter argued that Afrikaners should drop claims to racial identity and return to their ethnic base. Insisting on any form of group rights as constitutional means, he said, would not only feed political suspicions but also raise thorny questions of how to legally define groups. Venter affirmed individual rights as juridical guarantees of justice for individuals against the state as well as means for the prevention of group domination, whether racial or ethnic.

He thus suggested four foundational principles for constitutional policy. First, the state consists of all its citizens and must be ruled in the communal interest of all. Second, the cultural interests of voluntary groups should receive state protection, and individuals have the right to expect that their cultural interests (including religion, language and education) will be respected as long as the rights of other persons in the community as a whole are maintained. Third, the state should undertake in a reasonable and impartial way to enable all individuals to develop their talents, to protect their personal interests and to satisfy their rightful human needs. Fourth, actions in conflict with the above principles by the government or any government representative, or any other person or group of persons should be illegal. Venter clearly accepted Danie Strauss's critique of the Afrikaner *volkstaat* idea.

The first draft of his essay came under stiff attack from Judge Willem Booysen,[10] essentially on grounds similar to those of Piet Cillie in his reaction to the BSV document – the right of nations (*volke*) to self-determination (AB, 1992a). Power is not only exercised by the state, Boshoff said, but also by the nation as an aspect of the state. For him, self-determination through control of the state was manifestly the destiny of a genuine nation. At least at lower levels of the state (such as municipalities), he sought some form of group representation. Booysen thus insisted on a fifth foundational principle, namely that 'the greatest possible measure of self-determination be given to nations or groups that struggle for it through the devolution of power to regional and municipal governments or administrations' (AB, 1992a).

The Staatkundige Committee assigned Booysen and Andreas van Wyk to work with Venter on revising his document. The final version was much toned down, although it was still quite controversial (AB, 1992b). Venter had originally written, 'Group rights is a concept that has no clear meaning'. That sentence disappeared and a firm sentence, 'that group rights must also have ... protection' emerged. Finally, and most tellingly, a fifth foundational principle added Booysen's language about ethnic self-determination.

Judge Booysen had got his way, over-riding Venter's careful distinction between the state and 'the cultural interests of voluntary groups'. Booysen was trying to push the Broederbond back into the nationalism of a *volkstaat*, at least on local levels. Venter was obliged to abandon, at least in this *studiestuk*, the full development of his *regsstaat* ideas which then eventually re-emerged in his position paper for the constitutional negotiations.

CONCLUSION

Does the current South African constitutional state meet Van Wyk Louw's requirements for Afrikaner ethnic survival? Is there still a 'National Question' for Afrikaners? Solidarity and Afriforum, firmly in the Danie Strauss tradition, certainly think so.

Or is current widespread Afrikaner prosperity simply 'bare survival' in Louw's terms? Dirkie Smit, a theologian at Stellenbosch University, writes in scathing terms of contemporary Afrikaners:

> We are facing a brave new world, on our own, colour blind, free at last, walking tall, *boetmanne* without many *boete,* in short, as self-sufficient individuals, sometimes with families, a few friends, and perhaps a few fellow *taalstryders*, at the most (Weisse and Anthonissen, 2004: 139–41).[11]

What then of the ANC's own 'national' policy? Are we still haunted by racial conceptions of the nation: definitions inherited from colonialism and apartheid? Van Zyl Slabbert

(2011: 55–6) thought so, arguing that 'if you hold yourself hostage to a racist past, you can budget generously for a racist future'. And what of class, which I chose not to address in this paper? Dan O'Meara (1983) argued that Afrikaner nationalism was petty bourgeois at base. Could one not say the same for black 'national' advancement? Affirmative action is clearly essential, but in its South African form is it much more than a petty bourgeois class revolution, making use of racial categories abandoned by Afrikaner intellectuals only very late in the game?

NOTES

1 Much of my discussion of Louw's work is drawn from an earlier article (Moodie, 2009).

2 All translations from Afrikaans throughout this chapter are my own.

3 For a useful account of the political history of Verwoerd's conception of separate development, see Hermann Giliomee (2012:76–88).

4 Members of the Broederbond always refer to each other as 'friends' in their correspondence.

5 By no means do I seek to elevate Danie Strauss' political influence. He is well known in a small international circle of 'reformed' thinkers because of his expert knowledge of Dooyeweerd. His response to the BSV, however, is hidden deep in the Broederbond archives. None of his Broederbond colleagues, to the best of my knowledge, responded directly to his tightly argued paper. It is on his intellectual stance (*die wysbegeerte van die regs-idee*), not his political influence, that I draw here.

6 For the influence of Kuyper's ideas in South Africa, see Moodie (1975:52–72). I realise that I am sneaking into the argument here a set of assumptions, especially regarding Dooyeweerd's development of Kuyper, that should be more developed. There is simply not space to do so, although Strauss' formulation is remarkably clear. In classical Kuyperian argument the state was not a creation sphere (*verbindnes*). It was an institution (*verband*) established by God to oversee relationships between spheres because of human sinfulness.

7 Strauss includes such freedoms as freedom of assembly, freedom of speech, freedom of voluntary association, freedom to criticise and protest, and some form of universal franchise.

8 While Strauss represented a minority position, one ought not to forget that Tjaart van der Walt, Francois Venter, Chris Maritz and Johan Kruger – all major players at the end – had also been trained in the Kuyper/Dooyeweerd Gereformeerde (Dopper) tradition of clear, logical thinking and of *sowereiniteit in eie kring* (independence of each social circle) – as, for that matter, had Stoffel van der Merwe, F.W. de Klerk and his brother, Wimpie. All were essential players in the South African constitutional settlement.

9 The Boipatong massacre occurred in the middle of 1992, during a deadlock in the negotiations. Zulu-speaking hostel dwellers attacked and killed forty-five ANC supporters in a township south of Johannesburg.

10 One should perhaps note that Booysen, a Natal judge who was eventually obliged to resign from the Broederbond because his membership was perceived to create a conflict of interest, had been quite closely associated with the Natal Indaba which had dealt with the most ethnicised of the African groups in South Africa. Deals struck with Chief Buthelezi could certainly not be struck even with other African rural 'tribal' groups – let alone urban Africans.

11 The Afrikaans in this passage is almost untranslatable. It is also wry and very clever. *Boetmanne*, 'pals' or 'chums' (this is a reference to a cross-generational dispute between Chris

Louw and Wimpie de Klerk); and *boete*, 'penance' or 'penalty'. *Taalstryders* refers to those who continue to struggle for Afrikaans language instruction in schools and universities.

REFERENCES

Afrikaner Broederbond (AB) (1986a) *Basiese Staatkundige Voorwaardes vir die Voortbestaan van die Afrikaner* [Basic Political Policy Conditions for the Survival of the Afrikaner]. AB 10/32/2 (1). Afrikaner Broederbond archives, housed in the Erfenisstigtung at the Voortrekker Monument in Pretoria.

Afrikaner Broederbond (AB) (1986b) Responses to BSV document. AB 10/32/4. Afrikaner Broederbond archives, housed in the Erfenisstigtung at the Voortrekker Monument in Pretoria.

Afrikaner Broederbond (AB) (1992a) Willem Booysen's response to Francois Venter's *Waardes en Norme van die Afrikanerstaatkunde* document. AB 1/32/2 (3). Afrikaner Broederbond archives, housed in the Erfenisstigtung at the Voortrekker Monument in Pretoria.

Afrikaner Broederbond (AB) (1992b) *Waardes en Norme van die Afrikanerstaatkunde* (Values and Norms of Afrikaner Constitutional Policy – Various Versions.) AB 10/32/4. Afrikaner Broederbond archives, housed in the Erfenisstigtung at the Voortrekker Monument in Pretoria.

Alexander, Neville (writing as No Sizwe) (1979) *One Azania, One Nation: The National Question in South Africa.* London: Zed.

Botha, D.P. (1960) *Die Opkoms van ons Derde Stand.* Cape Town: Human & Rousseau.

Giliomee, Hermann (2012) *The Last Afrikaner Leaders.* Cape Town: Tafelberg.

Louw, L. (ed.) (1965) *Dawie 1946–1964.* Cape Town: Tafelberg.

Louw, N.P. Van Wyk (1986) *Versamelde Prosa I.* Cape Town: Tafelberg.

Moodie, T. Dunbar (1975) *The Rise of Afrikanerdom: Power, Apartheid and the Afrikaner Civil Religion.* Berkeley, CA: University of California Press.

Moodie, T. Dunbar (2009) N.P. Van Wyk Louw and the Moral Predicament of Afrikaner Nationalism: Preparing the Ground for 'Verligte' Reform. *Historia,* 54(1):180–210.

Norval, Aletta (1996) *Deconstructing Apartheid Discourse.* London and New York: Verso.

O'Meara, Dan (1983) *Volkskapitalisme.* Cambridge: Cambridge University Press.

Slabbert, Frederick Van Zyl (2011) Some do Contest the Assertion that I am an African. In *Becoming Worthy Ancestors,* edited by Xolela Mangcu. Johannesburg: Wits University Press.

Smit, P. and J.J. Booysen (1981) *Swart Verstedeliking: Proses, Patroon en Strategie.* Cape Town: Tafelberg.

Steyn, J.C. (2002) *Penvegter: Piet Cillie van die Burger.* Cape Town: Tafelberg.

Van Rooyen, J.J. (1971) *Ons Politiek van Naby.* Cape Town: Tafelberg.

Viljoen, Gerrit (1979) *Ideaal en Werklikheid: Rekenskap deur 'n Afrikaner.* Cape Town: Tafelberg.

Walshe. P. (1983) *Church versus State in South Africa.* Maryknoll: Orbis.

Weisse, W. and Carel Anthonissen (eds) (2004) *Maintaining Apartheid or Promoting Change?* New York: Waxman Munster.

7

NEVILLE ALEXANDER AND THE NATIONAL QUESTION

Enver Motala and Salim Vally

INTRODUCTION

Among the scholars, academics, political analysts and activists – even those not favourably disposed to Neville Alexander's political convictions and practices – there can be little dispute about his immense contribution to the discussions about the National Question in South Africa over the last several decades. He has played a critical role in the debates following the publication of his *One Azania, One Nation: The National Question in South Africa* under the nom de plume, No Sizwe (Alexander, 1979).[1]

In this chapter we will pay particular attention to this writing because it provided the most comprehensive statement of Alexander's views on the subject. In it he first set out the basis for a historical examination of the National Question, pointing to the wide range of perspectives from political analysts, academics and scholars and, most importantly, the ideas of the ideologues of liberalism and apartheid, and the views held by the organisations of the oppressed. In this work and in his subsequent writings Alexander explored the multiplicity of concepts relevant to the National Question such as race, nation, national group, ethnicity, separatism and the like. His coruscating critique subjected many of the prevailing conceptions on this issue to a thoroughgoing scrutiny that was important not only for proper theorisation in its own right but also for its construction of the strategic practices necessary for confronting exploitative and oppressive relations in South Africa.

We believe that his writings continue to inspire strong debate on the difficult questions of social change, and that they inform how we understand the nature of the contemporary conversations and policy pronouncements about South Africa's transformation, its development agenda, and indeed its revolution. In this contribution we set out to discuss Neville Alexander's work using the conceptual lens that he brought to the National Question. Such an examination will, in our view, be just as useful for what an examination of the National Question implies for the present – both theoretically and in practice.

Subsequent to the completion of his seminal work on the National Question, Alexander wrote several pieces which elaborated and clarified his views on this issue. We hope to provide a fairly coherent presentation of his ideas, given the space limitations of this chapter. We first set out a clear exposition of Alexander's views on the National Question, and then move on to deal with some criticisms of his ideas.

WHY DID ALEXANDER SET OUT TO ADDRESS THE NATIONAL QUESTION?

In a useful introduction, Alexander explains his purpose in writing the book on the National Question following his imprisonment on Robben Island, during which time he had occasion to engage with some of the strongest leaders of the liberation movement from across the range of political organisations.

> It should be stressed that my approach has been motivated throughout by the desire to facilitate the unification of the national liberation movement by fomenting a discussion on the *basis* of national unity and on the political-strategic implications of ideas about who constitutes the South African nation (Alexander, 1979: viii).

Key to understanding his approach was his intention to deal with the pervasive 'reactionary nationalisms' dominant both in the ideas of the apartheid regime and in much of the liberation movement itself, the need to refute the 'propagation of bogus nationalisms, the main purpose of which is to dissipate the force of the class struggle by deflecting it into channels that will nurture the dominant classes' (Alexander 1979: 4). For him these reactionary nationalisms conflicted with the interests of the working class, making it necessary to counteract the 'nefarious strategies' associated with them. Furthermore, because social relations were mystified as 'race relations', there was a need to 'illuminate the character of the *real* (socio-economic) basis of inequality and the *real* (ideological) forms in which it is expressed' (Alexander, 1979: 51). For him, 'bourgeois sociology', with its debilitating definitions, required a clarification of misused concepts such as race, nation, nationalism, ethnic group, colour caste and class.

AFRIKANER AND LIBERAL THEORIES OF THE NATION

Alexander begins his analysis of the National Question historically, with a careful examination of the orientations of both the National Party (NP) rulers and the various organisations of the oppressed. The National Party's theory of nationality arose from its struggle for hegemony against the background of the post-war development of capitalism in South Africa. It was based on the idea that 'whites, because of their "superior civilization" and their European heritage, were entitled to rule' (Alexander 1979: 11). Its Afrikaner sectionalism arose historically from the conflict between Dutch settlers and the British administration in the Cape Colony around 1834 to 1840. The Boer Republics they formed to the north of the Cape Colony continued in 'quasi-feudal anarchy' until the mineral discoveries of the latter half of the nineteenth century. The developing economic interests among the Afrikaans-speaking (white) population gave rise to a sense of nationality among them based predominantly on their common language. Several developments – including the conflicts over diamond fields, the emergence of an Afrikaans language movement in what is now the Western Cape and the organised response of emerging Afrikaner agrarian capital – gave impetus to Afrikaner nationalism. This was fostered by the formation of the Afrikaner Bond which was 'an association of bourgeois and petty-bourgeois white (predominantly Afrikaans speaking) farmers' (Alexander, 1979: 15). This 'class vanguard of Afrikaner nationalism' led the fight against British imperial interests in the Anglo Boer War. After the war a significant part of the old Afrikaner agrarian class had been dispossessed. This helped to force them into proletarian lives, competing for jobs with Africans. Both their 'class-based' antipathy to British imperialism and the 'caste-based' antipathy to black workers laid the basis for a 'sectionalist mass movement' exploited by the petty bourgeois leadership of what came to be known as the Afrikaner Broederbond (AB) (Alexander, 1979: 20). The resultant Afrikaner nationalism combined 'liberal' and 'neo-Fichtean' nationalisms, and enunciated a theory of nationality which Alexander summarises as follows:

> (1) Nations are divinely ordained, pre-destined categories, ideal forms, the historical context of which is determined in concrete struggles of congeries of peoples; (2) nations are communities of culture, defined by a set of values acquired and maintained in historic struggles; (3) this culture finds its main deposit in specific languages…. the 'badge of nationality'; (4) community of 'race' is an inherent attribute of a nation so that people of divergent 'race' cannot belong to the same nation (Alexander, 1979: 25).

Alexander deals with 'liberal' theories of the nation by examining the various perspectives of Jan Smuts, General Hertzog, 'the younger Hofmeyr', Margaret Ballinger and others – largely representatives of mining capital and urban English speakers. Their pluralist approaches to the idea of nation and the 'gradualist solutions' espoused by them hoped to steer the country to the idea of a 'confederation of racial groups' which existed under the domination of the 'white nation',[2] and simultaneously gave expression to the 'central question' of the supply of 'cheap black labour' (Alexander, 1979: 29). These approaches failed to transcend the limitations of their 'race-based' theorisations of the nation.

Alexander deals with the genesis of the reserve strategy following the growth of capitalism in South Africa, and especially the strategy of 'emancipating indigenous capital' from the metropolis so that the returns on capital investment supported the development of state-owned enterprises, import substitution policies and the growth of local production. Most critically, this had to be done in the context of maintaining a regular and controlled supply of cheap black labour. Cheap labour was a 'crucial component of the capitalist system' as it developed in South Africa. The reserves and later the bantustans were pivotal to the process of coercing labour into the emerging industrial, agricultural and commercial economy (Legassick, 1974a, b; Wolpe, 1972, 1988). They formed the objective basis for the passing of the various Land Acts, limiting access to land for the majority of the population, and the laws controlling the movement and supply of black labour, and restraining its resistance to exploitative and oppressive conditions. These policies attempted to reconcile the interests of the various sectors of the emerging capitalist economy and extended the policy of segregation, relying on the support of the Afrikaner 'nation'. However, they inevitably gave rise to the resistance against the migrant labour system that characterised South African capitalism from its inception.

THE BANTUSTAN STRATEGY

According to Alexander, the National Party's bantustan strategy speaks to its prescience in limiting the potential of an organised proletariat to lead the national liberation struggle. This represented a shift in strategy from a tribe-based conception of nation to a pretence that it was about the 'right of self-determination' of nations. The bantustan theory of nationality attempted to extend the idea of nation enunciated by the Broederbond 'to the different language groups and colour-castes amongst the oppressed' and, as Verwoerd said in 1958, 'giving the Bantu as our wards every opportunity in their areas to move along a path of development by which they can progress in accordance with their ability' (Alexander, 1979: 81). Quoting extensively from contemporary statements by representatives of the ruling class about this issue, Alexander shows that the evolution of the bantustan strategy is 'riddled with inconsistencies' (Alexander, 1979: 83).

Alexander deals similarly with the contradiction to be found in the 'liberal plural-ist' approach to the National Question, despite its terminological changes over time. Its underlying concerns were about the avoidance of 'violent conflict' and the retention of a framework of capitalist relations. Supporters of African nationalism among the pro-ponents of this approach had adopted a position of non-racialism and had been sym-pathetic to calls for one man one vote. This was the position of the former Liberal Party which pronounced its intention to use democratic and constitutional means in the pur-suance of its objectives – opposing totalitarian approaches such as communism and fas-cism (Alexander, 1979: 87). Other liberal approaches – such as that of the Progressive Federal Party (PFP), the progenitor of the present-day Democratic Alliance (DA) in many respects – adopted an orientation based on the idea that South Africa was com-posed of a plurality of groups, and were critical of the bantustan strategy because it rep-resented a 'Trojan Horse' danger to the growth of capitalism. Variants of these 'liberal' approaches made the case for a federation based on 'ethnic' groups in an attempt to stave off the attenuation of capitalist property relations. Alexander (1979: 90) asserts that the logic of these approaches shows how much a 'theory of nation' is in fact about 'the class struggle for national liberation'. The obvious political and economic imperative for the elaboration of the earlier separatist ideas was an awareness that the struggle against white rule could grow into a challenge to the capitalist system itself because, in the absence of a viable and prestigious black bourgeoisie, the liberation struggle could well be led by a radical proletarian leadership. For the National Party the only alternative was to wrest this leadership from its proletarian roots, to decapitate it and redirect it into sectionalist channels. The force of African nationalism as represented by the bantustan leaders would thus be harnessed in such a way that it dissipated an *inclusive* African nationalism.

In the final analysis, therefore, the only difference between the National Party and the liberals was in their assessment of the nature and potential of the African nationalist movement. Though they expressed the interests of different fractions of the capitalist class, their strategic goal remained the same – how to secure the free enterprise system and how best to disorganise the proletariat (Alexander, 1979: 91).

RESPONSES OF THE OPPRESSED BEFORE 1948

Alexander explains that three alternatives responses to conquest and dispossession might have been pursued by the oppressed: attempts to re-conquer the land; the religious option based on the Ethiopian movement; and the response of the emerging black educated petty bourgeoisie which sought a 'betterment of their own particular group'. This lat-ter response was represented, inter alia, by the South African Native National Congress (later the African National Congress), the African People's Organisation (APO), and the

Natal Indian Congress (NIC). These organisations, stated Alexander (1979: 48), reflected a 'craven subservience to Anglo Saxon culture'.

Organisations whose membership and orientation reflected the demands of the working class also emerged in the early twentieth century. Trade unions such as the Industrial and Commercial Workers' Union (ICU) grew from the process of proletarian development at this time. In 1921 the Communist Party of South Africa (CPSA) was formed, largely as a breakaway from the International Socialist League, itself a splinter group of the pro-war, whites-only South African Labour Party. While the CPSA was prepared at first to work with the 'petty bourgeois Afrikaner National Party' because of its anti-imperialist position, this position was abandoned in favour of a strategy of alignment with the 'liberal bourgeoisie' based, in theory and practice, on the 'conception of a two-stage revolution: first for bourgeois democratic rights and later for socialism' (Alexander, 1979: 50).

In the Communist Party, the debate on the National Question began in 1928. It took the form of a discussion about an independent native republic which arose largely from the need to reconcile the position of the CPSA with that of the Comintern and especially Stalin's formulation of the idea of a nation as a 'historically evolved stable community of language, territory, economic life, and psychological makeup manifested in a community of culture' (Alexander, 1979: 51). At the time, the slogan of an Independent Native Republic was meant 'either as a separate black state' within South Africa 'or one in which (black) Africans were to be regarded as a majority "nation" (or group of "nations") as against white, coloured and Indian "national Minorities"' (Alexander, 1979: 51).

This formulation was not without opposition since, as Moses Kotane was to argue, the language question itself posed some difficulties for the wholesale adoption of Stalin's formulation because it gave rise to questions about whether there was indeed one African nation or many distinct nations (Alexander, 1979: 51). Even those tendencies which were opposed to the CPSA, such as the Troskyists, viewed language groups as national groups and 'colour-castes' for practical purposes, suggesting to Alexander that there was a similar 'pitiable confusion' in their ranks.

Following the quest for 'non-European unity' at the time were two other organisations. These were the National Liberation League and the Non-European United Front of 1938, signalling a progressive shift from the caste-based orientations of previous organisations and seeking a united approach on behalf of all the oppressed. Later, other organisations following this trend were formed, including the Anti-Coloured Affairs Department (Anti-CAD) movement, the All-African Convention and, in 1943, the Non-European Unity Movement (NEUM).[3] The NEUM's approach to the idea of nation called into question the 'caste-based' approaches preceding it, and did not hesitate to declare its allegiance to the idea of a single nation based on a rejection of Stalin's definition of the nation, arguing that 'the ideological lag ... had to be bridged by means of a genuine national unity movement' (Alexander, 1979: 57). But Alexander (1979: 56) also criticised the NEUM, arguing that it continued to be confused about the concepts of nation and state. Furthermore, although ideas of separatism were anathema to the NEUM, questions about class leadership were not posed or resolved.

Yet the NEUM's approach had a significant impact on the subsequent approach of the Congress Alliance. Especially in the context of post-war developments, a younger group of ANC members sought a radical break with the bargaining and concession-seeking approach of its past leadership. Its explicitly Africanist Youth League saw no place for whites in the liberation struggle and insisted that Africans were responsible for their own destiny while being prepared to form periodic alliances for expedient purposes with caste-based organisations. Alexander characterises this as the view of the African petty bourgeoisie 'which wanted to use black chauvinism in a manner similar' to the Broederbond usage of Afrikaner nationalism – and which similarly failed to include all South Africans in its concept of nation (Alexander, 1979: 59).

PLURALIST APPROACHES AFTER 1948

The rise of Afrikaner nationalist power in 1948 and the torrent of legislation that came with it gave rise to a similar upsurge in the responses of the oppressed. It was marred, however, by the 'caste-bound' prejudices of these responses which prevented the development of a unified national liberation movement. The Freedom Charter itself was framed on the basis of four national groups and provided guarantees for each group's language, culture and customs. Soviet approaches to nationality continued to influence the Communist Party of South Africa. Ivan Potekhin, later director of the Moscow Africa Institute, argued that 'there are no grounds for assuming that one nation can be formed which would embrace the Bantu, the Coloureds and the Anglo-Afrikaners ... The Indians are a completely separate group' (quoted in Alexander, 1979: 98).

This approach, influential in the CPSA, was consistent with the view espoused by the Africanist leadership of the ANC (Alexander, 1979: 98).[4] It was responsible for what Ben Turok, a key member of the Congress Movement, recognised as the danger of talking about large national minorities in the absence of any clear formulation of the National Question (Alexander, 1979: 100).

According to Alexander, the Congress Movement and the CPSA were not unaware of the criticisms against their avowed position, and devoted an entire issue of the *African Communist* in 1976–1977 to the National Question. This was partly in recognition of the power and sway of the emerging Black Consciousness Movement (BCM), which rejected the pluralist approaches of the Congress Movement. Alexander points to the journal's references to the nation and to national groups, seemingly unaware of the contradictory

notions implied in these ideas. He criticises its historical falsifications about the indigenous owners of the land and uncritical references to the racial origin of various communities as well as references to the grievances of the 'other national groups'. And he points
to the considerable confusion about the question of class leadership in the struggle for
national liberation (Alexander, 1979: 103). For him such pluralist conceptions which echoed the views espoused by liberalism, and the inability to emphasise working-class leadership, left the Congress Movement vulnerable to the politics of the liberal bourgeoisie.

Alexander's own conception of the role of the black working class is best encapsulated
in his *Sow the Wind* speeches:

> The black working class has to act as a magnet that draws all the other oppressed
> layers of our society, organizes them for the liberation struggle and imbues them
> with the consistent democratic socialist ideas which alone spell death to the sys-
> tem of racial capitalism as we know it today. In this struggle the idea of a single
> nation is vital... 'Ethnic', national group or racial group ideas of nationhood on
> the final analysis strengthen the position of the middle-class or even the capitalist
> oppressors themselves (Alexander, 1985: 55–6).

Developing his arguments further Alexander (1986) deals with the 'four basic views'
about the nation in South Africa by both ruling-class political parties and oppositional
liberation organisations. Afrikaner nationalists regarded South Africa as a multinational
state composed of several nations, each entitled to seek their 'self-determination' and
even their independence. It is an approach reliant on the idea of ethnicity. Alexander
makes the point that the ideological power of such ethnic concepts of the nation need to
be recognised because of their influence on urban working-class and middle-class communities who were not averse to assuming such ethnic identities despite their acceptance
of being South African at the same time. The dominant position, however, remained the
idea of a four-nation thesis. In Alexander's view, this position was essentially about the
co-option of parts of the middle class and even of moderate elements in the liberation
movement. In the liberation movement itself, this thesis was given its fullest expression
in the writings of Anton Lambede and the ANC Youth League in the 1940s. As the Youth
League's manifesto declared in 1948:

> South Africa is a country of four chief nationalities, three of which (the European,
> Indians and Coloureds) are minorities, and three of which (the Africans, Coloureds
> and Indians) suffer national oppression (quoted in Alexander, 1986: 77).

Later the idea of four races is overtaken by more contemporary conceptions of non-
racialism, but how this notion was understood remained problematic (Alexander, 1985).

If it implied the rejection of the concept of race itself, denying the existence of races, the implication would be to reject those actions and practices which are reliant on such definitions.[5] In effect unless the use of 'non-racial' is attached to the struggle against all forms of racism, all talk of non-racialism would remain vacuous. Making the distinction between non-racialists who are in reality no more than multi-racialists and those who are steadfastly 'anti-racists, remains the critical defining factor' (Swartz, 2010).

INTERNAL COLONIALISM THESIS

For the CPSA and the ANC, the idea of the 'internal colonialism thesis' was critically defining. It was based on the 1962 programme of the SACP and argued, in essence, that 'non-White South Africa is the colony of White South Africa'. This notion was based on the differing access of whites and blacks to the productive assets (land and capital) of the country. Alexander (1979: 106) refers approvingly to Wolpe's criticism of the internal colonialism thesis – that the concept of internal colonialism failed 'to clarify the nature of the imperialist relationship between the two South Africas'. For Alexander the Party's neo-pluralist position in effect sanctioned the leadership of the liberal bourgeois. However, Alexander is critical of Wolpe's attempt to salvage the Communist Party's position through his elaboration of the relationship between the capitalist and non-capitalist modes of production as constituted in the urban and bantustan parts of South Africa (Alexander, 1979: 107). He suggests that the characterisation of South Africa as a colonialism of a special type is imprisoned within a pluralist approach which depends on a 'mystified' conception of race, leaving it open to 'the winds of sectionalist opportunism' (Alexander, 1979: 110).

Alexander turns his attention to the NEUM (after 1964, the Unity Movement of South Africa), believing that its approach was a considerable advance on that of the Congress Movement. But even in the NEUM's case there were occasional slippages referring to nationalities – and despite its claim to seek the unity of the oppressed, it was inherently unable to overcome its avowed aim to 'discard the divisions and prejudices and illusions which have been created and fostered by their rulers' (Alexander, 1979: 111). As a consequence, it was unable to bring together organisations across the racial divide and 'foundered on the rocks of petty-bourgeois opportunism', leading to a rupture in its ranks in 1959 'largely along lines of colour'. The Pan Africanist Congress (PAC), despite its rejection of the idea of multiracialism and the bantustan scheme, did not abandon its Africanist position. It aimed at 'government of the Africans by the Africans', a position Alexander characterises as the 'perfect instrument of the liberal bourgeois' opposed to Afrikaner sectionalism. He remained unconvinced about the PAC's subsequent shifts allowing coloureds and people of Indian origin to become members, referring to its ideological somersaults in exile which he regarded as no more than opportunistic. Alexander (1979) is critical of the BCM's position, too, despite its mutations over time, arguing that it had failed 'to understand clearly the relationship between colour-caste and class' because of its preoccupation with racial prejudice (see also Alexander, 2001). He concedes that the South African Students Organisation (SASO) presidential address of 1976 recognised class interests, rejected capitalism and adopted an anti-imperialist stance, and that the idea that the struggle for national liberation had to be understood beyond the idea of colour and 'in terms of class interests; skin colour has in fact become a class criterion in South Africa' (Alexander, 1979: 125).

CLARIFYING CRITICAL CONCEPTS

Alexander devotes an entire chapter in his book to clarifying some of the critical concepts used in the discussion of the National Question. The use of race as a concept is unavoidably associated with social hierarchy, prejudice, discriminatory practice and stereotypical depictions of members of society. He rejects the concept of race not only because of its reliance on phenotypical attributes, but because of the dangers inherent in racial (and racist) descriptions, and because the concept is so 'pregnant with confusion' and so given to opportunist usages in the political, economic and ideological domains. He seeks a new vocabulary about the usage of race, arguing especially that there is no logical reason 'for inferring the reality of "race" from the fact of racial prejudice'.

He refers similarly to the use of 'ethnic' as a 'humpty-dumpty' term because of the confusion it engenders by its nebulousness and the inability to explain the basis of the ostensible solidarities which are implied in it. The concept of ethnic groups and ethnicity, which have come to supersede race theory, is dealt with more fully in his collection titled *Sow the Wind* (Alexander, 1985). For him, confusions abound about the meaning and usage of the concept in the 'different tendencies in the liberation movement today'. Alexander (1985: 47) shows how an approach based on ethnicity reinforces separatism and how in fact its adherents played into the hands of organisations like Inkatha and the PFP in their advocacy of a federal constitution for the country. Alexander (1986: 50) did not, however, adopt a class reductionist approach to the National Question. For him, 'To deny the reality of prejudice and perceived differences, whatever their origin, is to disarm oneself strategically and tactically.'

As for the concepts of 'national group' and 'national minorities' and the potential and real confusions these have caused, he argues:

> The 'races' in South Africa are not 'national groups' precisely because they are not nations and because they do not desire separate statehood. The term 'national

group' like 'ethnic group' shifts the emphasis from alleged biological to alleged cultural and political attributes of the group. Whereas 'race', however, has either no political significance at all or, if it has, implies some state of inequality, the term 'national group' implies specifically a political dynamic towards separation or accommodation among various 'national groups' each retaining as much sovereignty as possible within a federal or confederal set up (Alexander, 1979: 139).

His main argument about the use of particular concepts, however, is that definitions are neither immutable nor uncontested and are given to socio-political practice reliant on the underlying theories – or lack of them – relevant to their usage (Alexander, 1979: 159ff).

Given his reservations about how the concepts are used, he undertakes an explication of the central concept of 'nation'. In this, he draws on Marx and Engels; in the Communist Manifesto they argued that:

> The working men have no country... Since the proletariat must first of all acquire political supremacy, must rise to the leading class of the nation, must constitute itself *the* nation, it is so far, itself national, though not in the bourgeois sense of the word (quoted in Alexander, 1979: 6).

Basing himself on this, he asserts that there can be no timeless definition of the concept affecting all circumstances and contexts. For him Stalin's definition referred only to the period of the bourgeois democratic world revolution. It was an arbitrary definition which required one to find a nation that met its definitional premises. Consequently, the nation could best be understood as historically determined in the specific circumstances and material relations between classes, and was dependent on the level of political consciousness attained by the classes through class struggle. It was directly influenced by the form of state bequeathed to colonial states because of the capitalist relations and markets it imposed on previously largely classless societies. It made whole peoples disappear, ruined cultural treasures and languages, and wiped out pre-existing boundaries, forcing some to congeal into proto-national units. It subordinated local leaders and 'mortgaged the incipient colonial bourgeoisie' to imperial capital. In Alexander's words (1979: 167):

> On general grounds all that one can say about nations in the modern world is that they will consist of antagonistic or potentially antagonistic classes... and that consciousness of nationality arises in the course of the struggle for national liberation.

Alexander's position (1979: 178) is based on the assertion that the nation was constituted by those who were 'prepared to throw off the yoke of capitalist exploitation and racist oppression' and who resisted and opposed any attempts at dividing the population 'on the basis of language, religion, tribe, or caste'.

National liberation could not therefore be interpreted either as the demand for territorial separation or the democratising of the political system within the framework of capitalist relations. This raised the important question of the permanency of the revolution, which was regarded as critical by Marxists in the NEUM and even by some thinkers in the CPSA. Somewhat prophetically, Alexander recognised (1979: 180) that 'because bourgeois democratic demands *are* revolutionary ... the nationalist tendency not only continues to have resonance among the people, but ... will continue to be the greatest danger to it, assured as it is of the full support of all the imperialist states'.

For him (1979: 180), the task facing the liberation movement was thus to propagate the 'fundamental distinction between *national* liberation, and the *nationalist* "liberation" proffered by bourgeois liberalism'. In his view (1979, 1986), this historical role could only be discharged under the leadership of a politically conscious working class. The working class alone was capable of producing national unity through the extension of democratic rights to the whole of the population, since that was not possible for the middle class given their relationship to the capitalist system. Only the working class, therefore, could assume the project of democratising the country and building the nation. This implied that:

> The nation has to be structured by and in the interests of the black working class. But it can only do so by changing the entire system. A non-racial capitalism is impossible in South Africa. The class struggle against racial oppression becomes one struggle under the general command of the black working class and its organizations. Class, colour and nation converge in the national liberation movement (Alexander, 1986: 75).

Alexander (1986: 68) also refers to the need to reverse the reality of landlessness and seize 'political power' as a sine qua non for the achievement of nationhood, and talks of the limiting nature of the idea that a common language is a condition for constituting a nation. Following Anderson, he argues that the development of print languages facilitate the rise of nation states because of its role in linking emerging capitalism to national consciousness. He does not, however, accept the idea that 'language is the badge of national consciousness', asserting that in fact nation states can be conceptualised without the requirement of language communality (Alexander, 1986: 73ff).

POST-APARTHEID EFFECTS

Writing about the post-apartheid period, Alexander (2012) suggests that even the middle class, which finds some resonance with the idea of the 'rainbow nation' and 'social cohesion', has largely abandoned these ideas given the social pathologies facing the post-apartheid state and society. In its place there is now even more confusion, engendered by a range of conceptions about national identity and 'a singular ineptitude of the country's cultural and political leadership to indicate the possible trajectories of national development'. This confusion is in part attributable to the unfamiliarity of those who engage in these issues with the historical development of the present state of affairs in South Africa. Tracing the development of the ideological positions adopted in the liberation movement and the contested notions of democratic transformation, Alexander argues (2012: 41):

> Indeed, one of the major challenges facing the post-apartheid dispensation is the creative resolution of the tension between the historically evolved ethnic and racial consciousness of the population and the intuitive aversion to group affiliation in the political sphere (given that apartheid had imposed racial and 'ethnic' categories in order to further the agendas of successive white regimes). The promotion of national unity, a national identity and social cohesion more generally... will ultimately depend on how this fundamental issue is approached.

Despite the pre-apartheid expectation that the concept of race would 'wither away' with the advent of a democratic polity, race consciousness has remained very alive. The period of mobilisation under the United Democratic Front (UDF) and the National Forum towards a non-racial position notwithstanding, the position that is now the dominant paradigm has reverted to the older multiracial tradition of liberalism, expressing the tenacity of its historical grip 'on the consciousness of the masses of the people' (Alexander, 2012). This has had undoubted consequences for the trajectory of the post-apartheid state, evidenced in the outcomes of the affirmative action strategies based on race (Alexander, 2006).

The potentially devastating consequences of this scenario are beginning to manifest themselves in the defensive racist attitudes of entitlement, professional incompetence that breeds inferiority complexes and, all too often, resentment of any kind of excellence. In addition, elitist attitudes and aspirations to glamorous lifestyles thrive amid the devastation of the townships and the former homelands, while the blight of corruption, fraud and outright theft continues to spread (Alexander, 2012).

In his *An Ordinary Country* Alexander (2002) further argues that after the abolition of the racist forms of political and economic control, South Africa was no more than an 'ordinary country', limited in its search for national sovereignty as a consequence of the 'logic of global production'. He criticises the leaders of the post-apartheid state for their '180 degree ideological and political turn... coming to terms with the most barbaric consequences of capitalist or free-market dogma'. He points to the impact of the political compromise that prevented the realisation of the goals of reconstruction and development, and of the electoral promises made by the parties that opposed racial oppression.

Alexander calls for the conscious development of a community freed of the blight of racist ideas and ethnic approaches, a community that will deal with the systemic roots of racism, economic marginalisation and exploitation to counteract the hegemony of the assumptions that underlie these approaches. He calls for the development of ideas and practices beyond the 'glib rhetoric about social transformation, national democratic revolution and an African Renaissance', and the recognition of the critical importance of the problem of wealth and inequality. Moreover, the continued promotion of the racial categories of apartheid is hardly a harmless practice since there are, as Alexander argues, other means to achieve the goals of redistributive justice not reliant on the usage of racist social identities.

Although the metaphor of the rainbow nation is used to foster unity, it unfortunately and unintentionally places the focus on different races, nations and cultures. Instead of this, Alexander pursues a new racial imaginary, employing the metaphor of the Groot Gariep (the Orange River), which views South African society as constituted by the confluence of different tributaries into the mainstream of a broader river. These tributaries symbolise cultural practices and beliefs originating from different parts of the world which together result in a more encompassing and humane South African society. He goes on to say:

> While some influences might be stronger than others, we need to recognize that in this integrative dynamic there is no dominant mainstream that should assimilate and submerge other influences. The essential point is to use this dynamic to build integration and a sense of nationhood without denying cherished practices and beliefs and without undermining diversity (Alexander and Vally, 2012: 17).

ALEXANDER'S DETRACTORS

As we suggested earlier, Alexander's ideas have been the subject of either neglect or misrepresentation. Most remarkably, a collection of writings on the National Question was put together by Maria van Diepen (1989) for the Dr Govan Mbeki Fund some ten years after Alexander's *One Azania One Nation* was published. Its contributors were drawn from arguably the most well-known theoreticians and strategists of the CPSA and ANC, including Joe Slovo, Francis Meli, Aziz Pahad, Mzala, Pallo Jordan, Harold Wolpe, Kader Asmal and Tessa Marcus. In examining the *References, Indexes and Notes* of Van Diepen's collection, we found only three references to Alexander's writing. Two of them were fleeting – one mentioning his 1986 article in *Transformation*, and the other referring derisively to 'Trotskyists like Neville Alexander' (Pahad, 1989: 93). The third, Slovo's 1989 paper, is no more than a restatement of the position of the SACP criticised by Alexander. It relies on the classics of Marxist-Leninist literature to which it refers copiously in a critique of what is called 'workerism', 'which denies that the main content of the immediate conflict is national liberation which it regards as a diversion from the class struggle' (Slovo, 1989: 1). It refutes Alexander's criticisms of the Colonialism of a Special Type (CST) thesis, arguing that CST

> (d)oes not imply a two-nation thesis, nor does it ignore class divisions within the communities. The CST thesis correctly describes the reality that, in the post 1910 period, the substance of the colonial status of the Blacks (*sic*) has remained intact even though its form may have altered. It is this reality which provides a correct starting-point for grappling with the complex problem of the relationship between national and class struggle. It is obvious that until the colonial status of Blacks is ended the process of building one nation cannot be completed (Slovo, 1989: 148).

The Van Diepen volume is evidence of the claim that the SACP simply airbrushed Alexander's oppositional ideas. If the Party ideologues were interested in debate, they certainly had no intention of seriously debating with Alexander. Even after the Van Diepen volume, Alexander has been dealt with in the most cavalier way. In a 2013 lecture, Pallo Jordan simply ignores what Alexander wrote for over three decades, referring only to his *One Azania One Nation*. In the section 'Neville Alexander and the National Question' there is little discussion of Alexander's position and more about Trotsky's ideas on the 'Black Republic', failing in fact to acknowledge Alexander's direct discussion of Trotsky's position on the 'Native Republic'. There is only a brief reference to Alexander's view of race, misrepresenting it by suggesting that 'he virtually implies that it was invented'. This is compounded by a number of non sequiturs in the arguments Alexander makes about 'national and class aspirations', leading him to attribute to Alexander the very opposite of what he has argued (Jordan, 2013: 6–10).

As for other criticisms of Alexander's writings on the National Question, we can refer to Tabata (1980), who is critical of Alexander's view of the BCM position. He asserts: 'Let it be categorically stated that the struggle in South Africa is NOT a colour struggle between White and Black. It is a CLASS STRUGGLE' (Tabata 1980: 5, emphasis in the original). Also reviewing *One Azania One Nation*, Brian Bunting (1980) makes this criticism:

> No Sizwe refers to 'Africans', 'Coloureds' and 'Indians' in quotation marks and calls them colour-castes … [This] has not enabled him to formulate either a national

theory or a programme of action more effective than that of the existing liberation movement headed by the ANC of which the Communist Party is an important component ... By this stage, however, it is too late for No Sizwe to come forward with new definitions. He has shot his bolt and revealed that all his agonizing is due to the fact that he does not understand the relationship between class and national struggle in the South African context. His theories, while interesting as semantic exercises, have no practical outlet and are therefore valueless to the liberation movement (Bunting, 1980: 31).

Among his last writings is Alexander's (2010) *South Africa: An Unfinished Revolution.* His essential argument is that no 'social revolution' has taken place since 1994, and in reality the post-apartheid state has extended capitalist relations. At best, South Africa has achieved what might be described as a 'regime change', signifying changes 'in the form of rule and the institutions of the state machine' without any alteration of economic power or of the 'management of the repressive apparatuses of the state' (Alexander, 2010: 2).

CONCLUSION

The implications of Alexander's views for the present should be obvious to any discerning reader, since the National Question remains not only unresolved but also mired in ever-greater mystification – in many ways forebodingly anticipated in Alexander's ideas. We are reaping the stormy consequences of the flawed concepts of nation which relied on problematic ideas of race, nation, ethnic groups, cultural groups, racial minorities and the like – descriptions which persist to this day as resolute beacons of a racist past. The desultory discourses of 'nation' based on such descriptions, especially in the vocabulary of South Africa's political leadership, attest both to the poverty of its ideas and the abandonment of any notion of a common humanity and a shared history in the struggles against a racist regime. Unsurprisingly, criticisms abound about the possibility of racialised and xenophobic genocide *à la* Rwanda and Yugoslavia, 'warring ethnic groups', the abandonment of the project of 'social cohesion' and a common South African identity.

A further implication of the debate on this issue concerns how and who writes history and whose politics can be hidden from view, because only those who have ascended to political power need be recognised as participants in history. Such a view violates the rich and contested traditions, political ideas and practices fundamental to the struggles against apartheid. The ascension to power is not the end of history or of the National Question – since it remains as contested today as it has ever been.

To conclude, we can do no better than to quote at some length Alexander's perceptive observations about the fate of the National Question in the very last article he wrote on this issue. In it he argued:

> Partly because of the racist and xenophobic incidents that became prominent in South Africa in 2008, discussions about whether or not there are any South Africans have brought two issues very clearly to the surface. On the one hand, it is obvious that the fading notion of 'the rainbow nation' is an expression of the end of the euphoria and catharsis that accompanied the release of Nelson Mandela and the subsequent historic events in South Africa. Fewer and fewer people, more specifically in the middle classes to whom the notion was most appealing in the early 1990s, now believe that a sense of national unity and 'social cohesion' is attainable in the prevailing circumstances of extreme social inequality, high unemployment, predominantly and continuing 'black' poverty, widespread violent crime and social insecurity, the ravages of the HIV/AIDS pandemic, as well as the ever-present threat of xenophobia. In short, quality of life is rapidly deteriorating for all. At the time of writing, shortly after the Football World Cup spectacular in 2010, many ideologues and naïve propagandists for one interest group or another are hoping against hope that the policy of bread and circuses, which has become a major part of the economic growth strategy of the ruling party, will revive the sense of hope and of a genuinely creative and constructive future that characterised the early years of the Mandela administration. These will remain vain hopes unless fundamental changes are made in economic, social and even in cultural policy (Alexander, 2012: 199).

He added:

> One does not need much imagination to see all the possible initiatives that can be taken by civil society and government if the commitment to a non-racial South African nation is to be realised. If, however, this vision is absent, we will inevitably stumble into the jungle of racial conflict and the fragmentation, rather than the expansion, supersession and transcendence of the national state. (Alexander, 2012: 212).

NOTES

1   Alexander clandestinely began writing this book on Robben Island and completed it during the period of his house arrest in Cape Town from 1974 to 1979. 'I wrote [the book] really

because of the debates I had with Mandela on the Island about post-apartheid South Africa, the new nation, nation-building, what it all means in terms of racial prejudice, racial attitudes, racial categories, class, gender and so on … The discussion took almost two years …'

2   Here referring to the capitalist ruling class supported by metropolitan capital.

3   Inspired largely by 'young Trotskyist and ex-Trotskyist intellectuals'.

4   There is a rich body of work which speaks to the continuity of this line of thinking about the National Question and especially about 'national minorities' in the pronouncements of the leaders. This includes work by Ben Turok, Joe Ngwenya and Ben Molapo, as well as policy documents of the ANC and CPSA.

5   In the 1980s, particularly during the mass mobilisations against the Tricameral elections and subsequently the Tricameral Parliament and the Koornhof Bills, Alexander belonged to organisations which were active consciously beyond historical group areas and produced literature for a mass audience rejecting the notion of races and racial groups. See, for example, Cape Action League (1986).

REFERENCES

Alexander, Neville (writing as No Sizwe) (1979) *One Azania, One Nation.* London: Zed.

Alexander, Neville (1985) Nation and Ethnicity in South Africa. In *Sow the Wind,* edited by Neville Alexander. Johannesburg: Skotaville.

Alexander, Neville (1986) Approaches to the National Question in South Africa. *Transformation,* 1: 63–95.

Alexander, Neville (2001) The Politics of Identity in Post-apartheid South Africa. In *Challenges of Globalisation: South African Debates with Manuel Castells,* edited by J. Muller, N. Cloete and S. Badat. Cape Town: Maskew Miller Longman.

Alexander, Neville (2002) *An Ordinary Country: Issues in the Transition from Apartheid to Democracy in South Africa.* Pietermaritzburg: University of KwaZulu-Natal Press.

Alexander, Neville (2006) *Affirmative Action and the Perpetuation of Racial Identities in Post-Apartheid South Africa.* Edited version of a lecture originally delivered at the East London Campus of the University of Fort Hare, 25 March 2006.

Alexander, Neville (2010) South Africa: An Unfinished Revolution. The 4th Strini Moodley Annual Memorial Lecture, University of KwaZulu-Natal, 13 May 2010.

Alexander, Neville (2012) The Unresolved National Question in South Africa. In *Pretending Democracy – Israel, An Ethnocratic State,* edited by N. Jeenah. Johannesburg: Afro-Middle East Centre.

Alexander, Neville and Salim Vally (2012) *Racism and Education.* Education Rights Project Series, Centre for Education Rights and Transformation, Johannesburg.

Bunting. Brian (1980) Reviews. No Sizwe, One Azania, One Nation: The National Question in South Africa. *Marxism Today,* 30(1).

Cape Action League (1986) Introduction to 'Race' and Racism – How does the Cape Action League see the Struggle against Racism? Cape Town: Cape Action League.

Jordan, Pallo (2013) Waiting for October: Revisiting the National Question. A Lecture in Honour of Neville Alexander. Nelson Mandela Metropolitan University, Port Elizabeth, 6 July 2013.

Legassick Martin (1974a). Capital Accumulation and Violence. *Economy and Society,* 2(3): 253–91.

Legassick Martin (1974b). Legislation, Ideology and Economy in Post-1948 South Africa. *Journal of Southern African Studies,* 1(1):5–35.

Pahad, Essop (1989) South African Indians as a National Minority in the National Question. In *The National Question in South Africa,* edited by Maria van Diepen. London: Zed.

Slovo, Joe (1989) The Working Class and Nation-Building. In *The National Question in South Africa*, edited by Maria van Diepen. London: Zed.

Swartz, Derek (2010) *Multiculturalism and Identity in Post-Apartheid South Africa: How far have we come?* Address at the Red Location Museum, Port Elizabeth, September.

Tabata, I.B. (1980) Review of Neville Alexander's Book: *One Azania One Nation*. From the Files of Unity Movement of South Africa, 14 March.

Van Diepen, Maria (ed.) (1989) *The National Question in South Africa*. London: Zed.

Wolpe, Harold (1972) Capitalism and Cheap Labour Power in South Africa: From Segregation to Apartheid. *Economy and Society*, 1(4): 425–56.

Wolpe, Harold (1988). *Race, Class and the Apartheid State*. London: James Currey.

THE MARXIST WORKERS' TENDENCY OF THE AFRICAN NATIONAL CONGRESS

Martin Legassick

The Marxist Workers' Tendency (MWT) of the African National Congress (ANC) grew out of the coming together of comrades from the ANC, the emerging internal democratic trade unions, and the Black Consciousness Movement (BCM) in Soweto and the Western Cape in the 1970s, together with comrades from the Mpondo revolt of the early 1960s. At its inception, it had a black majority membership. Among those from the ANC were George Peake and Nimrod Sejake, both former trade union leaders and treason trialists who had subsequently been forced into exile, as well as myself, who had worked throughout the 1960s with Mazisi Kunene, then ANC representative in Europe. Among those from the emerging unions were Dave Hemson, Rob Petersen and Paula Ensor, all three declared 'banned persons' and going into exile.

This chapter deals with the origins of the MWT and its early articulation of a programme and perspectives. It concludes with an examination of the MWT's approach to the National Question.

ORIGINS

The South African Congress of Trade Unions (SACTU), a federation of non-racial trade unions, had become defunct through repression in the early 1960s. It survived only as a small rump of officials in exile, oriented to solidarity work (Sithole and Ndlovu, 2006; Legassick, 2008). In the post-Soweto strengthening of the ANC in London, however, Rob

Petersen and Paula Ensor were employed by the SACTU office, the former as editor of the revived SACTU publication *Workers' Unity* and the latter as personal assistant to general secretary John Gaetsewe. Dave Hemson and I also worked on the paper.

The first issues of the paper placed primacy on building SACTU among factory workers underground – to assist in building and to guide the work of the emerging democratic unions.[1] These unions had already become schools of struggle, through which workers came together to discuss not merely factory issues but all the problems they faced and how to overcome them.

The independent trade unions, said *Workers' Unity* (1977b), were 'forced by repression to keep themselves cut off from the liberation struggle as a whole but we do not oppose them. Our policy is to fight for independent unions and to give these new organisations our support – in so far as they advance the workers' struggle.' The task was to build underground groups which could 'provide leadership and initiative, day by day, to all the workers in the factories ... establish links with similar groups in other factories and areas' and, in particular, 'guide and influence, firmly but carefully, the work of open trade unions, etc.' From these groups would come 'the initiative for action, on every issue from wages to the pass laws. Only by organising ourselves on this secure foundation can we be sure that our struggle will advance strongly, and the necessary link be maintained between our trade unions and our whole liberation struggle.'

John Gaetsewe's political report to the SACTU National Executive Committee (NEC) in January 1978 – drafted by Rob Petersen with input from others, including myself – subsequently appeared as *Looking Forward* and provided a context for these ideas. The tremendous upsurge of struggle inside the country since 1976, the report began, showed that capitalism and apartheid were bound together: 'The struggle against oppression cannot be separated from – and in practice has proved to be thoroughly bound together with – the struggle of the workers against the system of exploitation in South Africa.' At the same time, it noted a 'fundamental change' in the character of the period South Africa was passing through, from a sustained boom to a 'period of deepening and sustained recession' which was likely to continue, interrupted only by short upswings.

Politically, the report noted, 'under the heavy weight of the crisis, the old alliances and relationships are breaking up, or coming under increasing strain. We have entered a time of violent eruptions, in which sudden shifts in the political situation are likely to occur.' Since at least the 1920s the strategy of capital had been to rest on the political support of the white working class against the existence and potential resistance of the black working class. Now the ruling class was debating whether the black working class could be held back from revolution 'if a black middle class is not cultivated as a social buffer against them.'

The ruling National Party (NP) was thus riven with conflict between the *verkramptes* (speaking for the white workers and farmers) and the *verligtes*, speaking for capital. Prime

Minister John Vorster was a Bonapartist, 'balancing between the social forces and the factions which make up the ruling party, and for that matter the white community as a whole'. The concessions offered by the regime, however, were 'too little and too late'. *Looking Forward* presaged what took place in the 1980s when the State Security Council superseded the Cabinet and created the Joint Municipal Councils (JMC), and warned: 'the heads of the military and police forces may at some point be drawn more directly into the uppermost councils of the state' (SACTU, 1977: 3–4). Dan O'Meara (1982) soon used the concept of Bonapartism in his analysis of the 'Muldergate crisis' which led to the replacement of John Vorster by P.W. Botha as prime minister. Harold Wolpe (1988) subsequently criticised 'reductionism' and underlined the importance of the relative autonomy of the state.

With their experience in the unions, Rob Petersen, Paula Ensor and Dave Hemson opened up the networks through which *Workers' Unity* was circulated. The paper's ideas evoked a strong positive response from supporters of SACTU inside and outside the country. From early in 1978, however, Rob and Paula found themselves increasingly in conflict with other members of the editorial board from the South African Communist Party (SACP). As Petersen later put it:

> [A]fter the Soweto events of June 1976, when the black working class, young and old, were on the march, it was possible to put forward in *Workers' Unity – with the unanimous consent of the Editorial Board* – a clear revolutionary working-class position against national oppression and capitalist exploitation. This was fully consistent with the principles of SACTU laid down in our Constitution nearly 25 years ago (Petersen, 1979a: n.p., emphasis in the original).

But the forward movement began to ebb temporarily inside the country and led again to rigidity in ideas imposed from the top in exile.

The youth discussion group, for example, was viewed with some suspicion by ANC leaders in London and around this time it was arbitrarily closed down. The participants were told 'if you want to study Marxism, go to the CP' – where the 'Marxism' would of course be geared to proving the correctness of the two-stage theory of the 'national democratic revolution'. On the *Workers' Unity* editorial board, as Rob described it:

> ... mounting attempts were made to force the paper to retreat from its established political line, to abandon the standpoint set out in *Looking Forward*, and to hold *Workers' Unity* back from tackling the burning issues of the *practical struggle* of the oppressed workers at home. It became necessary for comrades who stood by the original ideas to wage a struggle on the [editorial board] to defend the paper [through] a determined struggle against the proposals and obstructions of the right wing (Petersen, 1979a: n.p.).

It emerged, for example, that there were serious differences on the editorial board regarding the attitude to be adopted towards the independent trade unions. Inside South Africa the position being taken by the highly conspiratorial ANC/SACTU remnant units was that emerging unions should be treated as mere 'signposts to MK' – that is, sources of military recruitment for exile (Lobban, 1996). This attitude was bitterly resented by worker activists trying to build those unions. The justification for it was provided by SACTU president Stephen Dlamini and others, who could not accept that independent democratic unions could exist in a 'fascist' country, and regarded them as 'yellow unions'. The SACTU rump in exile, correspondingly, was the 'only genuine messenger' of the South African working class. In the opinion of Rob, Paula, Dave and myself this was an attempt to elevate the military above the political (despite numerous injunctions by the ANC that such an elevation was incorrect).

The lack of political clarity on the editorial board, in our view, threatened the rebuilding of SACTU inside the country. After two years of the production of *Workers' Unity*, there was no sign that it was becoming rooted among workers in struggle and no feedback from any 'SACTU groups' in the country. Petersen submitted a memorandum (dated 8 April 1979) to the SACTU NEC, the body that had appointed him, arguing all this. Coincidentally, in the same month, the first federation of the new democratic unions was formed inside South Africa: the Federation of South African Trade Unions (FOSATU).

The NEC meeting in Dar es Salaam that month could have initiated a discussion on the issues throughout SACTU and the ANC. Indeed, in January 1979 a Commission had been established by the ANC leadership to undertake a major policy review, including of SACTU policy, in the wake of a visit by an ANC delegation to Vietnam in October 1978. It reported back to the NEC in August 1979. Rob's memorandum reached Dar es Salaam during the period of the Commission's existence. The Commission concluded that throughout the movement there were differences of interpretation 'in the vital areas of our approach to mass mobilisation, the character of our armed struggle, and the way we see it taking root and growing'. This Commission could have initiated discussion throughout the ranks of the movement on the way forward, including the ideas contained in Rob's memorandum – but it did not (Barrell, 1992, 1993; Karis and Carter, 2013).

President Tambo wrote in his personal notebook at the time of the visit to Vietnam:

> We've been forced by events into a false, a bad strategic situation in which armed struggle is and remains the basis of political struggle – *an impossible equation. [It is] necessary to correct this distortion* ... Necessary to recognise that our approach is an external approach: we see the struggle as being built up from outside, introduced from outside by people who are outside ... *This approach wholly excludes the*

people, the masses, as the decisive factor not only for victory, but for any progress at all in our struggle ... [We] see a serious strategic problem to solve before we can hope to make advances. Hence the view that we slow down on [military] operations and work for a change in the order of priority as between political work and military operation (emphasis added) (quoted in Callinicos, 2004: 527).

These were very similar to the conclusions that Rob and his colleagues had reached independently. We also believed that the strategy of rural guerrilla warfare proclaimed by the ANC since the 1960s was inappropriate for the liberation of South Africa, despite its successes in Cuba, Vietnam, Mozambique and elsewhere. We argued that in South Africa's urban conditions guerrilla action would degenerate into mere setting-off of bombs, which did not empower the masses but rather encouraged passivity – and at the same time drove whites further into the camp of reaction. We were not pacifists. The workers should be mobilised and, where appropriate, armed for self-defence of mass actions, and in doing so laying the basis for a new state through workers' insurrection (Petersen, 1979b: 33–5). The first issue of *Workers' Unity* had made clear that:

The rulers in South Africa are conducting a war against the black working people. Every imaginable form of brutality is being employed. To defend themselves against these attacks, to protect their organisations, and to ensure that the struggle is not defeated by the armed force of the apartheid regime, the workers themselves will have to arm. This will take place; it is inevitable (*Workers' Unity*, 1977a).

But the SACTU NEC did not even discuss the issues of Petersen's memorandum; instead they dismissed him as editor and from the editorial board. This resulted from the pressure of SACP leaders on the NEC. The excuse was that Rob was 'putting forward policies which were not those of SACTU' but despite repeated requests the NEC members refused to specify which policies were at fault. Subsequently, because of persistent requests from those of us who supported Rob for a discussion of the political issues, the NEC closed down the main SACTU organising committee in Britain.

We felt compelled to raise the issues with the movement inside the country, and did so in a discussion document that we circulated to subscribers of *Workers' Unity* (Petersen, 1979a). For this, on 26 October 1979, Paula Ensor, Dave Hemson, myself and Rob Petersen were suspended, not from SACTU but from the ANC, unconstitutionally, without even a hearing. We were told we had not sought resolution of our disagreements 'within the established structures of our movement', but instead had 'seen fit to attack the policies and leadership of the revolutionary alliance led by the ANC in public' (personal communication, Y. Zungu, 26 October 1979). It had hardly been in public; we had not even issued a press statement, but circulated the position solely to people in the movement. Meanwhile *Looking Forward* was withdrawn from circulation.

Later, at an ANC anniversary meeting on 8 January 1985, Labour Party MP Dave Nellist asked about the suspensions and was told by ANC spokesperson Francis Meli that they had taken place because we had 'pushed a line that was not SACTU policy'. Moreover, 'All questions that revolve around Marxism-Leninism the [South African Communist] Party is able to relate to, but not the ANC which is not a Marxist-Leninist forum' (*Inqaba*, 1985a: 33). It was not a question of the positions not being 'SACTU policy', but of not being SACP policy. Clearly the suspensions were purely for *political* reasons, and clearly behind them was the SACP, threatened by the challenge to its monopoly of the 'interpretation' of Marxism.[2]

We believed that the ANC-in-exile was dominated by the sectarian interests of the SACP, a rigidly controlled bureaucratic apparatus which leaned for support on workers in the ANC, but relied fundamentally on political and material aid from the Soviet Union. It proclaimed 'socialism' (Moscow-style) as its eventual goal. In this way, and by the use of guerrilla actions, it maintained its revolutionary credentials and held on to its working-class supporters. But at the same time, within the ANC it joined forces with and propped up the middle-class nationalist tendencies that wanted 'democracy' without a workers' revolution. It was hostile to the assertion by the South African working class of its leadership in the liberation struggle (*Inqaba*, 1985a).

We were never given the opportunity to discuss the differences in a comradely way within SACTU or the ANC in exile. We were simply suspended. (In fact, when we were selling our material outside an ANC meeting some of us were threatened by Stalinist hacks with more than suspension: 'You should be executed, and if you were in some countries you would be.') The first 'political' response came later, in the *African Communist* (A Reader, 1980). Much later, two other members of the editorial board referred to the events (though with big lapses of memory) in their autobiographies (Sibeko, 1996; Press, n.d.). And twenty-five years later I discovered, in the ANC archives at the Robben Island Museum and the Mayibuye Centre at the University of the Western Cape (UWC), some contemporary attempts at critique which we never saw.

Curiously, though these critics 'theorise' about *Workers' Unity*'s 'departure from SACTU policy' in its approach to trade unionism, not one of them makes a single reference to the actual rising trade union movement inside the country. One of the failings of which *Workers' Unity* was accused was an 'over-emphasis on the cities':

> Mass struggle in the cities undoubtedly turns those cities into main battlegrounds, but only at particular moments in history. The revolutionary experience of most modern struggles for national liberation shows clearly that the

enemy finds it relatively easy to control the cities, and that for long periods the main battleground of the revolution lies in the countryside. To emphasise the struggle in the cities and say not one word about the struggle in the countryside is to reveal an abyssmal [sic] ignorance of the objective revolutionary process (Anonymous 1, n.d.).

Yet throughout the 1970s and the 1980s the 'main battleground' of the South African revolution was the (urban) factories, the (urban) townships, and the (urban) schools. Even the actions of Umkhonto we Sizwe (MK), from its beginning in 1961, were overwhelmingly urban. That was because of the 'objective historical process'. Within the ANC, in fact, there was a complete lack of clarity on the strategy to be followed – which the anonymous writer's dogmatic assertions fail to deal with.[3]

It was equally regarded as a 'departure' for *Looking Forward* to have warned of the dangers of co-optation of the black middle class by capital. A document points out that the black middle class in South Africa was destroyed by imperialism. Therefore, 'each time an Oppenheimer speaks about the need to 'cultivate' a 'black middle class' we must remind the people of our history. The Robbites do the opposite. They give credance [sic] to the lie that the imperialists in our country seek to make amends *by creating what in fact they once destroyed*' (Anonymous 2, 1979/1980: 23). But who can say it was a 'lie' that throughout the 1980s – indeed, from the establishment of the Urban Foundation in 1976 – the capitalists tried to co-opt the black middle class to its support? President Tambo himself wrote in his personal notebook in 1982:

> Botha's Total Strategy ... to be assured of support among black bourgeoisie in urban areas and upper ruling class in Bantustans ... The people have been nurtured in capitalist expectations ... [The] racist strategy is to meet these expectations: (You want a big house and a big car – *voila!* You want to be a big businessman – Done! Dinner at the Carlton – *Pajalsta!* ... How [to] defeat its intention and counter its objective effects? How [to] expose enemy strategy as dangerous and win new opposition to [the] enemy over and against that strategy? (quoted in Callinicos, 2004: 536).

Yet, we were expected by this anonymous author to hide this truth from the working class in South Africa and internationally. Warning that capitalists might co-opt the middle class did not, however, mean writing them off. If the ANC had confidently put forward a socialist programme, it could have won large sections of the white as well as black middle class to the support of the working class.

In the pamphlet we circulated in South Africa in response to our suspensions we opposed the discussions which had just taken place between the leaders of the ANC and Gatsha Buthelezi, chief minister of the KwaZulu bantustan and head of the Zulu nationalist organisation Inkatha. We characterised him as 'an agent of capitalist interests and a figure upon whom the regime will increasingly lean in its attempts to hold back the tide of revolution' (Petersen, 1979b: 2). Soon afterwards, Buthelezi took offence at this:

> Gatsha Buthelezi this week uncovered a worldwide plot by communists and Marxists to discredit him as a leader of blacks in South Africa. The Chief said that a booklet entitled *The Workers' Movement, SACTU and the ANC* and subtitled *A struggle for Marxist policies*, which was compiled by four white South Africans, was being distributed around the world. He disclosed that Paula Ensor, David Hemson, Martin Legassick, and Robert Petersen ... were spearheading the move against him. Chief Buthelezi hit back, saying that Inkatha is the largest black organisation this country ever produced and that it is dominated by its worker membership ... 'These kind of journals reflect only the misbegotten concepts conceived in the incestuous relationships of twisted minds by people who are not in the struggle for liberation', he said (*Golden City Press*, 1982).

The continuation of the article merely confirmed that our assessment of Gatsha was correct:

> Last week Chief Buthelezi shared a platform with Harry Oppenheimer, head of Anglo American Corporation, at the opening of a technikon in Umlazi and Chief Buthelezi said to him, 'I am pilloried and castigated by some of my black brethren for what I am doing. I want here publicly to share a platform with you and say that South African blacks are deeply grateful for what you have done for us (*Golden City Press*, 1982).

More seriously, our criticism of Buthelezi as an enemy of the revolution was to be borne out in the counter-revolutionary vigilante role played by Inkatha in Natal against students, youth, the UDF and COSATU throughout the 1980s and right up until the eve of the election in 1994 (Maré and Hamilton, 1987). Indeed, some comrades of the MWT of the ANC were murdered by Inkatha thugs.

NATIONAL OPPRESSION AND NATIONAL LIBERATION

In 1981 the MWT of the ANC launched a three-monthly journal, *Inqaba ya Basebenzi*. Though the MWT of the ANC was often accused of ignoring the National Question, nothing could be further from the truth, as indicated by many quotations from *Inqaba*. For example:

> The coming revolution in South Africa is … clearly and inescapably a proletarian socialist revolution. Is this not contradicted by the fact that democratic demands, and above all the demand for national liberation, are to the forefront in the revolutionary struggle? Not in the least. The key to understanding this lies in the theory of 'permanent revolution' (*Inqaba*, 1985b: 9).

In the earliest documents of the MWT of the ANC we wrote:

> National liberation, democracy, and the basic material needs of the people, the MWT of the ANC argued, could not be secured by the black workers of South Africa on the basis of capitalism … There can be no separation of stages … between its national democratic and its socialist aims … Just as national oppression is rooted in class exploitation, so the national liberation struggle is rooted in class struggle (Petersen, 1979a: 31–3].

In part we took our standpoint from that of Leon Trotsky, replying to draft theses by comrades in South Africa, which he rejected because they ignored the National Question:

> Insofar as a victorious revolution will radically change not only the relation between the classes, but also between the races, and will assure to the blacks that place in the State which corresponds to their numbers, insofar will the Social Revolution in South Africa also have a national character. We have not the slightest reason to close our eyes to this side of the question or to diminish its significance. On the contrary the proletarian party should in words and in deeds openly and boldly take the solution of the national (racial) problem in its hands. Nevertheless, the proletarian party can and must solve the national problem by its own methods. The historical weapon of national liberation can be only the Class Struggle (Trotsky, 1996: 148–9).

After all, who could deny the reality of national oppression in South Africa? It was imposed by conquest, slavery and dispossession of the indigenous people, transforming them into cheap migrant labourers, and reinforced in the twentieth century by the mechanisms of segregation and apartheid. At the root of national oppression lay the stripping of the dignity of black people.

We were in fact applying to South Africa the theory of the permanent revolution, first advanced by Leon Trotsky before the Russian Revolution of 1917. He maintained that the foremost tasks of the revolution in Russia were those of bourgeois revolution – emancipating the peasantry from the rule of the landlords; replacing the regionalism of feudal rule with unified nation states; and replacing the rule of hereditary monarchs with forms of political rule reflecting the interest of the capitalist class. But the bourgeoisie, having developed later than the bourgeoisie in France, Britain and elsewhere, was too weak to carry out these tasks. Indeed, because it was allied to pre-capitalist classes, it would stand in the way of this. Though Russia was a backward country, the working class would have to take state power to carry out those tasks. Having done so, it could not and would not stop there. It would come into inevitable conflict with the capitalist class, and be compelled to end capitalism. Thus, he anticipated, in Russia bourgeois and proletarian revolution would become fused together into what he – following Marx and Engels – called a *permanent* revolution.

We maintained that the struggle for national liberation – one of the tasks posed for the bourgeois revolution – could not be carried to victory by black middle-class nationalists. The methods and ideology of nationalism could not end national oppression. In fact, a 'bourgeois revolution' had already occurred, though in a distorted way. While in other 'late-developing' Third World countries the emerging bourgeois class leaned for support on pre-capitalist landowning classes, in South Africa capitalism had triumphed in agriculture by subjugating the indigenous majority to land dispossession and deprivation. Equally, the rise of capitalism in mining and manufacturing had been achieved by imposing a cheap labour system on the black majority (and elevating white workers to privilege) on the basis of racial segregation and apartheid. Thus, apartheid and capitalism were bound together.

To undertake the abolition of apartheid and capitalism, the working class would – we asserted in 1979 – take up the banner of the ANC and it would need to build and transform the organisation on a socialist programme. A 'socialist programme' was not the 'pure class' programme set up by Slovo as the red-herring alternative to a programme of national liberation, but included national liberation and all the other 'democratic' tasks. The full implementation of the Freedom Charter would constitute most elements of a socialist programme. As I later put it:

> The nationalists take up solely the race issues and say 'we must combat racism'. We would agree, but add that can only be done effectively by class methods. The Communist Party says, 'There are race and class issues, but the race issues come first.' We would say, yes, there are both race and class issues, but both of them can only be solved by a movement of the working class to end capitalism. So combating racism and race discrimination (and all the other issues of democracy such as sexual discrimination, etc.), as well as fighting on class issues are included on a socialist programme (Legassick, 2002: 121).[4]

The MWT erred in failing to anticipate a negotiated settlement. We believed that the racial polarisation was too great, and the only alternatives were either a ghastly racial civil war or a workers' revolution. Commenting on the demands by big capitalists and President P.W. Botha in 1985 that the ANC must renounce violence and enter negotiations, we wrote that this demand meant that the ANC must:

> ... openly renounce the revolutionary overthrow of the state and agree to knuckle down under a system in which the capitalist class retains the monopoly of power defended by the present state monopoly of armed force. *This no black leadership could possibly accept without immediately appearing as sell-outs before the people.* ... It is not 'violence' which is at stake, in reality, but power. No ruling class surrenders its historical position of power without a fight. *The ANC leadership cannot yield to the bourgeoisie's claims without losing its own mass base of support and rendering itself impotent* (*Inqaba*, 1985b: 29; emphasis in the original).

Therefore, we concluded:

> Because a transfer of power to the black majority cannot take place without the revolutionary overthrow of the state in South Africa, it will be impossible for talks to succeed. That will remain the case even if the ANC leadership, on the one hand, and the South African regime on the other, wished to achieve a negotiated settlement with each other ... It is impossible because the constituencies, the respective class bases, on which the two sides rest are irreconcilable, even temporarily, in South African conditions (*Inqaba*, 1985b: 29).

In reality, a combination of factors, international and national, allowed the settlement to take place. The MWT had absorbed wrong perspectives from our international comrades. We did not anticipate the counter-revolution and restoration of capitalism in the Soviet Union, and had underestimated the resilience of capitalism in the advanced centres. The collapse of 'socialism' in the Soviet Union disoriented the active layer of South African workers and stood in the way of the mass rejection of a negotiated compromise that we had anticipated. In addition, there was the hugely changed balance of power in South Africa through black urbanisation, and the willingness of the white bourgeoisie to trade exclusive political power for a guarantee of their continued wealth and property.

There are those critics who caricature a class approach in South Africa as posing a necessary unity between white and black workers. Of course the white workers have long constituted a privileged layer. The position of the MWT of the ANC was that in the course of the struggle white workers would move to reaction. The main class force was the black working class. However, we argued that it was necessary to divide, confuse and if possible win over white workers – for the purely practical reason that they constituted the main social base of support of the repressive state machine.

The MWT – unlike some other left tendencies, the 'workerists' for example – did not oppose the concept of 'colonialism of a special type' (CST). It merely rejected the conclusion drawn from that by the Communist Party – the idea of a two-stage revolution, first democratic and then socialist (Legassick, 2007). Those left tendencies that opposed CST outright risked being accused of ignoring the National Question. Workerism compounded its errors in practice by failing to join the United Democratic Front in 1983 and struggle for a socialist programme within it. *Inqaba* was critical of the FOSATU unions and the General Workers Union (GWU) on this score. They compounded the error when in 1985–1986 they switched to uncritical support of the ANC within COSATU rather than struggling for a working-class programme.

The MWT of the ANC believed that the notion of a two-stage revolution was a Stalinist idea. By Stalinism we did not mean merely a system of dictatorship, but an ideology defending the interests of the bureaucratic caste that had usurped power in the Soviet Union – an ideology totally opposed to the struggle of the working class for workers' democracy.

The Communist Party argues for 'national democracy' because the working class needs to ally with the middle class (which does not oppose capitalism in their view). The MWT supported an alliance of the working class and middle class – but on the terms of the former and not of the latter. In reality, the middle class is also oppressed by bankers – the 1 per cent who are today the most hated by the other 99 per cent worldwide. The middle class would benefit from a workers' democracy. The middle class veers in its politics according to the balance of forces between the capitalists and the working class, turning to the left when the working class is ascendant and to the right when the working class has suffered defeats. Politicians (of the right, the centre and the reformist left) who claim to 'represent' the middle class in fact misrepresent it, and serve the interests of capitalism.

In reality the idea that South Africa is currently undergoing a national democratic revolution is increasingly divorced from the realities of repression (Marikana), corruption (Nkandla) and relative economic stagnation.

To this day the National Question has not been resolved. Imperialism stifles the equality of nations, imposing hierarchy instead. Domestically, capitalism reproduces the mainly white rich minority and the poverty-stricken black majority – and will continue to do so as long as it exists (allowing only a small minority of blacks to prosper). The economy generates unemployment and inequality – in education, health, housing and living standards. The cheap labour system has not been demolished. The massacre of workers at Marikana ordered by government and the bosses was an attempt to perpetuate cheap labour, against the fierce resistance of platinum workers demanding a living wage of R12 500 a month – and prepared in 2014 to undertake the longest strike in South African history (twenty-two weeks) to struggle for it. The same principles apply: just as national oppression is rooted in capitalist exploitation, so national liberation is rooted in class struggle – for workers' democracy in South Africa and indeed worldwide.

NOTES

1   Issue 1 tackled the lessons of Soweto and the road ahead. Issue 2 explained why it was necessary to fight for independent unions. Issue 3 discussed unemployment. Issue 4 raised a programme of demands. Issue 5 discussed how to organise. Issue 6 advocated a national minimum wage. *Workers' Unity* is available in the National Library of South Africa.
2   In her collection of O.R. Tambo's papers, Luli Callinicos has a note 'clearly [in] O.R.'s handwriting, unsigned, and in the middle of an otherwise blank page. It simply says, 'Leave Martin alone' (E-mail from Luli Callinicos to Martin Legassick, 6 June 2015). This must relate to discussion in a meeting regarding the suspensions and indicates Tambo's opposition to the action. The e-mail continues: 'In addition ... I recently had dinner with Norman Levy, who spontaneously remarked during our conversation that O.R. was very opposed to the expulsion of the MWT. I asked him how he knew that and he said he could not remember. But shortly afterwards he told me he is almost certain that Archie Sibeko told him when they were both in London.'
3   For example, the ANC Commission, meeting in Lusaka at the time, raised the question of a strategy of (urban) nationwide insurrection. However, on the Vietnam model, it opted instead for 'protracted people's war with a possible role for partial or general uprisings'. But it could not decide whether or not a peasantry, the essential basis for 'peoples' war' – rural guerrilla struggle – existed in South Africa. The question of insurrection and arming the people was endlessly debated in the pages of *Sechaba* and the *African Communist* during the 1980s.
4   The ANC Commission meeting in Lusaka at the time concluded, like us, that 'capitalist exploitation and racial oppression operate together and reinforce one another ... Real liberation is inconceivable without the overthrow of the economic and political power of this [ruling] class and the total destruction of its state apparatus'. But how could this be achieved without a struggle led by the working class at the head of all the oppressed? Yet the Commission rejected the essential means for this – the linking of national democratic and socialist tasks through workers' revolution. 'We debated,' it said, 'the extent to which the ANC, as a national movement, should tie itself to the ideology of Marxism-Leninism and publicly commit itself to the socialist option ... In the light of the need to attract the broadest range of social forces among the oppressed to the national democratic liberation, a direct or indirect commitment at this stage to a continuing revolution which would lead to a socialist order may undoubtedly narrow this line-up of social forces' (ANC, 2013: 720–34).

REFERENCES

African National Congress (ANC) (2013) Report of the Politico-Military Commission. In *From Protest to Challenge*, Volume 5, edited by Tom Karis and Gwendolyn Carter.
Anonymous 1 (n.d.) Untitled six-page paper which starts 'An Analysis'. MC, ANC Box 195, 'SALEP'.
Anonymous 2 (1979/1980) Iqaqa Alizi wa Kunuka: Basis of a Talk Given to the Islington Unit of the ANC [*c.*1979/1980] (Confidential) [document incomplete]. Mayibuye Centre ANC Box 65,

'SACTU Dissidents'. [Note that the ANC collection that was in the Mayibuye Centre has now been moved to Fort Hare.]

A Reader (Harold Wolpe) (1980) Role of Trade Unions in the SA Revolution. *African Communist*, 81(2). [The name of the 'reader' was identified from a draft of the article in MC ANC Box 65, 'SACTU Dissidents'.]

Barrell, Howard (1992) The Turn to the Masses: The African National Congress' Strategic Review of 1978–79. *Journal of Southern African Studies*, 18(1).

Barrell, Howard (1993) Conscripts to their Age: ANC Operational Strategy, 1976–1986. Unpublished D.Phil. thesis, Oxford, United Kingdom.

Callinicos, Luli (2004) *Oliver Tambo: Beyond the Engeli Mountains.* Cape Town: David Philip.

Golden City Press (1982) Commie Plot Against Me – Says Gatsha. *Golden City Press,* 18 April 1982.

Inqaba ya Basebenzi (1985a) Labour MP Protests Suspension of Marxists by ANC. *Inqaba ya Basebenzi*, 16/17 (January–June): 33.

Inqaba ya Basebenzi (1985b) Workers' Revolution or Racial Civil War? *Supplement to Inqaba ya Basebenzi,* No. 16–17.

Karis, Thomas and Gwendolyn Carter (2013) *From Protest to Challenge*, Volume 5. Report of the Politico-military Strategy Commission to the ANC NEC, August 1979.

Legassick, Martin (2002) The Past and Present: Interview with Alex Lichtenstein. *Radical History Review*, (Winter): 111–30.

Legassick, Martin (2007) *Towards Socialist Democracy.* Pietermaritzburg: University of KwaZulu-Natal Press.

Legassick, Martin (2008) Debating the Revival of the Workers' Movement in the 1970s: The South African Democracy Education Trust and Post-apartheid Patriotic History. *Kronos*, 34 (November).

Lobban, Michael (1996) *White Man's Justice: South African Political Trials in the Black Consciousness Era.* Oxford: Clarendon.

Maré, Gerhard and G. Hamilton (1987) *An Appetite for Power: Buthelezi's Inkatha and the Politics of 'Loyal Resistance'.* Johannesburg: Ravan Press.

O'Meara, Dan (1982) Muldergate and the Politics of Afrikaner Nationalism. *Work in Progress*, 22.

Petersen, Rob (1979a) Letter to NEC from Dismissed Editor, 17/7/1979. In *South Africa: The Workers' Movement, SACTU and the ANC – A Struggle for Marxist Policies.* Cambridge: Cambridge Heath Press.

Petersen, Rob (1979b) The Workers' Movement, SACTU and the ANC. Unpublished memorandum.

Press, Ron (n.d.) To Change the World! Is Reason Enough? Available online at http://www.anc.org.za/books/press1.html (accessed 11 October 2006).

Sibeko, Archie (1996) *Freedom in our Lifetime.* Durban: Indicator Press.

Sithole, Jabulani and Sifiso Ndlovu (2006) The Revival of the Labour Movement, 1970–1980. *Road to Democracy, Volume 2,* edited by SADET. Pretoria, Unisa Press.

South African Congress of Trade Unions (SACTU) (1977) *Looking Forward: SACTU's View of the Political Situation and the Tasks facing the Workers' Movement in South Africa.* London: SACTU.

Trotsky, Leon (1996) Remarks on the Draft Theses. In *South Africa's Radical Tradition: A Documentary History, Volume 1*, edited by Allison Drew. Cape Town: UCT Press.

Wolpe, Harold (1988) *Race, Class and the Apartheid State.* London: James Currey.

Workers' Unity (1977a) After Soweto: What Way Forward? *Workers' Unity*, No. 1.

Workers' Unity (1977b) How Do We Organise? *Workers' Unity*, No. 5.

THE NATIONAL QUESTION CONFRONTS THE ETHNIC QUESTION

Gerhard Maré

DISTURBING THE NATIONAL QUESTION

The National Question has predominantly been interpreted in the South African context as conceptualising the route to empowering an oppressed racialised majority. In this sense it has already been answered, it would seem, through the creation of a non-racial democracy based on shared citizenship. Black (as referring to a black African nation) majority rule was achieved with the overwhelming victory of the African National Congress (ANC) in April 1994. The consequence is that both '[c]lass and race mattered but, politically, race mattered more' (Friedman, 2015: 146). Ironically, this liberal argument may also describe the approach of some South African Marxist theorists, including those of the South African Communist Party (SACP). As a first stage towards the overthrow of capitalism, it seems certain from present conditions that the revolution has been postponed until power is transferred to another political imagination.

Such postponement may well be the reason why the National Question continues to be asked, alongside the (always) incomplete National Democratic Revolution (NDR), despite all achievements towards and since the overthrow of apartheid.[1]

However, my position is that it was never the right question to begin with, not in this recent (since 1910) nation state. The National Question relied on an assumed hegemonic and homogenising shared experience of racial domination among all black Africans. Steven Friedman writes about an anonymous article (revealed to be by Raymond Suttner,

Jeremy Cronin and David Rabkin, all political prisoners at the time) in *Africa Perspective* (Anonymous, 1983):

> ... the authors argued that ... the new Marxism [of the 1970s] did not understand how the 'actual experience' of black people under apartheid laid the basis for unity 'under the banner of African nationalism'. It [the new Marxism] ignored 'the National Question': Marxism had long known that national territory, language or culture could unite people across class lines (Friedman, 2015: 154).

The contradictions were effectively 'transcended' within the 'question' as framed (Anonymous, 1983: 90), but continue to leave extreme traces of conflict unattended, postponed and even denied, as had been the case during years of struggle against apartheid. The citizenry remains composed of difference and diversity – such as male and female, old and young, racialised groups re-confirmed, religions – and leaves perpetually demanding and threatening those outside the borders of the nation state, as well as the victims of inherited racial and increasing class inequality. Anonymous asked for commonly shared 'experience' of domination to create 'the nation', along with location within 'national territory' – the nation state of South Africa, that imperial and colonial container for capitalist placement, subject since 1948 to extensive and increased fragmentation though apartheid policy. Language and culture certainly did not disappear into the desired melting pot. The nation, it was implied, would occur despite the existence of apartheid ethnic 'homelands' – because of shared racist discrimination. Distinctions of collaboration, class, political allegiances, ethnicity and traditionalism had (largely) to be ignored.

As *the* National Question it dates back, in South Africa, to the 1940s (Mawbey, 2014), although the related 'black republic' policy within the Communist Party of South Africa (CPSA), the predecessor of the South African Communist Party (SACP), featured in 1928 (Mzala, 1988a: 50). The volumes of *From Protest to Challenge*, an archive of documents of resistance, make clear that solidarity and fragmentation were, unsurprisingly, seen in a variety of terms before and after the South African war – tension between Christian denominations in the late nineteenth century; acceptance of chiefly authority by some; arguing that tribal conflict was as intractable as the conflict between Afrikaner and English-speakers; and petition after petition calling for inclusion in forms of wealth and political democracy introduced through colonial conquest and rule. The elites were making their claims for participation within a new order, against the exclusionary form that was being created to accommodate colonial and Boer polities.

This National Question is an ideological notion, resting as it does on the constructed notion of 'the nation' – an 'imagined community' of inhabitants of nation states; of 'building the nation'; of what can be justified in the name of 'the nation'. Here it differs from the structurally located origin and existence of terms such as class, sex or gender. Social construction certainly does not mean there is no effect. As in the case of race, the most abhorrent actions, policies, beliefs and behaviours have flowed, and continue to flow, from the notion of nation.

I have previously argued against the notion of nation building – with the apparent goal an impossible and undesirable South African nation, or a black nation, or even a nation of the oppressed. Similarly, I have rejected mobilisation on the basis of ethnic identity as dangerous in the extreme (along with race or religion mobilised). Evidence since has not made me change my mind. This does not mean denying the rich existence of ethnicity in everyday life (Guy, 1991; Campbell, Maré and Walker, 1993; Sitas, n.d.) or rejecting the urgent need for common purpose among groups of people, at whatever scale of social life. On the contrary, such collective purpose is essential for avoiding conflict and, more positively, for resolving shared problems. Examples have to be recognised, discussed and supported. Such calls can vary, from action against inequality to calls for extreme engagement with the impending climate catastrophe, from sexism to xenophobia, from recovering public space as commons to education delivery.

In this chapter I constrain myself and focus on the place of ethnicity within a democratic society. Twenty-four years ago Jeff Guy (1991: 15) suggested that 'if any research is to be initiated in support of democratisation [in South Africa] then the question of ethnicity is an important one, and ... there is a real need to encourage such research in order to give a more nuanced, subtle, contextualised view of the topic ...'.

Jeff Guy's call is much neglected (or deliberately denied), but is still extremely relevant. In April 2015 the powerful holds of both ethnicity and nation were tragically displayed from within KwaZulu-Natal (KZN), now occurring in articulation rather than supposed contradiction. Despite denials, claims of misinterpretation, and defence of the perpetrator, there can be little doubt that King Goodwill Zwelithini, of the Zulus, while addressing a meeting of people so self- and other-identified, told foreigners to leave South Africa. Thousands were subsequently targeted as non-South Africans; their properties were looted; murders were committed; and they were driven from their homes into refugee camps. Although he did not directly call for violence, followers interpreted what he said as a call to action. At a meeting after the events, the king condemned the violence, but added that if he *had* called for direct action from 'his people', the 'warrior nation', South Africa would have been reduced to ashes. Large numbers of his followers dressed for the formal occasion in traditional regalia and carried traditional weapons. They jeered those of other 'races', religious groupings and nationalities who participated in the event. Such targeting can be identified from the 1980s onwards. Nor is the denial of responsibility and claims of misinterpretation anything new. Of even greater concern is the manner in which the status of 'the king of the Zulus' is protected by politicians, even in the assertion that criticising him will lead to unspecified 'consequences'.

Those consequences are illustrated here through a clash between ethnic and national mobilisation, during a period of struggle towards realisation of the National Democratic Revolution and answering the National Question. The episode illustrated competition over political identities and the social, political and economic power associated with contesting positions during a period of extensive instability and transition. I call for an approach that recognises complexity, both in understanding and in acting. This call remains necessary as the National Question retains rhetorical validity in the form in which it was asked throughout the twentieth century. The central role of calls to the 'Zulu nation' to provide the cement for Zulu-ness illustrates the power and plasticity of ethnicity in political mobilisation. Such adaptability allows ethnicity again to provide the basis of claims for power over subjects and for wealth.

The apartheid ethnic bantustan *strategy*, within a continuing racial and racist *ideology* (to utilise an analytical distinction by Neville Alexander (1979: 63)), overlapped with formulation and reformulation of the National Question within the ANC and other resistance organisations. The apartheid strategy was the 'smashing of African nationalism and black working-class consciousness', through an ideology of nationalities (Alexander, 1979: 63), but it also served to confirm the apparent correctness (or at least the appropriateness) of the National Question approach. Bill Freund (2014), in an excellent recent contribution to the very limited debate on the National Question, uses probably the most serious discussant of issues of national identity, Neville Alexander, as a starting point. Freund compares the ANC with the Indian Congress movement, to illustrate how, as Congress in India had done, the ANC excluded some from its notion of nation. Congress 'tap[ped] into a cultural imaginary that was fundamentally Hindu and thereby ... excluded both people outside the caste system who were not going to like the Hindu order of things and the huge number of non-Hindus' (2014: 25). Locally, the ANC 'from the period where it began to function as a mass force had to steer militant nationalism which often understood the enemy strictly in racial terms' (Freund, 2014: 25). This had, and still has, threatening implications for racialised minorities. In competition for resources in post-1994 South Africa, the frailty of racial solidarity, alongside its common-sense strength, becomes visible along ethnic and nationalistic fault-lines.

Two books, published within a year of each other in the second half of the 1980s, illustrate and grapple with the Zulu version of ethnic calls in the period immediately before 1994. The first to appear was *An Appetite for Power: Buthelezi's Inkatha and South Africa* (Maré and Hamilton, 1987). The second is *Gatsha Buthelezi: Chief with a Double Agenda* (Mzala, 1988a). Both books had Buthelezi, the president of the Zulu ethnic movement Inkatha and chief minister of the KwaZulu bantustan, on the cover. In one he was wearing a semi-military jacket, cravat, string of beads in the Inkatha/ANC colours of black, gold and green, and a Harrods scarf. In the second, Mzala's book, Buthelezi is in full Zulu regalia, much as you would still find displayed by those who today hold power at many events in the province of KwaZulu-Natal – leopard-skin ring around his head, leopard skin around his shoulders, carrying what might be an axe and an Nguni cattle-hide shield, and around his neck a string of what are probably lion claws.

The first book was written by two outsiders to Zulu-ness, but not to ethnic mobilisation and its consequences. It deliberately set out to debunk the many myths surrounding the man and his ethnic movement, myths essential to a particular vision of the future. The book clarifies Inkatha's location in the fundamental transformation of the country, away from racist apartheid, and draws attention to the dangers of ethnic mobilisation, to the class allies Buthelezi attracted, and to the creation of a new (black) bourgeoisie. Buthelezi and his supporters were openly in favour of deracialising capitalism; they were anti-communist, and were opposed to disinvestment and 'independence' for KwaZulu.

Mzala wrote from within Zulu-ness – and the National Question – and was committed to a Marxist understanding of the world. His book makes for a fascinating re-reading in relation to the narrower topic here, as much for the content and the argument as for who the author was. Jabulani 'Mzala' Nxumalo was an activist intellectual within the ANC and the SACP, prolific in his writing and in the range of issues on which he touched. A critical, and critically open, reading of his work would reward the effort, but here I will refer to only two sources (Mzala, 1988a, 1988b). I examine them in respect of the aspect relevant to the argument, namely the National Question and ethnicity, specifically as exemplified by Mangosuthu Gatsha Buthelezi and his Inkatha movement from the 1970s to the early 1990s. At Mzala's death in London in 1991 Brian Bunting noted in an obituary:

> He was endlessly fascinated and intrigued by the national question, and wrote and lectured extensively on the relationship between the national and class struggle in South Africa. Asserting that the aim of the South African revolution was to end the inequality between the nations, he believed this could only be achieved under socialism ...
>
> ... To be a member of the Communist Party did not mean that he was not equally devoted to the national interest of his people. He was immensely proud of Zulu history and culture, as any reader of his book, *Gatsha Buthelezi: Chief with a Double Agenda*, can testify. He believed that the bantustan system stifled the national drive and independence of the African peoples (Bunting, 1991: n.p.).

Here, note 'his people', 'the nations', and the plural in 'African peoples'.

Blade Nzimande, SACP secretary general and at present minister of higher education and training, draws attention to the same aspects:

> He [Mzala]wrote extensively on the national question. This has always been a difficult and controversial subject in South Africa, and in the course of the twentieth century communists themselves sometimes differed over how to analyse a South African society where race and class interact in complex ways. Mzala believed that for the national question to be resolved, the oppressed had to secure self-determination, not in the narrow, ethnic Bantustan sense as dictated by the apartheid regime. It had to be resolved, he believed, by achieving the kind of independence that would bring about freedom from oppression for the poor, who were mostly black, while liberating the oppressors from their fearful and fearsome domination (Nzimande, 2013: n.p.).

Note Nzimande's admission of the indeterminate status of the National Question and the ambiguity in saying that Mzala believed that 'for the national question to be resolved, the oppressed had to secure self-determination'.

In 1988, Mzala also had an article published – 'Revolutionary Theory on the National Question in South Africa'. The article stated the lack of certainty in debates on the National Question, except in the form in which it existed within a 'Marxist theoretical tradition': '... it is probably true that outside this ... theoretical tradition (as organised within the SACP), there have been few efforts to examine in detail the nature of the national question in South Africa' (Mzala, 1988b: 30).

Clarity within the Marxist tradition, but confusion around or lack of attention to the National Question? Is this why we have a prominent South African historian speculating on Verwoerd's (posthumous) approval for the continuation of chiefly authority in post-1994 South Africa (Beinart, 2014)? Is this why a king threatens violent action from the 'Nguni nations' unless colonial land occupation is addressed (Zwelithini, 2015). I will return to these central concerns. First, however, an overview of Inkatha ethnicity in contest with ANC racialised nationalism.

ETHNICITY, NATIONS, TRIBAL AUTHORITY AND TRADITION

Claims that 'the Zulus' are the best-known of all tribal/ethnic/national entities on the African continent have been voiced both from inside (Mahoney, 2012: 2) and outside the group itself. Since 1994, KwaZulu-Natal is the only province that still refers directly, in its name, to the bantustan effectively still existing within it. Tours of old battlefields are arranged as a profitable tourist attraction to examine the defeats by and of Zulu warriors in the nineteenth century (Guy, 1988; Hamilton, 1988). Films and TV programmes abound; the name 'Zulu' (and even more so 'Shaka') have been adopted by individuals, music groups, sports teams, an airport, an aquarium, homesick African-Americans, and politicians. Statues are erected, rejected and planned. The fearsome warlike status is adopted as genetically in the blood of the group, then and now (Maré, 1992; Waetjen, 2006). How do we make sense of it? And what is its importance to the National Question and, more relevantly, to living together in a modern republic?

Let me take the liberty of providing the amalgamated definition I utilised previously in dealing with ethnic mobilisation in apartheid South Africa. Ethnicity refers to social identity formation that rests on the following factors:

- culturally specific practice and a unique set of symbols and beliefs, the specific combination of which have, however, to be examined in each case;
- a belief in common origin and a common history ('the past') that is broadly agreed upon, and that provides an inheritance of origin, symbols, heroes, events, values, hierarchies;
- a sense of belonging to a group that in some combination ... confirms social identities of people (members) in their interaction with both insiders and outsiders. (Maré, 1993: 23).

What needs to be added to this definition is that ethnic mobilisation, as is the case with race mobilisation, is not class-neutral or gender-neutral in its populism. The call on tradition is one that confirms patriarchy, pre-dates capitalism and denies class difference.

Although Zulu-ness is often called upon, it is an invented, created, social identity and (hence) ethnic group. As with all ethnic groups (and nations), claim is made to historical continuity, to soften accounts of process and change. Buthelezi would use the term 'since time immemorial', a term strangely even used by Mzala (1988a: 113) in respect of the Zulu monarchy. In the same vein, Afrikaners and some other 'nations' claimed divine predestination.

In its employment in the region, and in calls made to 'Zulus' across the country, this social identity was given specific content. First, culturally specific practices and a unique set of symbols and beliefs were put forward to distinguish the Zulu group from other groups. As with race, there can never be just a single ethnic group – distinguishing features have to be identified, given credence and longevity, and repeated. While rejecting the creation of 'ethnic exclusiveness and isolation' by colonialism and apartheid, Mzala stated:

> Denunciation of tribalism and ethnic exclusiveness is not denunciation of the ethnic communities themselves. People's democracy does not mean that all cultural

and traditional distinctions between the various groups must disappear ... What is not needed are bantustans to preserve their cultural heritage (Mzala, 1988a: 220–1).

It had to be a sub-division of a larger existence, 'people's democracy'. But his discussion of the National Question does not clarify some continuing confusions (Mzala, 1988b: 54). Are ethnic communities included – along with African, Indian, coloured, Afrikaner and English – in nationalities that have to be united? And how does that relate to the 'solution of the national question ... only procee[ding] from the integration of the *two* nations', 'black and white'? (Mzala, 1988a: 231, emphasis added). Mzala contradicts himself to a certain extent, or confirms a deliberate ambiguity, when he says later in the Buthelezi book that 'the two items [of ethnicity and nationalism] do not form a single agenda for the national liberation movement'.

The belief in common origin and a shared history as a group is well illustrated, then and now, in the rhetoric of mobilisation employed by Buthelezi, the Zulu king, and those around them – including a number of academic supporters. This is how the process of construction, of invention, occurs and re-occurs. Followers, members, have to be told what existed and how to interpret and live that now. The field of creating 'the Zulu' (ethnic group, nation, nationality) was open to contesting experiences and loyalties from the start. Among those who should be Zulus there have been and remain dissidents. The issues of *contested construction* are all too visible and understandable in the present, once you have accepted Chapter 12 of the Constitution, the validity of historical identity in land claims, and regular salaries for incumbents of positions of traditional authority.

For the nineteenth-century process of creation of Zulu-ness, the study by Michael Mahoney (2012) and the fascinating exploration by Carolyn Hamilton and Nessa Leibhammer (2014) are relevant. Both draw attention to the important neglect of the quite distinct histories of African people living south and north of the Thukela river, the nineteenth-century boundary between Natal and Zululand. Hamilton and Leibhammer complement the detailed work on the Qwabe chiefdom that Mahoney presents, and the argument he creates for a set of identities south of the Thukela, not part of the developing Zulu-ness. They refer to this marginal part of what *became* accepted as an inclusive Zulu kingdom, but note that 'it has a regional history quite distinct from that of the nineteenth-century Zulu kingdom north of the Thukela', and to the manner in which the Zondi suffered under Shaka (Hamilton and Leibhammer, 2014: 160, 168, 173). Mbongiseni Buthelezi (2014) depicts the everyday living of distinct community identities in the twenty-first century in an unintended personal reflection.

And, finally, in employing the definition, a sense of belonging to a group is essential, holding on to a social identity in interaction with 'us' and 'them', the members and the outsiders, loyalists and traitors. In a powerful book on social identity, Anne Phillips

(2007) writes of two inevitable consequences of such mobilisation. First, leaders define acceptable behaviour, loyalties, traditions, and so forth – power lies with spokespeople (nearly always men). Second, the 'individuals, in all their complexity, disappear from view' (Phillips, 2007: 179). Mangosuthu Buthelezi cast the net wide and inclusively here – 'All members of the Zulu nation are automatically members of Inkatha if they are Zulus,' he told the KwaZulu Legislative Assembly (KLA) in 1975 (Maré, 1992: 75). That is the goal of all mobilisers of ethnicity or of the nation. Even then, aspects of an internal 'pure' group, chiefs and their followers north of the Thukela, shone through now and then in debates in the KLA. Clearly defined social identity, designating what the essence of belonging is, has to start with a top-down inclusivity, which then allows traitors to be defined and punished in various ways. *Amambuka* (traitors) can be named and punished, whether in the nineteenth (Mahoney, 2012: 195–6) or late twentieth century (Maré, 1995: 200), and into the twenty-first century.

Buthelezi linked the movement he started – or revived, if the earlier Inkatha of the 1920s is taken into account (Cope, 1993) – with all Zulus, here defined as speakers of the language and, problematically, all those allocated to KwaZulu by the state through its Population Registration Act and Bantu Authorities Act, even if they were located in the migrant hostels on the Witwatersrand.

CREATING AND MAINTAINING 'THE ZULU' AS ETHNIC GROUP

The central symbol of Zulu ethnicity, maintained by mobilisers (although not without rejection and dispute over the past 180 years or so) and the incumbents, is obviously the position of king. The most prominent historian of nineteenth-century Zululand and Natal has undoubtedly been Jeff Guy. Through a series of books, he explored the internal dynamics of Zulu society and colonial and settler power (political, military and economic) that shaped and was shaped by the former. Referring specifically to the Zulu monarchy in the twentieth century, including Goodwill, Guy writes that it played its part in

> ... attempt[ing] to make use of the monarchism deep in the culture of the Africans of KwaZulu-Natal [the province since 1994] and indeed beyond. The contradictions and ambiguities in such processes have contributed to the complexities of modern South Africa. But what has been constant is the emotional hold of the Zulu royal house, its central position in African tradition and, of course, in African history ... it has proved to be a social construct made up of strong and resilient historical memories, connecting the present with the past, and around which alliances continue to be made and battles to be fought (Guy, 2001: 448).

In his book on Buthelezi, Mzala also comes close to finding 'a past which fills a need in the present' (Guy, 2001: 448, emphasis added). Mzala wishes to save the Zulu king (Goodwill) from the control of a chief (Buthelezi), and writes:

> Never before in the history of the Zulu had their king been subject to the control of a chief. Yet the bantustan system was able to make it possible. From *time immemorial*, the social cohesion of *the Zulu state* had centred in all its facets on the king. *Tradition sanctioned* this symbolic nature of Zulu unity in him (Mzala, 1988a: 113, emphases added).

Michael Mahoney (2012: 3) confirms the centrality of Zulu kings to a changing constituency during the nineteenth century, and with a sometimes critical link during periods of the twentieth century: 'Zulu ethnicity and the Zulu king were the linchpins of the ideology of the movements led by the conservative elite.' Mahoney concludes that much has 'to be forgotten' (using Renan's phrase) in the building of the nation. In this case, conflict and divided loyalties between groups now mostly integrated, in claim and self-perception, into Zulu-ness have been largely obliterated in a common-sense presentation (Mahoney, 2012: 217). What is being 'remembered', though, I would argue, is the service kingship still provides to conservative elites.

In his mobilisation of Zulu people, Buthelezi obviously also drew on the king, at earlier times against his will, as there were other interests within Zulu-ness and within apartheid that attempted to hitch Goodwill's symbolic centrality to their wagon. Buthelezi needed him, as do the other claimants, for two reasons. The first is personal, to locate himself within the stream of 'the past' of Zulu-ness. Second, he wanted to have the essence of being Zulu, the one who can confirm what it means, within the vehicle being constructed. Goodwill Zwelithini offered the potential of a willing participant in the National Party's (NP) scheme of 'independence' for KwaZulu, the most significant of all the homelands – numerically, politically and in terms of international renown. Buthelezi deliberately prevented this option, largely through popular and chiefly support for himself. The king nearly derailed his value as symbol through an early attempt to create his own popular base – such as among migrant workers living in the hostels of Corobrick in Durban when they threatened to strike (IIE, 1974: 9–13; Maré and Hamilton, 1987: 118–19). Here, too, Buthelezi reined him in, leaving labour matters, at that stage, in the hands of the charismatic Barney Dladla, and later (in 1986) in his failed attempt to create the United Workers Union of South Africa (UWUSA) in opposition to the Congress of South African Trade Unions (COSATU). In 1986 the king also entered the fray, but now inseparable from Inkatha and Buthelezi. In a speech, preceding violence against National Union of Mineworkers (NUM) members at Hlobane Colliery, Goodwill committed himself to capitalism, and warned miners who insulted Buthelezi to desist. Buthelezi succeeded in locating the king initially within and later in firm relationship to Inkatha and to himself as 'prime minister'. So in 1991, with the formal ending of apartheid and with it the bantustan strategy, Buthelezi had the king at his side during the annual Shaka Day celebrations:

> Whenever I have to stand up to introduce His Majesty the King of the Zulu on these formal cultural occasions, I burn with a deep sense of pride. It is when one focuses on His Majesty representing the unity of the people in his person, and when you focus on His Majesty summing up Zulu history in his person, that you are confronted with an overwhelming sense of who the Zulu people actually are (Maré, 1992: 97).

In response the king confirmed Buthelezi.

In 1994 the Inkatha Freedom Party (IFP) (deliberately no longer a movement) very nearly derailed the elections with a threat of secession, or at the very least a federalism that would acknowledge the Zulu kingdom (Maré, 1995: 232–9; Humphries, Rapoo and Friedman, 1994: 158–63).

The king continued into the democratic republican order post-1994, making grandiose claims for his role in maintaining Zulu-ness, costing taxpayers millions of rands per year (with palaces and six wives and the accompanying material elements of status), and acting, with the full support of the ANC, to continue to 'sum up the history' and 'represent the unity' of the Zulu as he did under apartheid and in Inkatha. Monogamous Buthelezi is still there, but a shadow of his former self in comparison with the political presence he enjoyed in South Africa during the 1970s and 1980s. Now it is the polygamous president of the country who stands next to the king and who dons traditional gear.

CONFLICT: ETHNIC WAR OR POLITICAL STRUGGLE OVER IDENTITY?

During the period 1980–1994 some 16 000 people died in violent clashes between supporters of Inkatha and those within a broad support base of the ANC.[2] Freund (2008: 609) notes that '... a full-scale civil war did not materialise in Natal, perhaps because the ANC-Inkatha rivalry was not a battle over the legitimacy of Zulu culture'.

Freund is right in large part, as my references to Mzala's position, and closer examination of the ANC's relationship with Zulu-ness and tribal authority in the Natal province, would support. Rather, the battle was over who would control and interpret Zulu culture in a period when political power was increasingly fluid. However, the ANC was predominantly committed to being a nationalist movement, in which ethnic and certainly racial conflict and tensions existed but, along with gender and class, were treated as subordinate to the goals of the National Democratic Revolution. The ANC has at times claimed that it launched Inkatha as part of a strategy to gain access to rural parts of South Africa from which to wage armed struggle (Mzala, 1988a: 123). According to Mzala (1988a: 124), the ANC initially thought Buthelezi 'then displayed what the ANC considered "a democratic consciousness", however limited, [and] it thought it wise to deal with him'. That did not last long, and by the early 1980s virulent language was used by both sides – Inkatha and the ANC within the rapidly growing organised internal opposition to apartheid – which led to the extreme violence for the decade from roughly 1985 to 1995.

Inkatha was from the start caught in the irresolvable tension between ethnic and nationalist mobilisation. Buthelezi's speeches displayed 'the intricate and layered way in which [he] married the various legitimating traditions', ranging from Zulu lineages to prominent ANC leaders such as Albert Luthuli, from Zulu to 'Black' (Maré, 2000: 71) – in concrete terms between the Inkatha Cultural Liberation Movement and the ANC liberation movement's tradition of nationalism.

Mangosuthu Buthelezi straddled the distinction between nation and nationality, between strategically located resistance movement and apartheid ethnic national state, between the oppressed and the Zulu homeland. He succeeded, for a while. A number of books, both critical and hagiographic, were devoted to him and to Inkatha, and very many more academic studies and articles, while his politics dominated newspapers for two decades (Temkin, 1976, 2003; McCaul, 1983; De Kock, 1986; Maré and Hamilton, 1987; Mzala, 1988a; Smith, 1988; Buthelezi, 1990). He was feted by some leaders internationally, and many more were not embarrassed to receive him and be photographed with him. He nearly left the miracle of transition with a flaw that would have continued a war that had already cost thousands of lives, and that was inaccurately called 'black on black violence', but was really the National Question questioned. He also left post-1994 South Africa with the clearest symbol of an unresolved dilemma: ethnicity, tribalism, traditional structures and loyalties, citizens and subjects, and an additional far too tempting base for political mobilisation.

ETHNIC IDENTITIES POST-1994

The threat of creating a Zulu state in a federal post-1994 South Africa may have fizzled out. In large part this was because the retribalisation to which Ntsebeza (2006) and Beinart (2014) refer and the largely unexamined ethnicity which bothered Jeff Guy have meant that it has been created as a shadow presence – 'the Zulu kingdom'. Previously, apartheid had 'retribalised' black South Africans through the Bantu Authorities Act of 1951. The IFP and its monarch succeeded in strengthening provincial powers and gaining recognition for and protection of the position of the king within KZN post-1994 (and, hence, kings located elsewhere) (Ntsebeza, 2006: 272). Central to this process in KZN was the Ingonyama Trust Act of 1994, signed off days before the elections on 27 April 1994. This Act placed approximately a third of the land area in KZN (2.8 million hectares) in a trust, with King Goodwill as the sole trustee. A 1998 amendment established a board, chaired by the *ingonyama* (Goodwill) or a nominee. It is the base from which Goodwill makes claims of further restitution, including calls for all of KZN as putatively the Zulu kingdom as it was claimed to be in 1838.

The symbolic value of the king became slippery during the transitional period, from belligerent promoter of Inkatha (Nxumalo, Msimang and Cooke, 2003: 144–5), and fomenter of violence to this end, to bowing to the new political order reflected by the increasing power of the ANC in the new province of KwaZulu-Natal. His threats of action against critics, however, have not ceased. Despite Mzala's attempts to save Goodwill from responsibility, in his own right and not simply as a pawn in the scheme of Buthelezi, he was actively central to Inkatha in the 1980s and early 1990s. Since then he has actively, and expensively, continued to cement Zulu-ness as well as the territorial integrity of tribal authority and the Ingonyama Trust land holdings (on which Jacob Zuma also resides at Nkandla). In fact, King Goodwill has become active in extending his influence beyond the Zulu kingdom in strengthening traditional authority nationally. He prepares the way for the local equivalent of the Royal Bafokeng holdings in mining and not just boosting ethnic tourism as is already the case in KZN. As John and Jean Comaroff (2009: 1) have argued, 'while it [ethnicity] is increasingly the stuff of existential passion…ethnicity is *also* becoming more corporate'. In KZN it is not only the 'brand' – although that is everywhere – but also land and what can occur on it. The Comaroffs (2009: 12) draw attention to the brand, while Aninka Claassens and her colleagues argue for attention to what uses are planned on and under the land, but especially to the people located on it (CLS, 2014; Claassens, 2015). So, Thuto Thipe (forthcoming) asks 'how the democratic government has explained the spatial preservation of the former bantustans in a "new" South Africa', when 'boundaries of the former tribal authorities represented some of the crudest structural markers of racialised, tribalised inequality'. As justification she argues that the ANC government 'employs a history that presents tribal authorities as pre-colonial structures and then frames their retention as restoring the integrity of traditional leadership and governance institutions':

> That history…supports the idea of privileging traditional leaders' interests, or not emasculating them, by focusing on the structures that existed before colonialism without asking how these structures were distorted and traditional leaders' powers inflated under apartheid or, most importantly, how they serve people's interests in current contexts (Thipe, forthcoming: n.p.).

Lungisile Ntsebeza (2006: 257) writes that the legislation applying to the former bantus-tan areas, such as the Traditional Leadership and Governance Framework Act (TLGFA) (and the Ingonyama Trust Act, I would add), 'resuscitat[e] the powers they [traditional authorities] enjoyed under the notorious Bantu Authorities Act of 1951' – the Act that paved the way for the bantustans and that Buthelezi used in his consolidation of power.

Claassens (2015: 84) herself describes and analyses the process from 1913 to 2013, concluding that what is '[a]t stake is who controls the land rights of the 16.5 million peo-ple living in the former bantustans, and who profits from investment deals involving key mineral resources and valuable tourist land'.

The ANC post-1994 displays several ambiguities (deliberately using Shula Marks's [1986] term) in its rhetorical commitment to transformation of the apartheid past and attention to the 'poorest of the poor' (one of Buthelezi's own oft-used phrases), as well as policies and practices that increase inequality through support for the activities of a new bourgeoisie. Ethnicity and tribalism, under the guise of custom and a pre-colonial value and authority system, serves this trend very well. The National Democratic Revolution may be unfolding further, and the National Question may be in the process of being answered, but serious consideration of continuities and how to address them are mark-edly absent.

IN CONCLUSION

The ANC in power has been willing to ditch many previous principles and political commitments over the twenty-two years it has been in power. What is surprising is that nearly all relate to three important elements in the struggle against apartheid – race and racialism; capitalism in its core exploitative element; and the bantustan policy, with its reliance on notions of ethnicity, tradition and subjects (rather than full citizens). It is this last issue that has been the central concern in this chapter.

But why is an ANC government willing to increase the intensity of what Ntsebeza calls a 'dilemma' for itself? How is it possible to continue deliberately with the three dimen-sions of apartheid, in much the same form and with similar consequences? Answers have been argued for strongly in the case of ethnicity and its various presentations and existences – control over people and land, votes, and enrichment of segments of society. On a more abstract level, the National Question has largely stunted the imagination in thinking of alternatives. Ntsebeza (2006: 299) has, as an innovative example of an alterna-tive, 'proposed a new form of democracy for South Africa and elsewhere ... combin[ing] the participatory elements of pre-colonial indigenous institutions and the representative aspect of liberal democracy' – adding, importantly, that it would 'apply throughout the country, both urban and rural'.

It is to be hoped that Freund's (2008: 610) argument, against the assumptions of 'many doyens of African studies in the West' that 'ethnic identity is the motor force of political life', and that 'the fate of Zulu identity, a political force of national mobilization, shows the limits of such conjecture' proves to be accurate. I am less confident. Zulu ethnic social identity is simply too tempting to those who wish to mobilise against perceived threats and towards maintaining power, even if it should be less than national control. Mahoney (2012: 3) writes about much earlier periods in Zulu history: 'Zulu ethnicity and the Zulu king were the linchpins of the ideology of the [previous] movements led by the conservative elite.' That ideology now serves in control over and access to land and potentially access to votes, and tradition (in its malleable form) is credible currency within the National Question.

Directly and indirectly falling back on ethnicity puts paid to answering the National Question with racial solidarity, unless the answer incorporates some forms of tradition. And it demands another answer to growing inequality and divisions of gender, generation and nationality. Steven Friedman (2015: 194–9), in his intellectual biography of Harold Wolpe, raises the very important silence in theorisation and debates around Colonialism of a Special Type, the National Democratic Revolution and the National Question on the issue of gender and feminism. I have not explored the place of women in the material and social worlds of the previous and revived bantustans, but there is an extensive literature illustrating the additional burden borne by women under 'tradition'.

Why does traditional authority and Zulu ethnicity continue? The initial answer should be sought in the negotiations around the Constitution in a postcolonial African country and the (apparently unavoidable) compromises that it involved – in the pressures from the bantustans themselves (especially KwaZulu), from the acceptance of tribal/ethnic divisions within the ANC over the years, from the limited and limiting debate around the National Question, and more. However, in the twenty-first century it is impossible to imagine the rug of ethnicity being pulled from under the feet of a president with four current wives, a president who on many occasions wears leopard skins to show where his power lies, who expresses sentiments with regard to women and homosexuals that can be justified only by claiming conservative pre-capitalism as a model.

NOTES

1 In 2008 the author spoke at a protest meeting at the University of KwaZulu–Natal (UKZN) with Mac Maharaj. Maharaj tried, ineffectually, to convince the students that political victory over apartheid had been achieved, and that to claim ongoing victimhood and apparent lack of agency was counter-productive.
2 Jeffery (1997: 1) gives a figure of 11 600 killed in KwaZulu and Natal, with a further 25 000 or more injured. Many more were turned into refugees in their own province (Aitchison, Leeb

and John, 2010: 39–43). Jacob Dlamini (2011) writes: 'There are 25 000 people who died in the apartheid conflict in South Africa between 1960 and 1994. Of the 25 000, 16 000 were killed in the period 1985–1995 during clashes between supporters of the ANC and the Inkatha Freedom Party (IFP).'

REFERENCES

Aitchison, John, Wendy Leeb and Vaughan John (2010) *Political Violence in the Natal Midlands: The Unrest Monitoring Project Papers 1988–1994.* Pietermaritzburg: Centre for Adult Education, University of KwaZulu–Natal.

Alexander, Neville (1979) *One Azania, One Nation: The National Question in South Africa.* London: Zed.

Anonymous (Raymond Suttner, Jeremy Cronin and David Rabkin) (1983) Colonialism of a Special Kind and the South African State: A Consideration of Recent Articles. *Africa Perspective,* 23.

Beinart, William (2014) Verwoerd, Zuma and the Chiefs. Available online at http://www.custom-contested.co.za/verwoerd-zuma-chiefs (accessed January 2015).

Bunting, Brian (1991) An Obituary for Mzala. Available online at www.sacp.org.za/main.php?ID=2313 (accessed January 2015)

Buthelezi, Mangosuthu G (1990) *South Africa: My Vision of the Future.* London: Weidenfeld and Nicolson.

Buthelezi, Mbongiseni (2014) Fieldwork, Killing Time and Accidental Photographs. In *Uncertain Curature: In and Out of the Archive,* edited by Carolyn Hamilton and Pippa Skotnes. Johannesburg: Jacana.

Campbell, Catherine, Gerhard Maré and Cherryl Walker (1993) Evidence for an Ethnic Identity in the Life Histories of Zulu-speaking Durban Township Residents. *Journal of Southern African Studies,* 21(2).

Centre for Law and Society (CLS) (2014) Land Rights under the Ingonyama Trust. Pamphlet, August. Cape Town: Rural Women's Action Research Programme, University of Cape Town.

Claassens, Aninka (2015) Land, Law and Custom, 1913–2014: What is at Stake?. In *Land Divided Land Restored: Land Reform in South Africa in the 21st Century,* edited by Ben Cousins and Cherryl Walker. Johannesburg: Jacana.

Comaroff, John and Jean Comaroff (2009) *Ethnicity, Inc.* Pietermaritzburg: University of KwaZulu–Natal Press; Chicago: University of Chicago Press.

Cope, Nicholas (1993) *To Bind the Nation: Solomon kaDinuzulu and Zulu Nationalism 1913–1933.* Pietermaritzburg: University of KwaZulu-Natal Press.

De Kock, Wessel (1986) *Usuthu! Cry Peace: Inkatha and the Fight for a Just South Africa.* Cape Town: Open Hand Press.

Dlamini, Jacob (2011) The Death of Jacob Dlamini. Talk delivered at Nelson Mandela Foundation, 24 February 2011. Available online at http://www.saha.org.za/resources/docs/PDF/Projects/201102nmfdlamini.pdf (accessed December 2014).

Freund, Bill (2008) Zulu Identity in the International Context. In *Zulu Identities: Being Zulu, Past and Present,* edited by Benedict Carton, John Laband and Jabulani Sithole. Pietermaritzburg: UKZN Press.

Freund, Bill (2014) Nationalisms Inclusive and Exclusive: A Comparison of the Indian Congress Movement and the African National Congress of South Africa. *Transformation,* 86.

Friedman, Steven (2015) *Race, Class and Power: Harold Wolpe and the Radical Critique of Apartheid.* Pietermaritzburg: UKZN Press.

Guy, Jeff (1988) Battling with Banality. *Journal of Natal and Zulu History,* 18.

Guy, Jeff (1991) The Role of Ethnicity in the Homelands and Towns of South Africa. Paper presented at the International Conference on South Africa, Copenhagen, February 21–23.

Guy, Jeff (2001) *The View across the River: Harriette Colenso and the Zulu Struggle against Imperialism*. Charlottesville, VA: University Press of Virginia; Oxford: James Currey; Cape Town: David Philip.

Hamilton, Carolyn (1988) *Terrific Majesty: The Powers of Shaka Zulu and the Limits of Historical Invention*. Cape Town: David Philip.

Hamilton, Carolyn and Nessa Leibhammer (2014) Salutes, Labels and other Archival Artefacts. In *Uncertain Curature: In and Out of the Archive*, edited by Carolyn Hamilton and Pippa Skotnes. Johannesburg: Jacana.

Humphries, Richard, Thabo Rapoo and Steven Friedman (1994) The Shape of the Country: Negotiating Regional Government. In *South African Review 7: The Small Miracle: South Africa's Negotiated Settlement*, edited by Steven Friedman and Doreen Atkinson. Johannesburg: Ravan Press.

Institute for Industrial Education (IIE) (1974) *The Durban Strikes 1973*. Durban: IIE.

Jeffery, Anthea (1997) *The Natal Story: 16 Years of Conflict*. Johannesburg: South African Institute of Race Relations.

Mahoney, Michael R. (2012) *The Other Zulus: The Spread of Zulu Ethnicity in Colonial South Africa*. Durham and London: Duke University Press.

Maré, Gerhard (1992) *Brothers Born of Warrior Blood: Politics and Ethnicity in South Africa*. Johannesburg: Ravan Press.

Maré, Gerhard (1993) *Ethnicity and Politics in South Africa*. London: Zed.

Maré, Gerhard (1995) Ethnicity as Identity and Ethnicity Politically Mobilised: Symbols of Mobilisation in Inkatha. Unpublished PhD thesis, University of Natal, Durban.

Maré, Gerhard (2000) Versions of Resistance History in South Africa: The ANC Strand in Inkatha in the 1970s and 1980s. *Review of African Political Economy*, 27(83).

Maré, Gerhard and Georgina Hamilton (1987) *An Appetite for Power: Buthelezi's Inkatha and South Africa*. Bloomington and Johannesburg: Indiana University Press and Ravan Press.

Marks, Shula (1986) *The Ambiguities of Dependence in South Africa: Class, Nationalism, and the State in Twentieth-century Natal*. Johannesburg and Baltimore: Ravan Press and Johns Hopkins University Press.

Mawbey, John (2014) The Unresolved National Question in Left Thinking: Seeking Lineages and Hidden Voices. A draft concept paper commissioned by the Chris Hani Institute for the Workshop on the National Question under Apartheid, Hidden Voices: Unpublished Works 1950s to 1990, Johannesburg, 10–11 June.

McCaul, Colleen (1983) Towards an Understanding of Inkatha yeSizwe. SARS/DSG Dissertation Series 2. Johannesburg.

Mzala (Jabulani Nxumalo) (1988a) *Gatsha Buthelezi: Chief with a Double Agenda*. London: Zed.

Mzala (Jabulani Nxumalo) (1988b) Revolutionary Theory on the National Question in South Africa. In *The National Question in South Africa*, edited by Maria van Diepen. London: Zed.

Ntsebeza, Lungisile (2006) *Democracy Compromised: Chiefs and the Politics of Land in South Africa*. Cape Town: HSRC.

Nxumalo, OEHM, C.T. Msimang and I.S. Cooke (2003) *King of Goodwill: The Authorised Biography of King Goodwill Zwelithini kaBhekuzulu*. Cape Town: Nasou Via Afrika.

Nzimande, B.E. (2013) Foundation can help restore footprint of mercurial Mzala. *Sunday Independent*, 3 November 2013. Available online at www.iol.co.za/sundayindependent/foundation-can-help-restore-footprint-of-mercurial-mzala-1.1601249=VLY7X_wcMw

Phillips, Anne (2007) *Multiculturalism without Culture*. Princeton and Oxford: Princeton University Press.

Republic of South Africa (RSA) (1996) *Constitution of the Republic of South Africa,* Act 108 of 1996. Pretoria: Government Printer.

Sitas, Ari (n.d.) Class, Nation, Ethnicity in Natal's Black Working Class. Available online at http://sas-space.sas.ac.uk/4165/1/Ari_Sitas-Class,_Nation,_Ethnicity_in_natal's_black_working_class.pdf (accessed January 2015).

Smith, Jack Shepherd (1988) *Buthelezi: The Biography.* Johannesburg: Hans Strydom.

Temkin, Ben (1976) *Gatsha Buthelezi: Zulu Statesman.* Cape Town: Purnell.

Temkin, Ben (2003) *Buthelezi: A Biography.* London: Frank Cass.

Thipe, Thuto (2017, forthcoming) Bound by Tradition: Chieftaincy in a 'New' South Africa. In *Living Together, Living Apart,* edited by Christopher Ballantine, Michael Chapman, Kira Erwin and Gerhard Maré. Pietermaritzburg: University of KwaZulu–Natal Press.

Waetjen, Thembisa (2006) *Workers and Warriors: Masculinity and the Struggle for Nation in South Africa.* Pretoria: HSRC Press.

Zwelithini, Goodwill (2015) Zulu King's Call to Arms. *The Mercury,* 14 January 2015. Available online at http://www.iol.co.za/news/south-africa/kwazulu-natal/zulu-king-s-call-to-arms-1.1805077#.VLd1c_R5QYw.email

VARIATIONS ON A ZULU THEME

Ari Sitas

For Jeff Guy, Nafthal Mathiwane and Mvuse Mgeyane

There is a scientific and political imperative to stop thinking that a national consciousness is a deficit, some 'misrecognition' of interest or a distorted ideology. The historical idea of a belonging, a 'horizontal solidarity' to use Benedict Anderson's (1991) formulation, with its weaving together of territories, traditions and experience, is not as ancient as its narratives claim but it is a product of nation states and of hegemonic projects within specific boundaries. It received unique formulations in the colonial period of the late nineteenth century, particularly in racially structured settler societies such as South Africa's.

It is rather more to the point to ask what kind of consciousness it is, what its inflections are, and how it facilitates the emergence of non-racialism, anti-racism and class consciousness. By 'inflection' I mean that the national or horizontal comradeships it created differ in space and time: Cabral's articulation of the National Question is not Mobutu's, and what was articulated in *African Claims* in 1943 was not exactly what is being articulated now (Sitas, 1990; Hart, 2013).

Similarly, such horizontal solidarities are not merely a reaction to a structural constraint. There were many such constraints in the creation of South Africa's capitalist society: native reserves in the 1870s, pass laws in the 1880s, taxes culminating in the Poll Tax by the 1900s, the Union of South Africa and the Land Act by the 1910s, the Native Urban Areas Act and the Industrial Conciliation Act by the 1920s (Saul, 1979; Wolpe, 1990; Legassick, 1995; Mamdani, 1996; Guy, 1999) – all these cohered to define and construct the 'native', and as this construction was also 'tribal' the native's ethnicity was always at issue. Yes, such constraints were vital, but *agency* was and is important: it is equally vital to understand the emergence of the 'national idea' as an active, creative and ideomor-phic[1] narrative by those who were considered to be natives, and how these narratives came to use the jargon, a 'metanarrative' that is transmitted inter-generationally (Sitas, 2010). There is no one correct articulation of the 'national'.

Such an imaginative construction by the generation of the 1880s to the 1920s was trans-ethnic and involved a decisive shift from the 'native' to the 'African'. In its sym-bolic figurations it spawned parallelisms, inflections and ruptures. In this chapter, I will explore these three processes.

Parallelisms are discordant distances from existing movements that create alternatives but remain within the metanarrative of the original movement; they usually peter out. For example, in the period of the 1880s to the 1920s there were resistances to the national commonality of Africans; there were Zulu as much as there were Sotho particularisms. Although the Bambatha Rebellion has been used as a marker of a national rebellion against colonial and settler rule, nuanced studies show it to be a specific rupture in the politics of accommodation in KwaZulu-Natal (KZN) (Guy, 2006).

Inflections are shifting articulations and class biases within the main story. Competing voices give the national idea a specific character. For example, the way Clements Kadalie articulated the mission of the Industrial and Commercial Workers Union (ICU) in the Western Cape was not the same as the African nationalists of the day, nor was it the same as A.W.G. Champion articulated it in Durban and the Midlands. There was a different inflection to the story of 'national oppression'. The emergence of the labour movement as a class inflection within or a challenge without was at the heart of the KZN debates of the 1970s and 1980s.

Ruptures lead to the generation of new political formations. For example, the ICU started as an inflection that could have led to a rupture, but did not. The 1920s version of Inkatha in Natal could have, but did not (Marks and Trapido, 1987). The Zulu intelligent-sia of the 1940s and 1950s did not, but Inkatha and the Black Consciousness Movement (BCM) of the 1970s did (Hirson, 1979; Maré and Hamilton, 1987; Mzala, 1988; Pityana, 1991). None of them, however, can be understood outside the shifting inflections of the 'narrative.'

The formation of Inkatha was ab initio an attempt to create an inflection within the dominant tradition of the African National Congress (ANC). Chief Buthelezi solicited remarkable degrees of assistance from Jordan Ngubane and Joe Matthews, as much as he received it from Rowley Arenstein and Rick Turner (Arenstein, interview, 1984).[2] The ANC's Morogoro resolution in 1969 stated that the African working class was to lead the national democratic revolution. This created untold tensions with the emerging trade union movement.

The explosion of isiZulu orality and performance in the labour movement[3] challenged everyone deeply, but it did lead to violence and multiple ruptures in the Inkatha project.

Class played a significant articulatory role in creating parallelisms, inflections and ruptures, but class experience was dialectically shaped by them.

To understand such shifts in the symbolic figurations of nation, race and class and how they create parallelisms, new inflections or ruptures demands a careful analysis about how intellectuals crafted the range of possible imaginaries. A corrective has been Ntongela Masilela's (2012, 2013) project over the last fifteen years to define the intellectual sources of what he called the New African Movement from 1900 to the 1960s, and to collect and archive all the variations and emphases of a literate stratum of intellectuals that have in the main been ignored in South African social science (see also Couzens, 1985). His commitment to show the rich array of ideas, though, tends to bend the stick the other way: the differentiation of all this output into twenty-six clusters is wonderful archiving work, but there is no possibility of arriving at which was dominant and which was defining in national or class politics.

The question has to be asked the other way around: in looking at the black working class, its organisation and its forms of consciousness, what were the dominant ways the 'nation' was articulated in its formal and informal expressions? What can the historical record tell us? How does all this find expression in the political organisation of the South African Native National Congress, the African National Congress, the Indian Congresses, the Communist Party, the Pan Africanist Congress, the Inkatha Freedom Movement and the Black Consciousness Movement?

In this short chapter I will plumb the historical record to show, firstly, what I mean by parallelism, then by inflections within the dialectic of race, nation and class, and finally deal with rupture. It should throw some light on the backdrop from which national and class figurations are made possible in the contemporary period.

The attempts to formulate a hegemonic narrative of a horizontal comradeship weave narratives that combine the above five elements in different ways to achieve a discursive unity. These attempts, and the mobilisation of people around them, lead to parallelisms, inflections and ruptures.

PARALLELISMS

Let us take KwaZulu-Natal. The words native, black, African, Zulu, Indian, worker, and in isiZulu the words *bantu mnyama, izwe, inkhululeko*, Afrika, Zulu and *abasebenzi* find articulation from the days of the formation of the first pockets of a wage-earning class in Durban – at the railways and public works, in labour-tenant arrangements on the white farms, and later in the sugar cane plantations as black workers supplanted Indian indentured workers. If we take the period between the Bambatha Rebellion and the decline of the ICU, there was a great gap between what was being articulated by the emerging Zulu intelligentsia and the working class. But it was bridged, as Helen Bradford (1988) and Nicholas Cope (1997) showed; there was a disturbance among African labour tenants which the ICU was able to capture.

From our oral history records,[4] before and during the First World War there was a revival of African Christian ferment in the province. It was a re-run of the 1890s when Ethiopianism sent shock waves through the colony (Etherington, 1978). This time around, it was led by people like Cekwane, a peripatetic preacher who trained others to preach in their own locales (Mbelu, interview, 1989; Sitas, 2004). The congregations consisted of families that moved in after the Bambatha Rebellion, looking for land and labour tenancy arrangements (Zondi, interviews, 1986–87, 1989). They all learned the craft of the *imbongi*, the poet or praise-singer – although the imagery was rooted in oral biblical traditions, the formal expressions were a direct continuity with the Zulu past (Sitas, 2004). These refugee households, with their extended families, cattle and animals, were 'chief-less'. They shared much with other labour tenants on the same farm, but waited each Sunday for further connections linked to their prayer and sermon gatherings.

The ICU was particularly successful in inserting itself between labour tenants' grievances, white farmers' intransigence and attempts at evicting farmworkers. In a few years in the 1920s, the trade union's Natal membership was equally spread between town and country, and numbered more than 60 000 members (Simons and Simons, 1969; Wickins, 1978; Webster, 1979). However, it declined rapidly thereafter because, in the words of the Mbelu patriarch and his sons, they were 'swindlers' – they just 'wanted our money' (Mbelu, interviews, 1985, 1986, 1987, 1989).

Enter some class analysis: Leo Kuper (1965), in his study of class formation in Durban, differentiated between two aspirant bourgeoisies. The first group made their money in small business activities, and were in the thick of urban location and 'native reserve' affairs (clubs, burial societies, cooperatives, private enterprises, the traditional medicine trade and the like). The second group gained their position and status through education, and were concentrated in the professions and in the networks of the emerging political class which saw itself as the vanguard of a *national* consciousness.

Although mission-educated, Champion belonged to the former group and found fault with the latter. By the time he was asked by Clements Kadalie to become the ICU's Natal organiser, he was well ensconced in Johannesburg's black middle-class and white liberal networks, and enjoyed some of their patronage. He set about organising a serious presence in Natal. He was an anti-communist, and was at the forefront of ridding the ICU of communists in 1927. As a small businessman, he felt that the fraternity between the nationalist group and the Indians was idealistic, and saw himself in direct competition with Indian traders whom he wanted out of the way. For him, the Inanda moment of the Dubes and the Gandhis was far-fetched. In town it was Zulu against Indian, and the black working class was both a customer and a source of savings. It was trade unionism as a source of savings that animated his first steps as an organiser for the ICU. He could move between the worlds of the educated and the practical.

When the national office challenged Champion's leadership and activities, he played the ethnic card and led a Zulu split to form ICU yase Natal. He succeeded in retaining allegiance on an ethnic basis but lost it rapidly when he provided no socio-economic improvement for labour tenants and farmworkers. The decision to split the union coincided with his great effort to get closer to Zululand chiefs and headmen, to mobilise for a Zulu fund and, at the same time, to challenge the trans-ethnic nationalists who were getting worried about the machinations of John Dube towards a shift to what we have termed parallelism (Tabata, 2009). Champion's shift to a Zulu-centric nationalism did not mean an abandonment of trade union and location politics (Maylam, 1983; Marks, 1986; La Hausse, 1987). Indeed, he was banned after the disturbances of 1929–1930, and was removed to the Transvaal.

But whereas this self-identified Zulu petit bourgeoisie was close to black workers on a daily basis, the *amakholwa* and educated kept a safe distance. Their mission was the upliftment of the urban and rural masses from backwardness. This had a parallel process in the Indian community in the immediate post-Gandhi period, as a new middle class was trying to economically, socially and culturally uplift the workers who were moving into town after forty years of indenture (Marks and Trapido, 1987; Hughes, 2011).

Most important was the crafting of a national idea that combined elements of African-ness and Zulu-ness, and the construction of a version of Zulu-ness with Shaka as the epicentre of a Napoleonic ambition to unify Africans (Hamilton, 1998). Through that, a vision of the Zulu kingdom as the midwife of African solidarity and consciousness emerged with palpable force. The story of Bambatha came to define the consciousness of his real and metaphoric children. The real ones were the Zondi people who lost land and had to enter into wage or labour-tenancy agreements in the Midlands. Lawrence Zondi would be a direct descendant, labour tenant, proletarian, Sarmcol worker, militant of both the South African Congress of Trade Unions (SACTU) and the Metal and Allied Workers Union (MAWU) and, most importantly, an *imbongi*. The metaphoric was the symbolic importance of Bambatha's defiance as a marker of rebellion (Marks, 1978). Later, the Bambatha rebellion permeated the self-identity of an educated middle class, and the idea of rebellion and the spear endure down the years.

In the decade before the 1920s, the real children of Bambatha did not lack the metaphoric. Christian metaphors and Zulu orature combined well in the gatherings of congregations, but also in ICU gatherings in the hostile terrain of white farms in the Midlands.

The work on nationalism based on Benedict Anderson's (1991) insights and articulations is limited. It correctly identifies the bearers of such ideas as a bilingual intelligentsia – Anglophone at the national level, vernacular at the local sites of mobi-lisation. Concentrating on print capitalism and the written word as the medium for the creation of such imaginings ignores creations in the world of sound: orature, spoken language and song. Furthermore, Anderson's work on articulation ignores the processes and rituals of such constructions. Here, the archive needs careful reading because no oral history of such processes has been undertaken. What we do have is material about the generation following the post Second World War period. The gatherings of the ANC, of the other Congresses and of the labour movement are within reach. Although most black workers who were active in the 1950s and 1960s have passed away or are elderly, we have enough descriptions to understand what was inscribed in the songs, the oral poems and the rhetoric.[5]

Noting such limitations, we can only say that the agonistic aspect of the *imbongi* tra-dition around the formation of the Zulu kingdom, which centred around the praises of uShaka and the addition of Bambatha as a metaphor for rebellion, co-existed with the trumpets around the walls of Jericho, the suffering and the *siyakhala* of life and its neces-sary martyrdoms. The richest source is the stories Gladman Ngubo (a labour movement poet of the 1980s and a shop steward) heard from his father, a farm worker and a member of the ICU and later SACTU. It becomes fascinating to imagine what was deemed to be seditious in the 1890s and 1900s, and what led to them being re-imagined as being sedi-tious in the 1920s.[6]

It is obvious if we look at a more 'stable' tradition that has endured since the days when Shembe had the vision of a utopian congregation and of an African Christianity – a boul-der's roll away from what John Dube was doing with his Ohlange School and Gandhi's Phoenix settlement. All of them tried alternatives on the margins of Durban, searching for their own utopian spaces. The traces of the defiant oral lore were there. As an elder of the Shembe Church told me in 1987, 'Jesus for the whites, Gandhi for the Indians and Shaka for the Zulus', but 'Shembe is for all' (Magwaza, interview, 1987). After the first humanist codas, the praise poem of Shembe reads like a militant tract of struggle, with all the agonistic elements of the heroic poetry of the Nguni with Shaka as its prototype (Gunner and Gwala, 1991: 56ff). Jericho is echoed by the monotone horns of the Shembe church; the men dance with shields and short spears; the syncretic mix of word, gesture and sound (Gunner, 1988) is a distant but intimate cousin of the orature of the children of Bambatha who joined the ICU in droves.

On the writer's side, Benedict Vilakazi's work was emblematic. His *Zulu Horizons* (Vilakazi, 1973), his articles and poetry were part of a trans-ethnic national narrative but with a strong Zulu inflection. Its yearning for a Zulu past was in severe tension with a sense of underdevelopment, tribalism and backwardness. The Zulu kingdom was pre-cisely an indigenous attempt at modernity and a Bonapartean revolution. Colonialism was a dangerous phenomenon: it was the harbinger of education and Christian values, but it was also about callous national oppression and loss of culture and land (Koopman, 2005: 70–1). Here comes the class inflection as a metaphor: the African nation was reduced to toilers and destitution for white advantage. In poems about this experience we find the machines of the mines grinding out misery.[7] Alongside Vilakazi's machines, there were the musical compositions of Caluza, decrying the Land Act and its consequent immiseration.[8] The distance between this intellectual cohort and the emerging self-defined Zulu traders was marked and, despite metaphor and sympathy, the distance between them and the working population, let alone people in rural homesteads, was enormous.

But Vilakazi marks another dimension. His poetry is a recoil from the 'national'. Not only does he write in isiZulu but he writes from Johannesburg as if he was in exile. At the same time, though, he refuses to write as if his roots are the Zululand of the Amakhosi north of the Tugela. His 'KwaDendanendlale' which celebrates the beauty of the Valley of a Thousand Hills defines the four cardinal points of his homeland – with its borders south at the Umkomaas River, east to the Ocean, west to the Drakensberg and north to the uThukkela River and the Ndokakusuka flats (which he associates with Shaka's homestead). Although he does not say it, it is so obvious that Natal is Zulu throughout, colonialism is a problem, and Christianity is a real threat to Zulu traditions (Koopman, 2005: 72).

By contrast, Herbert Dhlomo moves sentiment in the opposite direction. His is a voice closer to the emerging New African consciousness. Although his brother wrote extensively in isiZulu, he chose English as his medium and proceeded to define Africanist sentiment much closer to the ideas the ANC Youth League would eventually adopt (Couzens, 1985; Sitas, 1994). His 'Valley of a Thousand Hills' is full of mellifluous rhyming but it is an undoubted statement of a colonial rejection and the stirring of a postcolonial idea (Couzens and Visser, 1985). The contrasts between the two poets are remarkable. Vilakazi's is the sensitive cry of pain and endurance, Dhlomo assumes the mantle of speaking for the 'masses mute', urging them to rise. For him, the contours of his nation-scape is South African and African (Sitas, 1994).

INFLECTIONS

The idea of class emerged through the tension between everyday experience of waged life and a sense of discord at the place of work, which often turned to an 'us' and 'them' and sometimes poured into strikes and informal ways of resistance. This led to forms of associational life, cooperatives, burial societies and in some cases the most sustained form of class organisation – trade unionism. Race was a constitutive factor that stopped white workers from permitting the organisation of black workers into trade unions. White trade unions entrenched job reservation and assented (in the main) that Africans as 'tribal' people should be excluded from the definition of 'employee' under the Industrial Conciliation Act of 1924.

Whereas this was seen in a positive light by customary leaders and chiefs in Zululand, Champion and his cohort emphasised the autonomy of class and the independence of trade unions. At the same time, he was aware that the customary authorities could buttress the resilience of black trade unions, have their members' homesteads looked after, pool worker savings for the creation of a Zulu fund, and use the Zululand reserve as the backbone of an economic project of self-reliance. His open talk of the exploitation of black people (Champion, 1982: 31) went hand in hand with the need to revive the Zulu kingdom. What he abhorred was the 'class talk' of the communists who were beginning to have some sway in the urban politics of Durban. He felt they were using the access his union was providing to dilute his project (Champion, 1982: 37).

I do not share the postmodern idea that class is a 'construction' among other 'constructions' of collective selves. Our science tells us that it exists as a structural constraint which in its material compulsions gets people to kill for access to a wage or livelihoods, and that those who accumulate do so on the basis of that biological need. How it is brought into language is a remarkable reworking of the main narrative. It occurs in struggle, in gatherings and in demonstrable experience that it is articulated through and despite the broader constructions of the national. Once again, constraint is one side; how people and workers create an imaginary of an 'izwe' does not drop out of a theoretical page, nor does it involve a spasmodic response to structure.

Milling, food processing and clothing were definitely the preserve of Indian workers and so was Dunlop, the first mass-producing rubber and tyre factory in Durban (Freund, 1995; see also Swanson, 1976; Hemson, 1979, 1996; Freund and Padayachee, 2002). The Communist Party of South Africa (CPSA) had made serious inroads in all these spaces by the 1930s, and managed to extend its influence in areas such as stevedoring (Hemson, 1996). By then, the CPSA's Native Republic thesis of 1928 allowed it to operate in class and national terms, as the struggle for a Native Republic was seen as an important stage on the road to socialism. This thesis, formulated a year after the expulsion of communists from the ICU, did not succeed in creating class unity nor could it exercise much influence over the direction in which national ideas were flowing. The stevedores, for example, were drawn from places as far-flung as northern Natal and Pondoland. They defined a robust Zulu-centric idea of ethnicity and class, and through the leadership of Zulu Phungula defined a tradition that spoke to people who were Christian and non-Christian, Zulu or Xhosa, but used the agonistic tropes of the Zulu epic and oral poetry to construct their militancy (Mdlalose, interview, 2006). This grass-roots ferment, instead of bridging any gap between them and Indian workers, achieved the opposite – it made them available to mobilisations against Indians in 1949 (Webster, 1978; Nuttall, 1991).

So as the Communist Party was making inroads into both Indian and African working-class communities, it lost its ability to create a common Afro-Indian class consciousness among the rank and file.

The year 1949 was a key turning point. The violence of that year resulted in an emotive split between those who strengthened their sense of Zulu-ness and their distance from Indians and whites (Ukpanah, 1993), and those who thought that the violence was a ruse of divide and rule by whites, and who looked for points of transcendence and ways to heal the rifts (personal communications, Phyllis Naidoo, A. Docrat and N. Mdlalose). The latter group bifurcated further. There were the humanists who tried to link the national idea with a common cause with the Indian community; they emphasised the importance of Gandhi and the traditions of Seme, Dube and Gumede. There were also the communists, who tried to keep alive the idea of a Native Republic; they also started extolling the value of Gandhianism. The latter group included members of the radicalised ANC Youth League who wanted action and a transformation of the African National Congress into an *African* National Congress.

Champion fronted the first trend. He was to lose. Luthuli captured the support of the other two groups as the best possible compromise. The syncretic mix of Gandhianism and Christianity was one side of Luthuli's appeal; the other was his openness to action and his strong belief that the apartheid government was a culmination of settler evil (Luthuli, 1961; Bhana, 1997).

The Luthuli era crystallised what the 'national' was: the Freedom Charter. However controversial and maligned by Africanists on the one hand and liberals on the other, it held sway and was endorsed in 1956 by the African National Congress. How such debates influenced the robust politics of everyday location life and the strong working-class sub-cultures of informal settlements is subject to debate (Ladlau, 1975; Edwards, 1988). For the South African Communist Party (SACP) the content of the 'national democratic revolution' – that is, the first necessary stage before socialism, the second stage – was to be the fulfilment of this. The achievement of this was to be the fulfilment of the national democratic revolution by the SACP. It was an idea that combined multiracialism, equality and freedom. By implication the culture-form of nationalism was diverse between African, coloured, Indian and white.[9] It was to be another fifteen years before the appellation 'African' would come to extend to other groups (Lambert, 1985).

This period signifies the clearest African nationalism in KwaZulu-Natal, with the scales tipping away from any Zulu-centrism. The 'trauma' to be fought against was colonialism, segregation and apartheid. Proletarianisation and dispossession were a shared fact, and the alliance between the ANC, SACTU and the Federation of South African Women (FEDSAW) was significant. By then the legitimacy lay not only in the founding moment of the ANC but also in the event of the Freedom Charter.

RUPTURES

The split of the Pan Africanist Congress from the ANC did not have enormous reper-cussions in Natal or Zululand. The Luthuli era slid into armed struggle. There were many authoritative oral accounts during the time of the repression of the early 1960s (Magubane, 2004). Let us start with the authoritative voices. Luthuli's banning and house arrest in Groutville did not stop him or his home from being an informal space for advice, thinking and consultation. Many of the Congress people who were freed after detention, or who received short sentences, kept the chief informed about politics. According to Mdlalose (interview, 2006): 'Perhaps we needed him much more than he needed us, but in the dark times we needed to feel that he was still in charge and that Congress was not dead.'

Although the first half of the 1960s appears to have been quiet, by the second half there were new stirrings. Black consciousness produced a rupture by the early 1970s, although some of its core ideas had been simmering since the mid-1960s (Stubbs, 1986). In Durban, artists and writers were beginning to articulate a black project (with African, coloured and Indian cooperation) after a rebellion against white patronage (Martens, interview, 1994; Badsha, interview, 2015). By the late 1960s, the black students of the University of Natal's Medical School, the Indian students at the University of Durban-Westville (UDW) and, most importantly, the University of Zululand students who were to be the new generation of anti-apartheid leaders, started finding voice and structure under the leadership of Steve Biko and others (personal communication, Bobby Marie and Strini Moodley, 1987). The language of a common oppression as blacks, the issue of English as the movement's lingua franca, the need for a psycho-cultural revolution, the rejection of the homeland system and their open attacks on Chief Buthelezi and his political and cultural project polarised the province (personal communication, Strini Moodley and Bennie Khoapa, 1992).

The creative success of black consciousness was enormous: the cultural associations of Durban, Hammarsdale and Pietermaritzburg with a plethora of radical plays, poetry and artwork was at the forefront (personal communication, Strini Moodley and Bobby Marie). Its spread through the university and the schooling system was rapid. By the 1970s, the idea of black emancipation was in competition with the ANC's strategy for lib-eration as articulated by the 1969 Morogoro Conference. Where it was not successful was in organising an alternative to the emerging trade unions of the 1970s, and keeping many of its stronger leaders within its fold once the ANC started resurfacing in the province. Dikobe Martins, Mafika Gwala, Diliza Mji, S'bu Ndebele, Terror Lekota, Sam Kikine, the Langa brothers, Tembeka Gwagwa, Brigitte Mabandla and Nozizwe Madlala were to lead in another way, but all of them started from the black consciousness ferment (personal communication, S'bu Ndebele, 1999).

The ferment in Natal obviously polarised black consciousness against the growing Inkatha Freedom Movement. The former was explicitly national in orientation and Anglophone in order to bring together all oppressed black people in the country; the latter was national in intention but Zulu in its symbolic and linguistic orature (Maré, 1992). One rejected participation in apartheid structures, and the other was totally involved in homeland structures. What is not obvious because of all the politicking in Natal and Zululand was that there were only two chiefs in Inkatha's central committee of more than a hundred people; indeed, its branches were purposely spread out to act as a counterpoint to the *amakhosi*. Furthermore, its Women's League became a powerful cultural epicentre in rural areas, and gave voice to the de facto backbone of the countryside when men were away working as migrants on the Witwatersrand and in Durban. These organisational efforts were buttressed by a version of ethno-nationalism that Buthelezi managed to construct. Its narrative combined a line running from Shaka to Cetshwayo, and placed Buthelezi himself as the titular, princely and hereditary prime minister of the royal line and a modernist.

What also needs to be said is that the 1960s were a period of rapid industrialisation. Durban's south was expanding rapidly, absorbing tens of thousands of migrants from Pondoland, dispossessed during and after the area's rebellion (Copelyn, 1974; Kepe and Ntsebeza, 2011). The Pinetown-New Germany complex started absorbing thousands of men and women in its metalwork and textile mills. The Mtunzini-Richards Bay-Empangeni belt was rapidly growing and absorbing black workers from northern Zululand. The decentralisation line running from Hammarsdale to Ladysmith and all the way to Newcastle started absorbing dispossessed farmworkers from the Midlands.

Then the 1973 strikes exploded and there was a strong belief that trade unions and their workplace resilience were going to create yet another rupture (Sambureni, 1977; Friedman, 1987). It remained merely a potential rupture, although it did create a real shop-floor tradition of democratic accountability. Nevertheless, the continuities with the Luthuli and SACTU era and its uneasy relationship with Inkatha continued. This focus on the 'point of production' was dismissed by networks linked to the Congress movement as 'workerism' – a characterisation that was simplistic, as it had many strands. The Non-European Unity Movement and a range of hybrids that developed away from Stalinist Marxism did not make a narrow 'point of production' argument. But there were others as well, because there were too many examples of how not to organise trade unions based on prior failures. The 'transmission belt argument' – that is, that trade unions had to be adjuncts to national independence movements and part of the post-colonial agenda – failed to deliver to workers in every case study undertaken in the broader African experience. Alongside that there was a critique that SACTU did not seek to advance workers' interests but sought to use their disaffection for non-working-class gains. There was also a mounting critique of bureaucratic and business unions in the West. Through all that, workers' control and democratic accountability became both a moral and practical argument in the regeneration of trade unionism in the post 1970s period.

Ruptures did lead to the Natal civil war from 1985 to 1995 (Morrell, 1996). It was precipitated by the split between Inkatha and the ANC in 1979 (Dhlomo, 1983; Marks, 1988). This created untold tensions in the trade union movement, exacerbated by the formation of an explicitly Charterist formation, the United Democratic Front (UDF). For a short while, 1979–1982, the Community Action Support Group in Johannesburg managed to keep the Charterist and the black consciousness traditions together in anti-apartheid activities. Already, there had been a split in the BC-inspired Black and Allied Workers' Union (BAWU) in Natal and the Eastern Cape to form the South Africa Allied Workers' Union (SAAWU), which was explicitly Charterist. So was the Food and Canning Workers' Union (FCWU); the Community Action Support Group had been founded around FCWU's Fattis and Monis strike.[10]

The leadership of the province was highly contested, but by 1991 Jacob Zuma emerged as the 'third way' – with the active support of the SACP and the Congress of South African Trade Unions (COSATU). He was seen as someone who could deal with Inkatha and end the carnage. He did, and he led the ANC's recovery in the province. In doing so, the language and imagery of this process mirrored Inkatha's conservatism and reading of history. Most commentators focused on Zuma's ideational populism and his evocations of Zulu-ness. What was ignored was a much subtler and ironic process: the use of Zulu-ness and the support of a highly organised working class to create an economic power bloc in the province; S'bu Ndebele, who was the founding Natal general secretary of the unbanned ANC and who was to become the first ANC premier in the province, had economic influence in and around Durban. He managed to create an inclusive *identity* politics – the African renaissance initiative – which combined black consciousness, Africanism, a modernising Zulu-ness, and an *amakholwa* sensibility with strong support among professionals. However, the Ndebele-centred initiative ignored the large dose of working-class and *amaqabane* workerism that was quite crucial to the Zuma bloc, who kept their distance believing that it was too close to Thabo Mbeki to survive his stewardship.[11]

Although the 1970s and 1980s produced ruptures, the ANC leadership in KZN managed for a while to be gargantuan – it could devour any nuance of 'we-ness'. If the cement between it and the masses was mixed around the promise of delivery, it could always deflect failure to the 'centre', the 'national'. According to key leader in the province:

> We were always committed to the RDP [Reconstruction and Development Plan]...We were always committed to a joint Economic and Social Council between government and labour...We even created a Workers' Parliament...that

is why we deployed Zuma back to the national ... to open up the prospects. But see what happened! (WM, interview, 2003).[12]

What was meant was that all kinds of ploys and set-ups were created to discredit and sideline Zuma. By deflecting failure to the national, the leadership could slide through multiple signifiers of the possible 'we' that constituted unity.

I argued during the height of the violence that there was a multiplicity of 'Zulu-nesses' at play in the province, that it was an unstable signifier that could be shifted to mean a range of experiences of dignity or prowess (Gunner and Gwala, 1991). It was not that it was used, it was how it was used to define a horizontal solidarity (Carton, 2008).[13]

The key link was the *amaqabane*, the heart of the 'comrades movement' in the 1980s (Sitas, 1992, 2010). They saw themselves as metaphoric *amakomanisi* even though many had not joined the unbanned Communist Party. They were the 'amaReliables' of the insurrection and the civil war. Such solidarities were extensive and culturally power-ful (Patel, 2005). It was not just an ethic of contingency, but a movement with poetics and nuance. I would not claim with Patel that they were the 'forgotten' after the transi-tion and the consolidation of the ANC, but they were at the core of its success. Samuel Mthethwa could reach the old Durban shop-steward councils, the Sydney Road workers and his Dunlop ex-workmates whom he had led for years, but also the rural homesteads of the Mthethwa clans all the way to Nongoma (Sitas, 1996). Don Gumede, son of Archie Gumede, Congress stalwart and ANC leader, could reach his ex-chemical co-workers and the *amakholwa* communities of Claremont and Chesterville.

New social movements in KZN had little purchase in such comradeships, although they managed to gain support from disaffected Inkatha networks in the urban and peri-urban areas or in the shacks that mushroomed astride so-called Indian townships. Despite their progressive ideas (Desai, 2002; Ballard, 2005; Naidoo and Veriava, 2005; Pithouse, 2006), they had no substantive purchase in black working-class politics in the province. This is so in the organised and stable industrial worker constituencies and the large numbers of survivalist workers in the informal economy (Valodia et al., 2006; Valodia, 2007; Scully, 2012).

The responses of those proletarianised in KwaZulu-Natal, and those leaders from the 'native' community who tried to establish a distinctive project of resistance and/or accommodation, re-worked multiple versions of Zulu-ness, always in relation to a trans-ethnic national project. Some gripped the emerging labour movement and allowed it to define a sense of dignity and cultural prowess, some were too distant to make sense to workers' immediate needs. They varied in how they defined the historical subject of their narrative, and in how they defined the originary trauma of the 'fall'. They varied in how they defined the social foundations of their alienation, and most certainly in how they defined in-groups and out-groups.

CONCLUSION

In my usage of terms like parallelism, inflection and rupture I have tried to show how pliant the symbolic landscape of nationalism and ethnicity may be, and how a careful study of what is signified can help to decipher the nature of nationalism and its specific magnetism. I have also argued that the 1970s and 1980s created ruptures which have been re-absorbed by the ANC leadership in its drive to establish its hegemony in competition with Inkatha. The latest public appropriations of it by the Zulu royal house has at its epicentre the 'House of Cetshwayo' and the demand that all land belongs to its customary control. This is not the only appropriation on the rise in this mutinous province.

NOTES

1　Ideomorphic refers to subaltern ideas that are influential but do not become hegemonic (Sitas, 2007).
2　Arenstein claimed that both he and Turner were involved in the drafting of Inkatha's Constitution.
3　See the Culture and Working Life Project Archive, and in particular the 1990 Dunlop Workers' Drama video recording in the Killie Campbell Africana Library, Durban.
4　Interviews conducted by the Natal Workers' History Project, 1983 to 1988.
5　The Culture and Working Life Archive is in two parts. One is with the Killie Campbell Library in Durban and includes ninety videos of actual rehearsals, performances and mass meetings. The rest is still being catalogued and digitalised, and is in my possession. This includes documents, transcripts and writings.
6　Discussions with Gladman Ngubo.
7　Vilakazi's (1973) *Zulu Horizons* has a very good translation of the poem *Ezinkomponi*.
8　Zondi (2011) has a fine analysis of the experience of mine work and its meanings in the poem.
9　Neville Alexander's critique that this was multiracialism and not non-racialism is apt.
10　I was part of this group as the link between politics and cultural/performance work.
11　Whereas the initiative displayed an olive branch to Inkatha by having a representative from it as a trustee, there was a marked absence of any of the key Zuma supporters save Mike Mabuyakhulu.
12　The Economic and Social Council was the provincial version of the National Economic Development and Labour Council (NEDLAC). It made sense in an Inkatha-led province because the Economic Development Department was controlled by the ANC.
13　See also my unpublished manuscript, 'The Flight of the Gwala-wala Bird', which is available at www.Arisitas.org.

REFERENCES

Anderson, Benedict (1991) *Imagined Communities*. London: Verso.
Ballard, R. (2005) Social Movements in Post-apartheid South Africa: An Introduction. In *Democratising Development: The Politics of Socioeconomic Rights in South Africa,* edited by P. Jones and K. Stokke. Leden: Martinus Nuhoff.

Bhana, S. (1997) *Gandhi's Legacy: The Natal Indian Congress: 1894–1994*. Pietermaritzburg: University of KwaZulu-Natal Press.

Bradford, Helen (1988) *A Taste of Freedom: The ICU in Rural Africa, 1924–1930*. Yale: The University Press.

Carton, Benedict (2008) Introduction: Zuluness in the Post- and Neo-worlds. In *Zulu Identities: Being Zulu, Past and Present,* edited by Benedict Carton, John Laband and Jabulani Sithole. Pietermaritzburg: UKZN Press.

Champion, A.W.G et al (1982) *The Views of Mahlathi*. Durban: Killie Campbell Library.

Cope, Nicholas (1997) *To Bind the Nation: Solomon Kadinizulu and Zulu Nationalism, 1913–1933.* Pietermaritzburg: University of KwaZulu-Natal Press.

Copelyn, J.A. (1974) The Mpondo Revolt. B.A. Honours dissertation, University of the Witwatersrand, Johannesburg.

Couzens, Tim (1985) *The New African: A Study of the Life and Work of H.I.E. Dhlomo.* Johannesburg: Ravan.

Couzens, Tim and Nick Visser (1985) *Collected Works of Herbert Dhlomo.* Johannesburg: Ravan.

Desai, A. (2002) *We are the Poors: Community Struggles in Post-apartheid South Africa.* New York: Monthly Review Press.

Dhlomo, O.D. (1983) The Strategy of Inkatha and its Critics. *Journal of Asian and African Studies,* 18:(1–2): 49–59.

Edwards, I.L. (1988) Mkhumbane Our Home: African Shantytown Society in Cato Manor Farm, 1946–1960. Unpublished PhD thesis, University of Natal, Durban.

Etherington, N. (1978) *Preachers, Peasants and Politics in Southeast Africa: African Christian Communities in Natal, Pondoland and Zululand, 1835–1880.* London: Royal Historical Society.

Freund, William (1995) *Insiders and Outsiders: The Indian Working Class of Durban, 1910–1990.* Portsmouth, NH: Heinemann.

Freund, William and V. Padayachee (2002) Durban: Structures from the Past, Pressures in the Present, Prospects in the Future. In *Durban Vortex: South African City in Transition,* edited by W. Freund and V. Padayachee. Pietermaritzburg: University of KwaZulu-Natal Press.

Friedman, Stephen (1987) Building Tomorrow Today: African Workers in Trade Unions, 1970–1984. Johannesburg: Ravan.

Gunner, Elizabeth (1988) Nazaretha, Power House, Prison House: An Oral Genre and its Use in Isaiah Shembe's Nazareth Baptist Church. *Journal of Southern African Studies,* 14(2).

Gunner, Elizabeth and Mafika Gwala (1991) *Musho! Zulu Popular Praises,* Michigan: Michigan State University Press.

Guy, Jeff (1999) *The Destruction of the Zulu Kingdom,* second edition. Pietermaritzburg: University of KwaZulu-Natal Press.

Guy, Jeff (2006) *Remembering the Rebellion: The Zulu Uprising, 1906.* Pietermaritzburg: University of KwaZulu-Natal Press.

Hamilton, Carolyn (1998) *Terrific Majesty: The Powers of Shaka Zulu and the Limits of Historical Invention.* Massachusetts: Harvard University Press.

Hart, Gillian (2013) *Rethinking the South African Crisis: Nationalism, Populism, Hegemony.* Pietermaritzburg: University of KwaZulu-Natal Press.

Hemson, David (1979) Class Consciousness and Migrant Workers: Dock Workers of Durban. Unpublished PhD thesis, University of Warwick, United Kingdom.

Hemson, David (1996) In the Eye of the Storm: Dock-workers in Durban. In *The People's City: African Life in Twentieth-Century Durban,* edited by P. Maylam and I. Edwards. Pietermaritzburg: University of KwaZulu-Natal Press.

Hirson, Baruch (1979) *Year of Fire, Year of Ash.* London: Zed.

Hughes, Heather (2011) *First President: A Life of John Dube, Founding President of the ANC.* Johannesburg: Jacana.

Kepe, Thembele and Lungisile Ntsebeza (eds) (2011) *Rural Resistance in South Africa.* Leiden: Brill Academic.

Koopman, Adrian (2005) Benedict Wallet Vilakazi: Poet in Exile. *Natalia,* 35.

Kuper, Leo (1965) *An African Bourgeoisie: Race, Class and Politics in South Africa.* New Haven: Yale University Press.

Ladlau, L.K. (1975) The Cato Manor Riots, 1959–1960. Unpublished MA dissertation, University of Natal, Durban.

La Hausse, P. (1987) The Dispersal of the Regiments: African Popular Protests in Durban, 1930. *Journal of Natal and Zulu History,* 10: 77–101.

Lambert, Robert (1985) Political Unionism and Working Class Hegemony: Perspectives on the South African Congress of Trade Union, 1955–1956. *Labour, Capital and Society,* 18(2) : 33.

Legassick, Martin (1995) British Hegemony and the Origins of Segregation in South Africa. In *Segregation and Apartheid in Twentieth Century South Africa,* edited by William Beinart and Saul Dubow. London: Routledge.

Luthuli, Albert (1961) *Let My People Go: The Autobiography of Chief Albert Luthuli.* Johannesburg: Collins.

Magubane, Ben (editor) (2004) *The Road to Democracy in South Africa, vol. 1, 1960–1970.* Cape Town: Zebra.

Mamdani, Mahmood (1996) *Citizen and Subject.* Princeton: Princeton University Press.

Maré, Gerhard P. (1992) *Brothers Born of Warrior Blood: Politics and Ethnicity in South Africa.* Johannesburg: Ravan.

Maré, Gerhard P. and Georgina Hamilton (1987) *An Appetite for Power – Buthelezi's Inkatha and the Politics of Loyal Resistance.* Johannesburg: Ravan.

Marks, Shula (1978) *Reluctant Rebellion.* Oxford: Clarendon.

Marks, Shula (1986) *The Ambiguities of Dependence in South Africa: Class, Nationalism and the State in Twentieth-Century Natal.* Johannesburg: Ravan.

Marks, Shula (1988) Inkatha and Contemporary Politics., *Journal of Natal and Zulu History,* 11: 175–87.

Marks, Shula and Stanley Trapido (1987) *The Politics of Race, Class, and Nationalism in Twentieth Century South Africa.* London: Longman.

Masilela, Ntongela (2012) *The Historical Figures of the New African Movement, Volume 1.* Trenton, NJ: Africa World Press.

Masilela, Ntongela (2013) *An Outline of the New African Movement in South Africa.* Trenton, NJ: Africa World Press.

Maylam, P. (1983) The 'Black Belt': African Squatters in Durban, 1935–1950. *Canadian Journal of African Studies,* 17(3): 413–28.

Morrell, Robert (editor) (1996) *Political Economy and Identities in KwaZulu Natal.* Durban: Indicator.

Mzala (1988) *Gatsha Buthelezi: Chief with a Double Agenda.* London: Zed.

Naidoo, P. and A. Veriava (2005) *Re-membering Movements: Trade Unions and New Social Movements in Neoliberal South Africa.* CCS Research Report No. 28. Durban: University of KwaZulu-Natal Press.

Nuttall, T.A. (1991) Race and Nation: African Politics in Durban, 1929–1949. Unpublished PhD thesis, University of Oxford, United Kingdom.

Patel, Ruksana (2005) Fragmented Lives: A 'Forgotten Generation' in Post-liberation South Africa. Unpublished PhD thesis, University of Cambridge, United Kingdom.

Pithouse, R. (2006) Struggle is a School: The Rise of a Shack Dwellers' Movement in Durban, South Africa. *Monthly Review: An Independent Socialist Magazine*, 57(9).

Pityana, N. Barney (editor) (1991) *Bounds of Possibility: The Legacy of Steve Biko and Black Consciousness.* Cape Town: David Philip.

Sambureni, N.T. (1977) The Apartheid City and its Labouring Class: African Workers and the Independent Trade Union Movement in Durban, 1959–1985. Unpublished PhD thesis, University of South Africa, Pretoria.

Saul, John (1979) The Dialectic of Class and Tribe. In *Race and Class,* XX(4).

Scully, Ben (2012) Development in the Age of Wagelessness: Labour, Livelihoods and Decline of Work in South Africa. Unpublished PhD thesis, Johns Hopkins University, Baltimore, USA.

Simons, Jack and Ray Simons (1969) *Class and Colour in South Africa.* Harmondsworth: Penguin.

Sitas, Ari (1990) Ethnicity, Nationalism and Culture in Natal's Labour Movement. *The Societies of Southern Africa,* edited by the Institute of Commonwealth Studies, 15(38).

Sitas, Ari (1992) The Making of the Comrades Movement in Natal. *Journal of Southern African Studies,* 18(2): 629–41.

Sitas, Ari (1994) Traditions of Poetry in Natal. In Elizabeth Gunner *Politics and Performance: Theatre, Poetry and Song in Southern Africa.* Indiana: The University Press.

Sitas, Ari (1996) The Sweat was Black: Working for Dunlop. In *The People's City: African Life in Twentieth-Century Durban,* edited by P. Maylam and I. Edwards. Pietermaritzburg: University of KwaZulu-Natal Press.

Sitas, Ari (2004) *Voices that Reason: Theoretical Parables.* Pretoria and Leiden: Unisa Press and Brill Academic.

Sitas, Ari (2007) *The Ethic of Reconciliation.* Durban: Madiba Press.

Sitas, Ari (2010) *The Mandela Decade: Labour, Culture and Society in Post-apartheid South Africa.* Pretoria; Unisa Press.

Stubbs, A. (ed.) (1986) *I Write What I Like: A Selection of His [Steve Bantu Biko's] Writings.* London: Heinemann.

Swanson, M.W (1976) The Durban System: Roots of Urban Apartheid in Colonial Natal. *African Studies,* 35.

Tabata, Wonga (2009) *A.W.G. Champion: Zulu Nationalism and Separate Development 1965–1975.* Unpublished Masters dissertation, University of Pretoria.

Ukpanah, I.J. (1993) Yearning to be Free: Inkundla Ya Bantu (Bantu Forum) as a Mirror and Mediator of the African National Struggle in South Africa, 1938–1951. Unpublished PhD thesis, University of Houston, Texas.

Valodia, I. (2007) Space, Place and Identity: Political Violence in Mpumalanga Township, KwaZulu-Natal, 1987–1993. Unpublished PhD thesis, University of the Witwatersrand, Johannesburg.

Valodia, I., L. Lebani, C. Skinner and R. Devey (2006) Low-waged and Informal Employment in South Africa. *Transformation,* 60.

Vilakazi, Benedict (1973) *Zulu Horizons* (trans F.L. Friedman). Johannesburg: Wits University Press.

Webster, Edward (1978) The Durban Riots: A Case Study in Race and Class. In *Working Papers in Southern African Studies,* edited by Phil Bonner. Johannesburg: Ravan.

Webster, Edward (editor) (1979) *Essays in South African Labour History.* Johannesburg: Ravan.

Wickins, Peter L. (1978) *The Industrial and Commercial Workers Union of Africa.* Oxford: Oxford University Press.

Wolpe, Harold (1990) *Race, Class and the Apartheid State.* Trenton, NJ: Africa World Press.

Zondi, N. (2011) The Protagonists in B.W. Vilakazi's 'Ezinkomponi' ('On the mine Compounds'). *Literator,* 32(2).

INTERVIEWS

Rowley Arenstein, 1984.
Omar Badsha, 2015.
Alfred Magwaza, 1987.
Dikobe Martens, 1994.
Inos Mbelu, 1985.
Sons of Inos Mbelu, 1986, 1987, 1989.
Naphtal Mdlalose, 2006.
W.M., Interview and discussion, March 2003. W.M. was a member of the ANC's Provincial Cabinet and a Central Committee Member of the SACP.
Zondi, Lawrence,1986–87, interviewed by Debby Bonnin.
Zondi, Lawrence, 1989, interviewed by the author.

BLACK CONSCIOUSNESS AS NATIONALISM OF A SPECIAL TYPE[1]

Xolela Mangcu

THE NATIONAL QUESTION: SOME EPISTEMOLOGICAL CONSIDERATIONS

Even though this chapter is primarily an exposition of the black consciousness approach to the National Question, it is ultimately an exploration of what an alternative conception of this question might have been outside of its dominant framing within twentieth-century Marxism. This conceptual re-framing is in the spirit of the Rhodes Must Fall campaign that started at the University of Cape Town on 9 March 2015. After concerted mobilisation – and resistance – the students succeeded in having the university agree to the removal of the statue of Cecil John Rhodes. The statue came down exactly a month later, on 9 April 2015. Central to the demands of the students was a call for all inherited and accepted knowledge systems – including Marxism, non-racialism and black consciousness – to be the subject of renewed critique from the perspectives of black people, and black women in particular.

In the ensuing debates, students and staff have questioned the scientific rationality that informs both liberal and Marxist epistemologies. This rationalist epistemology, Kwame Anthony Appiah (2005) argues, can be divided into two categories. On the one hand is the hard rationalism that refuses to entertain anything that has no foundation in scientific fact. Opponents of the Rhodes Must Fall movement dismissed it as too focused on pain and emotion. And because race does not have such scientific validity, they have been insisting that it should be barred from political discourse.

Isaiah Berlin (2000: 22) pointed out that this argument harkened to the Enlightenment idea that solutions to social problems will be obtained 'by the correct use of reason'. The logic is that 'there is no reason why such answers, which after all have produced triumphant results in the worlds of physics and chemistry, should not apply to the equally troubled fields of politics, ethics and aesthetics' (Berlin, 2000: 22). But Appiah also describes an alternative way of thinking about the world, and about race in particular, which he calls 'soft rationalism'. This allows for the fact that identities are 'unlikely to be settled by uncontroversially factual considerations' (Appiah, 2005: 178). Or as Patrick Chabal (2012: 33) puts it, the 'inability to conceive of other beliefs, other rationalities, confines our abilities to make sense of what we observe'.

This rationality is in turn based on a particular conception of progress as the 'transition from segregation to integration, from race consciousness to race neutrality, mirrors movements from myth to enlightenment, from ignorance to knowledge, from superstition to reason, from the primitive to the civilised, from religion to secularism' (Peller, 1995: 76). But as Cornel West (1999) argues, by bracketing out black cultural perspectives, both liberals and Marxists fail to get at the questions of identity that have been at the heart of the black response to European modernity. This inability to conceive of these other rationalities or 'multiple modernities' (Comaroff and Comaroff, 2012: 11) lies at the heart of the all too common reliance on 'service delivery' as the shorthand for describing the troubles that ail South Africa's black communities in particular. I shall later argue that a national identity will elude us for as long as we continue to ignore the psycho-cultural dimensions of black people's historical experiences.

The operation of scientific rationality is particularly evident in the critiques of black consciousness by Marxists in both the African National Congress (ANC) and the Unity Movement – even though they fail the empirical tests required of such rationality. These rather strange bedfellows are equally critical of the 'racial' politics of the Black Consciousness Movement (BCM), or what is today often derisively referred to as its 'identity politics'. On the one hand, the ANC's Comrade Mzala lambasted the black consciousness approach to the National Question as follows:

> In regard to the nationalism of the oppressed nation which sometimes goes under the term Black Consciousness in South Africa, suffice it to say that it will, like any other nationalism, pass through various phases, according to the classes that are dominant in the national movement at the time. Each class has its own view of the national question ... However, to uphold retrogressive nationalism in the name of liberation, a kind of nationalism that breeds hostility between the workers of different nations or nationalities, at a time when their unity is in fact an immediate historical need of the revolution, can only be described as petty bourgeois national opportunism (Mzala, 1988: 54).

Nelson Mandela (2001: 39) also criticised the Black Consciousness Movement for its clannishness: 'In a cosmopolitan environment where common sense and experience demand that freedom fighters be guided by progressive ideas and not by mere colour, the ideology of the BCM remains embryonic and clannish.'

In his comprehensive critique of the ANC's approach to nationalism, Neville Alexander also castigated black consciousness as no more than an anti-white movement:

> ... although they vehemently deny that they preach an anti-white philosophy and insist they are not, and indeed cannot be, racists, they teach hatred of whites because in South Africa 'whites' are the oppressors. Only rarely does any exponent of Black Consciousness attempt in a public analysis to demonstrate why whites as such are oppressors (Alexander, 1979: 123).

It is worth spending time on Alexander's thought on black consciousness because he has of late been recruited to a particularly conservative critique of affirmative action at the liberal white universities. But he is also appropriated by some on the left to reject race as a primary motive force in South African society (Maré, 2014: 35). Even though Alexander (1979: 135) regarded race as a social construct, he still saw it as a form of false consciousness.

In his biography of Chris Hani, Hugh Macmillan (2014) shows how much the communist leader appreciated the Black Consciousness Movement, which he described as 'an illustration of black anger and frustration'. Not only did he see in the movement the kind of heightened consciousness that was needed for the political education of ANC cadres; he also saw in it a source of recruits for Umkhonto we Sizwe (MK), the ANC's military wing (Macmillan, 2014: 69).

Alexander was so convinced of the inevitability of a class-based, scientific approach that he even saw a silver lining in the banning of the Black Consciousness Movement in 1977:

> ... with such a class approach all vestiges of a two-nation theory will be swept away and replaced by that of a single nation in a non-racial, socialist democracy. Indeed, the banning of the movement cannot but be conducive to the rapid development of the theory (Alexander, 1979: 125).

The banning of black consciousness did indeed pave the way for a triumphant non-racialism in the 1980s. But then, as the saying goes, be careful what you ask for – you might just get it. The triumphant non-racialism led not only to the emergence of a black capitalist class but also those tribal identities that Biko and his colleagues had done so much to combat. It also led to a rationalist, technocratic discourse in which the nation is stripped of any cultural dimension. This is symbolised by the fact that in government the Department of Arts and Culture is regarded as the most junior department.

However, not all Marxists held on to the same conception of class. Guinea Bissau's revolutionary leader, Amilcar Cabral, questioned the privileging of class as a social category in the analysis of non-European societies as follows:

> Does history begin only from the moment of class and, consequently, of class struggle? To reply in the affirmative would be to place outside history the whole period of life of human groups from the discovery of hunting, and later sedentary and nomadic agriculture, to cattle raising and to the private appropriation of land. It would also be to consider – and this we refuse to accept – that various human groups in Africa, Asia and Latin America were living without history or outside history at the moment they were subjected to the yoke of imperialism (Cabral, 1979: 124–5).

Scholars are mostly indebted to the Italian Marxist Antonio Gramsci for the departure from the orthodox Marxist position that the complexity and heterogeneity of social forces can be reduced to class. As Gramsci famously and eloquently observed:

> ... the claim presented as an essential postulate of historical materialism, that every fluctuation in politics and ideology can be presented and expounded as an immediate expression of the structure (i.e. the economic base) must be contested in theory as primitive infantilism, and combated in practice with the authentic testimony of Marx, the author of concrete historical and political works (Gramsci, 1971: 403).

The leading Gramscian Marxist and race theorist of the late twentieth century, Stuart Hall, also rejected the narrow scientific rationality and crude reductionism of many Marxists. He argued:

> ... the actual social and political force which becomes decisive in a moment of organic crisis will not be composed of a single homogenous class but will have a complex social composition ... it is implicit that its basis of unity will have to be, not an automatic one, but rather a system of alliances (Hall, 1996: 26).

Crucial to that alliance building is culture, which he described as 'the actual grounded terrain of practices, representations, languages, and customs of any specific historical society' (Hall, 1996: 26). It is these 'national-popular' cultural practices that define how and whether class will emerge as the primary driver of change in any given society. Hall

(1996) thus argued that 'the relative crudity and reductionism of materialist theories of ideology have proved a stumbling block' to our understanding of the operations of racism. He pointed to the working-class racism that provided support for Afrikaner nationalism throughout the twentieth century as an example of the limitations of crude class analysis.

Ernesto Laclau and Chantal Mouffe (1985) extended the Gramscian de-centring of class by extending the Gramscian concept of hegemony even further. Class became one of many subject positions – and not necessarily the decisive one. They argued that the working class thus has to 'abandon its class ghetto and transform it into the articulator of a multiplicity of antagonisms and demands stretching beyond itself' (Laclau and Mouffe, 1985: 58). In their hands the concept of hegemony meant that social categories operate more in articulation with each other to create a collective will. Whether the working class would be the decisive force was thus an empirical question. Thus, Hall (1996) argued that in South Africa the dominant ideology of white supremacy made unrealisable such articulation between the interests of white workers and those of black workers. Steve Biko (2004: 54) wrote that 'the greatest anti-black feeling is to be found among the very poor whites whom the very class theory calls upon to be with black workers in the struggle for emancipation. This is the twisted logic the Black Consciousness Movement seeks to eradicate.' A better-known phrasing of the same sentiment is his reference to the improbability of an alliance with an archetypal racist: '[Liberals] tell us that the situation is a class struggle rather than a race one. Let them go to Van Tonder in the Free State to tell him that. We believe we know what the problem is and we will stick by our findings' (Biko, 2004: 99).

Very little or almost no attention has been paid by social scientists to the latter part of this formulation: 'We believe we know what the problem is and we will stick by our findings.' And yet it goes to the very heart of the epistemological question of who actually has the licence to define the social reality of a people's lived experience. The transgressive nature of black consciousness as a political and epistemological project was to turn the question of who has license on its head by privileging the world views of black people. The revolutionary appeal of black consciousness among all the black political movements in South Africa lies in what it does to validate epistemological questions that black people have been asking since their encounter with colonialism.

PROTONATIONALIST LONGINGS

These epistemological and ontological longings are best understood within the context of Eric Hobsbawm's (1990) approach to the nation. While Benedict Anderson emphasised the role of print-capitalism in the rise of the nation, Hobsbawm (1990) argued that this did not in and of itself explain why people should have sought this particular institutional form in the first place:

> ... one reason may be that, in many parts of the world, states and national move-ments could mobilize certain variants of feelings of collective belonging, which already existed and which could operate, as it were, on the macro-political scale which could fit in with modern states and nations (Hobsbawm, 1990: 46).

Hobsbawm describes these pre-existing feelings as protonationalism, and identifies two types. First there is supra-local protonationalism, or what we today call the Diaspora. As Siphamandla Zondi argues in this volume, pan-Africanism is an example of supra-protonationalism. But there are also sub-national protonationalisms that are character-ised by claims made by groups of people who, while conscious of their nationality in a provincial or regional sense, have no desire to form a national state. In South Africa these sub-national identities became the raw materials for the construction of the colonial/apartheid state's ideology of tribalism. Archie Mafeje (1971) famously argued that the concept of 'tribe', which had historically described a self-contained community with con-trol over a small geographic area, was, in the hands of colonialists, stretched to describe people living in vast regions. The fact that those people spoke similar variations of a lan-guage or practiced similar variations of a culture did not, in Mafeje's view, mean that they constituted a tribe in the historical sense. This expansion of the concept, helped along by the conquering regimes of people such as Shaka, created a Zulu 'nation' out of disparate groups of people in KwaZulu and Natal, and Xhosas out of the same heterogeneity fur-ther south.

While sub-national protonationalism as tribalism was articulated by a genera-tion of homeland leaders between 1976 and 1994, supra-local protonationalism was in the main preached by the African National Congress but more spiritedly by the Pan Africanist Congress (PAC). Interestingly, the Black Consciousness Movement had more of a Third World than a pan-Africanist outlook, influenced as much by Julius Nyerere, Aime Cesaire, Frantz Fanon and Stokely Carmichael as by the writings of Paolo Freire, whose concept of *conscientisation* became central to the movement's polit-ical methodology.

But, as I have argued in my biography of Steve Biko, in as much as black conscious-ness was influenced by the global 'shared text of blackness', the movement's antecedents are properly grounded in the history of African discourses within South Africa, going back to the early encounter with European colonial modernity in the second half of the nineteenth century. Thus the movement had elements of both the supra-local and the sub-national. I will argue below that a new civil religion must be constructed out of these protonationalist and sub-nationalist longings through what Biko called a 'joint culture'.

These protonationalist and sub-national longings can be seen in the mid-nineteenth century, in the writings of Tiyo Soga, South Africa's first black university graduate and an ordained minister. At the very same time that Marx and his contemporaries were rethinking European societies, Soga was leading discussions on African identity precisely because of the cultural impact of colonialism. Contrary to the crude materialism that would come to dominate the liberation struggle, Soga made a pointedly cultural argument in an article welcoming the formation of the newspaper *Indaba* in 1860:

> ... the deeds of a nation are bigger than its cattle, its money and its food.... did we not have nations? Where is their history? Where are their customs, both good and bad? Where are the views of past chiefs? Did we not have poets and who were they praising? Where is the history? (*Indaba*, August 1862).

Soga's choice of a pseudonym for his articles was *U-Nonjiba wase-Luhlangeni*, which his biographer Donovan Williams (1983: 150) translates as 'an enthusiastic enquirer into cultural origins'. This quest for historical and cultural origins would have been a burning issue for Soga because of the cultural nature of colonialism. Karl Polanyi described the impact of colonialism on its victims in similar cultural terms:

> ... not economic exploitation as often assumed, but the disintegration of the cultural environment of the victim is [then] the cause of the degradation. The economic process may, naturally supply the vehicle of the destruction, and almost invariably economic inferiority will make the weaker yield, but the immediate cause of his undoing is not for that reason economic; it lies in the lethal injury to the institutions in which his existence is embodied. The result is a loss of self-respect, and standards, whether the unit is a people or a class... (Polanyi, 1957: 157–8).

Soga's inquiries into origins were not limited to South Africa. In another article, this time responding to a racist piece by his childhood friend, John Chalmers (who wrote that Africans were indolent and bound for extinction), Soga came to the defence of African people with examples from other parts of the world:

> Africa was of God given to the race of Ham. I find the Negro from the days of the Assyrian downwards, keeping his 'individuality' and his 'distinctiveness', amid the wreck of empires, and the revolution of ages. I find him keeping his place among the nations, and keeping his home and country. I find him opposed by nation after nation and driven from his home. I find him enslaved – exposed to the vices

and the brandy of the white man... I find him now as the prevalence of Christian and philanthropic opinions on the rights of man obtains among civilised nations, returning un-manacled to the land of his forefathers, taking back with him the civilisation and Christianity of those nations... looking forward to the dawn of a better day for himself and all his sable brethren in Africa (Soga, 1865: 39).

Joanne Davis (2012) has shown the personal networks that existed between Soga and the leaders of the pan-African movement. For instance, when he lived in Scotland he got engaged to Sara Weims, the daughter of Henry Highland Garnet, the leader of the Underground Railroad in the United States. Soga was in Scotland during Frederick Douglass's high-profile visit to that country. Davis borrows from Frank Ortiz the concept of transculturation to describe the influence of Africans in the Diaspora on Soga. In other words, the 'shared text in blackness' was not only local across generations but also transnational. This is the text from which African intellectuals in the Cape drew in developing what Chris Saunders (1973: 17) calls 'a new African Consciousness'.

While Davis's work is the closest anyone has come to locating Soga in the circle of other African intellectuals in the Diaspora, she does not offer any evidence of his inter-action with these individuals. Such a project awaits future researchers. It may reveal the influence of Africans in South Africa on the thinking of Africans in the Diaspora – that is, it may show the transcultural to have operated both ways, and thereby correct the exclusion of local Africans in Paul Gilroy's (1995) discussion of the Black Atlantic. By going into that archive, we can get a better sense of the local origins of Pan Africanism and its role in the conception of the nation in Africa as a supra-protonationalist imag-ining. Soga's defence of African culture has earned him the title of the father of black consciousness (Williams, 1978).

The quest for both supra-national and sub-national origins also continued among Soga's political and intellectual successors, though some of them would rather dissolve into the emerging European culture. Soon divisions emerged between the likes of John Tengo Jabavu, the proprietor of the first black newspaper *Imvo Zabantsundu*, and Walter Rubusana, the influential cleric and teacher at Peelton and later in East London, whose group included the likes of Allan K. Soga. This group would constitute the early founders of the South African Native Congress (SANC) in 1890. Rubusana articulated this supra-local vision as follows:

...the South African Native Congress's organisation is not complete; still it is already a power for good in the country, and will undoubtedly assume the posi-tion of the representative Native Association of the future (quoted in Odendaal, 2012: 145).

André Odendaal writes:

> ...from its formation in 1890, the SANC had clear national aspirations based on an African-centred approach to politics...From 1898 aspiration, opportunity and action converged to make possible the first concrete steps of a national movement. As its name, pronouncements and activities showed, the SANC, aimed to speak on behalf of all Africans throughout South Africa, and it came to have a direct influence in organisational politics in the other colonies (Odendaal, 2012: 210).

Odendaal highlights the syncretic nature of this new class as the Congress sought to balance African nationalist aspirations with 'Christianity, liberalism and African humanism' (Odendaal, 2012: 210).

But, as we shall see, Biko was not satisfied with this syncretism because he felt it always went in one direction:

> In our case this fusion has been extremely one-sided. The two major cultures that met and 'fused' were the African culture and the Anglo-Boer culture. Whereas the African culture was simple and unsophisticated, the Anglo-Boer culture had all the trappings of a colonialist culture and therefore was heavily equipped for conquest (Biko, 2004: 45).

I am not sure about 'simple and unsophisticated', and the influence was certainly not unidirectional. As Jean and John Comaroff (1991: 4) argue, as colonisers tried to impose Western modernity on the self-image of black Africans 'some people succumbed, some have resisted, some have tried to recast its intrusive forms in their own image'. While the succumbing and the resistance have been much documented, very little has been done on the recasting of colonial modernity by black people. And yet, as Comaroff and Comaroff rightly observe:

> ...in the long conversation to which [colonial evangelism] gave rise – a conversation full of arguments of words and images, many of the signifiers of the colonizing culture became unfixed. They were seized by the Africans, sometimes refashioned, put to symbolic and practical ends previously unforeseen and certainly unintended (Comaroff and Comaroff, 1991: 17–18).

But the general point about the unequal relationship between African and European culture is beyond dispute. As Biko (2004: 148) put it, 'this country looks...like a province of Europe. It has got no relationship rootwise to the fact that it exists in

Africa'. It is this inequality that S.E.K. Mqhayi sought to address by writing in his own language, thereby inviting the English to engage with him on his own terms (Schoots, 2012).

The quest for historical and cultural origins characterises Mqhayi's writings. He was arguably the most prolific and important African writer of the early decades of the twentieth century. In 1914 Mqhayi wrote the classic novel in isi-Xhosa, *Ityala Lamawele*, which presents African jurisprudence as centred more on reconciliation than on winners and losers. He wrote the novel *u Don Jadu* in 1929, which is one of the earliest literary expressions of a future South Africa with equal rights for men and women. A little-known fact is that Mqhayi wrote the bulk of South Africa's national anthem, *Nkosi Sikelel' iAfrica*. While Enoch Sontonga had first composed the song as a hymn with only two stanzas, Mqhayi added seven stanzas and published it as a poem titled 'Umhobe we Sizwe' (The National Anthem) in 1927. This subsequently became the national anthem of Tanzania, Zambia, Zimbabwe and Namibia. In addition to this own autobiography, *UMqhayi wase Ntabo Zuko*, Mqhayi also wrote the biographies of eminent leaders such as Elijah Makiwane, Walter Rubusana and John Dube. In *Long Walk to Freedom* Nelson Mandela writes that the day of Mqhayi's visit to his school at Healdtown was declared a public holiday. He describes Mqhayi's withering attack on British imperialism and how that changed his own perspective about white people as benefactors to whom he owed allegiance:

> Suddenly, the door [at the end of the school hall] opened and out walked not Dr Wellington [the headmaster], but a black man dressed in a leopard skin kaross and matching hat, who was carrying a spear in either hand. I could hardly believe my ears, his boldness in speaking of such delicate matters in the presence of Dr Wellington and other whites seemed utterly astonishing to us. Yet at the same time it aroused and motivated us, and began to alter my perception of men like Dr Wellington, whom I had automatically considered my benefactor (Mandela, 1994: 35–6).

The historian Colin Bundy (2012) describes how Fort Hare students such as Govan Mbeki, Epainette Moerane and Phyllis Ntantala regularly went to learn at the great man's feet in Ntabozuko, and Chinua Achebe (2013) lists Mqhayi alongside Amos Tutuola in the history of Africa's greatest writers.

These cultural themes were to be repeated by the group of young activists gathered around Anton Lembede and A.P. Mda in the ANC Youth League in 1943, and later around Robert Sobukwe when he led a break-away from the ANC in 1958. Sobukwe had first sounded his supra-local protonationalist ideas in the famous speech he gave as a student at Fort Hare in 1947. Then he had questioned the continued European domination and orientation of the university, calling for its transformation into 'a barometer of African thought'.

But contrary to the view that Africanism came into being with the Youth League, the strands of Africanist thinking can be found in earlier forms, particularly in the separatist Christian churches formed by the likes of Elijah Makiwane and Pambani Mzimba. As Odendaal (2012: 156) puts it, 'A wave of Africanist race consciousness swept throughout Southern Africa around the turn of the century'.

Like Sobukwe and Africanists before him, Steve Biko also lamented the neglect of African protonationalist longings in presentations of African history:

> We have to rewrite our history and produce in it the heroes who formed the core of our resistance to the white invaders. More has to be revealed, and stress has to be laid on the successful nation building attempts of men such as Shaka, Moshoeshoe, Hintsa. These areas call for intense research to provide some sorely-needed missing links. We would be too naïve to allow our conquerors to write unbiased histories about us but we have to destroy the myth that our history starts in 1652, the year van Riebeeck landed at the Cape (Biko, 2004: 105–6).

Biko viewed African culture as essential to an understanding of the nature of colonial oppression and exploitation. But even as he did that, he was acutely aware that he might be called 'essentialist' – even though that term might not have been in vogue yet. Anticipating such a critique, he wrote that culture 'emanates from a situation of common experience of oppression' (Biko, 2004: 50). African culture was necessarily a political culture that had 'withstood the bastardisation that came with colonialism', and was in subsequent years fused with Western culture to develop 'a culture of defiance, self-assertion and group pride and solidarity' (Biko, 2004: 50).

He concluded: 'I am not here making a case for separation on the basis of cultural differences; I am sufficiently proud to believe that in a normal situation Africans can comfortably stay with people of other cultures and be able to contribute to the joint cultures of the communities they have joined' (Biko, 2004: 50). It is this concept of the 'joint culture' that I believe it is at the heart of Biko's conception of a future nation. His position is not entirely consistent, however. At some points he speaks about a non-racial society in which individual identity will trump group identity, but at other points he seems to be advocating what we would today call a multicultural conception of the nation that has as its basis the recognition of group rights. He argued that the 'joint culture' would consist of both European and African experience because 'we have whites here who are descended from Europe. We don't dispute that. *But for God's sake it must have African experience as well*' (Biko, 2004: 148, own emphasis).

This rendition of African thought may appear to be too much of a seamless teleology, and that would be far from my intention. Any archive of African thought – or the 'shared text of blackness' – must of necessity include those African people who rejected the concept of race as the basis of the nation, and those who, from a Marxist tradition, saw it as secondary to class. But there is no questioning of the interpersonal relationships that existed among what was a small group of people in the small geographical area that is now the Eastern Cape, especially the area stretching between Alice, Fort Beaufort, King William's Town and East London. Alice became the centre of intellectual production because of the location there of the major educational institutions – Lovedale and the University of Fort Hare; Healdtown was in Fort Beaufort. These individuals moved to the growing industrial cities of King William's Town and East London where they became part of the small but influential black professional class consisting mainly of teachers, priests, journalists and court officials.

The appearance of a teleology could also be a result of the fact that African intellectuals often belonged to the same family and social networks and attended the same educational institutions, and would most likely have read each other's texts. Both Rubusana and Mqhayi wrote about the Soga family. As arguably the most influential cultural and literary figure of the time, Mqhayi became a source of inspiration for students at the University of Fort Hare. As an aspirant fiction writer and story teller, Sobukwe would have been influenced by Mqhayi. Biko's older brother Khaya was a leading member of the Pan Africanist Congress in the Eastern Cape. When Biko became a leader in his own right he met with Sobukwe a few times. This history of African nationalist thought is not so much teleology as it is what Paula Backscheider (1999: 210–27) described as the 'invisible lineage' of black history.

BLACK CONSCIOUSNESS AS A CIVIC REPUBLICAN IDEAL

The Marxist framing of the National Question has occluded investigations into this long history of thinking about the nation from African perspectives. As it is everywhere else in the world, the National Question in South Africa was framed in the image of Europe. As Europe moved towards a mass-based electoral politics, groups of people who had seen themselves as nations with provincial or regional identities now claimed sovereignty over much larger territories. According to Hobsbawm, nationalist movements around the world did no more than copy developments in Europe:

> The leaders and ideologues of colonial and semi-colonial liberation movements sincerely spoke the language of European nationalism, which they had so often learned from the west, even when it did not suit their situation. And as the

radicalism of the Russian Revolution took over from the French Revolution as the main ideology of global emancipation, the right to self-determination, now embodied in Stalin's texts, henceforth reached those who had been beyond the range of Mazzini. Liberation in what was yet not known as the Third World was now everywhere seen as national liberation or, among the Marxists, national and social liberation (Hobsbawm, 1990: 136).

This is in part the context for the importation of Joseph Stalin's (in)famous description of the nation into South African discourses. Stalin defined the nation as 'a historically constituted, stable community of people, formed on the basis of a language, territory, economic life, and psychological make-up manifested in a common culture'. But this conception of the nation could hardly have any applicability to a continent where national boundaries were drawn according to the interests of the imperial powers. European powers had gathered in Germany to slice up the continent in what became known as the 'scramble for Africa'. Adebajo (2010) writes that 'this epic drama involved squabbling colonial governments; devious explorers such as David Livingstone and Henry Stanley; vicious capitalist-politicians such as Cecil Rhodes and King Leopold; and sanctimonious Christian missionaries'. He concludes that it would be hard to find better examples of a single meeting that had such devastating political, socio-economic and cultural consequences for an entire continent.

Joe Slovo also criticised Stalin's linkage of the emergence of nations to a 'rising capitalism'. He pointed to the many nations (for example, Mongolia) that came into existence after the Second World War without having any roots in 'a new wave of rising capitalism' (Slovo, 1988: 144).

While Benedict Anderson (1983) emphasises the role of print-capitalism in the rise of the nation, Hobsbawm (1990) argues that capitalism does not in and of itself explain why people should have sought this particular institutional form in the first place. More importantly, Hobsbawm introduces collective *feelings* as the basis of nationalism:

> One reason may be that, in many parts of the world, states and national movements could mobilise certain variants of feelings of collective belonging, which already existed and which could operate, as it were, on the macro-political scale which could fit in with modern states and nations (Hobsbawm, 1990: 46).

In his later work, 'On the Goodness of Nations', Anderson (2011) argues that the enduring attraction of nations is in the manner in which they help individuals and societies make sense of the past, while also promising an innocent future. He also argues that, notwithstanding its chequered history, no other social formation has done more to secure human freedom:

> In the nineteenth century nationalism typically was found in popular move-ments against emperors, monarchs, and aristocracies, and nationalists in differ-ent regions regarded themselves as 'brothers' in a common struggle (Anderson, 2011: 109).

Ultimately, though, whether nationalism turns out to be bloody or a blessing depends on the political environment. For Appiah it is unhelpful to imagine nationalism away. What is more important is how to tame it:

> So nationality, for better or worse, has become a salient feature of the identities of modern men and women. However, the content of nationality – its meaning for each citizen – is the result of cultural work, not some pre-given commonality. That means there is a place for reflection in it: for working out, together, in the dem-ocratic spirit, what it means to be American or Ghanaian or, given where we are, South African. In doing this you will need some stories from the archive (Appiah, 2011: 107–8).

Appiah further argues that it is not so much what we have inherited from the archive that matters, but rather the interpretation of it in the present. He writes that 'the South African identity...like that of any living nation, is a work in progress. Its meaning will repose in an archive that remains to be written' (Appiah, 2011: 107–8).

The danger, as I have often argued, is that African nationalist leaders have too often claimed – and continue to claim – the right to be the sole authors and interpreters of their nations' experiences (Mangcu, 2008, 2011). In the process the victorious movements write history only in their own image. The claim to ownership of history is linked to a larger claim to the nation's resources. Ibbo Mandaza describes the behaviour of African nationalists:

> For African nationalists had – as their primary objective – and virtually as an end in itself – the need to inherit (State) power from the colonialists. In retrospect this was likewise the objective of the national liberation struggles in Southern Africa; the apparent adherence to an ideology devoted to (socialist) transformation dur-ing the armed struggle was merely expedient on the part of the leadership...so left to themselves the African nationalists – and their agenda and ideology – had no loftier goal than one of stepping into the coloniser's shoes, by inheriting the State and the (bourgeois capitalist) economy and, in general, the pursuit of

embourgeoisement, albeit in the vain hope that the majority, if not all of the people, would find the fullest fulfilment in the post-colonial dispensation (Mandaza,
2007: 6).

And if the people should show lack of appreciation of how much the postcolonial state
had done for them, then that same state is deemed to be within its rights to punish them
in order to send a lesson to everyone else. Mandaza (2007: 11) notes that as the colonial
state became increasingly unable to cope with the complexities of imposing its foreign
models on the local populace, it became 'more and more defensive, violent, autocratic'.

South Africa is the latest African country to see the state increasingly resort to violence
in response to protests. Joel Netshitenzhe argues that this has begun a vicious cycle of de-
legitimation of the state. Security agencies become the first line of attack for protesters,
but the spiral continues as the state responds in even greater measure.[2] The shooting of
protesting miners in Marikana stands as a tragic monument to this turn in the relationship between the state and the people in South Africa, and the xenophobic attacks on
foreign Africans as a reminder of nationalism gone terribly wrong. The question then is
not whether nationalism is good or bad but whether it is democratic and inclusive.

Nationalism's Achilles heel has been the extent to which it has rested on the subjugation of women. Not once does Biko address women's struggles. Neither have the other
nationalist leaders from other political parties, including those who have been running
South Africa since 1994. Nelson Mandela was notoriously anxious about participating in
public discussions of sexuality.

During his tenure as president, Thabo Mbeki introduced the idea of the African
Renaissance as the supra-national leitmotif of the new South Africa. Those of us from
the black consciousness tradition were first elated by the possibility that African protonationalist imaginings might become part of the official discourse of government.
Unfortunately, this project was dead on arrival because of Mbeki's inability to decentral-
ise it as the Black Consciousness Movement had done.

The strength of the Black Consciousness Movement lay in several aspects: the manner in which it had linked the supranational protonationalist idea, even though this was
tempered with a more Third World outlook; the national idea through the concept of
joint culture; and the sub-national protonationalism that peppered Biko's writings on
African culture. The movement's weakness, of course, was its inattention to questions of
gender and sexuality. Hence the irony of a movement that had women in political leadership positions while reproducing patriarchy in its social practices. Black Consciousness
was the first movement to elect a woman president when Winnie Kgware was elected
president of the Black People's Convention in 1971. The late Vuyelwa Mashalaba was
one of the most influential founders of the movement. Women leaders such as Debs
Matshoba, Nomsisi Kraai and Nombulelo Kobus were some of the leading voices of the

movement in the 1970s. In the Eastern Cape, the movement depended on the leadership of Mamphela Ramphele, Thenjiwe Mtintso, Nohle Mohapi and Pumla Sangotsha. These were often professional and highly educated women, which meant that their political leadership belied their social roles (this contradiction should be the subject of further inquiry).

To make black consciousness relevant it would not only have to create a new joint culture that confronts patriarchy. The new nationalism would thus not only de-centre class but also produce new processes of articulation, or what has more recently been called 'intersectionality', following the work of Kimberlé Crenshaw. One of the leaders of the Rhodes Must Fall movement at the University of Cape Town, Mbali Matandane, articulated the impact that new social movements are having on black consciousness:

> What I hope for is that people will look back at this movement one day and see how a small group of black feminists changed the politics of a black consciousness space – a space that has previously excluded these populations. They will remember how black women and members of the LGBTQIA [lesbian, gay, bisexual, transgender, queer, intersex and asexual] community became valued members of one of the most important movements in the university's history.

This is the archive of the nation that remains to be written by the young generation of women scholars and their male counterparts in these movements. In so doing they will hopefully bring alive a two hundred-year record of Black people have thought about the nation above and beyond the discourse of race and class. They must go to the works of their pioneers such as Nontsizi Mgqwetho, Phyllis Ntantala, Cissy Gool, Phyllis Naidoo and Vuyelwa Mashalaba.

The perspectives of these women can perhaps help us correct the abstract, rationalist modernism that continues to shape African nationalism. As bearers of culture in all of its complexity, women can perhaps help us understand what it would mean to move towards a cross-racial, anti-patriarchal joint culture. If it is to be enduring and meaningful, the idea of the nation must find its place in the hearts and minds of the people – not so much an economic process as a cultural process.

NOTES

1   I am indebted to Shireen Hassim for this formulation. I cannot say for sure that she meant it the way I have used it but it was attractive and appropriate enough for the purposes of a re-imagination of black consciousness and the nation in a way that centres the experiences and perspectives of women.

2   Joel Netshitenzhe, keynote address at the Mapungubwe Institute for Social Reflection Conference on 'The Role of Intellectuals in the State-Society Nexus', Liliesleaf, Johannesburg, 4 March 2015.

REFERENCES

Achebe, Chinua (2013) *There Was a Country: A Personal History of Biafra*. London: Penguin.

Adebajo, Adekeye (2010) *The Curse of Berlin: Africa and the Cold War*. New York: Columbia University Press.

Alexander, Neville (writing as No Sizwe) (1979) *One Azania, One Nation: The National Question in South Africa*. London: Zed.

Anderson, Benedict (1983) *Imagined Communities*. New York: Verso.

Anderson, Benedict (2011) On the Goodness of Nations. In *Becoming Worthy Ancestors: Archive, Public Deliberation and Politics in South Africa*, edited by Xolela Mangcu. Johannesburg: Wits University Press.

Appiah, Kwame Anthony (2005) *The Ethics of Identity*. Princeton: Princeton University Press.

Appiah, Kwame Anthony (2011) Identity, Politics and the Archive. In *Becoming Worthy Ancestors: Archive, Public Deliberation and Politics in South Africa*, edited by Xolela Mangcu. Johannesburg: Wits University Press.

Backscheider, Paula (1999*) Reflections on Biography*. London: Oxford University Press.

Berlin, Isaiah (2000) *The Roots of Romanticism*. Washington DC: Pimlico.

Biko, Stephen (2004) *I Write What I Like*. Johannesburg: Picador Africa.

Bundy, Colin (2012) *Govan Mbeki: A Pocket Biography*. Johannesburg: Jacana.

Cabral, Amilcar (1979) *Unity and Struggle: Speeches and Writings*. New York: Monthly Review Press.

Chabal, Patrick (2012) *The End of Conceit*. New York: Zed.

Comaroff, Jean and John L. Comaroff (1991) *Of Revelation and Revolution, Volume 1: Christianity, Colonialism and Consciousness in South Africa*. Chicago: University of Chicago Press.

Comaroff, Jean and John L. Comaroff (2012) *Theory from the South, or How Europe is Evolving toward Africa*. Boulder, CO: Routledge.

Davis, Joanne (2012) Tiyo Soga: Man of Four Names. Unpublished PhD thesis, Department of English, University of South Africa, Pretoria.

Gilroy, Paul (1995) *Modernity and Double Consciousness*. Cambridge: Harvard University Press.

Gramsci, Antonio (1971) *Selections from the Prison Notebooks*. London: Lawrence and Wishart.

Hall, Stuart (1996) Gramsci's Relevance for the Study of Race and Ethnicity. In *Stuart Hall: Critical Dialogues in Cultural Studies*, edited by David Morley and K.H. Chen. London: Routledge.

Hobsbawm, Eric (1990) *Nations and Nationalism since 1780: Programme, Myth, Reality*. New York: Cambridge University Press.

Laclau, Ernesto and Chantal Mouffe (1985*) Hegemony and Socialist Strategy*. London: Verso.

Macmillan, Hugh (2014) *Chris Hani: A Pocket Biography*. Johannesburg: Jacana.

Mafeje, Archie (1971) The Ideology of Tribalism. Journal of Modern African Studies, Volume 9, Issue 2, 253–261.

Mandaza, Ibbo (2007) Introduction. In *A Lifetime of Struggle*, by Edgar Tekere. Harare: Sapes Books.

Mandela, Nelson (1994) *Long Walk to Freedom*. New York: Little, Brown.

Mandela, Nelson (2001) In Maharaj, Mac (ed). *Reflections in Prison*. Cape Town: Zebra.

Mangcu, Xolela (2008) *To The Brink: The State of Democracy in South Africa*. Pietermaritzburg: UKZN Press.

Mangcu, Xolela (2011) *Becoming Worthy Ancestors*. Johannesburg: Wits University Press.

Maré, Gerhard (2014) *Declassified.* Johannesburg: Jacana.

Mzala (Jabulani Nxumalo) (1988) Revolutionary Theory on the National Question in South Africa. In *The National Question in South Africa,* edited by Maria van Diepen. London: Zed.

Odendaal, A. (2012) *The Founders.* Johannesburg: Jacana.

Peller, Gary (1995) Race Consciousness. In *After Identity,* edited by Dan Danielson and Karen Engle. New York: Routledge.

Polanyi, Karl (1957) *The Great Transformation: The Political and Economic Origins of Our Time.* Boston: Beacon.

Saunders, Chris (1973) Early Days: 1870–1900. In *Outlook on A Century: South Africa, 1870–1890,* edited by Francis Wilson and Dominic Perrot. Alice: Lovedale Press.

Schoots, Jonathan (2012) The Sociological Imagination of S.E.K. Mqhayi. Unpublished Master's dissertation, Department of Sociology, University of Cape Town, Cape Town.

Slovo, Joe (1988) The Working Class and Nation Building. In *The National Question in South Africa,* edited by Maria van Diepen. London: Zed.

Soga, Tiyo (1865) Defensor, Reply to Chalmers, *King William's Town Gazette and Kaffrarian Banner,* 11 May 1865.Varshney, Ashu (1993) Contested Meanings: Reconstructing Nations and States. *Daedalus, Journal of the American Academy of Arts and Sciences,* 122(3): 227–61.

West, Cornel (1999) *The Cornel West Reader.* New York: Basic Civitas.

Williams, Donovan (1978) *A Biography of Tiyo Soga, 1829–1871.* Alice: Lovedale Press.

Williams, Donovan (1983) *Umfundisi: The Journal and Selected Writings of Reverend Tiyo Soga.* Cape Town: Balkema.

POSTPONING THE NATIONAL QUESTION:
FEMINISM AND THE WOMEN'S MOVEMENT

Shireen Hassim

The 'Women Question' remains, arguably, the most unresolved in the history of democratic thought and practice in South Africa. In tracing the articulations of this question through the twentieth century and into the period of democracy it is evident that the dominant narratives of nationalist and class struggle relegated the demands for a society free of gender domination to a secondary status both in intellectual reasoning and in political projects. Although women were always participants in politics, it was only in moments of extraordinary mobilisation by women themselves that advances were made in defining an agenda for a good and just society in ways that referenced the particular, often-invisible conditions needed to liberate women. Indeed, the very idea of women's liberation was postponed to an indefinite future.

The subject of this discussion – women – is not definable without reference to a range of other markers such as class, ethnicity and race. The cultural meanings of 'woman' shift in relation to these markers of identity, and work in tandem with the ways in which capitalism mobilises ideologies of gender to normalise systems of economic exploitation. Although some women's movements, and some forms of feminism, have identified the elimination of patriarchy as the common interest of all women, patriarchy itself cannot be understood in ahistorical terms as separate from capitalism. Postcolonial feminists have argued that the ideological content of feminist consciousness should not be specified a priori according to abstract definitions. The archive of feminism, they argue, presents itself as universal but is indelibly marked by the specific historical trajectories of Western colonial-capitalist development. In this chapter, I therefore follow Chandra

Mohanty's (1991) advice and attempt to offer a discussion of women's struggles that is set not against a prescriptive test of ideological conformity but, rather, within the specific historical experience and political culture of South Africa. I suggest that as a working, open-ended definition feminism is the project of examining the particular ways in which power operates between the political, economic and social spheres. It is the complex interaction between these spheres that reveals how gender works to mark power and resource distributions.

The process of excavating theoretical and political archives that might offer up the imaginative components of a society that included women as full, equal and capable citizens involved – necessarily – a project of recovery. Women have been 'hidden from history', as Sheila Rowbotham (1975) argued. However, recovering alternative archives has proved to be both difficult, and insufficient for the project of transforming leftist thought. Despite a growing body of historiography of gender and sexuality, very few texts outside of feminist scholarship address gender power in their theorising. This lacuna remains puzzling, especially given the visibility of women in various political movements in South Africa. It seems a particularly retro comment to make in 2016 that most projects of theorising South African politics either ignore the vectors of gender and sexuality, or address them through a separate chapter on women.

I suggest that there are two reasons for this will to ignore. Firstly, the persistence of sharp distinctions between 'theory' and 'practice' pushes out of focus forms of understanding that are crafted in the messy, contingent and complex negotiations in families, households, workplaces and organisations. Archives of women's struggles do exist, of course, but are seen to be somehow separate from 'mainstream' archives. Rarely are the pamphlets and slogans of women's organisations accorded the status of theoretical interventions. Nor have the theorisations produced by the academic interlocutors of women's movements been treated as equivalent in leftist scholarship in South Africa to, for example, those of (male) working-class struggles. Women scholars have always been in the minority in the academy, and feminist scholars even more scarce. But that does not explain why the male left has not actively worked at integrating the work of its feminist comrades.

Secondly, problems of marginality of feminist insights are compounded by the extent to which the subject of male left theorising in South Africa tends to be a fixed, homogeneous category: worker, or black, or African. As I will suggest in more detail below, it is simply not possible to detach women's gendered struggles from their other markers of status and identities – that is undoubtedly the case for men, too (Cock, 1989). The argument about the entanglements of oppression is made powerfully by race theorists – not least Steve Biko – but frequently stops at theorising men as gendered and sexual subjects. For women, though, the effect is very particular: feminists reveal women and men as messy subjects who destabilise the certainties of socialist, black consciousness and nationalist analyses of South African politics. I would venture to say that this is the key explanation for why gender and sexuality are treated to obligatory but separate confer-ence panels and book chapters. The left simply does not know what to do with them. Yet surely we must agree that the continued deployment of fixed categories in theory impov-erishes all forms of theory.

The effects for political projects are very real. Women's participation in socialist and nationalist struggles paradoxically propelled their political agency and simultaneously restrained their abilities to imagine forms of liberation outside of the terms of male-dominated ideologies. Yet, the trajectories of struggle in South Africa have also shown how the containment of women's radical demands postponed the idea of the liberation of women and, at the same time, conceded ground to conservative approaches that could not stand up to the challenges of the post-1994 era. Consequently, we might be tempted to argue that despite the fact that the core demands of feminists were for substantive transformation, the post-1994 era saw gender equality redefined as formal equality and co-opted into new systems of ruling. Indeed, gender found its place in a government led by the African National Congress (ANC) not as a radical project but as the alibi for a thin form of state-managed social authoritarianism. That this emerging authoritarianism is unsuccessful must be ascribed, I argue, to a new form of feminism emerging outside the national liberation framing of debate.

I proceed by outlining the strands of feminist thinking in twentieth-century South Africa and then address the entangled alternatives: nationalism, equality and sexuality. Finally, I look at the ways in which the Women Question has played out post-1994 under a party in government that is, paradoxically, very much implicated in these multiple archives.

A CATALOGUE OF FEMINISMS IN SOUTH AFRICA

Elsewhere (Hassim, 2006) I identify four broad strands in the debates about women's lib-eration in South Africa – the Women Question approach, the radical feminist approach, the workerist position and the socialist feminist position. In retrospect, I would add two more. Although liberal feminism was only weakly developed in the mass movement, it laid out a manner of thinking about the dimensions of women's liberation that appears to have been adopted by the post-apartheid government. More recently, a sixth approach can be discerned which can be called 'queer feminism' as a shorthand term for a complex set of concerns.

Each of these approaches to feminism had strategic implications for the directions taken in political debate, and each produced forms of argument that clarified aspects of the complex formation of South Africa's political, social and economic institutions.

There were implications for political practice as well; in many instances the result was the formation of women's organisations with their own styles of work and their own agendas, as I will show below. These multiple approaches signal a thriving intellectual engagement with the realities of the bounded nature of feminist political practice. Despite the richness and complexity of the debates, these forms of theorising are thoroughly marginalised in the dominant narratives of political history, suggesting that simply making hidden histories visible does not necessarily achieve the political aim of deepening progressive agendas.

Liberal Feminism

The idea of universal political rights has a peculiar trajectory in South African gender politics. Women's suffrage was first raised by Voortrekker women in Natal, who argued that their participation in battles entitled them to equal rights with men. Although white women in the Cape had the right to vote on municipal matters (but not the right to stand for election), no women in South Africa could vote in national elections until 1930. The suffrage cause was taken up by white women almost immediately after Union, with the formation of the Women's Enfranchisement Association of the Union. The famous socialist and feminist Olive Schreiner was its first vice-president. However, the white suffragists' idea of universal rights did not extend to black people. When universal franchise for white people was introduced in 1931, it was directly tied to the diminution of the already small African vote, and eventually, by 1956, to the removal of the coloured franchise. The story of liberal equality for women was thus inextricably tied to race in South Africa, and the consequence was ironically that radical activists barely considered suffrage to be a key issue until the end of the twentieth century.

The Women Question in the ANC

The dominant position within the ANC until the 1980s was that the emancipation of women was secondary to and contingent upon national liberation. The task of women activists was to mobilise women for the broader struggle (Marcus, 1998). There were two tendencies within this position. In one strand, nationalism was emphasised as the primary concern. Frene Ginwala captured this position when she commented:

> In South Africa, the prime issue is apartheid and national liberation. So to argue that African women should concentrate on and form an isolated feminist movement, focusing on issues of women in the narrowest sense, implies African women must fight so that they can be equally oppressed with African men (Ginwala, 1986).

As I will show in the next section, this position was changed as more assertive forms of feminism gained traction in the ANC in exile and in women's organisations inside the country.

The other tendency within this broad categorisation was that of Marxist feminism. It followed the Communist Party approach that the struggle for liberation in South Africa was a two-stage struggle in which deracialisation of the bourgeoisie was the first aim and socialism the second stage. Women's liberation, it was argued, would only be achieved under communism, and until that point the national liberation struggle had to take precedence. Critics of the idea of women organising under a banner of feminism selectively invoked early twentieth-century socialist activists who were dismissive of feminism. For example, Rosa Luxemburg (1912: n.p.) worried that feminism was promoted by bourgeois women who were 'tools of the ruling classes'. As some feminists argued in the 1980s, this was a selective reading of Marxist archives. For example, Luxemburg had ended by quoting Charles Fournier that female emancipation was the 'degree and natural measure of the general emancipation'.

The radical feminist position

Radical feminism was always a relatively marginal ideology within the landscape of South African women's organisations. Nevertheless, it is discursively important in laying out the foundation for expanding understanding of the sources of women's oppression beyond class and colonialism. This position was primarily articulated by white feminists who worked to end violence against women, and especially to deal with rape survivors. Many radical feminists were based at university campuses, while others worked in the Rape Crisis Centres that were established in several city centres in the 1980s. A small number were also involved in anti-apartheid organisations such as the Black Sash and the Johannesburg Democratic Action Committee, which was affiliated with the United Democratic Front.

In the radical feminist understanding, the primary source of women's oppression lay in patriarchy, defined as an overarching structure of male power. Male-dominated organisations could thus not be trusted to advance women's interests. Women's organisations should be built as exclusively female organisations that would offer a safe organisational space to women. Such organisations would be characterised by a specific set of political values that included collective work, nurturing and mutual support.

The workerist position

Politically, the workerist position was articulated not in the space of the national liberation movements but in some trade unions. Indeed, it was distinguished by its rejection of nationalism as an ideological vehicle. In this strand of thinking, working-class women's organisations should be separate and autonomous from national liberation movements because women's demands would never be met by a nationalist movement dominated by the petty bourgeois interests of men. Women activists should associate themselves with the struggles of women workers and with the independent trade unions, and cross-class women's organisations should be of secondary importance. As with the Marxist feminists, it was argued that women's interests would ultimately only be met by the overthrow of capitalism.

The socialist feminist position

Socialist feminism was articulated most openly by women activists inside the country, many associated with the trade union movement and with the feminist media, as well as with some academics. A few activists in exile also self-defined themselves as socialist feminists. An early text, Olive Schreiner's (1911) *Women and Labour*, was extremely influential in Europe but surprisingly little known inside South Africa.

In this approach, women's organisations need relative autonomy from both the national liberation movement and the labour movement. That is, they should link women's struggles with national and workers' struggles while maintaining internal control over decision-making. Women's organisations should be shaped by a feminist approach that linked race and class to gender, and understood that women's interests were consequently also differentiated.

Queer feminism

This form of feminism emerged within public discourses on the left once the transition from apartheid began in the early 1990s. It was first associated with the progressive lesbian and gay rights movements of the 1980s and 1990s, which supported the ANC and sought to make sexual rights part of the liberation agenda. Their success in ensuring that sexual discrimination was a form of unfair discrimination significantly expanded and strengthened the equality clause in the Constitution. However, the ongoing violence against black lesbian women propelled a more explicit framing of anti-racist queer politics separately from mainstream politics.

Queer feminism focuses attention on the ways in which hetero-normative patriarchy intersects with race and class to fix people within a hierarchy of power. It draws attention to the problems with binary conceptions of gender, and argues that many women's organisations reproduce problematic conceptions of gender as entirely socially constructed. Queer feminism argues that power is embodied (literally and discursively) through ongoing processes of marking femininities and masculinities through violence. Rejecting that binary logic of male–female as the basis of either social identity of gender or biological category of sex, queer feminism destabilises the conceptual underpinnings of feminism. It argues for an intersectional approach that includes not only markers of inequality such as race and class, but also sexuality.

NATIONALISM AND SOME COMPLICATED ENTANGLEMENTS

As the catalogue of forms of feminism in South Africa demonstrates, there has been little consensus among women activists about the intellectual foundations of struggles for women's liberation or the appropriate forms of political organisation and mobilisation.

It is apparent that many of these framings took place in an entanglement with nationalism, and that the National Question acted as a kind of discursive master narrative. Women were not excluded from the nationalist struggle. On the contrary, they were invited into forms of collective agency and accorded political responsibility. They were treated as gendered political subjects.

Yet it has to be asked: what kinds of political subjects are possible within a nationalist framework? Feminism has always and everywhere been in a contestatory relationship with nationalism, and several scholars have shown why this is not surprising. Nira Yuval-Davis and Floya Anthias (1989) have provided a theoretically influential list of the ways in which nationalism is a gendered project:

- Women are the biological reproducers of nations and ethnic groups.
- The control of women's sexuality is central to the reproduction of the *boundaries* of groups.
- Women are positioned as the active transmitters (and sometimes producers) of national culture.
- National differences are symbolically signified through women.
- Women are active participants in nationalist struggles.

Yuval-Davis and Anthias argue that, for these reasons, nationalism cannot be studied outside of a theory of gender power. In particular, nationalism deploys ideas of the private into the public, centring the metaphor of family while eliding the differentiated power and interests within the family. It also deploys a particular language of unity that is resistant to dissident notions of the good society, that promote the redistribution of power in the public sphere of the state but also in the private spheres of the economy and family. Indeed, for some analysts in South Africa, the aim of nationalism was not so much to marginalise feminism as to silence it. By the end of the 1980s, the tensions were palpable between the mandarins in the ANC and internal feminism that was beginning to ask critical questions about whether national liberation would deliver a society that would address gender inequalities.

These differences came powerfully to the fore at the Malibongwe Conference held in Amsterdam in 1990. The conference presented the first opportunity for women activists inside the country and in exile to come openly into contact. At the cusp of the transition to democracy, it was a crucial event for addressing the shape of a post-apartheid society.

Analysing debates at Malibongwe, Charman, de Swardt and Simons (1991) conclude that the emphasis on national unity 'precluded a gendered analysis of both class and race in South Africa'.

A common defence of national liberation's approach to the Women Question is that nationalism itself was less a problem than its specific terms. The ANC's forward-looking, modernising nationalism is generally distinguished from, for example, Afrikaner nationalism. Deborah Gaitskell's and Elaine Unterhalter's (1989) comparative study of 'motherist' mobilisation in African and Afrikaner nationalism is emblematic of this approach. Zine Magubane (2009) makes similar arguments about the ways in which maternalism found progressive forms in the ANC. These readings suggest that even though nationalism has limits, these limits could be breached under certain circumstances. Favourable conditions for this include, for instance, whether there is an inclusive and porous understanding of the nation, whether there are democratic notions of equality in the framing of political demands by other political actors in a nationalist alliance, and the extent to which women are able to self-identify the content of their politics. Yet there remains a resistant kernel in nationalist politics, an inherent constitutive limit to the extent to which it can accommodate the full range of conditions necessary for women's liberation. I address these limits again below, in the section that deals with sexuality.

One last point needs to be made in relation to the tensions between the National Question and the Women Question. The pre-eminence of national liberation was by no means self-evident or inevitable. The catalogue of types of feminism provided in the previous section shows that alternative spaces existed in which feminists could locate their claims, and there are numerous examples of political movements among women that sought to pursue semi-autonomous paths. However, the hegemony of nationalism was an outcome of struggles within the left, one which reflected the persistent failure of male-dominated movements to address gendered inequalities.

SUBSTANTIVE EQUALITY

In this section, I want to note the idea of substantive equality as a commonly held idea across all of the variants of feminism described above. Substantive equality was understood as involving the removal of formal discrimination as well as positive interventions by the state to ensure that the systemic and economic bases of gender differentials would be eroded by the redistribution of public resources. The strength of these ideas can be plotted across several decades of debate within women's organisations, as I will show below.

I use three key texts to explore the conceptions of equality in the broadly defined women's movement. These are the two Women's Charters and the 1996 Constitution. The 1954

Women's Charter was drafted by the Federation of South African Women (FEDSAW), and the 1994 Women's Charter for Effective Equality by the Women's National Coalition (WNC). Although these two moments were very different in political, social and economic terms, the core idea of equality is surprisingly stable across five decades. Both documents understand equality to involve radical changes in the structure of society as well as in social and cultural relations. They note the complicities of the law in upholding inequalities, especially those in the private sphere, and demand the removal of the formal aspects of discrimination. Yet the demands go well beyond formal equality. In the 1954 Charter, for example, the demands include the rights to participation and representation in decision-making; full legal equality in respect of property, marriage and children; and the removal of legal restrictions on women's mobility. But, importantly, the document also addresses women as economic actors. It demands the right to work, and to equal pay for equal work. Recognising the disproportionate burdens of care that are placed on women as a result of the sexual division of labour, the Charter demands a radically redistributive approach to public policy including social provision of childcare, free education for all children and state provision of welfare services. The listing of custom and tradition as obstacles to the equality of women is also radical, in the sense that the drafters were prepared to name and tackle the private power of men.

This universalism was located in the vision of a modern society in which the traditionalist past would be superseded by a set of values that recognised the inherent equality of all citizens.

In 1994, the Women's National Coalition was more forthright in naming these practices as patriarchal when it stated that patriarchy was responsible for women's marginalisation.

The Charter also proposes stronger protection for women in the Constitution, demanding in Article 9 that 'custom, culture and religion shall be subject to the equality clause in the Constitution'. Article 7 calls for restructuring of traditional institutions in accordance with principles of equality, and demands women's right to participate in traditional institutions of decision-making and equal representation on traditional courts.

There are other significant shifts over the half-century in the ways in which equality was understood. The 1954 Charter was clearly hetero-normative in its framing of equality. It was assumed that the task was to be equal to men, both within families and in the public sphere. But the underpinning conception of families was that they were the product of conventional heterosexual relationships. The Charter paid attention to the destruction of tribal and kinship bonds as a result of the migrant labour system and urbanisation. It recognised that women had become wage earners in their own right, and wanted the reform of laws that rested on an older conception of women's status. The drafters were clear that while the traditional social structure of families had been disrupted, the protections offered to women in that system needed to be provided in other ways. Yet they do not offer any inkling as to their thinking about what alternative family and household systems might look like.

By 1994, these kinds of issues had been more widely debated – no doubt influenced by the intensification of urbanisation as well as the greater independence of women from traditional marriage and family systems. The 1994 Charter recognised the diversity of families, and includes a capacious demand that 'all family types have to be recognised and treated equally' as well as the right of all people to choose their partners. In various forms throughout the document, sexual and reproductive rights are introduced into the language of equality; these included the right to choose a partner and the 'right to decide in the nature and frequency of sexual contact within marriage and intimate relationships' (Article 8).

The 1994 Charter echoes its 1954 predecessor in calling for women to have equal rights in marriage, especially with regard to inheritance, property and the right to credit. This was a reflection of how little progress had been made in the intervening half-century with regard to women's formal equality. In 1994, modernity appears in the same political form as 1954, as a set of political rights claimed against the state, but this time it is a claim on the basis of human rights and democracy rather than the compromised idea of civilisation. The context is one in which a new Constitution was being drafted and new institutions of the state were being elaborated.

The Women's Charter for Effective Equality lists four principles that should underpin the state's provision of public services: social justice, equality, appropriateness and accessibility. The word 'effective' in the Charter's name was specifically chosen to describe the kind of equality envisioned: limited not just to political and legal equality but also to women's social and economic power.

New in the 1994 document was the inclusion of the strategy of affirmative action as a way of recognising and redressing disadvantages. This was part of the strategy for effective equality, by which was meant the equality of outcomes rather than the same treatment for all people. This position was strongly pushed by the ANC and its allies in the Women's National Coalition, and on several occasions it stood up to alternative framings by the Democratic Party which was keen to limit the demands in the Charter to political rights in the public sphere, leaving the family and economy out of the framing altogether on the grounds that these were beyond the state's sphere of influence (Hassim, 2006: 150).

Both documents see economic inequalities as substantially limiting any formal rights women may be granted. In 1954, the Women's Charter argued for women's right to work and equal pay for equal work, radical demands in the context of apartheid policies that sought to exclude women from the cities. The 1994 Charter recognised for the first time the impact of women's unpaid labour on their access to labour markets and on their gendered burdens in the household. It also noted the predominance of women in the precarious informal economy. The document makes significant links between the public and private sphere in other ways as well. For example, it considers that unless the power relations in households are shifted women will remain exploited and subordinate. Sexual and reproductive rights are one part of the solution, according to the Charter. The other is to ensure that 'all members of the household should endeavour to share in domestic labour' (Article 8) and that women should have access to household finances.

Several demands of the Women's Charter for Effective Equality were incorporated into South Africa's new Constitution in 1996. This was not achieved easily. The first draft of the Constitutional Principles, issued in May 1993, did not contain any explicit reference to the value of non-sexism, despite the numerous demands of gender activists. When the Women's National Coalition lobbied the Multi-Party Negotiation Process on the need to directly forbid sexism, the drafters stalled, arguing that a general clause on non-discrimination implied that non-sexism was valued. It was only when the Interim Constitution was finally presented to the Constitutional Assembly for ratification that the clause was finally included. This was due in no small measure to the concerted action of a substantial cohort of newly-elected women members of parliament.

The argument for an equality clause in the Constitution had an even messier political path. The Women's Charter for Effective Equality demanded that 'culture, custom and religion, in so far as they impact upon the status of women in marriage, in law and in public life, shall be subject to the equality clause in the Bill of Rights' of any new Constitution. But the WNC was thwarted by a coalition of traditional leaders, who were determined that their powers in areas under traditional authority should not be undermined. And although rural women were powerfully represented in the WNC by the Rural Women's Movement, traditional leaders in areas such as rural KwaZulu-Natal potentially had the capacity to foment unrest in an already fragile transition to democracy. The ANC convinced its feminist allies that it was committed to the reform of customary law and that it was 'simply a matter of implementing it in a politically less volatile environment' (Goldblatt and Mbatha, 1999: 104). The upshot was that in the final Constitution in 1996 rights to custom were allowed and gender equality was framed as a trump clause – precisely what the WNC had demanded. It seemed that implementation of the legislative reforms necessary to remove the second-class status of rural African women would proceed without a hitch. As subsequent developments were to show, the ANC proved to be an unreliable ally on this front.

SEXUALITY

The past two decades in South Africa have revealed a sharp schism in debates on gender rights. On the one hand, there is a category which might be termed 'virtuous' claims to equality – for example, demands for numerical increases in the representation of women in Parliament. On the other hand, claims to sexual rights and justice for people with non-normative sexualities, women living under the rule of traditional leaders and sex workers, have less purchase in the public sphere.

The narrative of democracy in South Africa is centred on a modernist idea in which the pinnacle is the formal sphere of the state and the Constitution. Remarkably – and paradoxically – despite the consensus about the importance of substantive equality in envisioning a free society, after 1994 ideas of formal gender equality began to dominate the strategies of political elites. The triumph of a form of feminism in South Africa that focuses only on access to places in institutional hierarchies is *the* instantiation of this modernist approach to containing the justice claims of women. These kinds of claims do not question the underlying structures of power in the relationships between citizens and the state – or at the very least they strategically suspend those questions. In South Africa, the outward manifestations of the state – personnel, institutions and policies – have been significantly stripped of their gender markers as a result. The numbers of women in the South African Parliament have steadily increased from nearly 28 per cent in 1994 to 35 per cent in 2014. By and large, this numerical increase in Parliament and government through the use of quotas has been relatively successful in disrupting the associations between maleness and political office.

The overall emphasis, in both representation and in interpreting the demands of equality in policy making, has been to use targets and quotas as the proxy indicator for women's empowerment. In that feminist strategy, women are positioned as a homogeneous and subordinate group, whose citizenship claims are encapsulated in a demand for equality of representation in already existing institutions of power. That is a modernist demand, in that it frames a demand for recognition in the context of the liberal democratic public sphere. From this perspective, social inequalities reflect the cultural lag between the democratic ideal of equality and the slowness of people to adjust their attitudes; it is a lag that will be resolved as institutions and norms spread more widely.

As Mohanty (1991) argues, however, this way of thinking about women in terms of their object status – how they are or are not affected by institutions and systems – does not confront the multifarious ways in which social categories of gender are constituted and reproduced. In order to grasp those dimensions of gender, a different kind of conversation is required. It should address the structures of meaning that link the public and the private spheres, and that address normative dimensions as part of a productive debate. This conversation should not be closed off by the insertion of an equality clause in the Constitution or the creation of group quotas but, rather, opened up by the recognition of women as persons. To recognise women as persons requires a recognition of their autonomy, individuality and agency – in other words, their capacity to act outside of the boundaries of nation.

But it is difficult to carve space for a conversation about the social without coming up against the difficulties of the politics of culture. And the experiences of the past two decades have suggested that cultural politics limits the space for feminist claims.

Two examples of contestations between feminists and their former ally – the ANC – illustrate the difficulties entailed in moving the project of equality beyond inclusion into existing institutions. One is the debate about the Traditional Courts Bill, and the other is the intractable problem of gender-based violence.

Thabo Mbeki and Jacob Zuma are frequently contrasted in journalistic analyses. Mbeki is characterised as the intellectual, modern Africanist committed to gender equality, while Zuma is portrayed as a traditionalist whose support for customary social relations is reflected in his personal choices. Mbeki certainly promoted women in Parliament and in his Cabinets, and during his time in office women advanced to the most senior positions. Indeed, it could be argued that by the time of the Polokwane Conference, the gender equality lobby was closely associated with the Mbeki faction in the ANC. When the chips were down, though, the ANC Women's League supported Jacob Zuma and were rewarded with the creation of a Ministry of Women and People with Disabilities. This was not sufficient, though, to ensure that women's demands for redistribution would be addressed. Under Mbeki's presidency, the innovative Women's Budget Initiative, which systematically tracked public spending on the reduction of gender inequalities, was shut down. This was a major setback for the feminist redistributive agenda, as without the hard economic instruments to measure progress women's demands were whittled down to the vaguest of 'good intentions'. The position worsened under the Zuma presidency. The introduction of the Traditional Courts Bill implied that even formal equality *between* women might be under threat, as black women living in tribal jurisdictions would have to contend with systems of governance in which they would have even fewer rights than under apartheid.

The other area in which the cracks in the ANC's commitments to substantive equality can be seen is in the area of gender-based violence. In the past two decades, gender-based violence has persisted at distressingly high levels, and it is prevalent across all economic and cultural boundaries. In particular, there has been an increase in crimes against black lesbians (Seedat et al., 2009), and the overwhelming evidence is that women are most at risk of attack by intimate partners (Vetten, 2007). Interventions at the legislative and policy levels have been minimally effective (Vetten, 2007). While the causes for the persistence of violence against women are complex and, to some extent, outside of the reach of the state, political leadership from the ANC has been weak. Instead of allying with feminists to drive a strong programme to counter the forms of male power that enable violence, both presidents have undercut real understanding and debate in the public sphere. Helen Moffett (2006) notes how Mbeki deflected public conversations about race by implying that feminists were caricaturing black men. Solidarities with black men became pitted against solidarities with women – an odd departure from the intersectional approach, the so-called triple oppression that had characterised ANC discourse in the past.

As an example, note the interchange in 2004 between Charlene Smith, a journalist who had herself been raped in 1999, and Thabo Mbeki. Smith (2004) was reporting on rape statistics released by the National Commissioner of Police in September 2004, which showed that the number of rape cases per 100 000 people had remained more or less static in the first ten years of democracy. Mbeki said Smith saw black men as 'barbaric savages': 'She was saying our cultures, traditions and religions as Africans inherently make every African man a potential rapist ... [a] view which defines the African people as barbaric savages' (Smith, 2004). Mbeki claimed that Smith stereotyped blacks. Whether Mbeki was misreading Smith is only part of the issue at stake. What he was giving voice to, and probably manipulating politically, was precisely the embeddedness of notions of rape in the marking-out of white supremacy. However, disempowering whiteness will not be sufficient to address the violent forms in which masculinity is articulated (not least because violence cuts across race and class).

Not only did Jacob Zuma do little to challenge this kind of discourse, he most certainly widened the gap between feminists and the ANC. In his rape trial, Zuma used arguments based on Zulu culture to justify his view that he was entitled to have sex with his accuser (Robins, 2008; Hassim, 2009). His widely reported statements in 2012 on the importance of motherhood and marriage for women added further evidence that a more conservative set of attitudes was emerging in government that would have an impact on the project of gender equality.

More women in Parliament, or a stronger Women's League in the ANC, have not staved off the rising conservatism. Indeed, at times the senior women leaders have been complicit in the discursive shifts. In August 2009, for example, the minister of women, youth and people with disabilities, Lulu Xingwana, walked out of an exhibition entitled 'Innovative Women' because it showed women in nude poses and various forms of love between women. Xingwana was offended at the exhibition, which she described as pornographic and immoral (Van Wyk, 2010). Although the exhibition was sponsored by Xingwana's government department and was part of the celebration of Women's Month, a series of activities held every year to honour the contribution of women to South African society, it clearly did not fit into the preconceived notion of what constituted virtuous female citizenship. Undoubtedly, the exhibition was unsettling to those for whom the narrative of democracy is twinned with the celebration of the presence of women in government. For them, to note the dissonances in democracy – the violence towards those who choose to live outside the given forms of gender, or who articulate intimacies that defy the pristine images of virtuous maternalist politics – is to disrupt the very core of the nation.

Twenty-two years after the party that was to represent the demands of women came to power, one stark fact remains constant. Women find themselves predominantly in the ranks of the poorest in society. The expansion of social grants by the ANC government, and particularly the introduction of the child support grant, has been a major poverty alleviation tool. However, it cannot compensate entirely for an economy with limited jobs and moreover one with large sections that are informal and outside of the regulations on working conditions that have been secured for formal sector workers. According to the National Planning Commission (NPC), women-headed households are more likely to be poor and, despite the virtual elimination of gender differentials in the quantity of education, continue to earn less than men. 'About 61 per cent of women live in poverty, and 31 per cent live in destitution, compared with 39 per cent and 18 per cent of men respectively' (NPC, 2011: n.p.).

As I have shown above, throughout the past two decades race and culture were invoked as rhetorical devices against the claims of women to the rights of personhood and autonomy. This is not accidental. Retaining the idea of women as central to the family and community is essential in an economy in which jobs are scarce and care needs are high. Women's unpaid labour within families is vital to sustaining households in crisis and, in a context of heightening food insecurity, the privatisation of the burden of meeting basic needs requires the normative underpinnings of conservative social values. When the delivery of important basic services such as accessible clean water, healthcare and affordable electricity is compromised, it is women who have to act as shock absorbers. The continued gender division of labour means that it is women who have to 'make do' for the household and community (Fakier and Cock, 2009).

Nowhere is this more glaringly apparent than in the rate of maternal mortality, a measure of the number of maternal deaths per 100 000 live births. It is a good proxy for measuring the quality of a country's healthcare system as well as the status of women in a society. The causes of maternal mortality may be immediately medical, but the underlying causes are a complex mixture of social, political and economic forces. This indicator relates to women's fundamental rights to health and life, and, from a feminist perspective, it is a good indicator of what difference it may make to have women in decision-making roles. After all, it is a gendered concern that should cut across differences such as class, race and ethnicity. It is also a developing country problem – 99 per cent of all maternal deaths occur in developing countries, with more than half occurring in sub-Saharan Africa. It is hard to think of a crosscutting gender issue that could be more important either to a government or to a women's movement. We know that when healthcare is paid out of household budgets, the health of women and girls is most at risk; they are the last priority for household spending on health.

Against the history of equality mapped in earlier sections of this paper, it is not unreasonable to expect that as women move into government they will have positive effects on healthcare spending. But the statistics show a different pattern – and we can read into them the complexity of making claims that there is a positive correlation between representation and outcomes. The line between the two – representation and outcomes – is broken in South Africa. Table 1 tells the story.

Table 1. Maternal Mortality Ratio (MMR) by five-year intervals

	1990	1995	2000	2005	2010
MMR for South Africa	250	260	330	360	300

Maternal Mortality Ratio (MMR) is the number of maternal deaths per 100 000 live births.
Source: http://www.childinfo.org/maternal_mortality_ratio.php

Outcomes matter for feminist politics. This single indicator shows the extent to which the failure to drive a redistributive project has affected the actual lives of women. The full story is doubtless more complex, and it is beyond the scope of this chapter to undertake an accounting of policy directions and implementation in democratic South Africa, but surely the maternal mortality ratio should give pause for thought.

CONCLUSION: DEMOCRACY AND POSTPONEMENT

The strongest legacy of the mobilisation of women in South Africa through the course of the twentieth century was the political consensus that not only should women have a greater voice in decision-making about public resources, but that those resources should be directed towards reducing the inequalities rooted in economic and social structures. That consensus is embodied in the Constitution. To be sure, one part of this relates to parity in representation, full legal equality for all, and a public commitment to the rights of women. But that was always understood among feminists inside and out of the ANC to be one side of the bargain; the other side was the redistribution of status and resources.

Yet the outcome of two decades of democratic rule has been the dismantling of that consensus in the face of economic pressures and the fight for political survival. Even though the ANC and its allies played a central role in establishing the normative consensus of the secular, universalist democratic value framework of the 1996 Constitution, it seems willing to trade this away for political survival in a brutal economic climate. Equality is espoused as a formal project of the state – a form of state-sponsored feminism – but its radical potential to enable women to be full citizens is undercut by its detachment from the complexities of power relations in society. What has happened in practice is what Nancy Fraser (1989) has shown so eloquently is happening in many parts of the world. Feminism has been reduced to liberal feminism, and the forms of feminism promoted (including by women) have proved to be remarkably friendly to capitalist democracy in the twenty-first century.

REFERENCES

Charman, A., C. de Swardt and Y. Simons (1991) The Politics of Gender: Negotiating Liberation. *Transformation*, 15: 41–64.

Cock, Jacklyn (1989) Keeping the Home Fires Burning: Militarization and the Politics of Gender in South Africa. *Review of African Political Economy*, 16 (45–46): 50–64.

Fakier, Khayaat and Jacklyn Cock (2009) A Gendered Analysis of the Crisis of Reproduction in Contemporary South Africa. *International Feminist Journal of Politics*, 11(3): 353–71.

Federation of South African Women (FEDSAW) (1954) *Women's Charter.* http://www.sahistory. org.za/topic/womens-charter.

Fraser, Nancy (1989) 'Mothers of the nation: a comparative analysis of nation, race and motherhood in Afrikaner nationalism and the African National Congress' in Yuval-Davis, Nira and Floya Anthias (eds.) (1989) *Woman-Nation-State.* Basingstoke: Macmillan.

Gaitskell, Deborah and Unterhalter, Elaine (1989) 'Mothers of the nation: a comparative analysis of nation, race and motherhood in Afrikaner nationalism and the African National Congress' in Yuval-Davis, Nira and Floya Anthias (eds.) (1989) *Woman-Nation-State.* Basingstoke: Macmillan.

Ginwala, Frene (1986) ANC Women: Their Strength in the Struggle. *Work in Progress*, 8: 12–15.

Goldblatt, Beth and Likhapha Mbatha (1999) Gender, Culture and Equality: Reforming Customary Law. In *Engendering the State: A South African Case Study*, edited by Catherine Albertyn. Johannesburg: Centre for Applied Legal Studies.

Hassim, Shireen (2006) *Contesting Authority: Women's Organisations and Democracy in South Africa.* Madison: University of Wisconsin Press.

Hassim, Shireen (2009) Democracy's Shadows: Sexual rights and Gender Politics in the Rape Trial of Jacob Zuma. *African Studies*, 58(1): 57–77.

Luxemburg, Rosa (1912) Women's Suffrage and Class Struggle. Available online at https://www. marxists.org/archive/luxemburg/1912/05/12.htm, accessed 25 June 2015.

Magubane, Zine (2009) 'Can we as Mothers Not Take Our Fight to the Enemy?': The Politics of Motherhood in South African Autobiography.' Cross Cultural Poetics: 48–75.

Marcus, Tessa (1998) The Women's Question. In *The National Question in South Africa*, edited by Maria van Diepen. London: Zed.

Moffett, Helen (2006) 'These women, they force us to rape them': Rape as a Narrative of Social Control in Post-apartheid South Africa. *Journal of Southern African Studies*, 32: 129–44.

Mohanty, Chandra (1991) Under Western Eyes. In *Third World Women and the Politics of Feminism*, edited by Chandra Talpade Mohanty, Ann Russo and Lourdes Torres. Bloomington: Indiana University Press.

National Planning Commission (NPC) (2011) [Title of article] http://www.npconline.co.za/pebble. asp?relid=123 (accessed 8 May 2014).

Robins, Steven (2008) Sexual Politics and the Zuma Rape Trial. *Journal of Southern African Studies*, 34(2): 411–28.

Rowbotham, Sheila (1975) *Hidden From History* [Publisher information?]

Schreiner, Olive (1911) *Women and Labour.* London: Unwin.

Seedat, M., A. van Niekerk, R. Jewkes and K. Ratele (2009) Violence and Injuries in South Africa: Prioritising an Agenda for Prevention. *The Lancet,* 374: 1011–22.

Smith, Charlene (2004) Rape has Become a Way of Life in South Africa. Available online at http://www.iol.co.za/news/south-africa/rape-has-become-a-way-of-life-in-south-africa-1.222663#.UmS_0BZVu2w.

Van Wyk, Lisa (2010) Xingwana: Homophobic Claims Baseless and Insulting. *Mail and Guardian,* 5 March 2010. Available online at http://mg.co.za/article/2010–03-05-xingwana-homophobic-claims-baseless-insulting (accessed 25 March 2013).

Vetten, Lisa (2007) Violence Against Women in South Africa. In *State of the Nation: South Africa 2007,* edited by Sakhela Buhlungu, John Daniel and Roger Southall. Cape Town: HSRC Press.

Women's National Coalition (WNC) (1994) *Charter for Effective Equality.* http://www.anc.org.za/content/womens-charter-effective-equality.

Yuval-Davis, Nira and Floya Anthias (eds) (1989) *Woman–Nation–State.* Basingstoke, UK: Macmillan.

WORKERISTS AND THE NATIONAL QUESTION

Alec Erwin

INTRODUCTION

The early 1970s saw the re-emergence of the non-racial trade union movement after decades of repression by the apartheid regime. Its sustained and effective effort carried through to the present day. This chapter will examine one of the major groupings within the resurgence: the Federation of South African Trade Unions (FOSATU), and its antecedents. FOSATU went on to form the core of the Congress of South African Trade Unions (COSATU) launched in Durban at the end of 1985.

FOSATU tended to place a heavy emphasis on shop-floor organisation and plant-based bargaining. As a result, critical activists often saw it as being syndicalist in orientation or, in the term coined in the 1980s, as 'workerist'. This chapter will assess the nature of the organisational form more carefully and identify what it offers in regard to the National Question.

The revival of non-racial trade union organisation was relatively widespread. The initial leadership was an interesting combination of experienced cadres coming off 'the island' (that is, activists who had been imprisoned on Robben Island), key officials in the registered unions, young left-wing intellectual activists, and a courageous and determined worker leadership that emerged out of intense – largely spontaneous – strike action. This combination was undoubtedly important in many ways.

FOSATU, formed in 1979, evolved and implemented a specific organisational approach. This was articulated in some detail in the Second FOSATU Congress in 1982, where an embryonic political philosophy can also be detected. This Second Congress coincided with a re-emergence of mass-based community action – the United Democratic Front (UDF) was formed the following year. There were distinct differences in approach of FOSATU's organising and that of the UDF, which led to a vigorous debate in the mid-1980s, usually styled 'populist versus workerist' – tags that masked more than they informed.

THE NATIONAL QUESTION AND WORKERISTS?

The National Question has long been a vexed issue within left thinking. It would be all too easy to tag the workerists as an expression of syndicalism and thereby conveniently disqualify them from such a grand dialogue. Although the workerists were not syndicalists, for many observers what they saw looked very like a form of syndicalism.

To fully understand this movement, we need to delve deeper into the exigencies of the time because they imposed certain imperatives upon the organisational practices. It was these exigencies, rather than grand theories, that shaped the praxis of the time. Out of such praxis, a proto-political philosophy emerged. It embodied a reasonably cogent approach to institution building, working-class organisation and social coherence that merits another look.

The debate on the National Question ranges across a wide range of politics, schools of thought and organisations, as illustrated by the existence and nature of this volume. At times the debates and positions adopted are not self-evidently related to the National Question. The workerist versus populist debate is a case in point; one needs to read carefully to define how it relates to the National Question – but relate it does!

THE JOE FOSTER SPEECH

At the Second Congress of FOSATU in 1982 General Secretary Joe Foster read out a speech entitled 'The Workers Struggle: Where Does FOSATU Stand' – often referred to as the 'Foster speech'. Two things about the speech are striking. The first is how it recorded a journey of unionisation over a few intense years, and the second is that it did indeed say something important that is worth reassessing in the present day.

Joe Foster delivered the speech, but there has been much speculation as to who the author was. The answer is important – there were many. The drafting process was one of the key moments in consolidating the thinking and organisational practice within FOSATU, and also had a major impact on how the Federation approached many subsequent challenges. This organisational approach came to dominate in the formation and early years of COSATU.

The Foster speech was a product of some months of meetings, discussions and laborious (usually hand-written) drafts by one or other scribe. The culinary staple was Kentucky Fried – the days before Nando's and laptops won the day. Participants were the 'intellectuals' – active, banned and associated with the unions. Then there were experienced unionists such as Fred Sauls, Joe Foster and Les Kettledas who had grown up in the registered union movement. A key group was the new worker leadership – either shop steward or organiser (a full-time union official). In those early days, the organisers had only recently left the shop floor.

This cadre of worker leaders was crucial for two reasons. First, they were the link to the factories. Second, as a result of the close proximity of the factories to the townships, they increasingly played a leadership role in communities. Worker leaders such as Chris Dlamini, John Gomomo and Moses Mayekiso were prominent in community activity in the East Rand, Uitenhage and Alexandra respectively. The leadership in Natal (which then included the bantustan of KwaZulu) – Jeffrey Vilane, Mike Mabuyakhulu, Bheki Ntuli, Willies Mchunu, Alpheus Mthethwa, Moses Ndlovu and John Makhatini among many – had an even more integrated and complex role in the community. This reality and their insights allowed for a more systematic assessment of the role the unions should be playing in community activism. The juxtaposing of localised worker organisation and community militancy was an important development, and the worker leaders rapidly developed strategic and tactical acuity. Their role in the drafting process was seminal.

Most of the actual collating and drafting was done in the FOSATU executive but many other meetings were held with participation from the wider group. This exercise in praxis was to inform a great deal of the subsequent educative and policy-making efforts within FOSATU and later COSATU.

THE FOSATU APPROACH TO ORGANISATION

It was the early and difficult years of organisation from the Trade Union Advisory and Coordinating Council (TUACC) through to FOSATU that were the dominant factor in shaping the content of the Foster speech. There was a determination to survive in order to establish unions, but there was also a longer-term objective, which was to strengthen working-class organisation. The Foster speech attempted to pull these threads together in an overall organisational and, indeed, a proto-political philosophy.

Conditions were difficult and it took persistence and courage to build these fledgling structures. This context influenced the mindset that informed the organisational practices. Banning and detention could neutralise organisational capacity and, accordingly, a robust organisation had to be built up quickly in order to survive. In particular, organisational structures had to be located where it was hardest for the repressive apparatus of the apartheid state to get to them. Clearly, this was on the shop floor.[1] The shop stewards had to be as self-sufficient as possible in their leadership roles, given the vulnerability of the organisers. This, then, informed the emphasis on training, study and debate. Not surprisingly, there was much study of the theories of guerrilla warfare – the factory-based leadership had to have a sense of strategy and tactics. The shop stewards were the fish swimming in the sea of factories, which could never be entirely drained by the repressive apparatus.

These organisational imperatives meant an emphasis on factories and a tactical caution about taking on losing battles – a form of 'guerrilla unionism'. In its form this looked very much like syndicalism intertwined with economism and, for many sceptics, even reformism. However, behind it there was a strategic intent to build a lasting working-class organisation as opposed to a purely trade union organisation.

A conviction grew that the meaning of 'working-class organisation' had to involve the effective and lasting organisation of workers in their workplaces – where their basic potential power lies. This organisation had to be structured in a manner that allowed them to influence wider community, social and political events in favour of the working class.

The Foster speech marked a pulling together of praxis and embryonic theoretical propositions about working-class organisation. However, it also has to be located in the basic reality that any attempt to organise non-racial unions in South Africa will automatically take the organisation onto the terrain of the National Question. This was further complicated by the existence of a powerful Zulu-based formation in the form of Inkatha, which will be dealt with more fully below.

ORGANISATIONAL INNOVATION

This view of working-class organisation also found expression in some very concrete organisational innovations and practices which also underlay the political propositions made in the Foster speech. Three abiding lodestars of organisational strategy at the time can be identified: survival, effectiveness and unity. These spawned the other essentials – the need for depth in leadership, a toleration of diversity of view and yet a capacity for collective discipline.

There were two important early developments in this evolving organisational approach. The first revolved around the debate on organising as many workers as possible as opposed to focusing on strategically located plants or clusters (Maree, 1986). The latter won the day, and it allowed the second important structural development, which consisted of the major changes made in the constitutions of the new unions.

The majority of the registered unions of the time built their decision-making structures on branch executive committees that were composed of individuals elected at annual general meetings. There was no, or a minimal, role for the shop steward or the shop-steward committee. This was a product of their evolution within the industrial council system. However, this was inadequate for the new unions built on a few factories. There was a critical need to strengthen factory-based leadership, so a new constitutional structure was developed.

An unintended consequence of the banning orders that plagued many activists was an outstanding cadre of labour lawyers. Two of them – Johnny Copelyn and Halton Cheadle – worked on the new union constitutions. The shop-steward committee became the building block of all decision-making structures within the union. These constitutional changes were first implemented in the TUACC unions based in KwaZulu-Natal and the Witwatersrand. It soon permeated all FOSATU unions.

The changes made factory or shop-floor organisation important. Decision-making structures were built around membership within a factory rather than membership of the union. To form a shop-steward committee there had to be significant factory-level organisation. In addition, the practice was that the shop stewards were elected within departments and shifts. This meant that the shop-steward committee reached into the far corners of the factory.

One important consequence of this was that where female workers predominated, then female shop stewards emerged. While not consciously conceived of, this outcome was to be important in developing greater gender consciousness over time. Many of these female shop stewards became a very powerful cadre of organisers and leaders.

The effect of this focus on factories was to contract the unions into fewer strategically located sites of organisation. This was a conscious decision, and it was to pay dividends. The strategically targeted factories were located in dense industrial concentrations where, by apartheid design, large townships were located relatively nearby. The massive Frame Group textile complex in Pinetown – in the region of 10 000 workers – with Clermont just a few kilometres away, was a graphic illustration of this. By the early 1980s, when the scope for organising improved, the organised factories were strong bases from which to move rapidly forward. Even more important, as the FOSATU shop-steward councils emerged, a key and natural nexus with community organisation in the adjacent townships also emerged. These local shop-steward councils were to play a key role in later community-based events.

INDUSTRIAL UNIONISM AND INDUSTRIAL COUNCILS[2]

Another important factor within the organisational approach was the choice made in favour of industrial as opposed to general unions. This was an early and crucial debate in TUACC, and shaped FOSATU. It was by no means a clear-cut issue and space precludes a full examination of the intricacies of the debate. However, it was in some respects the precursor to the populist-workerist debate.

The essential argument for general unions was that in favourable organisational circumstances it was best to expand organisation rapidly. Those in favour of industrial unions built their argument around the competitive imperative within capitalism – this was at its strongest within an industry. Therefore, they argued that the most effective organisational strategy was to deploy by industry, strategic plants and companies. By concentrating forces on key factories in a sector, gains could be made and then used in the next battle.

The reality was that the then industrial council structure represented a de facto truce between capital and labour. Capital had agreed to set industry-wide conditions by means of industrial councils, but in exchange the unions had surrendered their factory-based organisations and plant-based bargaining. The new plant-based unionism was to rock this boat.[3]

The emerging unions were built on factory-based organisational strength and this opened new strategic possibilities within the industrial council system. The factory-based organisation could be used to win plant-based agreements despite these not being contemplated in the legislation. This form of ratchet bargaining then uses the industrial council to spread the gains more rapidly than a plant-by-plant process. Since the industrial councils were a major structural feature of key sectors, it would be very difficult for capital to dismantle them in order to resist the new unions.

REFORMISM, OR LAYING THE BASIS FOR WORKING-CLASS ORGANISATION?

As the FOSATU unions implemented this strategy of using the industrial councils it inevitably gave rise to other actions that seemed to further reinforce the political perception that the workerists were guilty of economism and even outright reformism.

The prime objective was to build and sustain factory-based organisation and to consolidate the de facto power of the shop stewards. This meant increased use of the law. It was soon clear that common law could be used in place of the industrial legislation denied to the unregistered unions prior to the report of the Wiehahn Commission of Enquiry into Labour Legislation tabled in Parliament on 1 May 1979. The law of contract was the key, and it could be used at the plant level. De facto recognition of the new unions could be built up carefully through things like grievance and disciplinary procedures. Pulling all of this together in the form of a plant-based recognition agreement made eminent sense – and was also a platform upon which to build concrete solidarity links with international unions located in the same companies abroad.

The plant-based recognition agreements were pioneered by the famous Smith and Nephew agreement in the mid-1970s. Soon, factory after factory was succumbing and a de facto reality of plant-based bargaining was emerging. This reality was recognised by the Wiehahn Commission in 1979. There is an obvious paradox here – the unions were using a legal system that was fundamentally illegitimate. In doing so they were offering some recognition to the state behind it and for the purist this smacked of collaboration – especially when these unions chose to register and then enter the industrial council system after 1979.

Such an approach to organisation and mobilisation was bound to be in tension with the strategic imperatives of the African National Congress (ANC) and its international campaign for the isolation of the apartheid regime. For the Alliance – particularly its exile component – the tension revolved around the rapidly growing worker activity. This was to be welcomed, but its apparent willingness to accept various structural features of the apartheid state created consternation for many. Mass organisation was more aligned with ANC strategy. This would further increase the legitimacy of the external wing of the liberation movement and prevent the accusation that they were only external movements with no presence on the ground. From the perspective of the ANC this logic cannot be faulted.

For the SACP, a left-oriented movement was emerging that did not owe open allegiance to the party. Up till then, it had been the established, although not uncontested, leader of the working class.

However, for FOSATU such open alignment merely attracted further repressive attention. Tensions and mutual doubts arose around what the fundamental objective was – mass organisation to politically defeat the apartheid state, or intensive organisation to build worker power. In the former worker organisation could be seen as collateral damage, while in the latter protecting worker organisation for its own sake could be seen as syndicalism. This was an inherently tense situation and required sophisticated management.

In hindsight it is also easier to see why deep-seated doubts between groups emerged. Was the concept of a national democratic phase of the revolution being challenged? Was the socialist objective being abandoned? However, as came to be realised by the senior leadership of FOSATU, the prospect of a liberation struggle without a powerful mass movement such as the ANC seemed very remote. The essential challenge for this leadership was to establish working-class power within the growing mass struggle.

These basic tensions meant that at no time was TUACC or FOSATU a homogeneous political block. Divisions existed and it is important to understand this reality. Within both TUACC and FOSATU four tendencies emerged which contributed to ongoing tension. The comrades close to the ANC and SACP – usually through links to the rapidly growing underground network – were concerned that the organisational strategy did not fully align with that of the political movements, and were not fully convinced that their workerist comrades were at one with the Alliance. This suspicion was strengthened by the existence of two smaller tendencies within the unions. There were links with groups such as the Marxist Workers Tendency and other groups loosely defined as Trotskyist, and there was a network of links to the New Unity Movement (the latter were much closer to the workerists than the former). The fourth tendency essentially argued the factory-based and industrial union organisational strategy set out above – the workerists who came to dominate.

On all sides there were 'intellectuals' – some of whom could be regarded as being an independent left and some as SACP activists. There were experienced ANC and SACP activists and there were worker leaders. It is therefore an interesting question as to why the so-called workerist tendency came to dominate FOSATU policy. The answer is complex but in the end it probably boils down to the strategy being more effective on the ground, and more particularly that it resulted in real gains for workers in organised factories with recognition agreements. It is difficult to understate the importance of an increasingly strong leadership from the shop floor who were either full-time organisers or shop stewards. While it is enticing to see this as a clash of theories and, therefore, that the intellectuals were a salient factor, the reality is that the worker leaders were the final arbiters within the FOSATU structures. It was the group that focussed on industrial unions and shop-floor organisation that prevailed in the drafting of the Foster speech, the document that articulated their organisational, strategic and political perspective. It was this group that was labelled workerist.

It is important to understand that these substantive tendencies existed within FOSATU at all times but that despite them a high degree of unity within FOSATU was maintained. Underlying this ability to retain unity were the structures that we will examine further on.

However, mention must be made of a less well known but important factor. This was a modus vivendi developed between the top leadership of FOSATU and the top leadership of the ANC.[4] An acceptance grew on both sides that the two strategies would continue side by side. The success of the strategy based on industrial unions and the shop-floor organising was accepted by the ANC as building worker power. Equally, the need to isolate the regime and encourage mass organisation was accepted by the FOSATU leadership. In fact, following its own organisational practices, the local shop steward councils were rapidly proving to be very effective in this area. These two strategies were seen as components – despite being in tension – of the overall strategic imperative to isolate and defeat the apartheid regime.

This is an important strategic point that was to play out time and time again. In effect the senior leaders of the Alliance accepted that the workerists did constitute a distinct organisational movement with differing tactical and strategic objectives that did not, however, fundamentally conflict with the objectives of the Alliance, and therefore they should be worked with since they were manifestly effective. For their part, the FOSATU leadership eschewed syndicalist and 'socialism now' positions as they realised that a mass struggle was essential to defeat apartheid, and that restricting organisation to factories would not achieve that goal. To isolate the unions from the mass struggle was to be guilty of economism, while to replace factory-based organisation with mass struggle was to surrender a working-class power base. These choices and tension are at the very centre of the National Question and we will return to them.

THE TIGHT FEDERATION

What were becoming key distinguishing features of the FOSATU unions were the emphasis on the shop floor, industrial unions and the fight for plant-based recognition agreements. All of these were then carried over as a form of Trojan horse into the prevailing industrial council system.

Another key feature of the organisational practice was the relatively centralised structure of the Federation itself. The FOSATU structure was relatively complex. In each affiliate the decision-making was built up from the shop floor. This meant that the national structures of the affiliates had roots going back into the factories. However, there were three other important and often less remarked upon aspects of the Federation. These were the importance of FOSATU locals and regions in the structure, and the role of differentiated voting mechanisms in the decision-making structures.

As has been alluded to above, the local FOSATU shop steward councils played a very important role in local community politics. In an important sense the influence of FOSATU in communities was a result of this localised power – it took factory-based power onto the terrain of community affairs. The importance of this to working-class organisation may well be seminal. This nexus between factory-based organisation and locals and community affairs offered the potential for a wider working-class organisation.

In drawing inferences on the importance of the factory-community nexus for the larger National Question we need to focus on regions. Each FOSATU region had a structure modelled on the national structure. This allowed for the region to deal with its many specific socio-economic and political characteristics. The situation in KwaZulu-Natal and parts of the Witwatersrand was particularly difficult as the tensions with Inkatha grew from the mid-1980s. This serious and eventually violent tension had to be handled with care. Localised community politics differed widely across the country, and keeping a coherent approach to this complexity depended on having an experienced and effective worker leadership articulating these differences within the national FOSATU structures. The Federation had to deal with considerable diversity and yet embrace it in a common worker struggle.

The tension with Inkatha was a serious one and could easily have divided the fledgling Federation. By the mid-1980s the Alliance saw Inkatha as fully aligned with the regime, and many community activists in other provinces were only interested in isolating it. Yet again it was the ability of worker leaders who had to deal with the challenges on the ground that enabled the Federation to hold together. Many of the worker leaders in KwaZulu-Natal had to arm themselves for their protection, and many died. The union structures had to embody self-defence structures. Regional structures allowed a dialogue based on hard experience to hold the Federation together.

STRUCTURING NATIONAL ORGANISATIONS

Another important decision-making innovation was the voting system within FOSATU structures. Within executive committees or local shop steward councils of the Federation the formal voting structure was an equal vote per factory or affiliate, no matter the size of the factory or affiliate. The only place where voting was based on the size of the membership of an affiliate was in the regional and national congresses. This was based on the philosophy that within the Federation each affiliate was of the same worth and should benefit equally from the advantages of the Federation. However, where the key decisions were taken there should be respect for the number of workers represented by the affiliate. This was an important balance; it protected the smaller affiliates but also acted as an impetus to form larger unions. However, what might have been most important about it was that it allowed for diversity to be accommodated.

The conception of the Federation was always that it was a tight Federation. In effect, this was a carefully constructed system that attempted to use the organisational and survivalist benefits of factory-based organisation and industrial unions, yet to bind these together into a strong national structure covering the whole economy.

The regional structures of FOSATU were important but at no time did they override the national structures of either the affiliates or the Federation. This is not to suggest that all was plain sailing. Clearly, there were ongoing tensions, but the system had enough points of give to allow it to hold together.

The structures of the Federation and the affiliates were designed to deal with inevitable organisational tensions across regions and political viewpoints. What was central, however, was that the massive preponderance of workers in the decision-making process at key points meant that in the end one had to persuade workers of a position. Even more important was that these were not just members of the union; they were experienced leaders in their own right coming from a tough experience of the direct conflict with capital in the workplace. These were workers who were constantly involved in making tactical and strategic decisions, and therefore could make their own assessments of various positions and how that might have an impact on them and the members in the factories that had elected them.

Another important development in FOSATU was that at the outset it was a federation that embraced both registered and unregistered unions. Particularly important were the motor industry unions. The National Union of Motor Assembly and Rubber Workers of South Africa (NUMARWOSA), a registered union originating in the Eastern Cape, had formed a close working relationship with a union essentially formed by it, the United Automobile and Allied Workers Union (UAAWU). It then formed a link with the Western Province Motor Assembly Workers Union (WPMAWU), a smaller registered union in the Western Cape. There were also fascinating relics of another industrial age such as the Jewellers and Goldsmiths Union.

This absorption of registered unions was important for a number of reasons. The imperative of unity was at work here, leading to the pragmatic approach that worked with registered unions rather than attempting to drive them away or replace them. However, it also brought resources, experience and negotiating expertise into the Federation. Equally important, it meant the rapid growth of a national presence for the new Federation. A national unity was being built.

As unions entered the new Federation, a process of unity started toward the building of one industrial union in each sector. This unification process provided considerable experience in the formation of unions both at the factory level and through mergers with other unions. The latter is no easy process, as differing leadership cadres have to be merged. Once again there were advantages in building up from the shop floor. A worker leader had to have a base in a factory or workplace. From there other worker leaders would elect them to regional or national positions in the affiliate or the Federation. This contributed to a higher degree of accountability of the worker leadership. Furthermore, there were no significant additional material benefits in such a leadership position; on the contrary one exposed oneself to greater potential danger.

These processes were in effect 'a university in national politics' – or we could call it an exercise in nation building. Different racial, ethnic, political and pragmatic perspectives and situations were being melded into a single, well-coordinated, tight federation. It was at the core of the National Question.

Three areas need to be examined in order to assess what lessons can be learned from this whole unionisation process. These are the role of leadership and the importance of its structure, the ability to manage and integrate diversity and what was conceived of as working-class organisation.

WORKER LEADERSHIP

Leadership can be seen through the lens of the individual or the collective. From the foregoing, it will be evident that the preoccupation of the workerist grouping was to build a leadership collective that operated within a structure that was itself relatively complex and designed to handle diverse views and interests. Regrettably, space precludes an examination of how later external circumstances made an impact on collective leadership, and how they handled the transition from struggle to democracy. Here we deal with how the circumstances shaped the leadership collective.

FOSATU built a structured leadership cadre with links from the shop floor to the national level. This structure also straddled regional, ethnic and political divides but was bound in a common purpose of dealing with worker issues which had an impact on all, irrespective of race, sex or creed. The usual inference within democratic practice is that such a structured leadership would generate a high degree of accountability and must be important.

However, this layering of experienced leadership might be even more important. Shop stewards, as leaders, were an integral part of the everyday workplaces and communities grappling with intricate problems. This tried and tested leadership then also participated in wider local, regional and national structures – structures which, we have seen, were complex and capable of dealing with diversity.

Clearly, it is important not to idealise either leadership or organisational structures. All social formations are subject to continuous pressures and adjust to those pressures – they are dynamic, not static, formations. The insight explored is that the positions taken by the FOSATU unions were in large measure a response to organisational exigencies. However, in choosing certain organisational and structural responses to those pressures, the base was created to enable the achievement of wider working-class unity.

The proposition being explored here is that in forging a degree of cohesion in complex and latently divisive social and economic situations (a fair description of what the National Question is all about), deep layers of active and engaged leaders provide the basis for building a national cohesion.

In building on this potential it is necessary to create structures that allow the voice of this leadership to be heard at the national level without suppressing its localised or regional authenticity. The ability of leaders to deal with regionally specific issues must not be surrendered to a national imperative, yet at the same time regional issues must not be allowed to swamp wider national imperatives. This is an exceptionally difficult balance. The account of how FOSATU was structured is that of an attempt that emerged out of necessity to deal with these issues.

LESSONS FOR THE NATIONAL QUESTION

It is very evident that the ANC-led Alliance that came into power in 1994 was not blind to the shortcomings of the modern Westminster system as a state form. The Constitution and a host of policy choices show that there was both an awareness of the need for checks and balances and the recognition of specific collective needs – Section nine institutions; language equality; recognition of differing legal systems; traditional leadership recognition; the National Economic Development and Labour Council (NEDLAC) and policy choices around popular consultation in the form of *izimbizo* and ward committees. All speak to this awareness. Yet, despite this, there is a manifest and growing divide between the local and the overly national state power. Maybe it is the depth of structured leadership that is missing!

Strength at the base is crucial for integration of national diversity. Such strength in FOSATU proved capable of melding many differing political, sociological, cultural and ethnic divides by ensuring that those divides were never suppressed but, at the same time, were never able to overcome the larger common purpose.

What is important is that these capacities of the shop stewards cannot be ascribed to some idealised nobility of the working class towards the collective spirit. It has to be embedded in structures of decision-making that allow for high degrees of diversity and that protect the right of such diversity to exist. A democratic structure predicated only on one person one vote will not automatically lead to a national identity. There is no wisdom in numbers or in the vote per se. In fact, it is just as likely to be abused as it is to create harmony. The key issue is the process before the vote takes place and the sense of comfort and security for all after it has taken place. Lessons might well be learned from the strong shop-steward structures that were built.

Another insight arising from the organisational experience of FOSATU is worth a brief exploration. A three-way tension arose during that experience, and the participation of the 'intellectuals' heightened the tension. Representational democracy is complex when one pauses to reflect on it. The basic concept is that a person will be elected to represent the agreed collective views of a group of individuals. The first tension that might emerge is that the representative might become dislocated from the day-to-day activities of the group because they now need more time to effectively perform their representational functions – think of the concept of MPs who are away in Parliament for much of the time, and the effective and functional methods that have to be found to keep the representatives in touch with the group they represent. This can be complex even within the localised environment of a factory and the shop floor. It is hard for workers to effectively represent their peers and do the job they were originally hired for. In addition, the FOSATU unions placed emphasis on training, and this required time. The logical demand that was successfully made was for full-time shop stewards. The dynamic over time of this victory proved to be exceptionally complex, and we cannot explore it more fully here. However, the first area of tension is then in the interface between the shop steward and the group they represent. Keeping this effective and accountable cannot be taken for granted.

In order for the unions to function they need full-time functionaries. As indicated previously, the vast majority of such organisers came off the shop floor in the early days. These were not easy jobs. Recruiting workers could be a thankless task; the attentions of the apartheid Security Branch were endless; the hours were long and the payment meagre. In addition, significant new responsibilities and skills had to be assumed and learned as the union's dues were collected by hand in those days – creating serious temptations for shop steward and organiser alike.

The constitutional solution to ensuring that elected workers had primacy was to provide them with the power to vote and denying that to the organisers. This was important in form. In practice, however, the organisers had de facto power in many areas, as they were full-time, had access to information and easier access to the growing resources of the unions. In the days when the factory-based organisation was central, the shop stewards developed fast and their leadership of factory organisation gave them very real political power. In addition, many were relatively skilled workers able to fully understand the operations of the unions, and therefore they were in a position to exert real political power, giving substance to the form of the worker-organiser divide in the constitutions. However, the very success of the unions and the increased role of industrial councils inevitably had the effect of weakening this de facto power emanating from the shop floor. This tension between the effective political power of the elected worker leaders and the power that accrued from being a full-time organiser was persistent and moved over time to favour the latter (Hartford, n.d.).

The last important tension that we need to explore is that between industry-specific knowledge and the technical functions usually performed by professionals – accounting, legal matters, political economy analysis. All these areas are essential in a growing union movement that has to engage in serious collective bargaining. At one level these are services that can be procured, and as the unions got larger and more stable this is what happened to a large degree. However, such an understanding is very incomplete. The knowledge residing within these disciplines is crucial for successful strategising in the union movement, but only if it is complemented by the knowledge residing in worker leaders as to how the mass membership might respond. A scenario where such expertise is bought in and then assessed by worker leaders without that knowledge raises serious questions about the nature of worker control or, for that matter, citizen control of their destiny.

It is in this tension that the role of the intellectuals needs to be carefully assessed. They brought much technical expertise and theoretical capacity and thereby became the key interpreters of such information. This is a position of moral hazard for the intellectual, as it is a situation that can be abused in many ways. It is also a very risky situation for the unions, as key strategic considerations might be overly influenced by poorly tested technical and specialist advice. The intellectuals and the FOSATU union structures grappled with this tension in a number of ways. One of the first checks in place was the existence of many very capable and experienced unionists from the registered unions. Another was the presence of experienced ANC and SACP cadres who were always accessible. Then, as we have discussed, constitutional and operational checks and balances were put in place.

The most important check, however, was the development of a deep and active leadership that had real de facto power. Important steps were taken over time to deepen and empower this leadership even more. Here the experience in drafting the Joe Foster speech was seminal. This interactive process was then built on in many subsequent ways. Residential courses were held for shop stewards on history and economics; teaching methods became participative rather than passive; educative material was produced from the earliest days.[5] Once travel abroad became more possible, a systematic programme was undertaken, and the National Union of Metalworkers of South Africa (NUMSA) formed its research and development groups.

The point being explored here is the role of leadership in a situation where full-time representatives and functionaries emerge in an organisation and where it increasingly requires specialist, technical and professional capacities. To ensure the health of the decision-making process and its articulation with the many diffuse and often conflicting needs and interests of the membership base requires active, intelligent and functionally dynamic structures and practices within a national organisation.

WORKING-CLASS ORGANISATION

Thus far we have looked for possible insights from the organisational experience of the FOSATU unions. The likely hallmark of the workerists was their emphasis on building factory-based organisation and developing a deeply layered worker leadership anchored in that factory-based organisation. In the case of FOSATU, this made them capable of resisting a powerful oppressor and also of overcoming many social, ethnic and political divides in order to build an effective national organisation. The manner in which these diverse social currents were managed was through the engagement of leadership cadres in the common cause of building unions to advance the worker cause. The diversities had to be melded effectively to achieve this commonly supported greater objective. Stated in this way, it is the exact equivalent of nation building and therefore also at the centre of the National Question.

This chapter has also explored the reality that the forging of such common purpose cannot be taken for granted; it is not some subjective social urge that can be tapped by astute leadership. Institutional structures have to be built to maximise the scope for deep layers of engaged leadership and to deal with the many inherent tension that emerge within large national organisations – especially those based on forms of representational democracy. Constitutions and institutions are crucial. The FOSATU organisational experience was an intense period of grappling with these issues, and in the main it was a successful effort.

What is now worth assessing is whether the form of worker organisation that was developed and became also the dominant form of organisational practice within COSATU had any impact on the wider project of nation building. To do this we first need to see what in fact was conceived of as worker organisation.

Early in this chapter I suggested that there was in fact an embryonic political theory present in the Foster speech. In hindsight this is true, and what is also true is that it should have been more fully developed in the subsequent decades. What was articulated in the Foster speech was a well-disciplined worker organisation that had a national presence within the economy but that could also actively engage in local and regional matters and was conceived of as a working-class movement that would be so significant that the Alliance would have little option but to accommodate it and pay heed to working-class needs. It was definitely more than a trade union movement and the FOSATU unions took their involvement beyond the workplace and industrial councils into the communities and the cultural domain. This effective power base was seen as a guarantor of worker influence in the inevitable transition process (Friedman, n.d.).

However, a fair assessment would have to be that there was a dire need for a second Joe Foster speech process after the formation of COSATU, and then again after the democratic transition. The concept of worker organisation and a working-class movement articulated in 1982 was too vague to meet the two challenges that presented themselves at those times.

In 1985, the assessment made – not unanimously by any means – was that COSATU was strong enough to replace the South African Congress of Trade Unions (SACTU) as the union component of the Alliance. At one level this was obvious since SACTU was no longer effectively functional on the ground, but it did not automatically follow that COSATU should replace it in the Alliance. The decision to do so was heavily swayed by the need for unity in that conjuncture. The struggle was at its most intense and violent. In such a situation the rapid consolidation of the liberation movement was the imperative, and this view won the day and, even in hindsight, seems hard to fault.

What was missing, however, was a process to decide exactly how the well-organised worker formations would work with the Alliance. This was a complex issue as in reality COSATU was working with the UDF on the ground, and in that situation had no difficulty in holding its own as its formation formed a powerful component of the UDF. Alongside this, the COSATU senior leadership, in occasional meetings, was the formal point of contact with the formal structures of the ANC and the SACP.[6] Then, in 1990, following Joe Slovo's famous paper of 1988, many senior union leaders formally joined the SACP. This further increased the access of union leaders to the top decision-makers in the other Alliance partners. Given the exigencies of the time, this had many parallels with a 'war cabinet' type situation. In hindsight, though, this situation laid the basis for later inadequacies in building worker and working-class organisations.

It is difficult to see how the union leadership could have avoided such an active involvement with the Alliance. However, what was needed was a longer-term reflection on how the relationship between worker organisation and the Alliance should be structured. In particular, the relationship with the SACP, as a purportedly class-based party, should have been thought through. Key COSATU leaders such as Jay Naidoo stated time and time again that the unions were not a 'conveyor belt' for the ANC, and de facto on the ground, the COSATU structures remained very robust and very often dominant. However, there was a need for a serious process – similar to the Foster speech process – to work this through. This is not to suggest that nothing happened. A great deal was done to maintain unity in COSATU, and the tendencies that were described in FOSATU carried over into COSATU. Maintaining unity in this situation was a great achievement.

However, by failing adequately to foresee the dangers of an unstructured relationship within the Alliance and by paying insufficient attention to the need to find new ways of building working-class organisation, the workerist leadership missed a major opportunity to build working-class power. Whether the circumstances of the day and the subjective capacities of the leadership would have allowed them to define such new organisational structures and processes will remain one of the vexed issues of our own history. However, at the least there was an overestimation of how far towards worker organisation the Alliance could be cajoled, and there was an overestimation of the resilience of the worker leadership structures that had been built up within COSATU. The workerists were correct to place emphasis on worker organisation but failed to take further the embryonic position in the Foster speech.

The result of these processes was that the Alliance existed only at the top structures – national and regional. Below that no effective structure existed. Where workers were well organised they formed an important lobby group, but this seldom translated into a policy platform at that local level. In the main it veered toward lobbies around the election of particular leaderships. A frustrating and suboptimal stalemate developed. The ANC could not do without the unions when it came to the polls, and the unions had no platform which would allow them to organise to truly reshape government policy beyond the considerable success they had in labour law and industrial relations.

Faced with this stalemate, the union leadership decided to become kingmakers within the Alliance. Working with allies in the Alliance they mounted a silent coup in government. This was to take them onto ground – dangerous ground – well traversed on many occasions elsewhere in the world. By entering the political parties as kingmakers they merely invited the political parties into their structures to repay the compliment. Less obviously, they participated in a process that placed party politics above the national interest embodied in the democratic state form.

For reasons that I have discussed, the structures of the unions, the nature of their leadership and far-sighted leadership within the Alliance all contributed to keeping unity. This unity is now threatened and the only result of this is to weaken worker organisation. The split has all the hallmarks of the underlying issues that informed the populist-workerist debate, but the conditions are less conducive to unity.

Worker organisation and unity are key to nation building as it coalesces around more abiding common interests – basically, class interests. Strong working-class organisation acts as a discipline on more narrow and self-serving interests. The Scandinavian and social democratic states, while by no means any form of the dictatorship of the proletariat, are most certainly examples of the power of sustained working-class organisation. The achievements of China, Vietnam and Cuba are other testimonies to the benefits of sustained class-based organisation.

The successes of the workerists as organisers of worker power were built on several factors: depth of leadership; structured engagement by that leadership with their immediate communities; structures that articulated local, regional and national leadership; and processes that grappled with the inherent tensions of representational democracy within large democratic structures. For worker power to be built, it has to be built from the bottom again. It should be worker leaders who deal with the local issues of service delivery and they should then use their national power to ensure that delivery is provided. In so doing they will force the ANC to return to its own roots of representing the poorest of the poor.

Today's leaders in COSATU are faced with challenges every bit as great as those facing the founders – founders who did not take things quite far enough. It is time for the present to understand the past and to complete the job.

NOTES

1 We will use this term to describe all the different forms of workplace organisation.
2 Friedman (1987) provides a contemporary account of much of what is set out here.
3 Not all registered unions had accepted this 'truce' and it was around this time that TUACC found allies in the National Union of Motor Assembly and Rubber Workers of South Africa (NUMAWOSA) and the Western Province Motor Assembly Workers Union (WPMAWU).
4 In my experience the role of Thabo Mbeki and Chris Hani, in their different ways, was pivotal. I suspect that Oliver Tambo might have been the pivot in the background.
5 The role of the Institute for Industrial Education is a subject in its own right. The whole approach to education and training is worthy of much reflection.
6 In addition, a messy web of relations grew between prominent but banned activists and the formal union structures. For many in the ANC and SACP it was assumed that as the more senior parties in the Alliance they could transmit instructions to the COSATU structures.

REFERENCES

Foster, Joe (1982) The Workers' Struggle: Where does FOSATU Stand? FOSATU Occasional Publication No. 5. Available online at www.historical.papers.wits.ac.za.

Friedman, Michelle (n.d.) The Future is in the Hands of the Workers: A History of FOSATU. Historical Papers Labour Archive Project. Available online at www.historicalpapers.wits.ac.za.

Friedman, Steven (1987) *Building Tomorrow Today: African Workers in Trade Unions, 1970–1984.* Johannesburg: Ravan.

Hartford, Gavin (n.d.) The Mining Industry Strike Wave: What are the Causes and What are the Solutions? Available from gavin@esopshop.co.za.

Maree, Johan (1986) An Analysis of the Independent Trade Unions in South Africa in the 1970s. Unpublished PhD thesis, University of Cape Town, Cape Town.

Slovo, Joe (1988) The South African Working Class and the National Democratic Revolution. African Socialist archives.

RED, BLACK AND GOLD:[1]
FOSATU, SOUTH AFRICAN 'WORKERISM',
'SYNDICALISM' AND THE NATION

Sian Byrne, Nicole Ulrich and Lucien van der Walt

> *You, moving forest of Africa.*
> *When I arrived the children were all crying,*
> *These were the workers, industrial workers...*
> *Escape into that forest,*
> *The black forest that the employers saw and ran for safety.*
> *The workers saw it too*
> *'It belongs to us,' they said,*
> *'Let us take refuge in it to be safe from our hunters.'*
> *Deep into the forest they hid themselves and when*
> *they came out they were free from fear...*
> *Lead us FOSATU to where we are eager to go.*
> *Even in parliament you shall be our representative.*
> *Go and represent us because you are our Moses*
> *Through your leadership we shall reach our Canaan...*
> (Alfred Qabula, 'Praise Poem to FOSATU', 1984)

INTRODUCTION

After months of talks between unions associated with the Trade Union Advisory Coordinating Council (TUACC), the Federation of South African Trade Unions

(FOSATU) was inaugurated on 13 April 1979. FOSATU was the first federation of pre-dominantly unregistered trade unions with a truly national reach to operate openly in South Africa since the late 1960s.[2]

FOSATU membership reached 140 000 in 1985 (Baskin, 1991: 49); it was 'by far the strongest working-class organisation' opposing apartheid in the early 1980s (Schroeder, 1988: 54). The largest strike wave since the 1940s took place in 1981, and FOSATU played an integral role (Yudelman, 1984: 271). FOSATU was also associated with the distinct radical politics of South African 'workerism', and had a mass base among black workers.

'Workerism' was widely identified as the dominant political current within FOSATU in the early 1980s (for example, Mahomed, 1984). Although workerism was not the only current in the federation, and was not restricted to FOSATU (Byrne, 2012), its core posi-tions remain relatively unknown. This is partly because workerism was highly controver-sial at the time, the subject of fierce, often misleading polemics (for example, Toussaint, 1983; Comrades in Africa, 1984; Nhere, 1984; Nyawuza, 1985). Coupled with a lack of dedicated studies of FOSATU or its affiliates, this has left workerism's actual positions largely obscured from view.

This chapter is intended to provide a recovery of the politics and history of FOSATU, as well as a detailed investigation of how workerism engaged and sought to answer the National Question in South Africa. This discussion necessarily includes critiques of mis-leading claims about workerism – notably accusations that it was economistic, ignoring national liberation or issues beyond the workplace.

We retain the use of the term 'workerism', bearing in mind that FOSATU did not itself employ it and that it carries a certain historical baggage. However, it serves as well as any other term to describe the main political current within FOSATU and thus also the char-acteristic positions of FOSATU. Workerism, it should be stressed, was not the platform of an organised party; it was not monolithic, and it was an evolving project. Nonetheless, it was a pervasive current, with distinct and identifiable views.

Workerism is correctly remembered for its emphasis on strong, industrial, autono-mous unions, based at the point of production and outside of party tutelage. Its poli-tics, however, was far broader, and far more radical than this might suggest. Workerism viewed bottom-up worker-run unions as the heart of a larger 'working-class movement' (Foster, 1982: 6–8) for radical change. It nurtured working-class identity, culture and history, and campaigned for significant economic and political reforms, including within working-class communities, to strengthen workers and unions against both apartheid *and* capitalism.

Stripped of veils of misunderstanding, workerism stands revealed as having an insightful, left-wing, anti-capitalist and class-based approach to the National Question that remains of great interest (Byrne, 2012, 2013). Workerism questioned the notion that national oppression can, or indeed should, only be fought by nationalism: it aimed to fight racial domination through a radical working-class politics.

To remove racism required abolishing capitalism, something only a movement for workers' power could achieve. Immediate struggles, including for reforms, were steps to a new South Africa that was socialist; that involved a massive redistribution of power and wealth through the extension of workers' control of the workplace, the economy and the larger society; and that ended racial inequality and oppression. This required a movement separate from the nationalists, including the African National Congress (ANC), centre of the 'Congress' movement, from the Marxist-Leninists, including the South African Communist Party (SACP); and from the multi-class, nationalist popular fronts they promoted.

Workerism was a distinctive tradition, shaped by a kaleidoscope of left ideologies and initiatives, international and local, often refracted via the global New Left. It challenged the traditions of the ANC and the SACP, as well as other nationalist and left currents. However, the workerist position lies buried under an unsatisfactory historiography which elevates the authority of the Congress movement, the SACP and nationalism.

BEYOND THE 'WORKERIST-POPULIST DEBATE'

Much of the received wisdom about the political positions of FOSATU and workerism comes via the polemics generated by the so-called 'workerist-populist debate' of the 1980s, which pitted Congress-aligned 'populists' against FOSATU workerists.

These polemics shed more heat than light. Terms like 'workerism', 'economism' and 'syndicalism' were often used interchangeably, and workerism was described in wildly inconsistent ways. The SACP's journal, the *African Communist*, described FOSATU as having a revolutionary syndicalist programme, involving a union-led project of organising workers to directly take over 'the whole of industry and society', *and* as lacking any theory, strategy or left tradition (Toussaint, 1983: 40, 43, 44). 'Errors of Workerism', in the semi-official journal of the Congress-aligned United Democratic Front (UDF), *Isizwe*, simultaneously accused workerism of 'narrow' apolitical or economistic unionism, of British Labour Party-type social democratic reformism, of a revolutionary syndicalist project of 'attack on the apartheid government and bourgeois rule' by unions, and of a Trotskyist drive to a 'socialist, workers' party' (*Isizwe*, 1986: 17–26).

Evidently, the populist critique of workerism was somewhat incoherent, and it relied heavily on labelling and calumny. But it had enormous power. Thirty years on, 'economistic' and 'syndicalist' remain terms of contempt in the hands of the ANC and SACP (for example, ANC Today, 2007; Semudi, 2013). The populist characterisation of workerism has meanwhile been absorbed into scholarly accounts, as a recent literature review demonstrates (Byrne, 2012). For example, the semi-official history of the Congress of South African Trade Unions (COSATU), described workerism in almost exactly the same manner as did *Isizwe* (Baskin, 1991: 95–7). It cited no direct FOSATU or workerist sources to substantiate its characterisation.

A further difficulty in understanding workerism is a weak labour historiography. Until the 1970s, the key South African labour histories were produced by the left and the unions. From the 1970s, academic interest in South African labour history rose rapidly – giving rise to significant works, including unpublished work such as Johann Maree's (1986) PhD thesis. However, the field has declined sharply from the 1990s, and most current labour studies are focused on contemporary issues (see e.g. Buhlungu, 2009).

There remain enormous gaps. With no written history other than a popular commemorative volume (M. Friedman, 2011), FOSATU appears in studies mainly as part of the larger story of the rise of independent unions from the 1970s (MacShane, Plaut and Ward, 1984; Brown, 1985; S. Friedman, 1985; Kraak, 1993) or of COSATU. Most of these works are dated, published before 1994 (for an exception: Forrest, 2011).

Compounding the problems is a widespread tendency to conflate the history of black resistance in South Africa with the history of black nationalism, where the left (including the SACP) and labour (including the unions) are relegated to bit players – despite often being larger than any of the nationalist formations. In reducing South Africa's contradictions to national and racial ones, resolved through conflicts between white and black nationalists, this approach to 'the struggle' makes the implications of the country being a *capitalist* society quite secondary (Legassick, 1979); concomitantly, research on nationalists massively outstrips research on labour and the left.

FOSATU, WORKERS' CONTROL AND WORKERISM

By the early 1980s, FOSATU was the largest union centre based among black Africans, although it included significant numbers of coloureds and Indians, as well as a few whites (Malgas and Storey, 1982: 7). FOSATU had 45 000 members at its formation, 120 000 in 1984, and 140 000 in 1985 (Baskin, 1991: 49). Much of this growth centred on the Metal and Allied Workers' Union (MAWU), the largest FOSATU affiliate, which became the National Union of Metalworkers of South Africa (NUMSA) in 1987.

By contrast, the ANC-aligned South African Congress of Trade Unions (SACTU) had around 55 000 members at its height in the 1950s. FOSATU's registered contemporaries were initially larger: the Trade Union Congress of South Africa (TUCSA) claimed 299 455 members of all races in 1981, and the all-white South African Confederation of Labour (SACLA) claimed 138 864 (Imrie, 1979: 95; *The Star,* 27 January 1981: 21). However, by 1983 FOSATU was closing in on the registered union centres, and large numbers left TUCSA to join it (Botha, 1988: 689). Thus, from the time of its emergence and for a few years thereafter, FOSATU was the strongest black working-class organisation and opposition movement in the country (Schroeder, 1988: 54).

FOSATU's significance also transcended its size. First, it exemplified a remarkable model of trade union organising, involving a relatively bottom-up structure based on assemblies, shop-stewards' committees and representative bodies all the way up to national leadership. FOSATU focused on industrial unionism, and a 'tight federation' with common campaigns and inter-union solidarity, with inter-union 'locals' bringing together unionists from different affiliates. In this system, the 'worker member of the unions shall control and determine the objects, direction and policies of the unions' (FOSATU, 1982a: 12).

This system of workers' control differentiated FOSATU from looser formations such as the 1920s Industrial and Commercial Workers Union (ICU) and, later, SACTU (Maree, 1986; Ulrich, 2007). The ICU was plagued by chronic disorganisation. Some SACTU affiliates had strong shop-steward structures, but most were loosely organised, de facto general unions. FOSATU's workers' control system was intended to ensure its resilience, as well as ensure that ordinary worker members controlled the federation and its affiliates at all levels. This minimised influence from outsiders (state officials, political parties, academics and activist coalitions), and it limited the power of insiders such as paid officials (union appointees) and full-time office-bearers (elected union leaders).

This system was also meant to ensure that any use of courts and official collective bargaining machinery did not lead to state control over the unions. It was equally an attempt to steer clear of control by political parties. Many FOSATU activists believed that the demise of SACTU was largely *because* it was subordinated to the agendas of the ANC. This, they believed, had led SACTU into a range of futile campaigns that weakened its unions (Bonner, 1979; FOSATU, 1985e: 4–5). By the time that FOSATU was formed in 1979, SACTU was no longer functioning in the country. Its entire leadership was in exile, mainly in London. FOSATU reasoned that the end of SACTU could not be attributed solely to apartheid repression, as various African unions had remained operational during the repressive 1960s and 1970s. Furthermore, new unions like TUACC were able to grow rapidly in the 1970s by choosing their battles and by investing energy into building strong, democratic workplace structures that could remain operational – despite repression.

A further way in which FOSATU's significance went well beyond its rapid growth was that it gave rise to a new, innovative radical alternative political tradition: workerism. Of course it was primarily a trade union formation and organised workers regardless of their political views, and this meant that political tendencies existed alongside each other – including Congress, the Black Consciousness Movement (BCM), and various left groupings in favour of a workers' party. Workerism, however, emerged as the dominant political current within FOSATU, so much so that it was almost impossible to separate formal FOSATU positions from workerist ideas. This is not to suggest that FOSATU leaders always agreed, or that workerism itself did not contain different threads or internal tensions; but significant central tenets held it together, making it a distinct political current that had shared positions.

NATIONAL LIBERATION, CLASS AND NATIONALISM

FOSATU workerism was not against the nationalist goal of non-racial, majority rule in an undivided South Africa but it saw this goal as *inadequate* because it failed to ensure a new society in which workers controlled not just their own unions but also 'the production and distribution of wealth' and were centrally involved in 'decision making on the affairs of South Africa' (FOSATU, 1982a).

The workerist stress on workers' control was not simply about control of the unions, but about an extension of workers' power more broadly. It involved a socialist project, but one that rejected the Marxist-Leninist, pro-Soviet programme of the SACP; an anti-apartheid project, but one that that opposed apartheid while rejecting the nationalist and militarist traditions of the ANC; and a national liberation project, but one that denied that nationalism was the optimal response to national oppression in South Africa, as claimed by the ANC and SACP, or their rivals, the BCM and the Pan Africanist Congress (PAC).

Expanding workers' power across the economy and society required workers' struggles and organising for changes far beyond those of non-racial majority rule through a parliament – it was a direct challenge to capitalism. Workerists also held that apartheid itself was a product of capitalism and, therefore, that fighting apartheid required fighting capitalism. MAWU and FOSATU leader Moses Mayekiso argued:

> Apartheid is just an appendage, a branch of the whole thing – the tree of oppression of capitalism... Then if you chop the branch the tree will still grow. You have to chop the stem, straight, once and for all. South Africa's economy is at an advanced stage, where the workers can take over and direct the whole thing (quoted in Lambert, 1985: 19; also see FOSATU, 1983b).

FOSATU thus rejected SACP claims that South Africa's objective conditions required postponing socialism in favour of a stage of 'national-democracy'. For workerists, 'there are not two stages, but stages, continuous...' (Mayekiso, interview, 2010), and a 'suspicion... that once you've had the first stage you'd never have the second stage' (Fanaroff, interview, 2009).

Workerism also avoided alliances with nationalists, not just the ANC but its rivals, the BCM and PAC, because, it insisted, African nationalist governments routinely turned against trade unions and the working class after independence – not least because they were pro-capitalist (Bonner, interview, 2010). Nationalist movements could certainly defeat oppressive regimes, but always stopped short of complete liberation for the working-class majority: this had been the case in neighbouring Zimbabwe (Zimbabwe Trade Unions, 1985, also see FOSATU, 1983d).

Workerists tended to view nationalism – including the Congress, PAC Africanist and BCM varieties – as representing 'petit bourgeois politics' and 'capitalist' positions (Lambert, 1985; Dube, interview, 2009; Mayekiso, interview, 2010). While the ANC (1969) stated it would make significant economic changes in favour of the majority, its national democratic revolution – radical reform by an alliance of *all* classes and demo-crats – necessarily stopped short of socialism. Further, there was no reason to suppose that the ANC would be more tolerant of unions than any other independent nationalist, capitalist government.

SACP claims that the ANC had 'socialist-inclined policies' (Toussaint, 1983: 40) did not provide adequate reassurance, since the SACP's vision of socialism, the Soviet model, was itself viewed with scepticism. Workerists rejected vanguard-party control in favour of self-organised workers' organisations as the prime agent of change, and viewed social-ism fundamentally in terms of industrial and political democracy (FOSATU, 1982a: 14).

For workerists, the issue was not *whether* workers had 'political' interests, but how these were best to be realised without subordination to non-working-class projects. The solution lay in workers' organisations that 'should not allow themselves be controlled by non-worker political parties' or they would find their interests 'disregarded and their organisation and power gradually cut away' (Bonner, 1979: 5).

Workerism's class line meant, first, that it shared SACTU's stress on the need for the non-racial unity of all *workers*. However, unlike SACTU, and nationalists generally, it did not wish the workers' movement to be part of a larger multi-class popular front. Working-class unity was not only one component of a larger project of building a 'national dem-ocratic' movement (which would include the 'oppressed' middle and upper-class blacks and the liberal bourgeoisie). It was a *different project* for a *different goal*: the building of greater *working-class* power for participatory, anti-capitalist transformation, a transform-ative working-class movement (Foster, 1982: 6–8).

Workerism always clung tightly to the idea of non-racialism and a unified South Africa. In the 1980s, the language of 'non-racialism' formed part of a radical oppositional project. It was used by SACTU, the UDF, the Congress movement and the SACP, as well as by FOSATU and, later, COSATU, to signal a rejection of apartheid categories and rule, a rejection of the racially exclusive organisations favoured by the BCM and PAC, and a commitment to a transformed common society. 'Non-racialism' meant that anyone committed to the struggle could participate, regardless of race. This did not mean ignor-ing the history of racial domination, nor the ways this could manifest in interpersonal relations. It meant, instead, waging a common struggle, centred on the black majority, for radical change.

But for workerism, non-racialism served several additional purposes. It was key to the project of working-class mobilisation, provided a concrete practice of overcoming racial divisions, and was integral to the vision of a radically changed country. Racial and ethnic categories were seen as less important than *class* position as a basis for mobilisation. Workers everywhere existed within a shared struggle, and required a common, class-based, anti-racist, oppositional popular politics, reinforced through careful education (FOSATU, 1985d).

In 1983, for example, FOSATU called for opposition to the proposed Tricameral Parliament, viewing it as 'false and meaningless' and racially divisive (FOSATU, 1983a). General secretary Joe Foster explained that the federation was 'fighting for economic and political justice for all irrespective of race' and would have nothing to do with 'racially divided puppet parliaments'. The decision by the (mainly coloured) Labour Party to participate was denounced as playing a 'dangerous game of racial politics' (FOSATU, 1983b: 1). 'Employers and the State have built up racial division for their own benefit' so 'Only a united NON-RACIAL Trade Union movement can break it down' (FOSATU, 1980b: 3). What mattered was *working-class solidarity*: 'We do not care if you are black or white, if you are with management you can never lead the workers in their struggle' (FOSATU, 1980a: 4).

This approach differentiated workerism from the exclusivist Africanist movement, embodied in the PAC, as well as from the BCM. Africanism routinely argued that black Africans, as the indigenous peoples, should dominate Asian and European aliens; all whites were cast as a ruling class of foreigners and exploiters, with different spiritual and material interests to black Africans, cast as the only real workers (Raboroko, 1960: 25–26, 27). In the 1980s, this translated into the PAC programme of race war: 'for every African being killed by the racist security forces, a white person must be killed.... One racist, one bullet' (APLA, 1987: n.p.).

The looser BCM had some overlaps with Africanism, but rarely reached its levels of overt chauvinism. It argued instead for an alliance of all racially oppressed people, not just black Africans but also coloureds and Indians (jointly, 'blacks'), and a struggle against the oppressing 'white world' (Biko, 1972).

Workerism's non-racialism also differed from that of the ANC, which advocated nationalism based on equal, individual rights regardless of origin (Adam, 1994: 17, 24), and an inclusive South Africanism, albeit qualified by a strong tendency to a somewhat different project of African hegemony (ANC, 1997). Through the non-racial, national democratic struggle, both during and after apartheid, the ANC insisted a new nation would be formed, at once unified and diverse.

For the ANC, the mobilising category was the *nation*, explicitly as a territorial, multi-class formation. Workerism, by contrast, emphasised class divisions among both black

Africans and whites, rejecting elites in both camps. The mobilising category was the South African *working class*, explicitly seen as part of a global working class, with distinct interests. Embracing non-racial politics did not amount to accepting a white veto or the perpetuation of white rule, both of which, Africanists insisted, were the necessary price of non-racial organising (Raboroko, 1960: 26–7).[3] Rather, workerism stressed common class interests in a fight against apartheid and capitalism. Its non-racialism was a radical project of working-class solidarity. Class, here, was seen as a universal formation, albeit one imagined as segmented into national boundaries, so that a 'South African working class' existed as part of a global one.

WORKING-CLASS NATION

The workerist framing of issues throughout was thus *universalist*, in the sense of stressing common class interests and rejecting essentialist notions of fundamentally different racial or national interests, outlooks, epistemologies, spiritual characteristics, or destinies: at its founding congress, 'it was unanimously agreed that in being non-racial FOSATU was actually trying to eliminate racial conceptions' (FOSATU, 1979: 16).

Yet, workerism was focused on local circumstances, and a unitary South Africa was always a key reference. The notion that the homelands were, or could be, independent countries was consistently rejected by FOSATU workerists, as was the notion that whites or Indians were enemy aliens. Intellectually this also meant that the framing of FOSATU's understanding of labour history was *national* in character, in the sense that local labour history was seen in terms of the making of a *multiracial South African* working class (Bonner, 1979).

FOSATU made this viewpoint clear in a series of articles in *FOSATU Worker News* from 1983 to 1985 entitled 'The Making of the Working Class', which started with the founding of the Cape Colony by the Dutch East India Company in 1652. The key events in this story were not the congresses and resolutions of political parties, nor the lives and deaths of their leaders. Rather, it started with the origins of the working class through immigration and colonisation, and moved through a series of class rebellions – such as the 1799 Servant Rebellion – to strikes by white and coloured workers in the 1850s, to the rise of white labour from the 1880s, Indian workers' strikes in the 1910s, the ICU in the 1920s, non-racial communist and industrial unions in the 1920s to 1940s, the Council of Non-European Trade Unions (CNETU) in the 1940s, SACTU in the 1950s, to the new unionism of the 1970s and 1980s.

This history did not shy away from outlining the role of African kings and ruling classes in the sale of slaves and servants, in collaborating with colonialism, and in supplying migrant workers to capitalists. Nor did it fail to emphasise episodes of cross-racial workers' solidarity. By stressing *both* national oppression *and* class differences, it provided a powerful counter-narrative to black and Afrikaner nationalist visions of South African history as a perpetual race struggle – and inspiration for workerists' vision of a working-class movement (Foster, 1982: 6–8) able to change the country.

This stress on class-based mobilisation as both historical reality and contemporary strategy translated into workerists being deeply sceptical of movements and structures in which workers and the working class did not play the leading role. Thus, FOSATU's involvement in larger campaigns was always coupled to doing so 'in such a way that the working-class movement is strengthened' and 'democracy is not merely spoken, but also acted upon' (FOSATU, 1982a: 4).

In so far as workerism envisaged the transformed future in terms of a new and unified South Africa, it could be read as calling, at the least, for a working-class centred nation or, at most, for a working-class nation. This would be centred, not on indigeneity, race or ethnicity, nor even on a new South African identity that downplayed class, but on the interests of the working-class majority and the extension of workers' control.

FOSATU workerism was therefore a remarkable current. Workerist thinking combined anti-nationalist, anti-apartheid and anti-capitalist imperatives to make a distinct approach to the national liberation struggle. This would centre on a united, non-racial working class exercising workers' control – as opposed to a multiclass nationalist popular front, led by non-working-class elements, and often undemocratic (Byrne, 2012: Chapter 6). This project included a fight against capitalism and for industrial democracy (FOSATU, 1982a: 14).

Workerists wanted a 'just and fair society controlled by workers' (Foster, 1982: 2), where wealth was 'democratically produced and equally distributed' (FOSATU, 1982a: 3). Liberation meant 'having a voice in the wealth that you are creating and benefiting from' (Dube, Interview, 2009), where 'no group of people are going to sit in an office and issue instructions to workers' (Sauls, 1980).

BEYOND THE WORKPLACE

Workerism sought to build a strong workers movement by ensuring that black and other workers were well-organised at the point of production. However, this did not mean that workerism was economistic or sectional, as its opponents claimed. FOSATU's official political positions included demands for universal suffrage, the abolition of the homeland system and the end of apartheid security legislation (FOSATU, 1982a). Nor did workerism reject struggles beyond the workplace. FOSATU (1982a) stated that it would 'support any democratic organisation involved in struggles in the community' and 'participate in campaigns directed at the establishment of a more just society'.

FOSATU did not join the UDF, which it viewed as unduly controlled by the middle class, often undemocratic, and too closely linked to Congress (Byrne, 2012: Chapter 6). However, the federation supported township-based bus, consumer and school boycotts; opposed the detention of activists and trade unionists by the apartheid government; campaigned against the 1983 white referendum, the 1984 Tricameral Parliament and the black local authorities; participated in political strikes and work stoppages; championed gender equality at the workplace; fought influx control and provided radical union-based education (FOSATU, 1982a,b, 1983a,b,c,f,g, 1984a,b,c,d,e, 1985a,b,c,d,f,g). If a national liberation struggle is a struggle to end national oppression, then FOSATU workerism was certainly part of the South African national liberation struggle of the time.

Workerism was also concerned with issues related to state power and reform, in a way that contrasted sharply with Congress positions. ANC and SACTU populists posited that reforms were impossible under apartheid: claiming the system would only tolerate 'yellow' unions, they insisted that armed struggle was essential (SACTU, 1979, 1980a, 1981). Workerists, however, argued that it *was* possible to build strong, independent trade unions under apartheid, *and* to use them to win meaningful reforms.

Their position also contrasted with a common claim on the independent left – for example, by the independent Marxist Workers' Tendency (MWT) – that apartheid was so essential to the reproduction of capitalism that apartheid could not end without the destruction of capitalism itself (for example, *Inqaba ya Basebenzi*, 1982). The workerists rejected this claim. While recognising that capitalism benefited from and promoted apartheid, they evidently assumed that major changes could be made, short of socialist revolution, up to and including the installation of a post-apartheid black nationalist state.

Some workerists embraced the view, drawn from a reading of Gramsci, that the state was not 'a monolithic entity and purely functional instrument of capital, but a force which workers can affect by their struggles' (Fine, 1982: 55). This led logically to a politics of engagement, which showed there was a social democratic strand in workerism. Other workerists were more sceptical about the state but also tended to be pragmatic, and believed in using the courts and the statutory industrial relations system to win reforms.

When the apartheid state deracialised labour laws, expanding full union rights and participation in industrial councils to black African workers, the Congress movement called for a boycott. By contrast, workerists generally supported union registration in the reformed statutory industrial relations system as a means of opening up further space for union growth and influence. It was held that as long as workers' control remained central in the trade union movement, co-option into the official machinery could be avoided. Even the social democratic strand in workerism remained deeply committed to notions of workers' participation and self-management, differentiating itself from traditional Western European social democracy, which stressed labour parties and corporatism.

The building of organs of worker power was paramount (Erwin, interview, 2010). It was *possible* to have capitalism without apartheid, but it was not *desirable*, since the working class would remain oppressed and exploited. The unions should foster a larger 'working-class movement' including co-operatives, parties and newspapers 'linked to the working class' to help 'put workers in control of their own destiny' (Foster, 1982: 6–8). In townships, workers formed the majority, faced problems the middle class did not, and should bring to bear power and strategies otherwise lacking (Xipu et al., 1984: 6).

While workerism was labelled 'syndicalism' by the populists, the reality was more complex. Workerism shared with South Africa's earlier revolutionary syndicalists a stress on building an autonomous, democratic, radical workers' movement aiming at workers' control of the economy and society, and the notion of a class-based struggle against both capitalism and racism (see, for example, van der Walt, 2014). This was clearly different to the two-stage, party-led, statist strategy of the SACP: an independent capitalist republic with substantial reforms ('national democracy') as a stage towards a Marxist-Leninist state. In this sense, there was a strand of FOSATU workerism that can certainly be called 'quasi-syndicalist' (Byrne, 2012).

There were, however, no direct links between the earlier syndicalist movement and FOSATU workerism. It was mainly through the New Left that FOSATU imbibed, often indirectly, ideas from anarchists and syndicalists (Byrne, 2012: Chapters 5, 8). A notable conduit was the early Gramsci, with his 'early stuff – the factory councils' especially important (Bonner, interview, 2010; also Webster, interview, 2010). But more gradualist and reformist ideas, like social democracy and Poultantzas's Eurocommunism were also influences on workerism. It was not monolithic, and not a variant of revolutionary or anarcho-syndicalism.

WORKERISM AS MASS MOVEMENT

Many of the critiques of FOSATU workerism rest heavily on arguments that present nationalism as the natural politics of black people. These positions can be found not just in populist polemics against FOSATU, but in scholarly works which marginalise the left in the history of South African protest and resistance (see Legassick, 1979).

Congress populist polemics, for example, set up a number of conflations that effectively presented all rivals as inauthentic. The ANC was presented as synonymous with the national liberation movement, the SACP was presented as synonymous with the working class, and SACTU was presented as synonymous with the union movement. Thus, the bearer of the national struggle was presented as the ANC, which 'carries the present political aspirations of the majority of the black working class as well as other classes of oppressed South Africans' (Toussaint, 1983: 38). As for the working class, since unions alone cannot 'pass beyond the limits of economic struggle', it needed the distilled theory 'we call Marxism-Leninism', and thus, direction by the SACP (Toussaint, 1983: 35, 40–1, 45). In line with its two-stage theory, the direction that the SACP promoted was support for ANC nationalism, as bearer of the first stage.

Since the ANC was nationalist, in the classical sense of advocating a cross-class national movement for a national state, this sort of reasoning also meant presenting nationalism as the essential form of national liberation. And since nationalists and communists both viewed unions essentially as adjuncts to political parties, this also meant that unions, including SACTU, were viewed as political only to the extent that they took directions from the (correct) political parties. To set up any new movements must thus only have a 'disruptive and divisive effect' (Toussaint, 1983: 46).

The corollary of this type of reasoning was that alternative left traditions, among them workerism, were 'totally foreign to the reality of South African conditions' (Toussaint, 1983: 43). Since workerism rejected the ANC and SACP, populists reasoned, it obviously ignored national liberation (Toussaint, 1983: 43).

But how, if nationalism and Marxism-Leninism were the natural politics of black workers, could a large, mostly black formation like FOSATU come to reject both? For ANC and SACP ideologues, the explanation lay in FOSATU having the wrong leadership. FOSATU-type unions, claimed SACTU, were 'unions of black members run by one or two white organisers' (SACTU, 1980b: 4). Workerism was then presented as the politics of the small clique of whites, mainly university-educated, who were active in TUACC and FOSATU as educators, organisers and functionaries. Such 'forces amongst the intelligentsia' (Nhere, 1984: 80) supposedly imposed 'academic Marxism', 'very European in character' (Isizwe, 1986: 15), from their 'armchairs' (Toussaint, 1983: 43), blocking the nationalist instincts of black members.

Echoes of these arguments also appear in academic scholarship. One position argues that FOSATU forays into mass politics were a revolt *against* workerism by black workers (von Holdt, 1987). Another presents the workerist stress on class struggle as a self-serving attempt by middle-class whites to avoid the threat of race and maintain power (Ally, 2005). A third describes the decline of workerism in terms of the 'the labour constituency ... finding its own voice' for the first time with the rise of nationalist black leaders in the mid-1980s (Buhlungu, 2006a,b).

But such claims face several immediate problems. There is a major difficulty with presenting SACTU as a more authentic union than FOSATU, given that it stopped being a functioning federation in the 1960s. Individual SACTU activists played an important role in the 1970s independent unions, including TUACC and MAWU, but not as a coherent bloc (Hemson, Legassick and Ulrich, 2006). They were manifestly a minority, unable to win TUACC or FOSATU.

The notion that black unionists supported nationalism whereas white unionists supported a non-racial class or workerist position is incorrect. White activists in FOSATU were a tiny minority; black African and coloured members and worker-leaders dominated numerically at all levels; workerism successfully generated large numbers of black worker leaders and worker-intellectuals (Forrest, 2011; Sephiri, 2001: 70). Given FOSATU's bottom-up structures, there was no bureaucratic apparatus that could be manipulated to impose the will or views of any tiny layer (Byrne, 2012: Chapter 7).

The views of the black African and coloured majority in FOSATU were, by available evidence, indistinguishable from those of the whites. For example, Mayekiso bluntly rejected the ANC's Freedom Charter as a capitalist document, the notion of 'two stages towards liberation' as a waste of time and 'our struggle as part of the struggle of all workers internationally' (in Lambert, 1985: 20). The claim that workerism was white silences tens of thousands of workerist black African and coloured voices. And the fallacy of reducing politics to race is borne out by the simple fact that many of the ANC, SACP, SACTU and populist ideologues who attacked workerism were themselves white.[4]

There is also no reason to suppose that workerism would be any more alien to black workers than nationalism. Every major black nationalist movement in South Africa was founded by university-trained intellectuals, including the ANC, BCM and PAC, and Cyril Ramaphosa and Jay Naidoo, who led the nationalist charge against workerism in COSATU, were a lawyer and an ex-medical student, respectively.

In short, a neat mapping of workerism onto whites and of nationalism onto blacks, or of 'middle class' onto whites and 'working class' onto blacks, does not correctly represent the divisions. Nor – given that workerism *did* engage in the national liberation struggle – does a reduction of national liberation to nationalism ring true, since workerism exemplified an anti-nationalist mode of national liberation politics. To claim that class politics was adopted as a means to avoid uncomfortable racial realities not only amounts to a fairly instrumentalist view of ideas, but one that manifestly fails to explain why class politics, in various forms, was embraced by hundreds of thousands of black, coloured and Indian working-class people, not only in FOSATU, but in SACTU, the SACP and COSATU as well.

None of this is to say that South Africa did not have intense racial problems or that these did not pose real challenges in non-racial movements. The point is that a widespread socialist consciousness existed both in FOSATU and in parts of the UDF, which stressed class struggle centred on black workers as a means to a radical form of national liberation. The appeal of class, socialism and workerism reflected, at least partly, the fact that the black working class confronted not just racial oppression but class rule as well.

CONCLUSION: ECLIPSE

Bottom-up FOSATU unions were built to play a leading role in fighting both class exploitation and national oppression. A union-centred working-class movement was seen as the key site for the creation, from below, of a new nation – a nation reconstituted by the working class, where workers' control, in the broadest sense, was to be implemented.

The workerism of FOSATU engaged with political issues, while rejecting nationalist or communist tutelage. It opposed capitalism while rejecting Marxism-Leninism. It engaged in community politics while steering clear of multiclass popular fronts. And it used the courts and law while remaining committed to workers' democracy and autonomy from the state and capital. Most notably for this chapter, FOSATU workerism undertook anti-apartheid work, supporting national liberation, while rejecting nationalism in favour of a larger and more radical working-class politics.

Workerism's vision of the future was a radical one, in which the (non-racial) worker would have a direct say in the production and distribution of wealth, where the involvement of workers in 'all levels of decision-making in the production process' would be the safeguard for the needs and aspirations of 'the working people' (FOSATU, 1982a: 3, 14). This democratic and socialist system would not only overcome class division; apartheid oppression and race itself as a basis of inequality would be removed. This future was to be built in the present – by careful, methodical and democratic organisation, by winning gains through struggle, and through consistent investments in worker education as a means of building an alternative world view and developing the skills for workers' control.

Beyond these common points, and stress on prefiguration, there were a number of unresolved tensions and ambiguities in FOSATU workerism, including at the levels of longer-term strategy and social analysis that undermined its project (Byrne, 2012). One of the major issues that was not addressed was whether greater workers' control of the economy meant a left social democratic system of co-determination and corporatism, or complete worker self-management. Related to this was a larger question about how the working-class movement would relate to a new African nationalist-led government. Further, it was not entirely clear how exactly the working-class movement would carry out its socialist transition, and in doing so relate to forces like the ANC, the SACP and the BCM. Tensions between more social democratic and quasi-syndicalist strands of workerism were never resolved, and the workerist/populist clash ended in populist victory.

Workerism, as a project, declined rapidly in the later 1980s. Only fragments of its project remain in the unions. A full account of the dramatic eclipse of workerism by populism within COSATU by the start of the 1990s falls outside the scope of this chapter. However, since nationalism is only one current in national liberation struggles, and since workerism manifestly overshadowed nationalism for a large sector of the black population, the victory of nationalism cannot be viewed as inevitable or natural. Concrete political battles – and the weaknesses, ambiguities, tensions and contradictions of workerism itself – contributed to its eclipse. Obviously, nationalist currents did exist within FOSATU, but it was only in the late 1980s that Congress nationalism conquered COSATU. The influence of nationalism, or of parties like the ANC and SACP, must be explained, not assumed.

There is much to learn from workerism, which underlines the point that the hold of nationalism can be challenged, that a left project can have a great impact, and that the victory of the ANC and the SACP in the 1980s was not inevitable nor, indeed, need it be permanent. FOSATU workerism's insight is that the complete emancipation of the working class in South Africa, both in national and in class terms, requires self-activity, class-based and bottom-up mass movements, organised labour and a project of industrial democracy. This insight remains as relevant as ever. Workerism's ideas remain a jarring presence in South African resistance history, a radical challenge to the orthodoxies and hegemony of nationalism and Marxism-Leninism.

NOTES

1 Red, black and gold were the colours of the FOSATU banner – a red field upon which was superimposed a gold cog and three workers' fists, each holding a different tool.
2 Like TUACC unions, before 1980 most of FOSATU's unions were 'unregistered' – not formally registered in the state-run industrial relations system which effectively excluded almost all black Africans from direct participation. Laws in the 1950s further criminalised African strike activity, and prevented Africans from forming part of the registered unions. In the 1970s, before the reforms that followed the 1979 Wiehahn Commission report, black African workers and unions had no access to statutory industrial relations machinery, or protected strike action. 'Registered' unions represented only coloured, Indian and white workers, even if some, at some periods, had unofficial 'parallel' unions for black Africans.
3 This Africanist claim was also a caricature of ANC positions, which stressed that radical economic and political changes and majority rule were central to its aim of national democracy, and which theorised South Africa as marked by 'internal' colonialism (ANC, 1969).
4 For example, 'Nyawuza' of the *African Communist* was Joe Slovo; Jeremy Cronin was the author of 'Errors of Workerism' in *Iziswe*.

REFERENCES

Adam, H. (1994) Ethnic versus Civic Nationalism: South Africa's Non-Racialism in Comparative Perspective. *South African Sociological Review*, 7(1): 15–30.
African National Congress (ANC) (1969) *Strategy and Tactics of the ANC.* Document adopted at the Morogoro Conference of the ANC, Tanzania, 25 April – 1 May 1969. Morogoro: ANC.
African National Congress (ANC) (1997) *Nation-Formation and Nation Building: The National Question in South Africa.* Discussion document, 1 July. Johannesburg: ANC.

Ally, Shireen (2005) Oppositional Intellectualism as Reflection, not Rejection of Power: Wits Sociology, 1975–1989. *Transformation*, 59: 66–97.

ANC Today (2007) A Fundamental Revolutionary Lesson: The Enemy Manoeuvres but it Remains the Enemy. *ANC Today*, part 7, number 36. Available online at http://www.anc.org.za/anc-docs/anctoday/2007/at36.htm (accessed 15 September 2007).

Azanian People's Liberation Army (APLA) (1987) APLA Selects White Targets. *Azania Combat: Official Organ of the Azanian People's Liberation Army*, 4.

Baskin, Jeremy (1991) *Striking Back: A History of COSATU*. Johannesburg: Ravan.

Biko, Stephen (1972) White Racism and Black Consciousness. In *Student Perspectives on South Africa*, edited by H.W. van der Merwe and D. Welsh. Cape Town: David Philip.

Bonner, Philip (1979) Lecture delivered at the Inaugural Congress of FOSATU: The History of Labour Organisation in South Africa. Main FOSATU collection (AH1999), folder C.1.8.1, pp. 4–5. Historical Papers collection, University of the Witwatersrand, Johannesburg.

Botha, R.H. ([1985] 1988) Presidential Address to TUCSA's 30th Annual Conference. In *South African Industrial Relations of the Eighties*, edited by W. Bendix. Cape Town: IPC.

Brown, Gavin (1985) *Hard Labour: A Pictorial Survey of Labour Relations in South Africa since 1979*. Johannesburg: IR Data Publications.

Buhlungu, Sakhela (2006a) Rebels Without a Cause of their Own? The Contradictory Class Location of White Officials in Black Unions in South Africa, 1973–1994. *Current Sociology*, 54(3): 427–51.

Buhlungu, Sakhela (2006b) Whose Cause and Whose History? A Response to Maree. *Current Sociology*, 54(3): 469–71.

Byrne, Sian Deborah (2012) 'Building Tomorrow Today': A Re-Examination of the Character of the Controversial 'Workerist' Tendency associated with the Federation of South African Trade Unions (FOSATU) in South Africa, 1979–1985.Unpublished Master's dissertation, University of the Witwatersrand, Johannesburg.

Byrne, Sian Deborah (2013) Rethinking 'Workerism' and the FOSATU Tradition, 1979–1985. Paper presented at the Durban Moment Conference, Rhodes University, Grahamstown, 21–23 February 2013.

Comrades in Africa (1984) Ideological Struggle on the Trade Union Front. *African Communist*, 99: 106–09.

Federation of South African Trade Unions (FOSATU) (1979) Minutes of FOSATU congress. Main FOSATU collection (AH1999), folder C.1.8.1, p. 16. Historical Papers collection, University of the Witwatersrand, Johannesburg.

Federation of South African Trade Unions (FOSATU) (1980a) Ford-AUW Hits Back. *FOSATU Worker News*, 5.

Federation of South African Trade Unions (FOSATU) (1980b) TUCSA Tries Again. *FOSATU Worker News*, 7.

Federation of South African Trade Unions (FOSATU) (1982a) Resolutions Submitted to the Second FOSATU Congress, 10th and 11th April 1982.Main FOSATU collection (AH1999), folder C.1.8.2. Historical Papers collection, University of the Witwatersrand, Johannesburg.

Federation of South African Trade Unions (FOSATU) (1982b) Thousands Mourn for Neil Aggett. *FOSATU Worker News*, March.

Federation of South African Trade Unions (FOSATU) (1983a) Call for United Stand. *FOSATU Worker News*, February.

Federation of South African Trade Unions (FOSATU) (1983b) Labour Party's Dangerous Game. *FOSATU Worker News*, February.

Federation of South African Trade Unions (FOSATU) (1983c) New Bill Angers Workers. *FOSATU Worker News*, 19.

Federation of South African Trade Unions (FOSATU) (1983d) Profile [Chris Dlamini]. *FOSATU Worker News*, 22.

Federation of South African Trade Unions (FOSATU) (1983e) Strive to Build a Strong Working Class Movement [report on MAWU congress], *FOSATU Worker News*, 25.

Federation of South African Trade Unions (FOSATU) (1983f) Urban Rights for 300. *FOSATU Worker News*, 26.

Federation of South African Trade Unions (FOSATU) (1983g) We Say No. *FOSATU Worker News*, 26.

Federation of South African Trade Unions (FOSATU) (1984a) Deadline for Detainee Release, *FOSATU Worker News*, 33/34.

Federation of South African Trade Unions (FOSATU) (1984b) Maternity a Worker Right. *FOSATU Worker News*, 30.

Federation of South African Trade Unions (FOSATU) (1984c) Thousands Support Stay Away Call as Anger Rises in Transvaal Townships. *FOSATU Worker News*, 33/34.

Federation of South African Trade Unions (FOSATU) (1984d) What's the Use of Boots without Laces? *FOSATU Worker News*, 27.

Federation of South African Trade Unions (FOSATU) (1984e) Women Workers Speak Out at FOSATU Booklet Launch. *FOSATU Worker News*, 30.

Federation of South African Trade Unions (FOSATU) (1985a) Boycott. *FOSATU Worker News*, 40.

Federation of South African Trade Unions (FOSATU) (1985b) Over 100 000 Mourn Langa Dead. *FOSATU Worker News*, 38.

Federation of South African Trade Unions (FOSATU) (1985c) Stop Assaults and Detentions. *FOSATU Worker News*, 42.

Federation of South African Trade Unions (FOSATU) (1985d) The Making of the Working Class. Part 2: What is Education? *FOSATU Worker News*, 43.

Federation of South African Trade Unions (FOSATU) (1985e) The Making of the Working Class. Part 15: SACTU and the Congress Alliance. *FOSATU Worker News*, 42.

Federation of South African Trade Unions (FOSATU) (1985f) We Will Not Ride! *FOSATU Worker News*, Number 35/36.

Federation of South African Trade Unions (FOSATU) (1985g) 8 000 Mourn Langa Dead. *FOSATU Worker News*, Number 37.

Fine, B. (1982) Trade Unions and the State Once More: A Reply to our Critics. *South African Labour Bulletin*, 8(1): 47–58.

Forrest, K. (2011) *Metal that Will Not Bend: The National Union of Metal Workers of South Africa, 1980–1995*. Johannesburg: Wits University Press.

Foster, Joseph (1982) The Workers Struggle: Where does FOSATU Stand? FOSATU Occasional Publication, No. 5, in main FOSATU archive (AH1999), folder C1.7.3.16.3.10. Historical Papers, University of the Witwatersrand, Johannesburg.

Friedman, M. (2011) *The Future is in the Hands of the Workers: A History of FOSATU*, Johannesburg: Mutloatse Arts Heritage Trust.

Friedman, S. (1985) *Building Tomorrow Today: African Workers in Trade Unions, 1970–1984*. Johannesburg: Ravan.

Hemson, David, Martin Legassick and Nicole Ulrich (2006) White Activists and the Revival of the Workers' Movement. *The Road to Democracy in South Africa, Volume 2, 1970–1980*. Pretoria: Unisa Press.

Imrie, Ruth M. (1979), *A Wealth of People: The Story of the Trade Union Council of South Africa*. Johannesburg: TUCSA.

Inqaba ya Basebenzi (1982) Only Workers' Rule Can Replace Apartheid Dictatorship! *Inqaba ya Basebenzi*, 7.

Isizwe (1986) Errors of Workerism. *Isizwe – The Nation: Journal of the UDF*, 1(3): 113–31.

Kraak, Gerald (1993) *Breaking the Chains: Labour in South Africa in the 1970s and 1980s.* London: Pluto.

Lambert, Nigel (1985) Towards a Workers' Party? [interview with Moses Mayekiso]. *Socialist Worker Review*, October.

Legassick, Martin (1979) Review Article: Records of Protest and Challenge. *Journal of African History*, 20(3): 451–5.

MacShane, Denis, Martin Plaut and David Ward (1984) *Power! Black Workers, Their Unions and the Struggle for Freedom in South Africa.* Nottingham, UK: Spokesman Press.

Mahomed, Yunus (1984) State of Struggle. *AZASO National Newsletter: Discussion Series number 1.* FOSATU archives (AH1999), folder C4.5.Historical Papers, University of the Witwatersrand, Johannesburg.

Malgas, Rocco and Paul Storey (1982) Trade Union Unity: Which Way Forward Now? *Inqaba ya Basebenzi*, 7.

Maree, Johann (1986) An Analysis of the Independent Trade Unions in South Africa in the 1970s. Unpublished PhD thesis, University of Cape Town.

Nhere, Ruth (1984) The Dangers of 'Legal Marxism' in South Africa. *African Communist*, 99: 75–80.

Nyawuza (Joe Slovo) (1985) New 'Marxist' Tendencies and the Battle of Ideas in South Africa. *African Communist*, 103: 45–62.

Qabula, Alfred (1984) Praise Poem to FOSATU. *FOSATU Worker News*, 31: 12.

Raboroko, P. Nkutsoeu (1960) Congress and the Africanists: (I) The Africanist Case. *Africa South*, 4(3): 24–32.

Sauls, Freddie (1980) Interview with Freddie Sauls, Secretary of the National Union of Motor and Rubber Workers of South Africa (NUMARWOSA). *South African Labour Bulletin*, 6(2/3): 53–73.

Schroeder, Riyaad (1988) Trade Unions, Politics and the Working Class Struggle: The Food and Canning Workers Union, 1975 to 1986.Unpublished Honours dissertation, University of Cape Town, Cape Town.

Semudi, Jerry (2013) The Status of Trade Unions in Forms and Methods of Struggle. *The Thinker*, 53: 46–7.

Sephiri, Thabo Ezekiel (2001) The Emergence and Role of Black Intellectuals in the Development of the Trade Union Movement in South Africa: A Case Study of NUMSA, 1980–2000. Unpublished MA thesis, University of the Witwatersrand.

South African Congress of Trade Unions (SACTU) (1979) Wiehahn Commission a Con-trick, SACTU Chief tells ILO: Racists Plan More Chains for Unions. *Workers Unity*, 15.

South African Congress of Trade Unions (SACTU) (1980a) 1980: The Year of the Worker! A Call for Workers' Mobilisation. *Workers Unity*, 17.

South African Congress of Trade Unions (SACTU) (1980b) People United Cannot Be Defeated. *Workers Unity*, 23.

South African Congress of Trade Unions (SACTU) (1981) We Can't Use Apartheid Laws. *Workers Unity*, 24.

Toussaint (1983) A Trade Union is Not a Political Party: A Critique of the Speech 'Where FOSATU Stands'. *African Communist*, 93: 35–47.

Ulrich, Nicole (2007) 'Only the Workers Can Free the Workers': The Origin of the Workers' Control Tradition and the Trade Union Advisory Coordinating Committee (TUACC), 1970–1979. Unpublished Master's thesis, University of the Witwatersrand, Johannesburg.

Van der Walt, Lucien (2014) Revolutionary Syndicalism, Communism and the National Question in South African Socialism, 1886–1928. In *Anarchism and Syndicalism in the Colonial and Postcolonial World, 1870–1940: The Praxis of National Liberation, Internationalism, and Social Revolution*, edited by Steven J. Hirsch and Lucien van der Walt. Leiden: Brill.

Von Holdt, Karl (1987) Trade Unions, Community Organisations and Politics: A Local Case Study on the East Rand. Sociology of Work Research Report number 3, University of the Witwatersrand, Johannesburg.

Yudelman, David (1984) *The Emergence of Modern South Africa: Capital, State and the Incorporation of Organised Labour on the South African Gold Fields, 1902–1939.* Cape Town and Johannesburg: David Philip.

Xipu, Rolly, Amon Sibanyoni, Vincent Boshielo, Rusty Moagi, and D. Madupela, with Chris Dlamini, (n.d. [?1984]) The Worker in the Community, paper by panel of FOSATU shop stewards, Rolly in Taffy Adler Papers, (AH2065), folder CD15.3, Historical Papers collection, University of the Witwatersrand.

Zimbabwe Trade Unions (1985) Main FOSATU collection (AH1999), folder C5.3. Historical Papers collection, University of the Witwatersrand, Johannesburg.

INTERVIEWS

Philip Bonner. Interview with Sian Byrne, 18 October 2010, Johannesburg.

Daniel Dube. Interview with Sian Byrne, 21 July 2009, Port Elizabeth. FOSATU National Executive Committee, NUMSA President.

Alec Erwin. Interview with Sian Byrne, 23 July 2010, Cape Town. FOSATU General Secretary, FOSATU Education Secretary

Bernie Fanaroff. Interview with Sian Byrne, 27 November 2009, Johannesburg. MAWU National Organiser, MAWU Acting General Secretary.

Moses Mayekiso. Interview with Sian Byrne, 25 January 2010, Johannesburg. MAWU National Secretary, MAWU Treasurer, NUMSA General Secretary.

Eddie Webster. Interview with Sian Byrne, 20 November, 2010, Johannesburg.

NATIONAL DEMOCRATIC REVOLUTION MEETS CONSTITUTIONAL DEMOCRACY

Daryl Glaser

This chapter investigates the theory of National Democratic Revolution (NDR) and its implications for the construction of a post-1994 South African social order on a terrain of constitutional democracy. More specifically, it analyses the nexus between two fields of discourse and practice – NDR and South Africa's 1996 Constitution – tracing their genealogies to Marxism-Leninism and a left-inflected or social-democratic liberalism respectively. How have followers and practitioners of each of these discourses comprehended the other? To what extent can these fields of discourse and practice coexist, and on what terms? To what extent are they 'contradictory' in a Hegelian-Marxist sense, with the contradiction between them liable for future resolution on some or other (non-liberal?) basis?

The source of the tension between them is clear. NDR theory comprehends entire social formations, including economic substructures. It is class-focused and historical-teleological; it deals in the currency of struggle and power under the sign of a socialist telos. The ascendant discourse of government and power, namely constitutional democracy, is a formal and superstructural theory, one concerned with fair procedures, political pluralism, institutionalised contestation and limits to power. To be sure, constitutional democracy in South Africa is left-inflected in two ways that offer possible terms of reconciliation with NDR: it provides for certain elements of substantive social justice (reflected in socio-economic rights) and for participatory democracy (a concession to the orthodox Marxist critique of 'bourgeois democracy'). Even so, the nexus between NDR and democratic constitutionalism remains conceptually fraught. There is the further question of how it is actually construed by South Africa's principal political actors (particularly those in and around the ruling African National Congress (ANC)).

My interest, politically and normatively, is in drawing on the best of liberalism and the best of socialism. Unlike Marxist-Leninists, I consider it problematic to view these social orders or 'ideologies' in sequential terms, whereby a socialist stage supersedes a liberal-democratic one. An animating issue for me, therefore, is whether NDR theory conceptually allows its practitioners to pursue socially transformative goals on the terrain of constitutional liberal and social democracy, or whether it ultimately mandates its supersession. I consider the former possibility hopeful, the latter unsettling.

In the end, I argue, there are indeterminacies in the NDR constitutional-democracy relationship that cannot be definitively resolved. This is in part because the two theories speak past each other, having never expected to meet on ground where their respective ideologues would need to find a common language. I suggest two distinct ways of construing NDR, each of which has a different implication for constitutional democracy. One is essentially hostile to constitutional democracy. Its main features are economic and class reductionism, particularly in the analysis of the state, law and political forms; a quasi-deterministic theory of history; a teleological approach to politics; and a moral theory that, where not absent altogether, takes the form of what Lukes (1986: 221) termed 'long-range [moral] consequentialism'. This 'authoritarian' NDR conceives the people as collective, ideal, perfectible and purposive, yet also internally contradictory and transitional; its demos can be understood as ethnic, civic or both.

A second construal of NDR is more readily reconciled with constitutional democracy. It considers NDR to be an account of societal change offered by particular, fallible political actors. It generates a practical programme that acquires authoritative force only by revocable popular mandate. Furthermore, it acknowledges the legitimacy of procedural and essentially liberal-democratic rules of permissible political action. In other words, it is a substantive programme to be pursued within pre-established though not inflexible 'rules of the game' – with the proviso that all democratic constitutional orders require substantive design choices that NDR theory can legitimately inform, and arguably already does in South Africa's Constitution. In this 'democratic' NDR discourse, the 'people' is conceived as a plural body of citizens, as primarily civic-territorial rather than ethno-racial, as empirical rather than ideal, as irreducibly diverse, and as entitled recursively to decide between a range of futures for itself.

THE THEORY OF NATIONAL DEMOCRATIC REVOLUTION

Addressing the NDR-constitutionalism nexus requires that we first clarify the theories of NDR and constitutional democracy on their own terms.[1]

NDR theory originates in Marxism-Leninism, but represents a Marxism inflected by twentieth-century events. Among these, the victory of the Bolshevik Revolution, under Vladimir Lenin's leadership, is pre-eminent. NDR theory has often been appropriated by anti-colonial nationalists in whose hands it has sometimes become unmoored from its Marxist origins, a theory of, say, developmental nationalism. This appropriation is not accidental, given that NDR allies a Marxist class project to a nationalist, anti-colonial one. Even so, it is difficult to make sense of NDR except from a Marxist theoretical angle.

The Marxist-Leninist approach to the National Question is the product of a tension between a quasi-deterministic theory of history and unanticipated strategic opportunities. Specifically, the tension is between a theory urging that objective conditions are unripe for revolution and opportunities to seize revolutionary power in the here and now. The effort to resolve the tension has been intellectually and politically productive. In a lineage that includes Lenin, Trotsky, Stalin and Mao, practitioners of Marxism-Leninism identified and seized strategic revolutionary opportunities, justified doing so in recognisably Marxist terms, and turned their success into a revised historical theory that could frame subsequent revolutions led by Marxist parties and organisations (beginning in China in the 1920s).

The tensions arose because of four interconnected features of the societies in which Marxists had the opportunity to seize political power – features that ostensibly disqualified the societies as revolutionary candidates according to orthodox Marxist theory:

- Productive forces were insufficiently developed to sustain socialism, let alone communism.
- Capitalism had not been established and/or had not yet fulfilled its historical mission to create a modern economy.
- The class supposedly required to build socialism – the proletariat – was too small and/or insufficiently self-aware to provide revolutionary leadership.
- In many cases societies identified their principal sources of oppression not in internal class contradictions but in external colonial or neo-colonial domination.

Marxist-Leninist theory attempted to resolve these tensions in some combination of the following ways. In some cases, Marxists tried to prove that capitalism (and hence the working class) was further developed than commonly supposed, and therefore that proletarian revolution was possible. In other instances, they argued that the capitalist class was incapable of carrying out its historical mission of capitalist development, and that the working class would have to take over this leadership. (These apparently contrary notions were harmonised in Trotsky's theory of 'combined and uneven development'.) In either case, the working class rather than the capitalists would have to lead societies through a process of 'development'. This might include reproducing the primitive accumulation that capitalism was supposed to undertake (Liebman, 1975).

Given that the working class in these societies was too underdeveloped to provide leadership unassisted, Leninists insisted that it would have to be led by an advance guard of revolutionary professionals and class-conscious proletarians. Part of the vanguard's mission would be to bring the proletariat to a numerical and subjective point where it could perform the mission that capitalism was supposed to have readied it to do. Moreover, the proletariat would have to rule in – and over – an alliance of classes that shared its interest in carrying out the historical tasks that had to be completed before the construction of socialism could commence.

According to the Marxist-Leninists, the colonial domination of much of the world by European capitalist powers created an opportunity to attack advanced capitalism at its weakest link through support of anti-colonial struggles. They hoped that the seizure of power by leftists in less developed former colonial countries would precipitate a world revolution capable of bringing advanced capitalist economies into the revolutionary fold, thus drawing the new and classical Marxist theories back into alignment. From the 1960s Soviet theorists began to think of these new states as states of 'socialist orientation' capable of reaching socialism by a 'non-capitalist' path. In the meantime, they would strengthen the Soviet-led anti-imperialist camp.

These twentieth-century Marxist-Leninist responses crystallised in response to several experiences. The Russian Revolution inherited the Russian empire and in seeking the support of non-Russian nationalities Stalin and Lenin offered to recognise national self-determination for non-Russians within the former empire. Moreover, the Soviet Union had to demonstrate that it had liberated Russia's own colonial underlings in order to sustain its credibility abroad as an anti-colonial champion. In practice, the USSR granted self-determination to its own nationalities in limited, uneven or contradictory ways. Nevertheless, the theory of national self-determination worked out in this context contributed to Marxism-Leninism's openness to anti-colonial nationalist struggles (Martin, 2001).

A further unanticipated circumstance informed the new theory: the rise of fascism in inter-War Europe. Marxism-Leninism treated fascism as a case of capitalism in crisis, shorn of its bourgeois democratic veneer to reveal its underlying terroristic character in the face of a rising proletariat. Despite signalling a decaying finance capitalism, fascism also represented a dire threat to existing proletarian gains and a form of regression from bourgeois democracy. Like colonialism, it required a cross-class marshalling of forces against an immediate enemy, this time in the name of democracy.

Anti-fascism merged with anti-colonial struggle in the course of the Second World War, during which the Soviet Union backed anti-fascist forces against Nazi occupation in Europe and Japanese occupation in Asia. During the subsequent Cold War, the Soviet

277

Union backed efforts in the global South to throw off European rule and establish (as noted) states of socialist orientation. The Soviet Union also took advantage of the war's aftermath to establish satellite 'people's democracies' in East-Central European countries. At the same time the Soviet leadership's fear of a nuclear showdown with the West persuaded it to encourage moderate behaviour among Western European Communists. French and Italian communist parties sought not socialist revolution but to unite multiple class forces against state monopoly capitalism and American imperialism, and in favour of popular democracy and national independence. All of these circumstances and responses favoured cross-class alliances against immediate enemies rather than socialist revolution.

The upshot of these experiences was the delineation of immediate revolutionary or radical-reformist tasks that had a threefold character. They were: *national* (involving peoples against external powers); *popular* (involving mobilisation of whole peoples); and *democratic* (aiming for collective self-determination under bourgeois, popular or proletarian democracy). A fourth task was implicit: *development*.

According to one Marxist-Leninist account, the construction of socialism would have to be postponed until these prior tasks had been carried out. Alternatively, building socialism could commence at once owing to historical circumstances that rendered the capitalist stage redundant, including the presence in certain societies of elements of primitive communism that could be built upon (the Russian *mir;* pre-colonial communalism in Africa) and the availability of assistance from an advanced socialist power (the Soviet bloc).

All this raised the question of whether these immediate tasks constituted a 'stage'. Many Marxist-Leninists rejected mechanical stage-ism in favour of something more dynamic. Proletarian radicalism and/or the impossibility of realising the key demands of the proletariat and its allies under capitalism placed socialism on the agenda, they believed. After Trotsky, there was an implication that the national or popular-democratic moment would segue into the construction of socialism. Even so, critics on the Marxist left insisted that 'Moscow-line' communists (or 'Stalinists') were stuck in a stage-ist logic that blocked the transition to socialism. These arguments are familiar to South Africans.

THE THEORY OF CONSTITUTIONAL DEMOCRACY

South Africa's constitutional democracy belongs to a Western liberal tradition that gained traction in the seventeenth and eighteenth centuries, and that was modified by twentieth-century developments in social citizenship and human rights. Liberal constitutionalism originated as an intellectual and political movement to check royal despotism in Europe and North America by subjecting it to the rule of law, separation of powers and parliamentary oversight. Developing alongside market relations and in the aftermath of religious wars, it sought to relegate economic and religious life to an insulated private sphere while constituting the state as an impartial force regulating diverse private transactions from a distance. It aimed to protect a range of individual rights against arbitrary power, mainly as a series of negative-liberty protections. These included protections against suppression of free expression and association, against taxation without representation, against confiscation of property, and against attacks on the physical person in the form of unwarranted search, arbitrary arrest, cruel and unusual punishment and the partial ministration of criminal justice (Keane, 1988; Boucher and Kelly, 1994; Morrow, 2005).

Liberalism evolved in a variable relationship with two earlier traditions. One was republicanism. Originating in ancient Athens and revived in medieval Italy and later the American and French Revolutions, republicanism emphasised the collective, deliberative exercise of power by citizens, as a matter of civic duty and for the greater good of the state. Its relationship with a privacy-valorising, power-confining liberalism was complicated, as was its relationship with later forms of competitive party politics (Honohan, 2002). A second tradition was democracy, which also originated in ancient Greece, and which many liberals initially viewed with suspicion as a harbinger of majoritarian tyranny, potentially enabling a popular sovereign to exercise power as arbitrary as that earlier exercised by absolute monarchs (Macpherson, 1977; Dunn, 1992; Manin, 1997; Held, 2006; Tilly, 2007). Liberalism made peace with democracy via a modern coupling known as liberal democracy. This was largely on the basis of an institution that had developed in medieval Europe to protect the aristocracy against royal exaction – namely parliament. Liberalism established itself at a time when nation states were consolidating, and defended representative democracy as the democratic form best suited to modern states with their large populations and intricate divisions of labour. Parliamentarism also suited the liberal desire to filter majoritarian passion and a republican interest in collective deliberation.

Constitutionalism's history overlapped that of liberal democracy, but was not entirely coincident with it (Bogdanor, 1988; Elster and Slagstad, 1988). Its specific concern was the rule of a higher impersonal law that could constrain sovereign power (whether that power was monarchical or popular), minimise arbitrary power, and bind everyone from the chief executive to the lowliest citizen in an impartial fashion. Constitutionalism has been closely associated with parliamentary self-government in the Anglo-American natural law tradition. However, the Continental idea of a *Rechtsstaat* – a state which ruled on the basis of law – could, at least in its pre-Second World War versions, be adopted by authoritarian as well as democratic states. Despite classical Marxism's dismissal of law as a reflection of commodification and class division, twentieth-century Marxist-Leninist regimes themselves opted for socialist legality and a form of constitutionalism. Radical democrats remain suspicious of constitutionalism's institutionalising thrust, but the precepts of constitutional order have found wide ideological acceptance. At the same time its acceptance by liberals is not universal. Britain's system of parliamentary sovereignty is constrained by conventions and statutes rather than by a written constitution.

Like Marxism, liberalism and constitutionalism encountered twentieth-century realities that challenged their plausibility. Actually, prior to the late nineteenth century we should talk of the limits of liberal practice rather than of realities that contradicted it. For a long time, liberalism served as a doctrine announcing the rights of materially better-off white males in metropolitan centres. Its universalism was thus contradicted by its limited reach. Much of the subsequent history of liberalism, but also of constitutionalism and democracy, has been about the conflict-laden expansion of its range of rights-bearing subjects via suffrage reform and decolonisation. These processes involved the universalisation of liberal principles, not a recasting of them.[2]

What did challenge the plausibility of liberalism could not have been fully anticipated in the seventeenth and eighteenth centuries. It was the concentration of unaccountable power within the private economic sector and its democracy-distorting spillover into the political realm. Corporations came to look like the large impersonal organisations against whose power liberalism sought protection for individuals. Equally, and thanks to feminism, it became clear that the private non-economic abode hid its own power hierarchies. Treatment of families as singular moral personalities publicly represented by male household heads contradicted the liberal insistence on equality of rights between persons. Yet, liberalism lacked the conceptual language for justifying rights-equalising state intervention in the realm of the intimate.

Liberalism and constitutionalism responded to these challenges in various ways. Right-libertarians attacked private monopolies and crony capitalism in the name of a purified free market. In practice, however, they proved far more suspicious of state intervention than of private power, and remain so in their more recent neoliberal incarnation. Their response to the 'discovery' of patriarchy did not go further than the advocacy of a formal equality between sexes and the criminalisation of private male violence against women; certainly it did not extend to, say, 'market-distorting' affirmative action.

The development of a left or social liberalism is more interesting (Gutman, 1980; Waldron, 1993; Rawls, 1999; Kymlicka, 2002; Glaser, 2014). Many reforming middle-class liberals began to argue that the realisation of liberal values such as freedom and equal rights required state intervention to ensure a more even distribution of resources in society. Whereas small-scale property remained sacrosanct, corporate power became a legitimate target of liberal attack. Liberals played a significant role in the extension of the welfare state in Britain and North America. Communitarian-minded liberals such as T.H. Green insisted that individuals flourished in contexts of social cooperation. In the 1970s, John Rawls initiated the philosophical movement of 'liberal egalitarianism'; his own most famous precept is that deviations from absolute equality in the provision of primary goods can only be justified where these benefit the least advantaged in society (Rawls, 1999).

Perhaps of most immediate relevance here is the later twentieth-century adoption by left-liberals and constitutionalists of socio-economic rights (Fredman, 2008; Langford, 2008). The embrace of second generation rights formed one moment within the development of a widened notion of human rights. If human rights formed the basis of a searing critique of Marxist-Leninist regimes, the more specific idea of socio-economic rights ironically – or perhaps logically – was given its first institutional boost by Stalin's 1936 Constitution, and found its way into international human rights discourse partly through the Soviet challenge to Western liberal human rights during the Cold War. A number of newly democratising countries have since constitutionalised socio-economic rights. If core liberal rights bound majorities with negative prohibitions, the new rights bound majorities and their representatives with positive obligations of social provision. Many liberals remain doubtful of the justiciability of socio-economic rights; many radicals insist that constitutionalism cannot be a substitute for redistributive politics. But the expansion of rights has provided a rubric under which left-leaning forces have been able to reconcile themselves with liberal constitutionalism, as they have done – for the most part – in South Africa.

NDR AND LIBERAL CONSTITUTIONALISM IN SOUTH AFRICA

White rule in South Africa was weakly constitutional. It amounted to a system of parliamentary sovereignty, entrenched in the British Parliament from 1909 and South Africa's Parliament from 1961. Notoriously, South Africa's basic constitutional form was negotiated exclusively between the UK and the white settler minority, to the exclusion of blacks.

Black exclusion set up the 'National Question' (Van Diepen, 1988; Fine, 1991; Drew, 2000). The question was actually twofold: what was required to liberate black people from political, economic and cultural domination, and what new form of South African nationhood might replace the scheme of segregated, ethnically-defined nationhood imposed by apartheid after 1948. All significant black groups concerned themselves with the National Question. Although explicit references to a national democratic revolution only began to appear in ANC documents in 1962, following the appearance of this notion in post-war Soviet theory, the concept built loosely on the 'native republic' thesis of the Communist Party of South Africa (CPSA), adopted in 1928. Variants of NDR theory (under differing names) were adopted by other Marxist-Leninist and nationalist formations in the country. From the Marxist-Leninist standpoint, the National Question in South Africa was not simply about how to end minority rule but also about how to introduce socialism in a country where the race question predominated. The answer chosen by most Marxist groups was to enter into an alliance with one or other strand of African or black nationalism – the ANC in the case of the CPSA, the Non-European Unity Movement (NEUM) and the Azanian People's Organisation (AZAPO) in the case of the Trotskyists – and to prioritise national and democratic over socialist tasks.

While opposition forces adopted various aspirational charters and programmes, the question of whether the future state would be 'constitutional' was not on their horizon. Equally, the specific programmatic content of both the national and the democratic in the NDR was left vague.

White rule in South Africa after 1910 presented twentieth-century Marxists with a challenge and opportunity distinct from that posed by either colonialism or fascism, namely a domesticated white settler colonialism operating in a developing capitalist economy. South Africa arose out of European settler colonialism, but so did the United States and the British dominions. In this respect, it seemed no more obviously colonial than post-independence Canada, Australia or the United States. In addition, South Africa established a significant national bourgeoisie, including a manufacturing sector with a substantial industrial proletariat. Its white political system contained many features of capitalist parliamentary democracy. These considerations suggested that the prospects for a class struggle directed towards socialism – in a manner predicted by orthodox Marxist theory – might be more favourable in South Africa than in many other 'developing' countries (especially in Africa). Could it be that there was in fact no National Question in South Africa, but only a class one?

In the main, the South African Communist Party (SACP), the descendant of the CPSA, chose to reduce white rule in South Africa to the phenomena of fascism and colonialism (albeit 'colonialism of a special type'). And indeed the country retained obviously colonial features, including rule by whites over an indigenous majority, racial discrimination in favour of whites, and white indirect rule over Africans in rural 'reserves'. The fascism theme also resonated, given that in the 1930s and early 1940s Afrikaner nationalists had flirted with Nazi race theory, extra-parliamentary militias and models of corporatist rule. In power, the National Party (NP) became increasingly repressive, banning opposition organisations and newspapers, detaining and banishing dissidents without trial, censoring the press and literature, and introducing Christian National Education and militia training in white schools. The colonialism and fascism analogies were adopted by other leftist strands, including Trotskyists, sometimes with even greater conviction.

The Communists formed a close alliance in the 1950s with an increasingly radicalised ANC. In line with the thinking enunciated above, the CPSA/SACP and the ANC both adopted roughly the following understanding of the National Question after the Second World War. As indicated, white-ruled South Africa was colonial and fascist, meriting a cross-class, cross-racial and cross-ethnic popular alliance (usually presented as being under African working-class leadership) to deal with these immediate enemies and to create a national-democratic state. On the political plane, NDR required an alliance between Marxist and black nationalist organisations, and a programme that proclaimed the emancipation of 'Africans in particular and black people in general' (to use a later formulation) (SACP, 1997). The NDR, once it achieved power, would create a non-racial, inclusive state. It would also address urgent political and economic tasks, such as eliminating monopolies and resolving the land question in favour of dispossessed blacks. The national-democratic state would either precede the struggle for socialism or (in the leftist version) trigger socialist revolution. The ANC would lead the NDR. Whether the SACP would take over leadership in a subsequent period of socialist construction was a matter that could be deferred.

Although the pre-war ANC had a Christian-liberal and constitutionalist orientation, there was little either liberal or constitutionalist about post-war ANC-SACP thinking. The ANC-SACP alliance did not talk much about the character of a future state, but the two organisations, and in particular the SACP, enjoyed strong ties to the Soviet Bloc. The Freedom Charter was capable of being construed as a social-democratic document, but the dominant rhetoric of the SACP – and much of the ANC – was Leninist and anti-liberal during the exile period. The ANC-SACP alliance romanticised guerrilla opposition and subsequently 'people's war' – strategies lending themselves to militarism, hierarchy and secrecy. To the extent that there was any image of what the political system of the NDR period might be, it was of radical-nationalist or Afro-Marxist one-party states such as those established by allied liberation movements in post-independence Africa. The ANC's internal ally during the 1980s – the United Democratic Front (UDF) – practised a more pluralistic, grass-roots politics, but its own rhetoric remained in the Marxist-Leninist anti-liberal mould. To the extent that the internal movement supplied any model of a future state, it was the one prefigured by people's power in the townships from 1985 – essentially a councilist pyramidal model of government under overall Charterist stewardship, and one associated uneasily with the 'red terror' of township comrades.

Signs of the coming encounter between the logics of the NDR and democratic constitutionalism were clearly visible by the later 1980s. The prospect of negotiations required the ANC to think about the terms that whites could accept, including possible protections for minorities. The ideological self-confidence of the Communist Bloc was already waning before the East-Central European revolutions of 1989. By the time open negotiations began in the early 1990s, it had disappeared. Liberal democracy was suddenly globally triumphant, and transmitted to post-independence Africa by the conditionalities of international financial institutions, as well as by demands from below for an end to failed dictatorial rule across the continent. The ANC's own allies in the trade unions and civic organisations wanted to preserve some autonomy for civil society. Radical nongovernmental organisations (NGOs) and human rights lawyers provided an additional impetus towards ANC acceptance of core liberal and social rights. In short, the SACP-ANC had to contemplate a future that was liberal-democratic in previously unanticipated ways.

The Constitution negotiated in South Africa was an amalgam of liberal constitutionalism, African traditionalism and social democracy. It was the expansive conception of rights – their expansion, specifically, to encompass rights to housing, health, education and water – that enabled progressives to view the Constitution as going beyond liberal formalism to embrace a 'transformational' agenda. Given constitutional mandates for socio-economic rights and participatory democracy and the likelihood of ANC electoral victory, there appeared to be no contradiction between the NDR and democratic constitutionalism: they pointed in the same direction, more or less.

Even so, tensions soon became evident after 1994. The Constitution's counter-majoritarian provisions sometimes impeded the decisive governance sought by the ANC. The Constitution cast the ANC and SACP not as bearers of a constitution-transcending mission, but as ordinary rule-bound political parties. Constitutional liberties gave space to what many in the ruling alliance considered to be counter-revolutionary forces, whether of the left or the right. The ruling alliance responded to these facts by threatening to restrict liberties and weaken counter-majoritarian institutions. Successive electoral majorities placed it in a position where it could suborn state power to its partisan ends. While liberals and some leftist opponents appeal to constitutional provisions against ANC excess, other left oppositionists share with many ANC members the view that the constitutional settlement represented a sell-out to white and capitalist interests. They challenge the ANC in a language of anti-institutional populism and a practice of low-level civil insurgency. In other words, both the ruling alliance and key opponents talk and act in ways that imply that their acceptance of constitutionalism, where not null, is largely instrumental.

CONCEPTUAL CONTRASTS

Until now this chapter has tracked the separate histories of NDR and constitutional democracy, both globally and in South Africa. There is value in comparing and contrasting them in a more conceptual way, the better to understand what is at stake in their encounter.

This section draws deliberately simplified contrasts between the two discourses. South African democratic constitutionalism straddles some of the specified binaries, as does the ANC's rhetoric and practice. Further, NDR and democratic constitutionalism constitute diverse bodies of thought, and their adherents are not always theoretically explicit on matters dealt with here. To some extent, then, the following relies on a particular reading of their underlying logics. The main points of difference are the following.

First, orthodox NDR theory attends primarily to what Marxists think of as questions relating to the substructure, or the socio-economic base, of society. NDR views constitutional and institutional designs as part of the superstructure, and thus as products of underlying economic and class relationships. This holds for both the national democratic and socialist 'stages', each of which will exhibit corresponding political forms. The detailed political-institutional forms are indeterminate, products of conjunctural revolutionary requirements and structural constraints rather than abstract and decontextualised lawyerly blueprints. Even so, the national-democratic stage typically takes the political form of a cross-class bourgeois or popular democracy, expressed in a parliamentary government or in leadership by a single mass party or proletarian vanguard party. The subsequent socialist stage is usually thought to require proletarian democracy, conceived along roughly the councilist lines glimpsed in the Paris Commune. This will represent a 'truer' form of democracy than parliamentary democracy, which classical Marxism deems an apparatus of bourgeois domination. For those subscribing to this thinking, the South African constitutional order can have no more than the tactical or strategic value that Lenin ascribed to parliamentary participation, or must be understood as the product of a capitalist stage or temporary class compromise. Its destiny is to be superseded by more radical forms of democracy and social organisation.

In addition, NDR theorists see themselves as addressing real material questions, whereas constitutionalism is conceived of by them as mere 'ideas on paper'. Alternatively, constitutionalism is conceived of by NDR thinkers as a set of norms, belonging to an epiphenomenal realm of moral or ethical injunction. In either event, the ideas and norms only matter to the extent that they are supported by interests and power – or, more specifically, by interests that possess actual power in some form. These interests and powers are located outside the constitutional apparatus itself, usually in the basic social structure. Ideas and norms, and even their institutional office-bearers, generally lack efficacy, at least compared to whatever fundamental interests and powers they 'serve'. In this sense NDR theory is 'realistic' – focused on how power plays out in practice rather than on formalistic descriptions of how it is or ought to be exercised.

There is a further tension around the matter of power – the capacity to realise goals, whether or not there is resistance. NDR and constitutional democrats both acknowledge power as a primary fact about the world. Both implicitly acknowledge that power has two faces: 'power to' and 'power over'. Both consider the former a necessity and potentially benign and the latter a potential source of domination that must be curtailed in an ideal world. (Indeed, Marxist utopians might be more convinced of power's ultimate eradicability than constitutional democrats, who are primarily concerned about dealing with the persistent fact of it.) Nevertheless, in any given conjuncture prior to the realisation of a communist order, Marxists and NDR-ists will tend to view power, including power over, as a valuable thing that is desirable to accumulate in the hands of progressive forces. Constitutional democrats, on the other hand, will view power, or at least power over, as a problem, and its excessive accumulation in the hands of any one actor (however progressive) as bad. In short, constitutional democracy is partly about frustrating power rather than enabling it. The constitutionalists see power accumulation as a source, perhaps even a form, of despotism. Power must be limited or checked or balanced. This feature of democratic constitutionalism rubs up against those practitioners of NDR who seek commandist leadership, and who, in a South African context, see constitutional constraints as hostile to democratic majoritarianism.

This is not the same as a claim that NDR theorists will resort to any means to achieve a desired end. There are two strands in revolutionary Marxist thinking about the means-end relationship. Both foresee a future communist society in which power as domination is dissolved in a stateless and classless order. One, however, envisages a long transition of proletarian dictatorship, marked by ruthless power over the previous dominant classes, and for this strand the ultimate communist end indeed justifies the means. Another strand romanticises 'prefigurative' communism – the possibility of practising, within liberated zones of the here and now, the kind of life that communism will ultimately transform into a general human condition. The celebration of 'people's power' in South African townships in the mid-1980s was predicated on such radical prefigurative hope (Suttner, 1986; Morobe, 1987). But, complicating matters further, this prefigurative communism does not seek to abolish power, even power over; it is a moment within transitional revolutionary dictatorship, and coexists with it. Indeed, the people exercise power over adversaries both internal and external. In the case of people's power, these included the national state, councillors, police, suspected infiltrators, collaborators of various descriptions, and apolitical and rival organisations. Moreover, the sovereign people were not expected to form spontaneously on township streets or to be free at once of false consciousness, and the vanguard – the civic and, beyond it, the United Democratic Front and the ANC – was always expected to be present, exercising a more or less visible guiding hand. In NDR, then, a subordination of means to noble ends jostles with an excitement about the possibility of anticipating noble ends in noble means.

Neither route, however, is to be conflated with the democratic constitutionalist worry about power as such – a worry that fixes on, inter alia, the dangers of precisely the anti-institutionalist, crowd-based participatory majoritarianism that anarcho-Marxists champion. Democratic constitutionalism insists that power should observe limits and rules. These rules institutionalise ideological and partisan disagreement rather than treating it as an occasion for zero-sum struggle. For some prefigurationists, political disputation is a sign of the persistence of the interest-driven power politics that the anarcho-communal space is meant to expel, whereas true communist egalitarianism is marked by harmony rather than politics. Democratic constitutionalism rejects this depiction of a good polity, suspecting that the exclusion of disagreement in the name of egalitarian unity itself involves a masked exercise of illegitimate power.

The means-end conundrum connects to another tension between NDR and democratic constitutionalism. This is the tension between politics understood as teleological and purposive, directed towards particular outcomes, and politics understood as procedure or process, open in principle to multiple outcomes. NDR promotes the former understanding, democratic constitutionalism the latter.

This distinction should not be mischaracterised. Democratic constitutionalists acknowledge the legitimacy of substantive projects; indeed, procedural democracy is designed to accommodate diverse and competing goals. Moreover, they mostly argue that procedural democracy ultimately delivers better end results overall – in terms of human rights, economic development and other desirable ends. Conversely, NDR-ists can see developmental value in democratic processes and have no principled objection to democratic debate about tactics, strategy and policy detail. Even so, the two discourses weigh things differently. NDR *is* a substantive project, whatever internal differences it can accommodate about the means to implement it. To the extent that NDR is mandated by history, it is a substantive purpose that transcends the niceties of process. Democratic constitutionalism, by contrast, is in important measure *about* formal democratic processes, which it defends as both procedurally just and instrumentally valuable.

The difference identified here has deontological and consequentialist dimensions. The defence of constitutional democracy is usually partly deontological: it champions constitutional democratic institutions as intrinsically just or as expressions of values that are just in themselves, such as liberty and equality. NDR, by contrast, originates in discourses that are sceptical about Kantian deontology, or the idea of normative limits to human action, preferring instead to focus on long-range goals like socialism or communism. While a plausible democratic constitutionalism takes consequences seriously, it constrains the range of permissible means for realising even good results.

An epistemological contrast is also at work here. The discourse in which NDR is located proceeds from a high degree of certainty about the type of social arrangement that works best for humanity. Democratic constitutionalism, on the other hand, institutionalises epistemic uncertainty and experimentalism. Even if a particular democratic constitutionalist, wearing a politician's hat, is confident about the characteristics of a good society, he or she lacks the epistemic certainty that could justify either constitutionalising just one ideological or programmatic choice or coercively imposing it outside of constitutional constraints.

A final set of tensions between NDR and democratic constitutionalism concerns the character and boundary of the demos.

DISTINCTIVE CONCEPTIONS OF THE DEMOS

Both NDR and constitutional democracy defend rule by the people. They both assert the governing authority – indeed, sovereignty in a certain sense – of the body of adult persons bound by the laws and rules of a given polity. That is their shared democratic premise: it is why democracy figures in both terms. However, there are implicit differences between the way the demos is conceptualised in the two discursive orders. One difference has already been noted: the democratic constitutionalist demos is constrained by counter-majoritarian protections for individual and minority rights in a way that the NDR demos is not. In other words, in constitutional democracies current majorities are constrained by the decisions of the people previously assembled for constitution-founding purposes. But my concern here is with the actual nature and specification of 'the people' rather than with the conditions under which they exercise power.

NDR deals with three groups who appear to have a sequential relationship with each other. Its immediate subject is 'the people', an expansive cross-class population bounded in one or another fashion (typically by nationality or citizenship, sometimes more narrowly by race or ethnicity). The successor subject is the working class and its most immediate but generally subordinate class allies, who in turn segue (at some distant future point) into the collective producer of communism. This is not a case of physically distinctive populations replacing each other (except in the intergenerational sense). Rather, unity gives way to antagonistic subdivisions as class contradictions manifest, only to be resolved in the future when parasitic non-working social categories are sociologically eliminated as all persons become absorbed into a collectively empowered, universalised body of workers. The power of NDR's 'people' is thus fulsome but terminal, delimited by an evolutionary theory of history whose custodians have the power to declare its existence over when the time is right. The 'people' of constitutional democracy is constrained but (in principle) temporally indefinite – lacking a theoretically pre-ordained future, it retains sovereignty. The democratic power of the NDR demos is thus in one sense more contingent and uncertain than the demos of constitutional democracy.

The NDR itself is the initial stage in which the cross-class 'people' exercises sovereignty, guided by a national liberation movement. It is collectively conceived; its individual constituents are products of common experience, called to joint action and capable of being socialised into collective life. The demos of constitutional democracy is different; it consists of individual citizens, separately capable of rational autonomy. These citizens are diverse in their interests and values, yet unified enough to agree to common rules and a thin set of common liberal, democratic and social values. Their acceptance of these rules and values enables them to sort out their differences through institutionalised competition or deliberation. They enjoy protected private lives, yet join together democratically for collective action where this is needed (and it is generally thought to be needed on fewer occasions than under NDR). They have no higher collective purpose; they strive towards plural individual and collective ends, and the political order accommodates, and within limits facilitates, their distinctive personal goals. Constitutional democrats are uneasy about invocations of a 'people', especially when such a group is understood to possess a unified will capable of being represented by a dominant liberation movement or to require fealty from its individual members.

Although NDR explicitly refers to a 'nation' in a way that democratic constitutionalism does not, both conceive of the people as national *in some sense*. Both radical nationalism and democratic liberalism fastened historically onto the Westphalian nation state. It is the territorial nation state that delimits the popular sovereign's jurisdiction. NDR has a particularly close relationship with national struggles for self-determination, but in modern constitutional democracies sovereignty also invariably resides in nation states. Moreover, nations tend to possess an at least partly ethno-cultural character – most typically a common language, but often also other ethnic or cultural markers that form what Kymlicka (2004: 55) terms a 'societal culture'. States that lack a societal culture are often perceived as multinational rather than as nation states. They are also often seen to be more fragile, especially where they are composed of ethno-national groups aspiring to autonomy or separate statehood.

And yet NDR and constitutional democracy do invoke distinctive senses of nationhood. NDR is the banner of a pre-state people aspiring to statehood. Such groups vary, but they commonly possess an ethnic character to some degree. This is because they are struggling to separate themselves from another group of people, typically from a distant place, marked by a distinctive language, religion, lifestyle or physiognomy. At the same time, the nationalists seek self-determination for a *territory*, a logic that inclines them to mobilise all those who live in that territory, irrespective of their ethnicity. Those appealed to can include domesticated colonial settlers. Here is the germ of a tension internal to NDR itself – between ethnic and civic-territorial concepts of the people.

Many African states have confronted a multi-layered instability of popular identity. In challenging white Europeans, African national liberation movements led peoples unified by black ancestry and shared experience of discrimination, but they also liberated peoples divided into ethnic groups that were potentially nations in their own right. Nation building was (at least in its negative aspect) the post-independence effort to forestall further fragmentation. In South Africa, the picture is further complicated by an inheritance of four apartheid-designated 'races', each internally differentiated by language, religion or extra-territorial national origin. All races lay claim to either abo-riginality or long-established rootedness, though some (coloureds and Africans) more plausibly than others (whites, Indians). As in America, settler whites fought for inde-pendence from metropolitan powers. As in America, settlers won independence. But unlike in America, they then faced a new national liberation struggle – this time of 'non-whites' fighting to free themselves from domestic white settler domination. Yet those fighting white rule in turn had an array of ethnic and national self-definitions to choose between: South Africans of all races, conceived either non-racially or as sepa-rate nations; all 'non-whites', defined positively as 'black' by the Black Consciousness Movement; particular 'black races', like bantu-language African or Indian; and even par-ticular ethno-linguistic groups, like the Zulu. The NDR vision advanced by the ANC repudiated narrowly 'tribal' mobilisation of the ethno-linguistic kind, but 'tried on' many of the other conceptions of its national 'people' – non-racial, multinational, mul-tiracial, black and African.

Democratic constitutionalism's 'ideal' nation is formed around the state rather than a pre-state ethno-cultural entity. While it benefits from the existence of a shared civic and political culture, its boundaries are territorial rather than ethnic. It directs national loyalty towards universal ideals embodied in common citizenship rather than the par-ticularistic ends of ethnic sub-groups. In its nation-building mode, NDR points in the same direction. From the standpoint of democratic constitutionalism, however, the dan-ger is that a civic-nationalist NDR could collapse into an ethnic-nationalist NDR; equal citizenship could transmute into a differentiated and hierarchical citizenship that priv-ileges particular ethno-racial subjects and encourages group chauvinism and division. Conversely, for South African NDR proponents, a colour-blind reading of rights and entitlements would frustrate legitimate efforts to put right the wrongs of the past and correct ongoing racial inequalities.

GROUNDS FOR RECONCILIATION?

As already signalled, the abstract tensions which exist between NDR and constitution-alism are mitigated in practice by a number of factors, including the particular nature of the South African Constitution and its accompanying jurisprudence. The Constitution is not simply an outline of decision-making procedures and 'negative' liberties; it man-dates specific substantive changes and policy directions, notably in its specification of socio-economic rights. Moreover, it permits 'fair' discrimination in favour of historically disadvantaged groups. It does not merely stand guard impartially over the political and civil interplay of citizens but envisages a positive process of transformation towards a particular kind of society, one in which racial imbalances are corrected and essential social needs are met. Democratic constitutionalism can take different forms that depart in some ways from the ideal-type employed in the preceding sections; and South Africa follows a post Second World War trend in proclaiming a range of social aspirations and rights that bind majorities and their representatives in the same way that do core liberal rights.

Further, the ANC and its allies helped to write, signed up to, and have for the most part observed the rules of the democratic constitutional game. The ruling Alliance's own practical record, and some of its rhetoric, attests to a willingness to advance NDR and simultaneously to respect democratic constitutionalism, finessing whatever difficulties this dual commitment generates. Politics is about more than the realisation of abstract principles. Tensions visible in logical exposition can be reduced in the real world by the 'art of the possible' – and the ANC and its allies have governed pragmatically rather than ideologically. They are keen to hold the political and social order together, and they will, if necessary, use diverse languages and employ divergent logics – often tailored to audiences – in order to satisfy their own base that a radical NDR is underway and middle-class 'public opinion' that constitutional democracy is safe.

Some of the tensions between the two ways of thinking can be resolved conceptually. Constitutionalism does not require that political actors operate by its own regulative logic of impartiality. It seeks impartial ways of reconciling divergent political and ideological projects; and it defines routes by which – and the limits *within* which – particular partisan or ideological programmes legitimately come to enjoy the backing of law and to be implemented over objections. In so far as NDR is conceived as 'merely' a party-political project, enforceable within liberty-respecting limits by dint of revocable popular mandate, it becomes just one of the competing substantive visions whose rivalry constitutional democracy anticipates, supervises and, up to a point, celebrates. Conceived in these terms, NDR submits itself to constitutional primacy; but the Constitution in turn grants policy leeway to the ruling party or coalition of the day.

In any event, a simple formal-substantive distinction is implausible. Constitutional design is never entirely neutral. When formulating constitutions, substantive choices have to be made about which rights are to be protected, which electoral systems are to be employed, which fields of power are to be subject to democratic control. These choices will shape the balance of advantage among competing political actors and programmes, and ideological and partisan concerns will inevitably influence how these matters are discussed. Proponents of NDR can reasonably argue that their concerns should carry weight in these debates; and there is evidence that they have done so in South Africa, in the constitutionalisation of social rights, affirmative action, 'cooperative governance' and participatory democracy. Proponents of NDR cannot legitimately rig the Constitution in their favour, and must (in constitutional-democratic terms) justify their design preferences in terms that can be accepted by reasonable opponents. But within these limits they are entitled to argue for provisions that ensure that their own historically disadvantaged constituents are fairly and properly served by the constitutional order.

Even so, the tensions between NDR and constitutionalism are far from rendered null by these considerations, and there are circumstances in which they can flare up. Each of the above reconciling considerations comes with built-in limits and caveats.

While socio-economic rights give positive substantive content to the Constitution, they are necessarily flexibly formulated. They are to be realised over time, by means rationally related to the goal of their realisation, in light of available resources. They are thus not as decisively justiciable as first-generation rights. While they have concrete implications for policy, these rights, and the judges who interpret them, cannot dictate economic policy in the round. Ideological economic choices remain to be made. It is thus doubtful that the Constitution could reliably serve the ANC as the constitutional expression of NDR. It cannot guarantee policies that align with the ruling alliance's notion of NDR. There remains room for disagreement about what the socio-economic rights mandate. Moreover, some constitutional clauses will be experienced by any radical NDR party as constraining positive action. The Constitution does not permit the kind of decisive command that some in the ruling party – inspired, for example, by China's success – hanker after.

As noted earlier, the ANC's own pragmatic reconciliation of NDR and democratic constitutionalism often looks fragile. The ruling party seems impatient with opposition from civil society, the media, the arts, the judiciary and Chapter Nine institutions. Senior political figures have talked the Constitution down as a compromise forced on the liberation movement, and have called for less emphasis on liberal freedoms and more on substantive freedoms. The ANC's electoral pre-eminence has enabled it to act with impunity – for example, in evading corruption charges– and to 'deploy' loyal cadres throughout the state apparatus, including in supposedly independent bodies. Moreover, the pragmatic accommodationism of the ANC may be premised on the party's continued electoral success. The question of whether it will respect constitutional rules when they no longer yield results favourable to the ANC awaits an answer.

Finally, it is far from clear that the ANC fully accepts the subordination of NDR to the Constitution. Its documents and leaders often appear to regard the NDR as a transcendent historical task, and the Constitution as its instrument. They continue to regard the ANC as the true custodian of the national-democratic project. Nor is this an implausibly partisan reading of NDR theory; this way of thinking constitutes a reasonable interpretation of its requirements. If NDR is pitched at the big issues of economy, society and historical destiny, and the Constitution is merely formalistic legalism inserted into the objective course of developments, then it follows that NDR must enjoy precedence.

CONCLUSION

Early 1990s South Africa hosted an encounter between two logics whose relationship remains unresolved. One arises out of the adaptation of Marxist theory and politics to revolutionary opportunities in underdeveloped countries, and from experiences of cross-class alliance-building to fight fascism, colonialism and 'state monopoly capitalism'. The friction between Marxist theory and unanticipated realities sparked a great deal of intellectual productivity, of which NDR constituted a key product. Its essential lesson was that a revolution – under leftist leadership and capable of launching socialist construction at some reasonably near future point – was possible in ostensibly unpropitious circumstances, provided the strategy and tactics were right. Getting them right meant joining nationalists against colonial enemies. And, indeed, revolutionary breakthroughs were achieved on this basis in a number of countries of the global South. Many factors contributed to the subsequent failure of these efforts of socialist development, but their failure may in part attest to the limits of the kind of imaginative reconfiguration that marked NDR theory. It is possible that the underdeveloped, peasant-majority, culturally conservative countries of the global South were in fact not ripe for socialism, just as orthodox Marxist theory predicted. And it may be that some of the brutality of these regimes resulted from efforts, eventually involving physical force rather than ideas, to synchronise recalcitrant realities and theoretical requirements.

This thesis never encountered a South African test, because in this country there has been no radical socialist experimentation. South Africa's democratic transition occurred at a moment when previous NDR-guided experiments had exhausted themselves, and when another logic was dominating the field and demanding engagement. This was the logic of constitutional democracy. In the form handed down to late twentieth-century democratisers, including in South Africa, this amounted to a synthetic legacy heavily marked by its liberal origins, reworked by more recent recognition of human and social rights and an expanded idea of citizenship. Yet, however 'transformational' its objectives in a South African context, democratic constitutionalism's logic is basically procedural and formal, concerned with the limitation of power. As the limits of South Africa's market-friendly path have become visible, voices are heard blaming constitutional constraint for the failure of South Africa to evolve in the more radically egalitarian direction envisaged by NDR. The ANC's uneasy accommodation with constitutional democracy – and that of other leftist forces – is thus increasingly strained. This has caused consternation on the part of the many who look to the Constitution to secure both liberal and socio-economic rights against powerful public and private actors.

This chapter has argued that there are genuine points of friction between NDR and constitutional-democratic logic – genuine, because rooted in the underlying logics of these positions. NDR is concerned with the substance of social and economic change for human betterment, whereas democratic constitutionalism classically attends to form. NDR seeks power, whereas democratic constitutionalism seeks to constrain it. NDR is realist, democratic constitutionalism apparently a product of legal and moral philosophy. More than that, they differ in their conception of the demos. NDR sees it as collective, ideal and perfectible. For constitutional democracy, on the other hand, it is individuated, empirical and marked by an irreducible pluralism of interests, values and conceptions of the good. On top of that, NDR's nation is ambivalently both civic and ethno-racial, whereas constitutional democracy's is civic and, for the most part, territorial.

Despite their discordant relationship, the two logics are not irreconcilable. Everything depends, I have argued, on how their nexus is conceptualised. The version of NDR compatible with democratic constitutionalism posits NDR as the substantive, primarily socio-economic programme of particular parties. Constitutional democracy specifies game rules that determine the conditions under which the advocates of such programmes legitimately occupy government and exercise 'power over' others. The two logics clash to the extent that NDR is conceived as a higher project, and democratic constitutionalism as either its currently useful instrument or the arrangement that corresponds to a national-democratic phase. In terms of conceptions of the people, an NDR friendly to democratic constitutionalism will insist on equal citizenship and inclusive nation building, even while allowing special measures to benefit those who have suffered past injustices or suffer current deprivation. An NDR conceived as the project of a particular racial and ethnic group will, by contrast, grate against constitutional democracy.

Would an NDR that subordinates itself to constitutional democracy fail to deliver the social gains that the black poor expect? Doubtless, constitutionalism will hamper decisive decision-making in certain instances, sometimes in ways that frustrate needed redistributions. But in defence of the possibility of a socially egalitarian democratic constitutionalism, I offer the following considerations. First, there are grounds to believe that democracy will be better than dictatorship in delivering development equitably and at an acceptable human cost (Caldwell, 1986; Brown and Hunter, 1999; Shandra et al., 2003; Sen, 2009; Christiano, 2011). Second, South Africa's specific variant of constitutionalism allows – even mandates – substantive pro-poor social and economic change. Third (and perhaps a corollary to the second), there is reason to think that the failure to address poverty and inequality more effectively in South Africa has less to do with the Constitution than with absent political will and structural constraint (factors that have nevertheless not stopped the implementation of some of the largest housing and social grant programmes in the developing world). Fourth, many of the judicial, media and civil society pressures that 'check and balance' the state issue from a progressive, pro-poor direction and impede state actions that harm the poor. They are thus far from inherently 'counter-revolutionary'.

For all these reasons, constitutional democracy is fundamentally attractive, and ought to be conceptualised as an enduring (if amendable) source of pressures and constraints on South African governance. It should not be conceived as a tactic or phase to be super-seded by some better set of arrangements being borne towards us by underlying his-torical and economic forces. Whether proponents of NDR do – whether they logically can – accept this limitation is something that we cannot yet say for sure.

NOTES

1   An excellent source for several of the historical and theoretical developments touched on in this section is Fernando Claudin (1975). A more updated source on both Soviet and South African approaches to NDR, and which benefits from access to Soviet archives, is Irina Filatova (2012).
2   Here I draw upon Losurdo (2011) and also take issue with him. He exposes the limits of lib-eralism's reach but wrongly treats these as logically inherent in liberalism.

REFERENCES

Bogdanor, Vernon (ed) (1988) *Constitutions in Democratic Politics*. Gower: Alldershot.
Boucher, David and Paul Kelly (eds) (1994) *The Social Contract from Hobbes to Rawls*. London: Routledge.
Brown, David and Wendy Hunter (1999) Democracy and Social Spending in Latin America, 1980–92. *American Political Science Review*, 93(4): 779–90.
Caldwell, John C. (1986) Routes to Low Mortality in Poor Countries. *Population and Development Review*, 12(2): 171–220.
Christiano, Thomas (2011) An Instrumental Argument for a Human Right to Democracy. *Philosophy and Public Affairs*, 39(2): 142–76
Claudin, Fernando (1975) *The Communist Movement: From Comintern to Cominform*, Volumes 1 and 2. New York: Monthly Review Press.
Drew, Allison (2000) *Discordant Comrades: Identities and Loyalties on the South African Left*. Pretoria: Unisa Press.
Dunn, John (ed.) (1992) *Democracy: The Unfinished Journey, 508 BC to AD 1993*. Oxford: Oxford University Press.
Elster, John and Ruth Slagstad (eds) (1988) *Constitutionalism and Democracy*. Cambridge: Cambridge University Press.
Filatova, Irina (2012) The Lasting Legacy: The Soviet Theory of the National Democratic Revolution in South Africa. *South African Historical Journal*, 64(3): 507–37.
Fine, Robert (1991) *Beyond Apartheid: Labour and Liberation in South Africa*. London: Pluto.
Fredman, Sandra (2008) *Human Rights Transformed: Positive Rights and Positive Duties*. Oxford: Oxford University Press.
Glaser, Daryl (2014) Liberal Egalitarianism. *Theoria*, 61(140): 25–46.
Gutman, Amy (1980) *Liberal Equality*. Cambridge: Cambridge University Press.
Held, David (2006) *Models of Democracy*, third edition. Stanford: Stanford University Press.
Honohan, Iseult (2002) *Civic Republicanism*. London: Routledge.
Keane, John (1988) *Democracy and Civil Society*. London: Verso.

Kymlicka, Will (2002) *Contemporary Political Philosophy: An Introduction,* second edition. Oxford: Oxford University Press.

Kymlicka, Will (2004) Nation-building and Minority Rights: Comparing Africa and.the West. In *Ethnicity and Democracy in Africa,* edited by Bruce Berman, Dickson Eyoh and Will Kymlicka. Oxford: James Currey,

Langford, Malcolm (ed.) (2008) *Social Rights Jurisprudence: Emerging Trends in International and Comparative Law.* Cambridge: Cambridge University Press.

Liebman, Marcel (1975) *Leninism under Lenin.* London: Merlin.

Losurdo, Domenico (2011) *Liberalism: A Counter-History.* London: Verso.

Lukes, Steven (1986) Marxism and Dirty Hands. In *Marxism and Liberalism,* edited by Ellen Frankel Paul, Jeffrey Paul, Fred D. Miller Jr and John Arens. Oxford: Basil Blackwell.

Macpherson, C.B. (1977) *The Life and Times of Liberal Democracy.* New York: Oxford University Press.

Manin, Bernard (1997) *The Principles of Representative Government.* Cambridge: Cambridge University Press.

Martin, Terry (2001) *The Affirmative Action Empire: Nations and Nationalism in the Soviet Union, 1923–1939.* Ithaca, NY: Cornell University Press.

Morobe Murphy (1987) Towards a People's Democracy: The UDF View. *Review of African Political Economy,* 40: 81–7.

Morrow, John (2005) *History of Western Political Thought,* second edition. Basingstoke: Macmillan.

Rawls, John (1999) *A Theory of Justice,* revised edition [first edition 1971]. Oxford: Oxford University Press.

Sen, Amartya (2009) *The Idea of Justice.* Cambridge, MA: The Belknap Press of Harvard University Press.

Shandra, John M., Jenna Nobles, Bruce London and John B Williamson (2003) *Dependency, Democracy, and Infant Mortality: A Quantitative, Cross-national Analysis of Less Developed Countries.* On-Line Working Paper Series, California Center for Population Research. Los Angeles: University of California. Available online at http://escholarship.org/uc/item/1wm303dg. Accessed May 2012.

South African Communist Party (SACP) (1997) *Strategy and Tactics.* Available online at http://www.anc.org.za/show.php?id=2424.

Suttner, Raymond (1986) Popular justice in South Africa today. Paper presented to the Sociology Department, University of the Witwatersrand.

Tilly, Charles (2007) *Democracy.* Cambridge: Cambridge University Press.

Van Diepen, Maria (ed.) (1988) *The National Question in South Africa.* London: Zed.

Waldron, Jeremy (1993) *Liberal Rights.* Cambridge: Cambridge University Press.

BIOGRAPHICAL NOTES

Basil Brown is the president of the New Unity Movement, Port Elizabeth.

Sian Byrne studies work and labour movements. She was a researcher for the National Labour and Economic Development Institute (NALEDI) in Johannesburg, linked to the Congress of South African Trade Unions (COSATU). Winner of the Ruth First scholarship at Rhodes University, South Africa, she is working on a PhD comparing the Federation of South African Trade Unions (FOSATU) in South Africa and Solidarność in Poland in the early 1980s from a global labour history perspective. She is a guest researcher at the Berlin Social Science Centre (WZB) with the Globalisation, Work, and Production Project Group.

Luli Callinicos is a social historian and the author of *Gold and Workers* (Ravan Press); *Working Life: Factories, Townships and Popular Culture* (Ravan Press); and *Oliver Tambo: Beyond the Engeli Mountains* (David Philip). She was appointed to the Arts and Culture Task Group in 1994, was the chair of the National Heritage Council from 2004 to 2007, and currently serves on the Transformation of the Heritage Landscape task team.

Jeremy Cronin is the deputy general secretary of the SACP, and the deputy minister of Public Works. A political activist during the apartheid years, Cronin served seven years in Pretoria Maximum Security Prison. He was a member of the ANC/SACP negotiating team at the Convention for a Democratic South Africa (CODESA) and co-convened the Reconstruction and Development Programme (RDP) Drafting Committee.

Alec Erwin was the general secretary of TUACC and FOSATU, the education secretary of COSATU, and held positions in NUMSA and the National Union of Textile Workers (NUTW). He was deputy minister of Finance in the Mandela Administration and later minister of Trade and Industry and of Public Enterprises. He served on the WTO Disputes Panels, and is now involved in strategic consulting projects in Africa.

Mallet Pumelele Giyose is a political activist working in the areas of rural development and apartheid debt.

Daryl Glaser is associate professor in the Department of Political Studies at the University of the Witwatersrand and has a longstanding interest in democratic theory and practice in South Africa. He has worked in the disciplines of democratic theory and normative analytic philosophy and is the author of *Politics and Society in South Africa* (Sage).

Shireen Hassim is a professor of Political Studies at WISER at the University of the Witwatersrand and the author of *No Shortcuts to Power: Women and Policymaking in Africa* (Zed Books) and *Women's Organisations and Democracy: Contesting Authority* (University of Wisconsin Press). She is a member of the Editorial Advisory Committee for UN Women, and an academic expert for the Section 6 Committee of the Commission on Gender Equality.

Martin Legassick was emeritus professor of History at the University of the Western Cape, a member of the Marxist Workers Tendency of the ANC, and a political activist. He published extensively on South African history and political economy, including *Towards Socialist Democracy* (University of KwaZulu-Natal Press). He passed away in March 2016.

Xolela Mangcu is a professor of Sociology at the University of Cape Town, Harry Oppenheimer Hutchins Fellow at the Hutchins Center for African American Studies at Harvard University and Visiting Chair of Commonwealth Studies at the School of Advanced Study and the Institute for Commonwealth Studies at the University of London.

Gerhard Maré is an emeritus professor at the University of KwaZulu-Natal and fellow at the Stellenbosch Institute for Advanced Study. He wrote extensively on ethnicity during the 1980s and 1990s. He is the author of *Declassified: Moving beyond the Dead End of Race in South Africa* (Jacana).

Alex Mohubetswane Mashilo is the SACP national spokesperson and head of Communications. He worked in the auto industry and served as a trade union official at the national level. He has been a member of the Young Communist League (YCL), the ANC Youth League, and the ANC, and served in leadership structures at the branch, provincial and national levels.

John Mawbey is a historian. He joined the emerging trade union movement over forty years ago, first as an editor of the *South African Labour Bulletin*, and later as an organiser, educator and researcher among metal workers and in the South African Municipal Workers Union (SAMWU).

T. Dunbar Moodie is an emeritus professor of Sociology at Hobart and William Smith Colleges in New York, and an honorary research associate at the Society, Work and Development Institute at the University of the Witwatersrand. He is author of numerous articles and books including, *The Rise of Afrikanerdom* and *Going for Gold,* both published by the University of California Press.

Enver Motala is a researcher at the Nelson Mandela Institute for Rural Education and Development at the University of Fort Hare. He has worked for more than thirty years in a variety of educational environments including non-governmental organisations, a university-based policy development unit, and in government.

Hamilton Petersen, a former teacher and political/community activist, is the joint secretary of the New Unity Movement, Uitenhage.

Ari Sitas is now a professor of Sociology at the University of Cape Town after many years at the University of KwaZulu-Natal. He chairs the National Institute for the Humanities and Social Sciences and is the author of *The Mandela Decade: Labour, Culture and Society in Post-Apartheid South Africa, 1990–2000* (Unisa Press) and co-authored *Gauging and Engaging Deviance, 1600–2000* (Tulika Press).

Charles Thomas is an activist and is currently convener of the New Unity Movement's Publications Bureau in Cape Town.

Nicole Ulrich is a labour historian based at Rhodes University, interested in the organisation, political ideas and identities of labouring classes in southern Africa. She researches workers' organisations in the 1970s, and the solidarities and transnational connections forged by slaves, servants, sailors and soldiers in the early colonial Cape. In Johannesburg, she has been involved in the Workers' Library and Museum and the History Workshop, and at Cambridge University, the Centre for African Studies. Her work has appeared, *inter alia*, in the *International Review of Social History,* the *Journal of Southern African Studies*, and the *South African Historical Journal.*

Salim Vally is director of the Centre for Education Rights and Transformation at the University of Johannesburg and an associate professor in the Faculty of Education. He is a visiting professor at the Nelson Mandela Metropolitan University.

Lucien van der Walt works at Rhodes University, South Africa. He is involved in union and working class education and movements, and has published widely on labour, left history and political economy. Notable works include *Anarchism and Syndicalism in the Colonial and Postcolonial World, 1880–1940* (2010/2014, with Steve Hirsch), and *Negro e Vermelho: Anarquismo, Sindicalismo Revolucionario e Pessoas de Cor na Africa Meridional nas Decadas de 1880 a 1920* (2014). He was southern Africa editor for *The International Encyclopedia of Revolution and Protest* (2009) and won both the *Labor History* and Council for the Development of Social Science Research in Africa (CODESRIA) PhD prizes.

Robert van Niekerk is the director of the Institute of Social and Economic Research (ISER) and Matthew Goniwe Chair in Social Policy at Rhodes University. His academic work focuses on the institutional history and ideologies of social policy in South Africa and policy aimed at overcoming inequality and building an inclusive social citizenship.

Edward Webster is a research professor in the Society, Work and Development Institute (SWOP) at the University of the Witwatersrand. He was the director of the Chris Hani Institute from 2012 to 2015 and has published widely in the field of labour studies. His current research interests are work, informalisation and democracy.

Allan Zinn is the director of the Centre for the Advancement of Non-racialism and Democracy (CANRAD) at the Nelson Mandela Metropolitan University.

Siphamandla Zondi was at the time of writing the head of the Institute for Global Dialogue associated with the University of South Africa (Unisa). He is also a faculty member on African political economy and renaissance at the Thabo Mbeki African Leadership Institute at Unisa. He works on Africanisation and decolonisation, Africa's agency internationally, and the Global South in a changing world.

INDEX